Southern Perspectives on the Post-2015 International Development Agenda

At the turn of the millennium, the unanimous adoption of the Millennium Development Goals (MDGs) by the United Nations General Assembly marked a new chapter in international development. However, voices from the Global South were noticeably absent in shaping the agenda. Fifteen years later, the global context has changed so much that it would have been inconceivable not to have taken voices from the South into account when planning the new Sustainable Development Goals (SDGs). Since its inception in 2012, the Southern Voice on Post-MDG International Development Goals (Southern Voice), a network of 49 think tanks from Africa, Asia and Latin America, has generated a substantial body of original research to feed into various aspects of the post-2015 development agenda, such as the missing dimensions of the MDGs, ways to mitigate existing challenges in delivering on aspired outcomes, and new issues, goals, targets and indicators that are crucial for the next global development framework.

Southern Perspectives on the Post-2015 International Development Agenda consolidates this research and stitches together development realities and policy experiences from the global South, infusing unique local perspectives to the global debate on the post-2015 agenda. The compendium addresses the overarching themes underpinning the new international development framework by focusing on issues such as sustainability and growth, inclusion and social policies, governance and capacities, and financing of the new agenda. Southern Voice seeks to challenge the "knowledge asymmetry" afflicting the global knowledge system by channelling evidence-based policy analyses produced by centres of excellence, located in the global South.

This is a valuable resource for academics and researchers, policymakers and practitioners, and concerned students in search of alternative views on sustainable development.

Debapriya Bhattacharya is the Chair of Southern Voice on Post-MDG International Development Goals and a Distinguished Fellow at the Centre for Policy Dialogue (CPD), Dhaka, Bangladesh.

Andrea Ordóñez Llanos is the Research Coordinator for Southern Voice on Post-MDG International Development Goals.

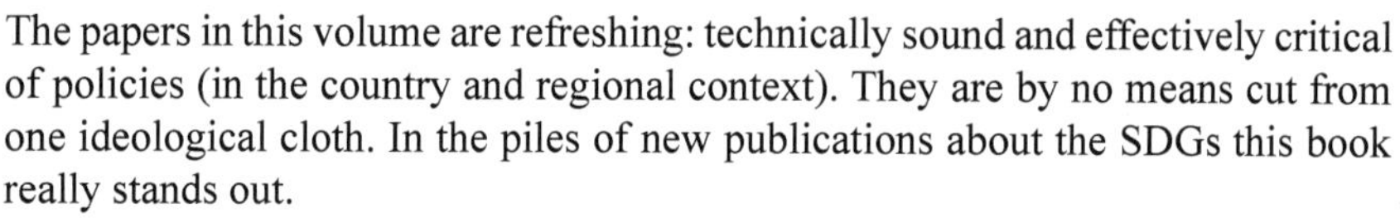

The papers in this volume are refreshing: technically sound and effectively critical of policies (in the country and regional context). They are by no means cut from one ideological cloth. In the piles of new publications about the SDGs this book really stands out.

— *Nancy Birdsall, Founding President, Center for Global Development, USA*

Routledge Explorations in Development Studies

For a full list of titles in this series, please visit www.routledge.com

This Development Studies series features innovative and original research at the regional and global scale.

It promotes interdisciplinary scholarly works drawing on a wide spectrum of subject areas, in particular politics, health, economics, rural and urban studies, sociology, environment, anthropology, and conflict studies.

Topics of particular interest are globalization; emerging powers; children and youth; cities; education; media and communication; technology development and climate change.

In terms of theory and method, rather than basing itself on any orthodoxy, the series draws broadly on the tool kit of the social sciences in general, emphasizing comparison, the analysis of the structure and processes, and the application of qualitative and quantitative methods.

The Political Ecology of Climate Change Adaptation
Livelihoods, Agrarian Change and the Conflicts of Development
Marcus Taylor

China's Foreign Relations and the Survival of Autocracies
Julia Bader

Democratic Accountability and Human Development
Regimes, Institutions and Resources
Kamran Ali Afzal and Mark Considine

Rural Livelihoods in China
Edited by Heather Xiaoquan Zhang

Global Food Security and Development Aid
Ivica Petrikova

Southern Perspectives on the Post-2015 International Development Agenda
Edited by Debapriya Bhattacharya and Andrea Ordóñez Llanos

Southern Perspectives on the Post-2015 International Development Agenda

Edited by Debapriya Bhattacharya and Andrea Ordóñez Llanos

LONDON AND NEW YORK

First published 2017 by Routledge

2 Park Square, Milton Park, Abingdon, Oxfordshire OX14 4RN
711 Third Avenue, New York, NY 10017

Routledge is an imprint of the Taylor & Francis Group, an informa business

First issued in paperback 2018

British Library Cataloguing in Publication Data
A catalogue record for this book is available from the British Library

Library of Congress Cataloging-in-Publication Data
Names: Bhattacharya, Debapriya, editor. | Ordóñez Llanos, Andrea, editor.
Title: Southern perspectives on the post-2015 international development agenda / edited by Debapriya Bhattacharya & Andrea Ordóñez Llanos.
Description: Abingdon, Oxon ; New York, NY : Routledge, 2016. | Series: Routledge explorations in development studies
Identifiers: LCCN 2016026343 | ISBN 9781138186996 (hbk)
Subjects: LCSH: Economic development—Developing countries. | Economic assistance—Developing countries. | Economic policy—International cooperation. | International economic relations. | International relations.
Classification: LCC HC59.7 .S5964 2016 | DDC 338.9009172/4—dc23
LC record available at https://lccn.loc.gov/2016026343

ISBN: 978-1-138-18699-6 (hbk)
ISBN: 978-1-138-61522-9 (pbk)

Typeset in Times New Roman
by Apex CoVantage, LLC

The chapters included in the book were prepared with support from the Southern Voice on Post-MDG International Development Goals.

Disclaimer: The views expressed in the chapters of the volume are those of the respective authors alone and do not necessarily reflect the views of the Editors, the Southern Voice on Post-MDG International Development Goals, or any other organisations that they are affiliated with.

Contents

Annexes, tables, figures and box

Annexes

Tables

Figures

Box

Foreword

In the piles of commentary and the mountain of new publications about the Sustainable Development Goals (SDGs) agreed to at the United Nations General Assembly in the fall of 2015, one stands out: this book developed under the auspices of Southern Voice, a network of 49 think tanks from Africa, Asia, and Latin America. The SDGs reflect a truly global conversation about universal values and goals, and their framing is likely to influence the debate in the developing world about the meaning and purpose of economic growth and social development, and about the nature and relevance of environmental justice and political rights, for the next decade and beyond. Although the SDGs are officially the product of an intergovernmental process, in fact they are also a product of a world-wide set of conversations and convening, in which civil society organisations, student groups, universities, networks of professionals, and finally and most notably, think tanks in the South as well as the North, participated.

As the head of a think tank in the rich world, I believe there is no substitute for the kind of contribution think tanks in the developing world can make to their own countries' economies and democracies, and to the global debate about what is, in fact, "sustainable development." But as the editor and founding inventor of Southern Voice, Debapriya Bhattacharya, notes in his overview chapter, the number of peer-reviewed publications mentioning the SDGs that have been generated in the South is, as has been the case with the Millennium Development Goals (MDGs), far smaller than the number generated in the North. The difference is no surprise, given the wealth of the latter compared to the former. But it raises a troubling challenge for implementation of the SDGs. Compared to the MDGs, effective implementation of the SDGs in developing countries, with their explicit emphasis on inclusion, rights, jobs, and environmental sustainability, requires a more local, more evidence-based, and more "political" conversation within developing countries – about taxes, discrimination, corruption, and democratic politics itself. That implies the need for a local and independent research community within countries that can play a greater role in the future than its small size and heavy dependence on outside funding allowed in the past. It also requires at the international level greater engagement with independent research "voices" from the South to enrich what has sometimes been an international discussion focused more on outside aid financing than on insiders' evidence of what works given local political and social realities.

The papers in this volume are refreshing: technically sound, while quietly and effectively critical of policies and programmes in the writers' own countries and regions and on the part of the international community. They are by no means cut from one ideological cloth: One author applauds the greater focus of the SDGs compared to the MDGs on growth itself; another notes the failure of the SDGs to explicitly tackle the interaction between growth and long-term environmental sustainability. Social policies tackled include the aging of populations in the South and the question of affirmative action for women and other groups experiencing discrimination.

I recommend these essays to readers and hope there will be more avenues for seeking and listening to Southern voices working in independent think tanks – both within developing countries and at the global level. This volume should be the first of many in the next decade.

Nancy Birdsall
Founding President, Center for Global Development
May 2016

Acknowledgements

In June 2012 in Cape Town, Southern Voice on Post-MDG International Development Goals emerged as a network and platform for the global South to contribute to the discourse on the post-2015 international development agenda at a meeting of the Think Tank Initiative (TTI). In 2013 and 2014, Southern Voice launched two rounds of research grant calls for network members to interpret their work in the context of the post-2015 agenda and highlight issues of importance to developing countries. The present volume comprises the studies generated by this process. Sincere thanks are due to the authors who have contributed their time and efforts to prepare and update their studies for this volume.

Submissions under the research grant calls went through multiple rounds of peer review, from the proposal through the first and second draft stages. Southern Voice is particularly indebted to the following peer reviewers for their insightful comments: *Vaqar Ahmed*, Sustainable Development Policy Institute (SDPI), Pakistan; *Nisha Arunatilake*, Institute of Policy Studies of Sri Lanka (IPS); *Ivan Borja*, Universidad San Francisco de Quito (USFQ), Ecuador; *Ibrahima Hathie*, Initiative Prospective Agricole et Rurale (IPAR), Senegal; *Saleemul Huq*, International Institute for Environment and Development (IIED), United Kingdom; *Rounaq Jahan*, Centre for Policy Dialogue (CPD), Bangladesh; *Towfiqul Islam Khan*, CPD; *Fahmida Khatun*, CPD; *Blandina Kilama*, Policy Research for Development (REPOA), Tanzania; *Shannon Kindornay*, Norman Paterson School of International Affairs (NPSIA), Carleton University, Canada; *Donald Mmari*, REPOA; *Khondaker Golam Moazzem*, CPD; *Muhammed Muqtada*, formerly of the International Labour Organization (ILO), Geneva; *Mustafizur Rahman*, CPD; *Shakeel Ramay*, SDPI; *Shekhar Shah*, National Council of Applied Economic Research (NCAER), India; *Sarah Ssewanyana*, Economic Policy Research Centre (EPRC), Uganda; and *Mireya Anabell Villacís Taco*, Centro Ecuatoriano de Derecho Ambiental (CEDA), Ecuador.

Southern Voice has been sustained by the 49 think tanks from Africa, Latin America and Asia that make up its network. Active participatory roles have been played by members of its Steering Committee, namely *Martín Benavides*, Grupo de Análisis para el Desarrollo (GRADE), Peru; *Bitrina Diyamett*, Science, Technology and Innovation Policy Research Organization (STIPRO), Tanzania; *Karin Fernando*, Centre for Poverty Analysis (CEPA), Sri Lanka; *Khalida Ghaus*, Social

Policy and Development Centre (SPDC), Pakistan; *Ibrahima Hathie*, IPAR; and *Carmen Ortiz*, Asociación de Investigación y Estudios Sociales (ASIES), Guatemala. Many of these members also served as peer reviewers.

Since the inception of Southern Voice, the support of the TTI, particularly that of *Peter Taylor*, Programme Manager, TTI, International Development Research Centre (IDRC), Ottawa, has been instrumental in taking the network forward. Support received from Peter and his colleagues is gratefully acknowledged.

Without the generous support of the William and Flora Hewlett Foundation, Southern Voice could not have achieved what it did over the past two years. The encouragement received from *Ruth Levine*, Programme Director, Global Development and Population Programme, and *Sarah Lucas*, Programme Officer, Global Development and Population Programme, is particularly appreciated.

The UN Foundation, New York, has taken great interest in the activities of Southern Voice and created opportunities for the network to transmit its messages to official processes at the United Nations and beyond. I would like to put on record our appreciation for the helpful cooperation extended by *Minh-Thu Pham*, Senior Policy Director, and *Jenna Slotin*, Deputy Director, of the UN Foundation.

The key role played by CPD as the Secretariat of the Southern Voice network merits special mention. I would like to thank all my colleagues at CPD for making Southern Voice a success. Under the able leadership of *Mustafizur Rahman*, Executive Director, core contributions have been made by *Anisatul Fatema Yousuf*, Director, Dialogue and Communication; *Fahmida Khatun*, Research Director; *M Shafiqul Islam*, Additional Director, Administration and Finance; *Khondaker Golam Moazzem*, Additional Research Director; and *Towfiqul Islam Khan*, Research Fellow.

Within the Southern Voice Secretariat, *Mahenaw Ummul Wara*, former Research Associate; *Umme Shefa Rezbana*, Senior Research Associate; and *Maeesa Ayesha*, Programme Associate, have played essential roles in organising and managing the smooth implementation of the research programme and other activities undertaken by the network. The volume benefitted from excellent professional editing by *Michael Olender* and *Oliver Turner*. *Nazmatun Noor*, Deputy Director, Publication, served as the coordinator of this volume and received able assistance from *Tarannum Jinan*, Administrative Associate. *Avra Bhattacharjee*, Deputy Director, Dialogue and Outreach, oversaw the graphic works and other technical issues at various stages of the publication.

Rehman Sobhan, Chairman, CPD, has been a source of overwhelming inspiration and the Southern Voice network has always benefitted from his guidance.

Andrea Ordóñez Llanos, Research Coordinator of the Southern Voice, has demonstrated exceptional commitment and competence in managing the research programme of the network and deserves special thanks for her contribution as the co-editor of the volume.

When approached with the request to write a foreword for this volume, *Nancy Birdsall*, Founding President, Center for Global Development (CGD), Washington, DC, readily responded. It is indeed gratifying to have words of appreciation from a person of her experience and stature.

Finally, genuine thanks to Routledge for showing interest in the work of Southern Voice and providing this opportunity to bring the network's intellectual contribution to a wider readership.

Debapriya Bhattacharya
Chair, Southern Voice on Post-MDG International
Development Goals and Distinguished Fellow, CPD
Dhaka
June 2016

List of contributors

Adedeji Adeniran is a PhD student at the Department of Economics, University of Witwatersrand, South Africa. He previously worked at the Center for the Study of the Economies of Africa (CSEA), Nigeria. His research interests include public finance economics, development finance and poverty analysis.

Mashfique Ibne Akbar is a Public Sector Specialist at the World Bank and a Lecturer at North South University. Previously he was a Senior Research Associate at the Centre for Policy Dialogue (CPD). Particularly curious about econometrics and macroeconomic issues pertaining to developmental concerns, Akbar is especially interested in blending theoretical constructs with numerical applications.

Mohd. Sahil Ali is a Senior Economist at the Center for Study of Science, Technology and Policy (CSTEP), India, working on energy efficiency and demand-side management, mitigation strategies and sustainability issues. He specialises in systems modelling, economic forecasting, resource planning strategies and techno-economic and policy analysis.

Muhammad Al Amin is doing his PhD in Economics at the University of Mississippi. He is a Senior Research Associate at the Centre for Policy Dialogue (CPD), Dhaka. Al Amin completed his MS in Applied Economics from the University of Wyoming. His publications concentrate on international trade and climate change.

Debapriya Bhattacharya, PhD, is a macro-economist and public policy analyst. Currently he is the chair of two global initiatives, viz. Southern Voices on Post-MDG International Development Goals and LDC IV Monitor. He is a Distinguished Fellow at the Centre for Policy Dialogue (CPD) in Dhaka, where he had been earlier the Executive Director. He is Bangladesh's former Ambassador and Permanent Representative of Bangladesh to the WTO and UN Offices of Geneva and Vienna. He has published extensively on trade, investment and finance-related issues of the LDCs and the post-2015 agenda.

Boris Branisa is a Senior Researcher at the Institute for Advanced Development Studies (INESAD) in Bolivia. He received his PhD in Economics from the University of Göttingen, Germany and has worked as a consultant for various international organisations. His main research interests include development economics, applied econometrics and impact evaluation.

Carolina Cardona is a Researcher at the Institute for Advanced Development Studies (INESAD), Bolivia. She holds a Master of Health Science in Health Economics from the Johns Hopkins University, Bloomberg School of Public Health. Her main research focus are health economics, applied econometrics and demography.

Subrat Das is the Executive Director of Centre for Budget and Governance Accountability (CBGA) in New Delhi. He has worked extensively on government financing of social sectors, fiscal policy and social inclusion, and some of the structural issues in the federal fiscal architecture in India.

Bitrina Diyamett is the Executive Director at the Science, Technology and Innovation Policy Research Organization (STIPRO), Tanzania. Her research focus is on science, technology and innovation policy. She holds a Masters in Science and Technology Policy from the Lund University, Sweden, and a PhD from the University of Dar es Salaam.

Karin Fernando is a Senior Research Professional at the Centre for Poverty Analysis (CEPA), Sri Lanka. She has over 10 years' experience of working in the development sector. Her interests are in natural resource management and sustainable development. She has an MA in Sustainable International Development from Brandeis University, USA.

María Fernanda Mora Garcés is a PhD candidate at the Environment and Sustainability Program at the University of Saskatchewan, Canada. Her research interests include interculturality and knowledge decolonisation, water governance, environmental governance and community-based tourism.

Khalida Ghaus, PhD, is the Managing Director of Social Policy and Development Centre (SPDC), Pakistan. She has over 30 years' teaching/research experience and has extensively worked on foreign policy, development and gender issues. Former Chairperson, Department of International Relations, University of Karachi, she is an author of a book and several monographs.

Nihit Goyal is a PhD candidate at the Lee Kuan Yew School of Public Policy, Singapore. Previously, he was a researcher at the Center for Study of Science, Technology and Policy (CSTEP), India. He is interested in the areas of climate change, energy policy, ICT4D and sustainable development.

Vagisha Gunasekara is a researcher at the Centre for Poverty Analysis (CEPA), Sri Lanka. She received her PhD in political science from Purdue University, USA. Her broad research interest lies in understanding the effects of development interventions in post-war contexts.

Prasanthi Gunawardena, PhD, is the Head of the Department of Forestry and Environmental Science of University of Sri Jayewardenepura, Sri Lanka. Her current research interests include green accounting, environmental ethics and environmental valuation. She has been teaching environmental economics for over 15 years in Sri Lanka.

Ibrahima Hathie is the Research Director for the Initiative Prospective Agricole et Rurale (IPAR Senegal). He holds a PhD in Agricultural and Resource Economics from the University of Connecticut, USA. His research focuses mainly on agricultural performance, youth employment, climate change and the post-2015 development agenda.

Towfiqul Islam Khan is an economist and a Research Fellow at the Centre for Policy Dialogue (CPD), Bangladesh. Over the last decade, Khan has conducted several research studies on fiscal policies and illicit financial flows. Recently, he has published several journal articles, book chapters and research reports on global development agenda.

Fahmida Khatun is the Research Director at the Centre for Policy Dialogue (CPD). She has a Masters and PhD in Economics from University College London and a Post-Doctorate from Columbia University. She was a Visiting Fellow at the Christian Michelsen Institute, Norway, and the Korea Institute for Industrial Economics and Trade, South Korea.

Luis Linares is Executive Secretary of the Asociación de Investigación y Estudios Sociales (ASIES), Guatemala. Previously, he worked at the Ministry of Labour in Guatemala. He holds a degree in Law and Social Sciences from the University of San Carlos. At ASIES, he is the coordinator of the project Supporting Social Dialogue for Decent Work.

Andrea Ordóñez Llanos is the Research Coordinator for the Southern Voice on Post-MDG International Development Goals and a Research Fellow at the United Nations University – Maastricht Economic and Social Research Institute on Innovation and Technology (UNU-MERIT). Her main area of interest is the impact of research on national and international policies for development.

Rodrigo López has an MA in Energy Governance from FLACSO-Ecuador. He is currently a Professor at the Cultural Historic Tourism Faculty at the Central University of Ecuador and works as a researcher on environment and climate change topics.

Musambya Mutambala works for the Science, Technology and Innovation Policy Research Organization (STIPRO), Tanzania, as Research Fellow. In the past, he has also worked for UNIDO-Tanzania. Mutambala is pursuing PhD studies in Development Studies, and has published in the area of science, technology and innovation.

Katerine F. Saravia Olivarez was a research assistant and supported projects in the areas of political economy and public policy in ARU Foundation, Bolivia. She is also a Professor Assistant of Negotiation and Conflict Conciliation. She graduated from Universidad Mayor de San Andrés and is continuing further studies at the Universidad Católica Boliviana.

Wilson Jiménez Pozo is a founding member of ARU Foundation, Bolivia. He has worked at UDAPE and INE in Bolivia and for UNDP. He was involved in research and analysis projects related to poverty, inequality, decentralisation and economic development in various organisations. He obtained his Masters from the Universidad Católica Boliviana.

Julio Prado is a researcher at the Asociación de Investigación y Estudios Sociales (ASIES), Guatemala, where he is responsible for the Decent Work Observatory. He holds degrees in Industrial Engineering from University Rafael Landivar and the University of Pittsburgh and a Masters in Computer Science from West Virginia University.

Nidhi S. Sabharwal, PhD, is an Associate Professor at the Centre for Policy Research in Higher Education, National University of Educational Planning and Administration. Previously, she was Director of the Indian Institute of Dalit Studies. Her research focuses on the impact of caste and gender discrimination on inequalities in human development.

Muhammad Sabir is Principal Economist at the Social Policy and Development Centre (SPDC), Karachi, and provides technical support to the Government of Sindh in negotiations of the 9th NFC. He also served as a national expert on Gender Responsive Budgeting Initiative at the Ministry of Finance, Government of Pakistan, during 2005–2007.

Shweta Srinivasan is a researcher at the Center for Study of Science, Technology and Policy (CSTEP). She works on low carbon energy policy and mainstreaming climate mitigation interventions using co-benefits approaches. Other research interests include natural resource access and governance. She graduated with an MA from the Institute of Development Studies.

Mireya Anabell Villacís Taco has a Masters in Environmental Policy from the Lincoln University, Christchurch, New Zealand. She has a background in the management/coordination of environmental and social projects within civil society organisations. Her interests include issues related to sustainable development and participatory governance.

Ganga Tilakaratna is a Research Fellow and the Head of Poverty and Social Welfare Policy Unit of the Institute of Policy Studies of Sri Lanka. She holds an MPhil in Economics from the University of Cambridge, and a PhD in Development Policy and Management from the University of Manchester, UK. Her key research interests include poverty, microfinance, social protection and employment.

Eberechukwu Uneze, PhD, is an Executive Director at the Asset Management Corporation of Nigeria. He has worked on global development and has published several articles. His research interest cuts across public economics and policy analysis, development finance, results-based public financial management, and outcome and impact evaluation.

Acronyms

ADB	Asian Development Bank
ADF	Augmented Dickey Fuller
AfDB	African Development Bank
AIC	Akaike Information Criterion
ARA	Amazonian Regional Articulation
ARDL	Autoregressive Distributed Lag
ASEAN	Association of Southeast Asian Nations
ASIES	Asociación de Investigación y Estudios Sociales [Association for Research and Social Studies]
AU	African Union
AUC	African Union Commission
BMI	Body Mass Index
BPRS	Bolivian Poverty Reduction Strategy
BRICS	Brazil, Russia, India, China and South Africa
CAP	Common African Position on the Post-2015 Development Agenda
CBGA	Centre for Budget and Governance Accountability
CES	Consejo Económico y Social [Economic and Social Council] (Guatemala)
CIMDM	Comité Interinstitucional de las Metas de Desarrollo del Milenio [Interagency Committee of the Millennium Development Goals] (Bolivia)
CISE	Consejo Interinstitucional de Seguimiento y Evaluación [Interagency Council for Monitoring and Evaluation] (Bolivia)
CO_2	Carbon Dioxide
CPI	Consumer Price Index
CSO	Civil Society Organisation
CSR	Corporate Social Responsibility
DAC	Development Assistance Committee
DNT	De-Notified Tribe
EAP	Economically Active Population

EC	European Commission
ECM	Error Correction Model
EFA	Education for All
EKC	Environmental Kuznets Curve
ENDSA	Encuesta Nacional Demográfica y de Salud [National Demographic and Health Survey] (Bolivia)
ENEI	Encuesta Nacional de Empleo e Ingresos [National Survey of Employment and Income] (Guatemala)
ESRP	Education Sector Reforms Programme (Pakistan)
FATA	Federally Administrated Tribal Area
FDI	Foreign Direct Investment
FIU	Financial Intelligence Unit
FSI	Failed State Index
FTT	Financial Transaction Tax
GDP	Gross Domestic Product
GDT	Gross Devolution and Transfers
GHG	Greenhouse Gas
GID	Gender, Institutions and Development (Database)
GLS	Generalized Least Square
GNI	Gross National Income
GPI	Gender Parity Index
GRAP	Gender Reforms Action Plan (Pakistan)
GTQ	Guatemalan Quetzal
G-20	Group of Twenty
HCR	Head Count Ratio
HDI	Human Development Index
HIES	Household Income and Expenditure Survey
HIPC	Heavily Indebted Poor Countries
HLC	High-Level Committee
HLP	High-Level Panel of Eminent Persons on the Post-2015 Development Agenda
ICT	Information and Communication Technology
IDRC	International Development Research Centre
IEA	International Energy Agency
IFF	Illicit Financial Flow
IHDS	India Human Development Survey
ILO	International Labour Organization
IMR	Infant Mortality Rate
INE	Instituto Nacional de Estadística [National Statistics Institute] (Bolivia)
IPCC	Intergovernmental Panel on Climate Change
IPoA	Istanbul Programme of Action
IT	Information Technology
LDC	Least Developed Country

LIC	Low-Income Country
LIFS	Low-Income Fragile States
MDG	Millennium Development Goal
MIC	Middle-Income Country
MIFS	Middle-Income Fragile States
MNC	Multinational Corporation
MPCE	Monthly Per Capita Expenditure
MSE	Micro and Small Enterprise
NEAS	National Education Assessment System (Pakistan)
NEP	National Education Policy (Pakistan)
NFC	National Finance Commission (Pakistan)
NFHS	National Family Health Survey (India)
NGO	Non-Government Organisation
NSE	National Secretariat for Elders (Sri Lanka)
NT	Nomadic Tribe
OBC	Other Backward Classes
ODA	Official Development Assistance
OECD	Organisation for Economic Co-operation and Development
OLS	Ordinary Least Square
OWG	Open Working Group
PCEC	Per Capita Electricity Consumption
PCGDP	Per Capita GDP
PDS	Public Distribution System (India)
PIHS	Pakistan Integrated Household Survey
PNBV	Plan Nacional del Buen Vivir [National Plan for Good Living] (Ecuador)
POLS	Pooled Ordinary Least Square
PP	Phillips-Perron
PPMCC	Pearson Product-Moment Correlation Coefficient
PPP	Public-Private Partnership
PRGF	Poverty Reduction Growth Facility
PRSP	Poverty Reduction Strategy Paper
PSLM	Pakistan Social and Living Standards Measurement
PSPS	Public Service Pension Scheme (Sri Lanka)
RBA	Regional Bureau for Africa
RUDE	Registro de Estudiantes [Register of Students] (Bolivia)
SAARC	South Asian Association for Regional Cooperation
SC	Scheduled Caste
SCP	Sustainable Consumption and Production
SDG	Sustainable Development Goal
SDSN	Sustainable Development Solutions Network
SE4ALL	Sustainable Energy for All
SIAS	Sistema de Información de Agua y Saneamiento [Water and Sanitation Information System] (Bolivia)

SIC	Schwarz Information Criteria
SIE	Sistema de Información para la Educación [Educational Information System] (Bolivia)
SIGI	Social Institutions and Gender Index
SIS	Statistical Information System
SISAS	Sistema de Información Sobre el Agua y Saneamiento [Information System on Water and Sanitation Sector] (Bolivia)
SISFIN	Sistema de Información de Financiamiento Externo [External Financing Information System] (Bolivia)
SITDG	Sistema de Indicadores de Trabajo Decente para Guatemala [System of Decent Work Indicators for Guatemala]
SNIA	Sistema Nacional de Información Ambiental [National Environmental Information System] (Bolivia)
SNIS	Sistema Nacional de Información en Salud [National Health Information System] (Bolivia)
SPDC	Social Policy and Development Centre
SSA	Sub-Saharan Africa
ST	Scheduled Tribe
STAR	Stolen Assets Recovery
STIPRO	Science, Technology and Innovation Policy Research Organization
TTI	Think Tank Initiative
T-Y	Toda-Yamamoto
UDAPE	Unidad de Análisis de Políticas Sociales y Económicas [Analytical Unit for Social and Economic Policies] (Bolivia)
UN	United Nations
UNDP	United Nations Development Programme
UNECA	United Nations Economic Commission for Africa
UNEP	United Nations Environment Programme
UNGC	United Nations Global Compact
UNICEF	United Nations Children's Fund
UNSG	United Nations Secretary-General
UN-ECLAC	UN Economic Commission for Latin America and the Caribbean
UN-OHCHR	UN Office of the High Commissioner for Human Rights
UN LDC IV	United Nations Fourth Conference on the Least Developed Countries
USD	United States Dollar
VAR	Vector Autoregression
VECM	Vector Error Correction Model
VIF	Variance Inflation Factor
VIPFE	Viceministerio de Inversión Pública y Financiamiento Externo [Vice-Ministry of Public Investment and External Financing] (Bolivia)

WAP	Working-Age Population
WDI	World Development Indicators
WEF	World Economic Forum
WHO	World Health Organization
WTO	World Trade Organization
W&OP	Widows'/Widowers' and Orphans' Pension Scheme (Sri Lanka)

1 Exploring the post-2015 development agenda from Southern perspectives

Debapriya Bhattacharya and Andrea Ordóñez Llanos

Why Southern Voice

At the turn of the millennium, the most ambitious major innovation in international development was the unanimous adoption of the Millennium Development Goals (MDGs) by the United Nations (UN) General Assembly. This set of goals, targets and indicators was purported to reflect a shared global vision for a world where the needs of all humans are both respected and promoted by national governments and the international community. Not long after, the MDGs became the blueprint for the work of government institutions, philanthropic organisations, multilateral institutions, and of course, the UN system as a whole.

It is now widely agreed that one of the fault lines of the MDGs was that they were designed behind closed doors, primarily with inputs from the governments and think tanks of the developed world and UN officials. The marginal representation of developing country governments in shaping the MDGs was probably a shortcoming of the negotiation process, but a record of low participation in global discussions also suggests that capacity deficits often afflict delegations from the developing world. Such deficits are outcomes of an interplay of factors, including the lack of dedicated public and private resources available for the purpose.

Moreover, there was low participation by researchers, policy experts and development practitioners from the global South.[1] Southern actors usually have limited access to global knowledge networks. They often confront structural impediments in engaging with others due to, *inter alia*, locational disadvantage, practices and procedures that mitigate against effective engagement, and inadequate resources and capacities.

These problems persisted throughout the 15-year implementation period of the MDGs. An analysis of journal articles indexed on the Web of Science[2] indicates that authors who publish on MDG issues in international peer-reviewed journals are mostly from the United Kingdom, the United States and multilateral institutions. There are individual institutions in the United Kingdom with over 100 publications on MDG issues, whereas only two countries from the global South have more than 20.

Fifteen years after the adoption of the MDGs, the global context has changed, as it is now unimaginable that a global process would not take all voices, particularly those from the South, into account. It is in this context that the post-2015 development agenda, namely the Sustainable Development Goals (SDGs), are designed in a much more participatory manner through an intergovernmental process, where countries at various stages of development from different regions played key roles in negotiating the final outcome document, *Transforming Our World: The 2030 Agenda for Sustainable Development* (United Nations, 2015). Although the SDG process has embedded broader political participation from the global South through governmental and non-governmental processes, it has yet to be translated into wider diversity in knowledge generation on the SDGs. Consequently, the knowledge asymmetry in global development discourse and practice continues to be perpetuated.

The Web of Science demonstrates that the structure of knowledge generation on the SDGs is similar to that on the MDGs. As shown in Figure 1.1, only one country from the global South, South Africa, appears among the top 10 countries publishing on SDG and MDG issues. Pakistan and Uganda have produced research works on the MDG issue, but not on the SDG issue, yet. While there are more resources available in languages other than English and outside the Web of Science, researchers with the ability to publish in English-language international peer-reviewed journals are probably more likely to exert influence on global discourse and practice. Researchers who publish in other languages and journals appear to have less impact on international readership.

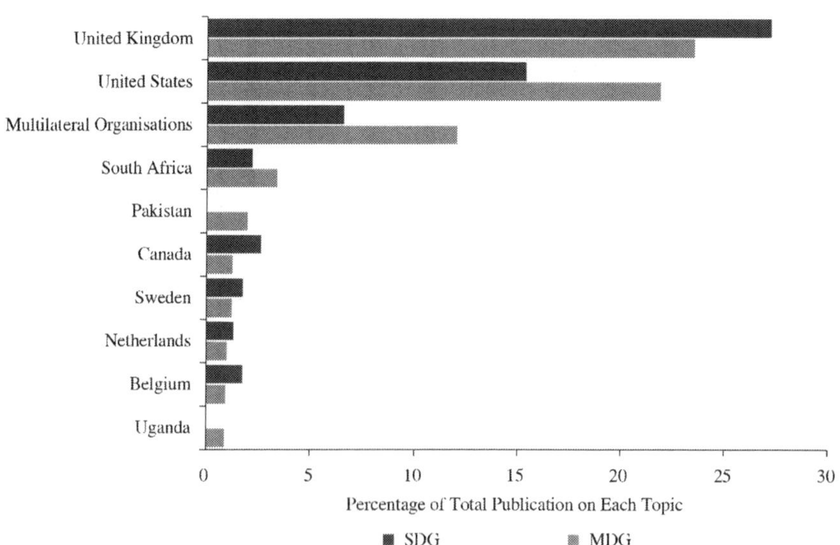

Figure 1.1 Concentration of publications on SDGs and MDGs by country

Source: www.webofknowledge.com [Accessed: 30 September 2015].

Note: Data included herein are derived from Thomson Reuters Web of Science™.

These assertions are confirmed by our own research of the inputs received by the UN System Task Team on the Post-2015 UN Development Agenda during the design period for the SDGs.[3] More than 80 per cent of inputs came from Northern institutions and another 10 per cent came from Southern experts working in Northern institutions. Only a residual 10 per cent of inputs came from Southern research centres and think tanks. These numbers come as a surprise because such Southern institutions are the best repositories of expertise and experience regarding the implementation of the MDGs. They are established sources of rich knowledge about what works and what does not in terms of development policies and programmes in their specific country contexts.

Participation shortfalls and capacity deficits on the part of Southern research centres and think tanks, as well as knowledge asymmetry in global development discourse and practice, are structural constraints that will very likely affect the implementation of the SDGs. There is a compelling need to tackle these constraints at the international level, particularly through international policy processes. Notably, there is an opportunity to promote better coordination among relevant national, regional and global platforms. There is an implication here that Southern institutions could produce high-quality knowledge on development in general, and the SDGs in particular, and communicate it to a wide audience. Researchers, policy experts and development practitioners from the global South will first need full access to the global knowledge network and then to deploy it within the concrete context of their countries. At the same time, global policymakers and Northern researchers need to better acknowledge and fully consider the work of their counterparts from the South. Only then can Southern institutions realise their full potential.

The present volume has been inspired by the above-mentioned perspectives and seeks to contribute to ongoing discussions on the SDGs as they move from the topic of articulation to delivery.

From concept to practice

Southern Voice on Post-MDG International Development Goals was conceived in Cape Town in June 2012. Members of 49 think tanks from Africa, Asia and Latin America met at an awardees meeting of the Think Tank Initiative (TTI), a multi-donor programme managed by the Canadian government's International Development Research Centre (IDRC).[4] They perceived the negotiations on the post-2015 development agenda to be an opportunity to engage in policy debates at the subnational, national and regional levels, with a view to inform the international agenda by applying and building upon their research and analyses. They decided to take their discussions forward with the objective of channelling evidence-based policy inputs from the participating think tanks to ongoing global discussions on the next development agenda.

The Southern Voice initiative was launched in January 2013 at an expert group meeting in Dhaka, which established a network of the above-mentioned 49 think tanks with the objective to serve as an open platform for contributing to global discussions on what should succeed the MDGs. A Steering Committee was elected from amongst the network members to operationalise and oversee the network's various activities; later on three regional coordinators were designated from Africa, Asia and Latin America to strengthen the network's operational capacity. The Centre for Policy Dialogue (CPD) in Dhaka was assigned the task of hosting the Secretariat for the Southern Voice network.

The Dhaka meeting also led to the production of a document titled *First Approximations on Post-MDG International Development Goals* (Bhattacharya, 2013). This was the first time that network members put forward a collective position on the post-2015 agenda. The document was later shared with the UN Secretary-General's High-Level Panel of Eminent Persons on the Post-2015 Development Agenda and discussed at a number of meetings in New York during March and April of 2013.

Given significant experience in conducting empirical policy-relevant research across different developing regions as well as shared thematic expertise, Southern Voice members are uniquely placed to reflect on the post-2015 agenda. During the first two research phases in 2013 and 2014, members had the opportunity to both reinterpret their existing research findings and highlight new issues in the context of the ongoing discussions.

The present volume brings together a selection of papers that were produced under the first two phases of Southern Voice's research programme and that focus on key issue areas characterising discussions on the post-2015 agenda to date, including defining the agenda, implementation of the SDGs, and monitoring and accountability. These research outputs passed through internal and external peer-review processes from the proposal stage to the final drafting of chapters. Authors also came together at the first Southern Voice Research Conference in Istanbul in February 2015 to receive feedback on their research.

In addition, Southern Voice developed an innovative research programme called the *Post-2015 Data-Test: Unpacking the Data Revolution at the Country Level*, which evaluated the state of data availability, quality and accessibility to monitor and assess the implementation of the post-2015 agenda.[5] To test the proposed universal nature of the agenda, research was conducted by research centres and think tanks in Bangladesh, Canada, Peru, Senegal, Sierra Leone, Tanzania and Turkey, which represent a range of low-, middle- and high-income countries. Furthermore, Southern Voice was one of the strategic partners involved in the preparation of *European Report on Development 2015: Combining Finance and Policies to Implement a Transformative Post-2015 Development Agenda*, which discussed the financial challenges of implementing the post-2015 agenda (ODI et al., 2015). In these cases, Southern Voice members informed global discussions by bringing national and regional knowledge, along with a sense of realism and pragmatism, to the table.

Southern Voice has also informed global discussions through several strategic engagements at the global and regional levels. The network has organised more than 30 events in national capitals such as Dhaka, Dar es Salaam, Nairobi and New Delhi to disseminate its members' research findings and analyses. Moreover, the Chair of Southern Voice has been invited to address many high-level platforms including the stock-taking session of the intergovernmental negotiations on the post-2015 agenda at the UN, sessions of the UN High Level Political Forum on Sustainable Development and UN General Assembly's Open Working Group (OWG) on SDGs, as well as the British Parliamentary Association, United States Department of State and the European Union. Southern Voice is now moving forward with the delivery of the 2030 Agenda by conducting 11 country studies on the challenges of implementing the SDGs that will support the development of national implementation plans.

The issues covered by the present volume critically concern the post-2015 agenda. It touches on topics that are fundamentally important for defining the agenda as well as its delivery. These topics will have enduring relevance during the implementation of the agenda in the years to come. These topics will also impinge upon the monitoring and accountability processes that are yet to unfold.

Distinguishing features of the Southern Voice perspective

When Southern Voice was launched, the perspective that the network would adopt was not immediately evident. Moreover, it was unclear whether the platform should have one voice or be a collective expression of a number of voices. While the authors of the chapters in the present volume were free to develop their conceptual categories and analytical constructs, six recurring themes emerge across chapters. These themes include economic transformation, social inclusion, integrated approach towards economic, social and environmental issues, governance challenges, systemic concerns and new forms of global partnership. Together, these themes constitute a framework for understanding the Southern Voice perspective on the post-2015 agenda.

Economic transformation refers to fundamentally changing the economic structures of developing countries to set them on a path of higher sustained growth driven by enhanced factor productivity. Such structural changes necessitate improvements in productive capacities that lead to more and better jobs and higher incomes. The authors emphasise the importance of the expansion of the manufacturing sector, modernisation of agriculture, diversification of exports and improvement of infrastructure. They discuss the inclusion of specific post-2015 goals and targets for economic transformation with a sustainable perspective, since they were missing in the MDGs.

The emphasis on *social inclusion* was prompted by the MDG experience, where the focus was on aggregates and averages. A number of chapters raise the issue of inequality – not only in terms of income. Concerns for distributive justice underscore the need to allocate additional resources and policy support towards ensuring gender parity, addressing rural–urban disparities, ameliorating youth unemployment and mitigating discrimination against minorities. Instead of implicit targets and indicators, the authors indicate their preference for specific measurable goals in these respects.

While it was clear that the economy, society and the environment would constitute the three pillars of sustainability in the post-2015 agenda, the authors maintain that interdependent economic, social and environmental issues have to be addressed in a *holistic* way and in an *integrated* fashion. This entails breaking away from the so-called silo approach and promoting synergies among the core objectives of the new agenda. Along with horizontal integration across the three pillars, the authors recommend the proper alignment of new goals and targets across global, regional, national and subnational policy platforms.

Governance challenges at the national level may be singled out as another element of the Southern Voice perspective. A common aspiration for developing countries, good governance, could have been considered the fourth pillar of the post-2015 agenda. In addressing governance challenges, the authors reiterate the need for institutional makeovers and policy reforms in their respective countries in order to accelerate inclusive economic growth. A related set of issues in this regard includes the need for citizen participation in development policy making, management and implementation, which would likely contribute towards greater transparency of development processes, efficiency of resource use and accountability for outcomes.

The authors highlight *systemic concerns* about the functioning of the global economy. They hold that without development-friendly changes in global economic governance that result in greater voice for developing countries, more policy space for this country group and enhanced coherence among different aspects of developed countries' development and economic policies, it will be quite difficult for developing countries to actually implement the post-2015 agenda. The issue of illicit financial flows exemplifies these concerns. While income-poor countries mount efforts to raise their ratios of tax to GDP (gross domestic product), large parts of the mobilised domestic resources illegally flow out of the countries to tax havens. Distortions in international financial taxation, global trade and intellectual property rights systems must be effectively addressed in order to make the new agenda work in practice.

Finally, the authors contend that the post-2015 agenda has to be bolstered by a firm commitment to promote a revitalised *global partnership* with strengthened international development cooperation at its core. Recognising that financial resources for implementation of the agenda will not come exclusively from official development assistance (ODA), they still expect that developed countries will keep their commitments to provide 0.7 per cent of gross national income (GNI) as ODA and strengthen global economic ties by concluding the World Trade Organization's (WTO) Doha Development Round. They stress the importance of ongoing climate change negotiations, particularly since the new agenda intends to effectively integrate environmental concerns into operational modalities. At the same time, the authors affirm that the revitalised global partnership has to suitably accommodate expanding South–South cooperation for the overall benefit to the global economy.

Overview of the volume

The diversity of issues across the present volume illustrates the challenge of putting forward an agenda that is meaningful at both the global and subnational levels. The chapters have wide geographical coverage, addressing issues of interest to middle-income countries, least developed countries (LDCs) and fragile states. The authors strive to bridge discussions from the subnational to the global level. In certain instances, they adopt novel approaches and categories of analysis to understand the specificities of the ongoing discussions. For instance, one of the chapters explores the issue of carbon emissions for the LDCs and sheds light on the special needs of this group of countries. In another chapter, the issue of gender institutions in fragile states is examined, underscoring the need for attaching special attention to the interplay of contextual factors.

An overview of the volume can be broken down according to the following five broad topics:

- Overarching issues of the post-2015 agenda
- Sustainability and growth
- Inclusion and social policies
- Governance and capacities
- Financing the new development agenda

Overarching issues of the post-2015 agenda

National development agendas have evolved differently across regions over the past 15 years. Even though the MDGs were of limited scope, their implementation demonstrated the range of variance in agendas between and among regions and countries. The challenge for the post-2015 agenda is to be relevant for national and subnational governments while remaining meaningful at the global and regional levels. Goals, targets and indicators must be adaptable to all levels of economic development, ecosystems, and social and cultural characteristics. Chapters in the volume depict marked differences between regions that need to be reconciled at the national level during the implementation of the global agenda.

Ibrahima Hathie explores the debates within Africa as summarised in the Common African Position on the post-2015 agenda. He highlights the importance of the political process to attain this common position and identifies it as the first step in strengthening the region's hand in global discussions. Political and technical coordination on priorities is strong in Africa. Notably, there is consensus that structural economic transformation is crucial for the region's successful implementation of the new agenda. To attain the SDGs, low-income countries will require structural economic changes, with new sectors and jobs being essential. Only such changes can break the vicious cycle of poverty, low productivity and low incomes. Attention should be focused on bringing the benefits of science, technology and innovation to low-income segments of populations in order to stimulate productivity and ensure higher returns on labour.

In their chapter, Mireya Anabell Villacís Taco, María Fernanda Mora Garcés and Rodrigo López offer a perspective from Latin America, where certain governments are applying the new concept of 'Good Living' as a modern paradigm for development. 'Good Living' proposes the respect of the social and cultural rights of citizens while maintaining a respect and harmony with nature. There is some scepticism about this direction, but such debates illustrate efforts in a region that continues to struggle with unique challenges. The authors argue that the post-2015 agenda must ensure that development outcomes are shared, particularly by traditionally disadvantaged groups, in order to meet the SDG commitment to 'leave no one behind.' To this end, governance should be people-centred, respect traditional knowledge and territorial diversities and operate in harmony with nature.

The development debates preoccupying minds in the global South provide insights into the complex settings in which the post-2015 agenda will be implemented. All historical contexts have been complex, but the contemporary context, characterised by great advancements in science and information technology, is arguably the most complex. Partial and limited solutions are no longer economically justifiable and socially acceptable. Authors in the volume argue that the new agenda has to be implemented as an indivisible package – not as standalone goals and targets – to deal with both traditional and new development challenges.

Sustainability and growth

In retrospect, the MDGs' social focus was a major limitation. Even though the social agenda remains unfinished, as not all goals and targets were met and many were incorporated into the SDGs, not tackling economic and environmental concerns makes any social agenda unattainable. Interestingly, as Karin Fernando and Prasanthi Gunawardena show in their chapter, while social goals and targets in the post-2015 agenda are clear and ambitious, the same is not the case for economic and environmental goals and targets. They identify environmental goals and targets as being the weakest and least ambitious. Furthermore, the interaction between economic growth and environmental sustainability is not explicitly addressed. Tensions between the two are therefore expected to arise during the implementation of the agenda. As Fernando and Gunawardena argue, the fact that economic, social and environmental dimensions have not been fully integrated into the agenda may lead to sub-optimal performances, especially under the weakest goal areas.

Mohd. Sahil Ali, Nihit Goyal and Shweta Srinivasan outline the challenges of integrating economic, social and environmental dimensions in the domain of energy provision. They examine the energy sector in India and define the sustainability of a system as its ability to maintain long-term functionality – to withstand and recover from shocks and stresses – without compromising well-being, equity or the environment. The specific characteristics that a sustainable system must possess, among others, are stability, resilience, durability and robustness. Failure of a system to be endowed with such features will pose risk of compromising the post-2015 agenda's target on universal access to energy, which brings out negative implications in social and economic terms. To address such complex challenges, the authors recommend the introduction of a sustainability assessment framework that gauges threats to sustainability through a quantitative and qualitative evaluation of the likelihood of disruptions and their impacts on access. This is an example of the types of policy tools that can support an integrated approach to economic, social and environmental issues during implementation of the post-2015 agenda. Without such tools, the isolated achievement of goals in one area might have negative impacts on others.

Acknowledging that sustainability may involve trade-offs, Fahmida Khatun and Muhammad Al Amin study the trade-offs between economic growth and carbon dioxide (CO_2) emissions in LDCs. Using co-integration and vector error correction modelling, they assess short- and long-term approaches to sustainable development, a necessary strategy given that development policies may deliver substantive results within a few years, but will also likely have negative impacts in the decades that follow. The authors conclude that deforestation and higher energy usage in LDCs will most likely increase emissions over the long term, but there is a window of opportunity in terms of agriculture, one of the main economic activities in this country group, an important source of employment for the poor, and a key challenge given that it is a major source of emissions. They suggest a focus on sustainable agriculture and a balanced, efficient use of chemical fertilisers and pesticides going forward. Such research supports the promotion of sustainable agriculture at early stages in national and international development, breaking from traditional practices in light of the evolving global context.

Bitrina Diyamett and Musambya Mutambala contribute to the discussion of economic growth in Africa by looking at the case of Tanzania, which demonstrates that not all growth is equal when it comes to its capacity to reduce poverty and promote economic transformation. Like many other countries in the global South, Tanzania's growth is based on the extraction of natural resources, not industrialisation. The authors show that from a social perspective, a different type of economic growth is necessary. Both this chapter and that by Ali, Goyal and Srinivasan exemplify that the incorporation of an economic agenda in the SDGs is an improvement over the MDGs, but its inclusion does not come without challenges to an integrated approach.

These chapters suggest that a flexible sustainable development approach is clearly necessary. Developing countries still operate within their national biocapacity limits and can stay within these limits by strategically using existing knowledge and technology.

Inclusion and social policies

Authors agree on the importance of strengthening the link between social issues in the post-2015 agenda and the economic and environmental dimensions of sustainability to improve income generation and reduce poverty. For example, Luis Linares and Julio Prado analyse the challenges of employment in Guatemala, with a specific focus on the informal economy and limited opportunities despite educational training of individuals. More than half of unemployed people in the country have completed either secondary or tertiary education, and still there is persistently a high level of informal employment. This points to structural problems, with the economy unable to grant opportunities even to those who are trained, and perhaps problems in the educational system, which may not be providing young people with the skills required to enter the labour market. While the original MDGs had a significant focus on improving access to education, there was no explicit focus on education quality and education that would lead to broader employment opportunities, which can be implicated in unequal access to labour markets. Moving forward, the post-2015 agenda must be more ambitious in linking better education with broader economic opportunities in order to maximise the positive impacts of investments.

In her chapter, Vagisha Gunasekara looks at the links between inequality, poverty and labour markets in middle-income countries (MICs). While many of these countries have been successful in reducing poverty, statistics usually hide the high proportions of people who live barely above the poverty line. These populations might not be poor, strictly speaking, but they live in precarious situations, especially in terms of employment since most people remain in low-productivity jobs. In fact, these populations face similar realities to those who are officially considered poor. As the author summarises, "the fleeting gains made on one score, poverty reduction, often get lost on account of unabated or worsened unemployment and inequalities that token policies often fail to address in meaningful ways."

Inequalities in the labour market are, of course, also visible through the lenses of gender, ethnicity and social construction. Nidhi S. Sabharwal explores social exclusion of groups based on their identities in India, particularly in the case of scheduled castes who are socially deemed as the 'untouchables'. An analysis of MDG attainment in India shows that these socially excluded groups have performed worse than the general population of the country, across the board, due to persistent discrimination. Economic vulnerabilities are often embedded in social constructs. To tackle such vulnerabilities, relevant local institutions and groups should be integral in development discourse and treated as partners in development processes. The author suggests that affirmative action policies for specific groups, in addition to better universal social projects, are an effective option that can be used to address social exclusion and level the playing field for those who have been traditionally excluded.

Another challenge not directly tackled by the MDGs is that of aging, specifically the aging of populations of the LDCs and MICs that may be reaching retirement age without social protection systems in place. Ganga Tilakaratna explores the issue in Sri Lanka, where the share of the population over the age of 60 will double by 2040, meaning that approximately one-fourth of the population will be above 60 years of age. Informal markets and fragmented social protection systems in the developing world leave a significant number of people in precarious situations when they become too old to work. Although cash transfer programmes may become parts of solutions, properly planned and funded retirement schemes are necessary to cover the needs of aging populations. Furthermore, social protection is an important strategy that reduces inequalities and social exclusion.

In another analysis of social issues, Boris Branisa and Carolina Cardona show how fragile states have completely different social institutions that relate to gender inequality relative to other country groups, suggesting that a specific approach is needed. These social norms relate to long-lasting values, codes of conduct and traditions that determine the roles that men and women play in society. There is an explicit need to tackle the issues of security, legitimacy and slow economic growth in fragile states. The authors explore the dimension of gender inequality and conclude that it is in fact a central feature of state fragility. This finding attests to how highly interconnected the aforementioned issues are and how differentiation in the implementation of the SDGs is necessary to maintain an agenda that is both universal and relevant for different country groups.

Social issues found in the post-2015 agenda are part of the unfinished agenda of the MDGs. The challenge remains as to how to attain the original goals and targets while at the same time tackling emerging issues, especially those that are linked with the economy such as labour market opportunities and the social protection schemes. These chapters underscore the need to adopt and enhance the human rights approach, with goals and targets not just being checked off in reports, but rather used as stepping stones to the well-being of all people. Successfully operationalising the human rights approach would help prevent the formulation of policies that only have short-term impacts or that are too narrowly focused on small, targeted populations. Furthermore, a human rights approach would cover individuals throughout their lives including when they are elderly, a period when people are poorly attended, maybe as a reflection of how little attention older generations received in the MDGs.

Governance and capacities

Governance by and capacities of government institutions are incorporated into the post-2015 agenda. Governance and capacities are both considered goals in their own right and key to achieving the agenda.

Subrat Das discusses the link between governance and capacities, arguing that the lack of skilled personnel and resources are major limitations to governments being more participative and accountable. He provides the case study of India to demonstrate the link. He also highlights that the issue of capacity in a country is related to the ability and willingness of the government to make long-term public expenditure commitments, which are in turn based on the government's resource mobilisation policies.

Katerine F. Saravia Olivarez and Wilson Jiménez Pozo go over the institutional challenges of setting up a framework to monitor the MDGs in Bolivia to draw lessons for the SDGs. They find that MDG adoption had two effects on data availability and quality, and conclude that while more attention was given to data needs, there were no substantial improvements in the quality of data, especially those from surveys. They also note that the monitoring framework overemphasised outcomes above processes and focused too much on the ability of governments to comprehend what was driving achievements and what was hindering them.

Khalida Ghaus and Muhammad Sabir examine public expenditure in Pakistan and suggest that prioritising the increase of financial resources in the post-2015 agenda will not be enough for realising the envisaged development outcome.

Adopting a gender-sensitive perspective, they present the case of budget transfers to subnational governments and the limited impact that they have had on the improvement of education. Their findings indicate that there should be a stronger connection between financial resources and planning processes during the implementation of the agenda.

These chapters draw attention to the processes of implementing the post-2015 agenda and the possible unintended consequences of a new global agenda on national processes. While the agenda provides national governments with a strong role in the design and execution of national implementation plans, a global process that supports and facilitates the work of governments should also be put into place.

Financing the new development agenda

Finally, one of the most critical aspects of the post-2015 agenda is how to finance it, especially since the agenda is universal in coverage and encompasses more themes.

On the topic of new sources of finance, Towfiqul Islam Khan and Mashfique Ibne Akbar explore the issue of illicit financial flows as both an obstacle to financing and an opportunity to finance the agenda. They suggest that the issue requires a two-pronged approach, where illicit funds are part of both the agenda's goals and financing mechanisms. A significant share of resources that could be mobilised, especially for developing countries, include proceeds of tax evasion and laundered commercial transactions along with proceeds of corruption, including theft and bribery, and criminal activities including drug trafficking, racketeering, counterfeiting, trading contraband and terrorist financing. Khan and Akbar suggest that certain ambitious global policies could be used to support domestic resource mobilisation, such as those on the disclosure of the beneficial ownership of companies, trusts and foundations, reforms in the tax rules for multinational corporations, and mandatory reporting of funds paid to governments for natural resources. This issue exemplifies that some issues, such as illicit financial flows, cannot be tackled at the national level without a broader international framework and coordination.

Tensions between country ownership of development processes and the need for international commitments may arise during the implementation of the post-2015 agenda if sufficient financial resources are not mobilised. Unlike in the past when developing countries often depended on the international commitments to provide resources, the new agenda draws mainly on domestic resources and innovative financing options. In exploring the financing options for Sub-Saharan African countries, Eberechukwu Uneze and Adedeji Adeniran find that in reality many countries cannot design strong fiscal policies. Weak institutional capacities and susceptibility to corruption limit the capacities of governments to mobilise domestic resources for the financing of development. Hence, efforts to increase domestic resource mobilisation must go hand in hand with plans to strengthen institutional capacities, especially those related to revenue collection and fiscal accountability. As a first practical step during implementation of the new agenda, governments should carry out country-level assessments of their financial options and institutional capacities to determine whether there are any gaps. Such assessments would also boost country ownership and help reduce the misallocation of resources.

Looking ahead

This volume provides a distinct set of Southern perspectives and recommendations on shaping the post-2015 agenda. As the new agenda stabilises, a new set of challenges emanates as the world moves towards actualisation of the new development framework. Resolution of these new sets of challenges in diverse settings will demand more policy and programme innovations and other creative institutional interventions that should be informed by empirical research and evidence-based policy analysis. Southern research centres and think tanks must remain engaged with the post-2015 process by generating the needed knowledge and analyses to support the successful implementation of the agenda. Their efforts have to support, *inter alia*, integration of the SDGs into national plans, policies and programmes, creation of adequate national institutional mechanisms, mobilisation of sufficient financial resources, and generation of necessary data, statistics and information.

The next major task for Southern research centres and think tanks is to contribute to the establishment and operationalisation of a robust monitoring and evaluation system that can be applied nationally, regionally and globally to improve the transparency of outcomes and efficiency of resource use. Southern researchers, policy experts and development practitioners are expected to devote significant amounts of their professional time to developing a global accountability mechanism to keep the new agenda legitimate.

Southern researchers will continue to strategically engage in global discussions on policy, data and innovation by widely disseminating their research and analyses. Given the 15-year journey that lies ahead, Southern researchers would be well advised to mentor the next generation of researchers fit for the purpose of also contributing to these discussions.

This volume is a humble beginning towards those lofty aims.

Notes

1 The term 'South' is used across this chapter interchangeably with developing countries. The global South has been defined as all countries that are not members of the Development Assistance Committee (DAC) of the Organisation for Economic Co-operation and Development (OECD).

2 The Web of Science is a scientific citation index maintained by Thomson Reuters that contains over 90 million scientific records and more than 12,000 journals (see Thomson Reuters, 2015).

3 This has been referred in Kenny (2013) based on a presentation by one of the authors at a round table organised by the Center for Global Development on 20 February 2013.

4 For more information, see www.thinktankinitiative.org

5 In conducting this research programme, Southern Voice collaborated with the CPD and the North-South Institute and later the Norman Paterson School of International Affairs at Carleton University in Ottawa. For details and research outputs, see www.post2015datatest.com

References

Bhattacharya, D. (ed.) (2013) *First Approximations on Post-MDG International Development Goals.* Southern Voice Occasional Paper Special Issue 1. Dhaka: Southern Voice on Post-MDG International Development Goals.

Kenny, C. (2013) Southern voices in the post-2015 debate. *CGD Blog*. Washington, DC: Center for Global Development (CGD). Available from: http://www.cgdev.org/blog/southern-voices-post-2015-debate [Accessed: 25 September 2015].

Overseas Development Institute (ODI), in partnership with the European Centre for Development Policy Management (ECDPM), the German Development Institute (Deutsches Institut für Entwicklungspolitik) (GDI/DIE), the University of Athens (Department of Economics, Division of International Economics and Development) and Southern Voice on Post-MDG International Development Goals. (2015) *European Report on Development 2015: Combining Finance and Policies to Implement a Transformative Post-2015 Development Agenda*. Brussels: European Union.

Thomson Reuters. (2015) *Web of science*. Available from: http://ipscience.thomsonreuters.com/product/web-of-science [Accessed: 30 September 2015].

United Nations. (2015) *Transforming Our World: The 2030 Agenda for Sustainable Development*. New York: United Nations.

Overarching issues of the post-2015 agenda

2 The post-2015 development agenda

Favourable enough to Africans?

Ibrahima Hathie

Introduction

The last three years have witnessed extensive discussions on the post-2015 international development agenda. Alongside the United Nations (UN)-led global consultations, several autonomous processes have provided key inputs to the global debates. These include institutional proposals (such as the High-Level Panel of Eminent Persons on the Post-2015 Development Agenda (HLP); United Nations Sustainable Development Solutions Network (SDSN); United Nations Global Compact (UNGC); and United Nations Secretary-General (UNSG)) and civil society contributions which have gradually shaped the future Sustainable Development Goals (SDGs) (SDSN, 2013; UNGC, 2013; United Nations, 2013a; UNSG, 2013). In September 2013, a special event by the UN General Assembly designed a roadmap towards the adoption of the post-2015 development agenda. At this special session, world leaders advocated for an "inclusive and people-centred post-2015 development agenda," calling for "a transparent intergovernmental process which will include inputs from all stakeholders including civil society, scientific and knowledge institutions, parliaments, local authorities, and the private sector" (United Nations, 2013b, 3).

One of the challenges of this process was to build a single framework and a set of universal goals, while recognising national differences and taking into account the primacy of national policies and priorities. Bergh and Couturier (2013) examine the plethora of documents emerging from the global debates and discussions and present the areas of consensus and divergence in the post-2015 goals. Their conclusions show (i) a strong consensus on the importance of goals such as education, health, gender, energy and poverty; (ii) a weaker consensus on goal areas such as governance, food security, water and sanitation, inclusive growth and employment; and (iii) that a few goal areas capture little attention: urbanisation, social inclusion, infrastructure and technology.

Parallel to the institutional proposals and civil society contributions, the Open Working Group (OWG) – an emanation of the Rio+20 processes – held several thematic sessions from March 2013 to February 2014. Then from March 2014 to July 2014, the OWG focused its discussions on its draft report including goals and targets. The final outcome document published on 19 July 2014, at the end of the

13th and final session, displays 17 goals and 169 targets, a solid consensus on the SDGs (Open Working Group, 2014).

Building on Bergh and Couturier's work and taking stock of the progress made, this study examines how the consensus on the Sustainable Development Goals is consistent with priorities set out by Sub-Saharan Africa (SSA) through its 'Common African Position on the Post-2015 Development Agenda', otherwise known as the CAP.

During the last three years, the United Nations Economic Commission for Africa (UNECA), the African Union Commission (AUC), the African Development Bank (AfDB) and the United Nations Development Programme's Regional Bureau for Africa (UNDP/RBA) held several national, regional and continental consultations to articulate an African position on the post-2015 development agenda. These initiatives were reinforced in July 2012 when the African Union Heads of State (Assembly/AU/Dec.423 (XIX)) mandated the AUC, in close consultation with member states and Regional Economic Communities, to identify Africa's priorities for the post-2015 development agenda, with the support of AfDB, UNDP/RBA and UNECA. In May 2013, the African Union (AU) established a High-Level Committee (HLC) of 10 heads of state and government,[1] chaired by Liberian President Ellen Johnson Sirleaf, to work towards the CAP (Assembly/AU/Dec.475 (XXI)). The mandate of the HLC was to finalise a demand-driven joint African post-2015 perspective and to build regional and intercontinental alliances around it. With the backing of a technical support team,[2] the HLC committed itself to include the outcomes of the various national, regional and continental consultations held in Africa into the draft CAP.

Alongside these initiatives, AUC, UNECA and AfDB led a process to develop SDGs that are compatible with African interest. This process culminated with the Africa Regional Consultative Meeting on the SDGs held in October–November 2013 and aimed at drafting Africa's sustainable development priorities and goals. Organisers clearly stated their hope to use the meeting outcome document as a technical input to HLC's CAP draft document (Ogiogio, 2013). The 22nd African Union Summit held on 31 January 2014 (Assembly/AU/Dec.503 (XXII)) adopted the CAP on the post-2015 development agenda with recommendation to the HLC for further refinement, suggesting additional concern for peace and security. The HLC crafted and launched the final CAP document on 28 February 2014 in Ndjamena, Chad.

For countless reasons, Africa has a lot at stake in the post-2015 development agenda. Most social and economic indicators depict a gloomy picture for the continent. African countries are at the bottom of the Human Development Index (HDI) list and display high levels of poverty and vulnerability. Climate change, environmental degradation, youth unemployment and rising inequalities are among key challenges that Africans have to cope with. Recent positive signs have surfaced, including record economic growth rates in several countries of the continent, even though these have not translated into real poverty reductions. Given the above conditions, it is imperative that Africans participate in the global debate on the post-2015 development agenda to ensure that their interests are accommodated. Unfortunately, information asymmetries and sometimes a lack of capacities prevent proficient contributions. This research can offer guidance to SSA stakeholders on ways to have their voice heard.

The following section describes the methodology used as well as the data mobilised for the study. The next section presents the results and discussions with emphasis on (i) CAP on the post-2015 development agenda, (ii) institutional proposals and their alignment with the CAP, and (iii) the match between the CAP and the SDGs emanating from the OWG. The last section of the chapter presents the conclusions and policy implications.

Data and methods

This paper has mainly drawn on a desk review to undertake the proposed analysis. First, it describes the CAP elaboration process and its content (for further process and content analyses). Next, the CAP is analysed, focusing on its strengths and weaknesses. Additionally, three countries are selected in West Africa as a case study to complement the analysis at the regional and continental levels. Second, the study takes stock of the analysis of the institutional proposals at the global level and the consensus on the SDGs. Third, it compares the CAP with the institutional proposals and the SDGs and assesses its departure from these outcomes. The overall analysis is based on key documents such as African Union resolutions, outcome documents stemming from technical meetings and regional/continental consultations.

Results and discussions

The main priorities set out by Africans: the Common African Position on the Post-2015 Development Agenda

The CAP on the post-2015 development agenda, which reflects Africa's development priorities, is based on six pillars: (i) structural economic transformation and inclusive growth; (ii) science, technology and innovation; (iii) people-centred development; (iv) environmental sustainability, natural resources management and disaster risk management; (v) peace and security; and (vi) finance and partnerships (African Union, 2014).

Pillar 1 – Structural economic transformation and inclusive growth

This first pillar is by far the biggest of Africa's development priorities.[3] It promotes inclusive growth which reduces inequality and creates decent and productive employment, sustainable agriculture, food self-sufficiency and nutrition. It also calls for a diversified economy and more processing of primary commodities through national value chains development across sectors, as well as development of the services sector. Infrastructure development is indispensable for this transformative process to succeed. This pillar is designed to reverse Africa's dependence on a cluster of primary commodities and develop solutions to issues such as the concentration of African growth in relatively few sectors and its limited employment effects, the weak intersectoral linkages of the economy and rising inequalities.

Pillar 2 – Science, technology and innovation

This second pillar is critical for the transformative agenda. It includes enhancing technological capacities, enabling a financial and regulatory environment to support innovation, increasing support for research and development, and inducing optimal utilisation of space and geospatial technologies through increased investments and human resources development.

Pillar 3 – People-centred development

This third pillar contains three key goals of the current Millennium Development Goals (MDGs), i.e. poverty reduction, education and health. Specifically, it focuses on eradicating poverty, developing human capital and providing universal and equitable access to quality healthcare. Other items include gender equality and women's empowerment, responding to population dynamics and development, harnessing the strengths of Africa's youth and expanding access to sustainable human settlements.

Pillar 4 – Environmental sustainability, natural resources management and disaster risk management

To date, the exploitation of Africa's natural resources and biodiversity base has provided limited results in terms of economic returns and employment opportunities. Thus, this pillar focuses on improving natural resource and biodiversity management; enhancing access to safe water for all; responding effectively to climate change; addressing desertification, land degradation, soil erosion, flooding and drought; and contributing to natural disaster risk reduction and management.

Pillar 5 – Peace and security

This fifth pillar focuses on addressing the root causes of conflict and preventing the outbreak of armed conflicts. This pillar was added during the final phase of the CAP formulation process and is an indication of the low level of consensus on the theme on security and peace. A closer look at the draft of Africa regional experts' report on the SDGs shows that most regions rated very poorly on this theme. Not surprisingly, only the Central Africa group ranked it as the highest priority.

Pillar 6 – Finance and partnerships

This last pillar consists of two components: finance and partnership. Finance includes improving domestic resource mobilisation; maximising innovative financing; implementing existing commitments; and promoting high-quality, predictable external financing. Partnership, on the other hand, comprises promoting mutually beneficial partnerships, strengthening partnerships for trade and establishing partnerships for managing global commons.

Beside these six pillars, the CAP defined factors enabling implementation. These include good governance, transparency and fighting corruption; enabling governance architecture; human rights for all; sound macroeconomic policy; private sector development; a credible and viable participatory process; strengthened national statistical capacities; and effective monitoring and evaluation systems.

Strengths and weaknesses of the CAP

One voice for Africa

The CAP is a genuine success as Africa will speak with one voice and present a unified set of priorities in the upcoming negotiation process. This will also strengthen Africa's bargaining power and increase the likelihood of getting the African position fully integrated into the global development agenda. Moreover, the AU has urged its member states to use the CAP as a negotiation instrument. Another feature of the CAP is its departure from externally driven initiatives, with an emphasis on domestic resources. Africa now calls for "a fully open, transparent and inclusive global negotiation process in which parties are treated equally and their voice carries equal weight."[4]

Inclusiveness of the process

From the onset, Africa endorsed the participatory approach of the process by which the post-2015 development agenda is being formulated. The 30 national consultations, four regional consultations and online surveys, jointly coordinated by UNECA, AUC, AfDB and UNDP/RBA, provided a unique opportunity to different stakeholders to give their inputs. The synthesis from these meetings has greatly influenced the final version of the CAP. For instance, four pillars out of six were already well formulated and visible from the outcome document of the last regional consultation on the post-2015 development agenda held on March 2013 in Hammamet, Tunisia. Only Pillar 4 on *environment sustainability, natural resources management and disaster risk management* and Pillar 5 on *peace and security* were absent from the stakeholders' priorities.

CSOs' involvement

In spite of this success, the elaboration process of the CAP is not free from criticism. African civil society organisations (CSOs) have criticised the process, especially with regard to the development of the roadmap and the drafting of the CAP. The process was limited to member states (through the HLC and the Sherpas), AUC, UN agencies and key regional institutions such as the AfDB. African CSOs have lobbied in vain for the inclusion of CSO representatives within the technical team of the Secretariat of the AU to ensure that the content of the CAP reflects the aspirations and needs of the communities they represent. Finally, some have voiced concern about the influence of key African institutions and states on shaping the CAP and have urged other African stakeholders to engage in the next phase of translating this CAP into goals, targets and indicators.

Gender, governance and youth employment: three hot topics hard to discard

Although gender is mentioned within Pillar 3 as *gender equality and women's empowerment*, African women's rights advocates have reacted vigorously and urged the HLC to consider a standalone pillar on gender equality and advised mainstreaming gender across the entire framework. The same is true for youth employment. The weight of Africa's young is recognised under the same pillar as *harnessing Africa's youth population*, but its visibility does not reflect its crucial role with respect to the fate of the continent. Surprisingly, governance is absent and considered only as an enabler despite its crucial role in securing economic and social development. There is no doubt that poor governance has been an impediment to progress and is still a key problem in Africa.

The CAP displays a level of consensus at the continental level. It is, however, useful to complement and contrast this official view through two channels: (i) exploring the differences within and between countries stemming from national consultations by selecting three countries in the Sahel and (ii) integrating a more global perspective (Africa region) through the use of the MY World 2015 tool.

Post-2015 national consultations: case studies of Mali, Niger and Senegal

In West Africa, Mali, Niger and Senegal share many commonalities. They belong to the same monetary region, have to cope with similar climate and environmental challenges, and often face regional insurgencies. The first two are landlocked, while Senegal is a coastal country. It is therefore worth looking at how people within these countries have formulated their expectations towards the post-2015 development agenda (République du Mali, 2013; République du Niger, 2013; République du Sénégal, 2013).

A closer look at the priorities stemming from the national consultations reveals the following key findings (see Table 2.1):

- Governance is a priority for all three countries although it does not seem to resonate loudly at the continental level (CAP). Bergh, Menocal and Takeuchi (2014, 2) show that "people across the world care deeply about governance, but some dimensions of governance emerge as more important to them than others. People's top priority is for governments that are honest and effective and can deliver on their needs and expectations."

Table 2.1 Summary of country priorities resulting from national consultations

Senegal	*Mali*	*Niger*
Strengthening the social base of human development	Governance, peace and security	Food security and nutrition
Promoting a competitive economy which creates decent jobs	Inclusive growth	Youth employment
Establishing a favourable governance for sustainable development	Education and technological innovation	Equitable and quality access to education, health, water and sanitation
Peace and security	Sustainable human development	Governance
		Environment and access to energy
		Women empowerment and equal opportunities

Source: République du Mali (2013); République du Niger (2013); République du Sénégal (2013).

- The main priorities are centred around three pillars of the CAP, namely Pillar 1 on *structural economic transformation and inclusive growth*, Pillar 3 on *people-centred development* and Pillar 5 on *peace and security*.
- There are limited references to Pillar 2 on *science, technology and innovation* and Pillar 4 on *environmental sustainability, natural resources management and disaster risk management*. There is no reference to Pillar 6 on *finance and partnerships*.
- Results of these three national consultations are consistent with the general picture of the output from the regional consultations.

A look at MY World 2015 – What are the African priorities?

The United Nations global survey 'MY World' is a platform that allows the general public to choose six issues considered to matter most. An analysis of the survey results provides interesting and useful learning both at the global and African levels (MY World 2015, 2014).

Surprisingly, the first seven priorities are the same for the world and Africa, the only difference being the switched ranks of 'better job opportunities' and 'an honest and responsive government'. For Africa, the seven priorities are in the following order of importance (number of votes obtained is shown in Figure 2.1):

a A good education
b Better healthcare
c Better job opportunities
d An honest and responsive government
e Access to clean water and sanitation
f Affordable and nutritious food
g Protection against crime and violence

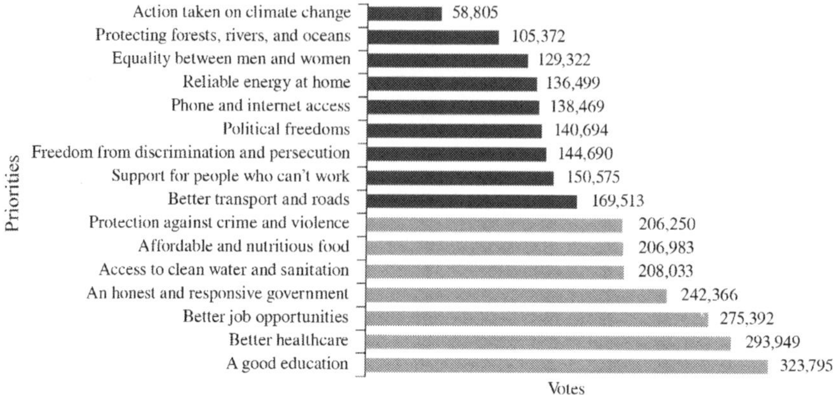

Figure 2.1 African priorities – votes from MY World 2015

Source: MY World 2015 (2014).

These seven priorities are found almost entirely in Pillar 3 (education, healthcare and job opportunities) and to a lesser extent in Pillars 1 (affordable and nutritious food) and 5 (protection against crime and violence). In contrast, the priority on governance (an honest and responsive government) is not supported by the pillars of the CAP.

Focus on the key institutional proposals: yes, but not far enough . . .

According to Berg and Couturier (2013), the key institutional proposals agree on 12 priorities at the goal level: education, health, gender, energy, poverty, food security, water and sanitation, inclusive growth and employment, peace and stability, governance, environmental sustainability, and a global enabling environment. Some of the proposals present a few outliers such as infrastructure and technology, urbanisation and social inclusion. From their analysis, they derive three clusters of goals.

The first cluster consists of *education*, *health*, *gender*, *energy* and *poverty*. There is a broad agreement on eradicating poverty, focusing on improving education and acting on key health issues (for example, by reducing or even eliminating maternal and child mortality, HIV/AIDS, tuberculosis and malaria and expanding immunisation rates). There is also consensus on gender (for example, improving women's empowerment and enhancing equal rights and opportunities). For energy, there is an emerging consensus on achieving universal access to sustainable energy and on the importance of energy efficiency. The apparent consensus on these goal areas, however, hides some divergence on how these goals will be implemented (targets and indicators).

The second cluster of potential goals consists of *food security*, *water and sanitation*, *inclusive growth and employment*, *peace and stability*, *governance*, *environmental sustainability*, and a *global enabling environment*. The following facts are worth noting:

- Although the institutional proposals agree that a goal on food security should aim to end hunger, malnutrition and stunting, other basic components are missing. These include self-sufficiency, rural–urban linkages, employment along food supply chains and social protection.
- For water and sanitation, there is consensus on sustainable water management, universal access to drinking water and sanitation. However, a few proposals suggest better governance of water systems management or more effective funding mechanisms.
- Most proposals consent to tackle climate change, but the institutional proposals are far away from the advanced position of civil society.
- For the potential goal on governance, most institutional proposals agree on the need for transparency and accountability, strong institutions and fighting corruption.
- With respect to 'peace and stability', there is consensus on the link between peace and development, the importance of rule of law and effective, inclusive institutions.

The last group consists of *infrastructure and technology*, *urbanisation* and *social inclusion*. These potential goals are almost outliers with little chance to make it as a goal. The proposed goal on social inclusion focuses on social and economic inequities and shows the need to end discrimination on the basis of gender, ethnicity, disability, geographic location or other groupings. This is popular among CSOs but retains little attention among institutional proposals. The same is true for potential goal areas such as infrastructure and technology or urbanisation. Their best chance might be to figure in the final proposal as targets.

The institutional proposals do not meet the CAP expectations

It is noted that issues such as *infrastructure and technology* and *social inclusion* are areas low on the institutional proposals and would have little chance of being included in the list of goals post-2015. However, these goals are considered essential for Africa's development. For instance, infrastructure and technology represent critical ingredients for the transformative agenda called for by African leaders and stakeholders. Likewise, African CSOs value highly *social inclusion* and deploy a lot of energy to advocate policies that address social and economic inequities. Ending discrimination on the basis of, for example, gender, ethnicity, disability and geographic location cannot be set aside, especially in a context in which Africa has experienced high growth rates that have not translated into tangible social and economic progress for the majority due to record inequality levels. There is a growing consensus that tackling the inequalities which hamper human progress should be part of the new set of SDGs after 2015 (Melamed, 2014).

CAP is Africa's offer of its transformative agenda to the world. A glance at the six pillars reveals three different outcomes when one assesses the possibilities of consensus and divergence between the CAP and the institutional proposals for the post-2015 development agenda.

a The first two pillars (*structural economic transformation and inclusive growth*; *science, technology and innovation*) dedicated to the transformative agenda are unlikely to arouse the enthusiasm of the institutional proposals even though they are fundamental to Africa. Pillar 1 is extremely important but there is little probability it can gain support in the international arena. Pillar 2 is also unlikely to generate international support but is crucial to the transformation process of Africa.
b The next two pillars (*people-centred development*; *environmental sustainability, natural resources management and disaster risk management*) are the most likely to get full support from the international community. For instance, Pillar 3 contains those human development goals that are present in the current MDGs and are not subject to any controversies. Likewise, Pillar 4 is extremely important for Africa given its natural resource endowment and the fragility of the management of these resources. This is also an area where world attention is gained.

The last two pillars pose different sets of questions. For Pillar 5 on *peace and security*, Africa should first consolidate its consensus within the continent. The paper has already mentioned all the talks that have fuelled the debate around this theme and the circumstances that led to the adoption of Pillar 5. The situation of Pillar 6 on *finance and partnerships* is a bit different. Although the international community was called upon to respect its promise, the decision was reached to rely first on domestic resource mobilisation and private sector involvement. There is a risk, however, that resource-rich countries may concentrate on international financing and investments, thus eroding the current consensus of the CAP.

Outcome of the open working group: closer to African priorities

The review of the institutional proposals has showed that key components of the African transformative agenda are missing from most of these proposals. Luckily, the outputs of the OWG seem to compensate for most of the drawbacks identified within the institutional proposals. As a consequence, it is not surprising that the 24th Ordinary Session of the Assembly of the Union held in Addis Ababa, Ethiopia, on 30–31 January 2015 (Assembly/AU/Dec.560 (XXIV)) recognises the fact that the OWG results constitute a good representation of African priorities and fully endorses its content (African Union, 2015). Thus, based on the proposal of the HLC on the post-2015 development agenda, the Assembly of the Union:

a SUPPORTS the decision to use the proposal from the OWG on the Sustainable Development Goals (SDGs) as the main basis for negotiations as it captures the essential elements of the Common African Position (CAP) priorities and should not be reopened for further discussion;

b ENDORSES the formation and the Terms of Reference of the African Group of Negotiators on the Post-2015 Development Agenda which shall be the single negotiating body acting on behalf of the continent;

c REAFFIRMS that the CAP remains the sole negotiating document for Africa and CALLS UPON all African Member States to adhere to its provisions during all negotiations relating to the Post-2015 Development Agenda.

How perfectly does the CAP match the proposed SDGs?

The proposed SDGs provide a comprehensive coverage of the CAP's Pillar 1 *structural economic transformation and inclusive growth* and represent an excellent step forward. The noticeable differences are two-fold: the first one relates to the African choice of food self-sufficiency while the international consensus focuses on food security. Additionally, the development of the services sector (improved linkages between services and real sectors, innovation in service delivery) called for by the CAP are absent from the SDGs.

The second pillar on *science, technology and innovation* gets a great echo from the SDGs. Goal 9 and its targets are centred on building resilient infrastructure, enhancing scientific research, upgrading technological capabilities, encouraging innovation and significantly increasing access to information and communications technology. Targets 17.6 to 17.8 of Goal 17 provide additional opportunities on technology.

These two pillars, central to the African transformative agenda, are close to the SDGs in content, unlike what was observed with the institutional proposals.

The other four pillars are completely covered by the proposed SDGs. This is why the African leadership fully endorsed the outcome of the OWG and called for the use of this document as the main basis for the intergovernmental negotiations.

Conclusions

The Common African Position on the Post-2015 Development Agenda is a vital tool as it provides a negotiation framework for Africa. Ownership of these African priorities and a willingness to align with them in the course of the international negotiation process is critical in getting Africa's voice heard. The creation of the African Group of Negotiators on the Post-2015 Development Agenda as the single negotiating body acting on behalf of the continent and the use of the CAP as the sole negotiating document for Africa constitute a genuine milestone. While it is early to assess how and if individual African countries have abided by the AU decisions and the real impact of this shift, there is no doubt that this new path constitutes an improvement.

Beyond the consensus built within the continent, the African leadership should find the appropriate links and partnerships with the global South to make their voice heard. Failure of the Africa Group's proposal to the OWG is an interesting example. Indeed, because the new model of Africa's economic development focuses on structural transformation and Pillar 1 of the CAP shows how critical this new path is to the future of Africa, the Africa Group had proposed a standalone goal on structural transformation to the OWG for SDGs sessions. This proposal did not get enough support. Fortunately, the adopted SDGs encompass all the key components of the transformative agenda. The challenges foreseen during the implementation process reinforce the need for partnership with the global South. These partnership efforts should be undertaken without further delay to facilitate global coordination and minimise the risks of failures.

Notes

1 Algeria, Chad, Congo, Ethiopia, Guinea, Liberia, Mauritania, Mauritius, Namibia and South Africa.
2 Members of the HLC had each a representative called Sherpa who met several times to prepare the inputs for the 10 heads of states and government. The AUC, UNECA and UNDP provided key technical guidance and support.
3 The 'Africa Group' has proposed to the OWG sessions for a standalone goal on structural economic transformation.
4 Keynote address by H.E. President Ellen Johnson Sirleaf at a special event 'Getting ready for the post-2015 development agenda', Rome, Italy, 4 April 2014.

References

African Union. (2014) *Common African Position (CAP) on the Post-2015 Development Agenda*. Addis Ababa: African Union.

African Union. (2015) *Assembly of the Union, Twenty-Fourth Ordinary Session, 30–31 January 2015, Addis Ababa, Ethiopia: Decisions, Declarations and Resolutions*. Assembly/AU/Dec. 546–568(XXIV). Addis Ababa: African Union.

Bergh, G. and Couturier, J. (2013) *A Rough Guide to Emerging Consensus and Divergence in Post-2015 Goal Areas*. London: Overseas Development Institute (ODI).

Bergh, G., Menocal, A. R. and Takeuchi, L. R. (2014) *What's Behind the Demand for Governance? An Assessment of People's Views*. London: Overseas Development Institute (ODI).

Melamed, C. (2014) *Inequality in Post-2015: Focus on the Targets, Not the Goals?* London: Overseas Development Institute (ODI).

MY World 2015. (2014) *What are the African priorities?* Available from: http://vote.myworld2015.org/ [Accessed: 12 May 2014].

Ogiogio, G. (2013) *Draft Africa Regional Report on the Sustainable Development Goals*. Ethiopia: United Nations Economic Commission for Africa (UNECA), African Union (AU) and African Development Bank (AfDB).

Open Working Group. (2014) *Introduction to the proposal of the Open Working Group for Sustainable Development Goals*. Available from: http://sustainabledevelopment.un.org/content/documents/4518SDGs_FINAL_Proposal%20of%20OWG_19%20July%20at%201320hrsver3.pdf [Accessed: 7 August 2014].

République du Mali. (2013) *Rapport des consultations nationales sur l'agenda de développement de l'après 2015*. Bamako: Government of the Republic of Mali.

République du Niger. (2013) *Consultations nationales post-2015 – Niger*. Abuja: Government of the Federal Republic of Nigeria.

République du Sénégal. (2013) *Le Sénégal que nous voulons – Rapport des consultations nationales sur l'agenda de développement Post-2015*. Dakar: Government of the Republic of Senegal.

SDSN. (2013) *An Action Agenda for Sustainable Development*. Report for the UN Secretary-General. New York: Sustainable Development Solutions Network (SDSN) of the United Nations.

UNGC. (2013) *Corporate Sustainability and the United Nations Post-2015 Development Agenda – Perspectives from UN Global Compact Participants on Global Priorities and How to Engage Business towards Sustainable Development Goals*. Report to the UN Secretary-General. New York: United Nations Global Compact (UNGC).

United Nations. (2013a) *A New Global Partnership: Eradicate Poverty and Transform Economies through Sustainable Development*. Report of the High-Level Panel of Eminent Persons on the Post-2015 Development Agenda. New York: United Nations.

United Nations. (2013b) *Special event outcome document*. Available from: http://www.un.org/millenniumgoals/pdf/Outcome%20documentMDG.pdf [Accessed: 13 December 2013].

UNSG. (2013) *A Life of Dignity for All: Accelerating Progress towards the Millennium Development Goals and Advancing the United Nations Development Agenda beyond 2015*. Report of the Secretary-General (A/68/202). New York: United Nations Secretary-General (UNSG).

Annexes

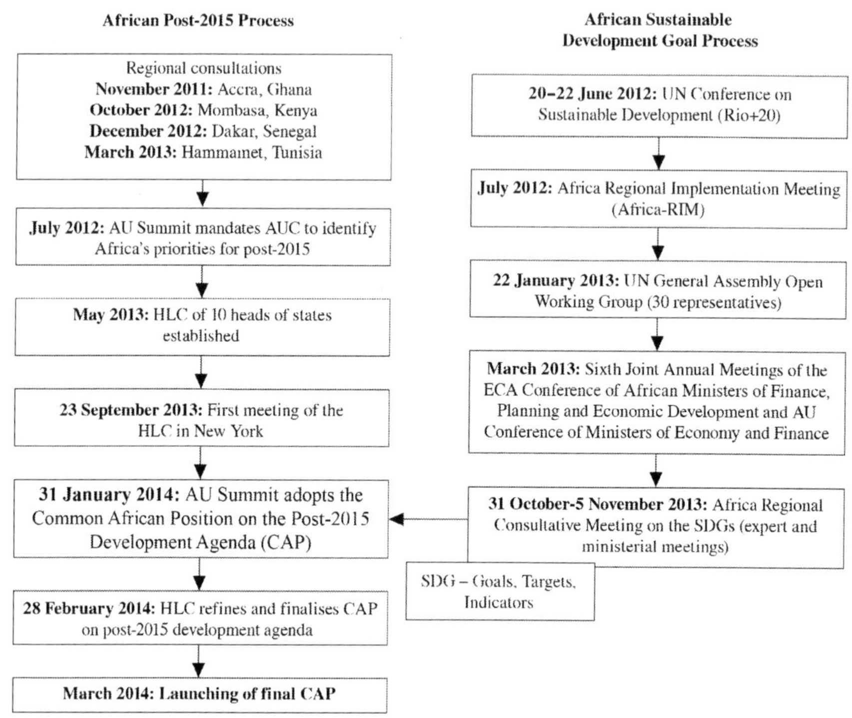

Annex 2.1 Formulation process of the Common African Position on the Post-2015 Development Agenda (CAP)

Source: Prepared by the author.

Annex 2.2 Common African Position on the Post-2015 Development Agenda (CAP)

	Pillar 1: Structural economic transformation and inclusive growth	*Pillar 2: Science, technology and innovation*	*Pillar 3: People-centred development*	*Pillar 4: Environmental sustainability, natural resources management and disaster risk management*	*Pillar 5: Peace and security*	*Pillar 6: Finance and partnership*
a)	Inclusive growth that reduces inequality	Enhancing technological capacities for Africa's transformative agenda	The eradication of poverty	Improving natural resource and biodiversity management	Addressing the root causes of conflict	Improving domestic resource mobilisation
b)	Sustainable agri-culture, food self-sufficiency and nutrition	Building enabling environment for innovation	Education and human capital development	Enhancing access to safe water for all	Preventing the outbreak of armed conflicts	Maximising innovative financing
c)	Diversification, industrialisation and value addition	Increasing support for research and development	Universal and equitable access to quality healthcare	Responding effectively to climate change		Implementing existing commitments and promoting quality and predictability of external financing
d)	Developing the services sector	Optimal utilisation of space and geospatial technologies	Gender equality and women's empowerment	Addressing desertification, land degradation, soil erosion, flooding and drought		Promoting mutually beneficial partnerships
e)	Infrastructure development		Leveraging population dynamics for development	Natural disaster risk reduction and management		Strengthening partnerships for trade
f)			Harnessing Africa's youthful population			Establish partnerships for managing global commons
g)			Improving access to sustainable human settlements			

Source: African Union (2014).

3 Alternatives for development or alternatives to development?

Mireya Anabell Villacís Taco, María Fernanda Mora Garcés and Rodrigo López

Introduction

Context and justification

As stated in the Report of the High-Level Panel of Eminent Persons on the Post-2015 Development Agenda (HLP), no one can deny the important role that the Millennium Development Goals (MDGs) have played around the world. Among other positive indicators, data show that "there are half a billion fewer people living below an international poverty line of USD 1.25 a day. Child death rates have fallen by more than 30 per cent, with about three million children's lives saved each year compared to 2000, deaths from malaria have fallen by one quarter" (United Nations, 2013, 7). However, the Panel also recognised that there were many issues the MDGs did not address, such as the devastating effects of conflict and violence on development; the important role played by good governance and institutions in guaranteeing the rule of law for ensuring development; free speech; open and accountable government; the need for inclusive growth to provide jobs; and the integration of the economic, social and environmental aspects of sustainable development, which includes the promotion of sustainable patterns of consumption and production.

The HLP suggested that the post-2015 agenda should be supported by dynamic partnerships, to help ensure compliance with the new goals. According to the Panel, these goals are bold yet practical, and like the MDGs, not binding. The Panel highlighted the fact that progress is possible and that there is an opportunity to solve the problems associated with attaining development targets, if all relevant actors (governments at all levels, businesses and civil society organisations (CSOs), multilateral institutions) act together and are willing to change the current paradigm.

On 2 August 2015, the United Nations (UN) member states agreed by consensus on a post-2015 development agenda, which will be transmitted for consideration and adoption during the Summit in September 2015. This agenda is in line with the recommendations made by the HLP and emphasises that this is a "plan of action for people, planet and prosperity." It recognises that "eradicating poverty in all its forms and dimensions" is the greatest challenge and the main requirement for sustainable development.

With this in mind, this paper is based on an analysis of the applicability of the current 2030 Agenda for Sustainable Development in the Ecuadorian Amazon. The aim is to generate findings and recommendations that are relevant to the region in the context of the newly adopted Sustainable Development Goals (SDGs).

Why the Amazon region?

The Amazon region covers more than 7.5 million km of South America spanning eight countries: Bolivia, Brazil, Colombia, Ecuador, Guyana, Perú, Surinam and Venezuela. This region is of strategic importance not only for the countries located within the region, but also to the rest of the world. This territory accounts for the largest tropical rainforest and highest biodiversity in the planet. It provides vital ecosystem services for the welfare of humanity and protects one of the largest ethnic and cultural diversities of the world. The Amazonian population is estimated at 34.1 million people, who constitute 10 per cent of the total population of South America. From this population, approximately 1.6 million people belong to 375 indigenous groups (Celentano and Vedoveto, 2011, 12). The average population density (4.5 inhabitants per km^2) is almost five times lower than the South American average. The annual population growth between 1991 and 2007 was 2.3 per cent, where immigration primarily accounted for the increase (Celentano and Vedoveto, 2011, 12).

Economic development in the Amazon region varies greatly among countries. According to the available data, it was estimated that from 2005 to 2010, regional gross domestic product (GDP) reached an annual figure of 330 billion dollars, of which Brazil accounts for more than 70 per cent. The average per capita GDP in the region is USD 5,500 per year, but varies greatly from one country to another. For instance, GDP per capita is lowest in Bolivia (USD 1,200) and highest in French Guiana (USD 18,800) and Venezuela (USD 9,300). The main productive activities in the region are mining, oil production, forestry, agriculture and livestock, which are often associated with environmental degradation and social conflicts (Celentano and Vedoveto, 2011, 12).

Although GDP is considered the main indicator of economic growth in a country or region, it does not reflect the quality of life of people and social inequality. Furthermore, GDP does not take into account the loss of natural wealth or assets of a country. Unfortunately, national accounts do not reflect the rate of depletion and/or degradation of these resources. Therefore, it is necessary to adopt other variables for wider social, environmental and economic development discussion (Celentano and Vedoveto, 2011, 12).

The Ecuadorian Amazon covers an area of approximately 116,000 km^2. This represents almost half of the land area of the country (248,574 km^2) and around 2.5 per cent of the Amazon basin. Twenty-six per cent of the Ecuadorian Amazon territory is protected through the National System of Protected Areas. Ten of the 15 existing indigenous communities in Ecuador live within this region, each upholding its own culture and language. In the provinces of Orellana and Pastaza live the Tagaeri and Taromenane, two indigenous groups who maintain voluntary isolation from the rest of society (Onofa, Rodríguez and Ponce, 2012, 19–22).

The discovery of large oil reserves in these areas in the 1960s brought great changes to the Amazon that feature rapid population growth, higher occupancy spaces, indiscriminate felling of forests, unplanned urbanisation without basic services, and a strong cultural impact on indigenous peoples. The construction of a definition of development and associated indicators therefore need to take into account the particular characteristics of the Amazon region in Ecuador and in the whole basin (Onofa, Rodríguez and Ponce, 2012, 21).

Research questions

- How is development defined and measured? Is this applicable to all countries and regions alike?
- How is poverty defined? How is it measured (if indeed this is possible) in the Amazon region?
- How are the indicators of quality of life applicable to the Amazon region?
- Are only national targets possible, or is it also necessary to establish regional objectives and indicators? What are those?
- Who should be involved in formulating the definition and subsequent monitoring of the objectives and goals? How can the participation of most marginalised actors be ensured?

Paper layout

The theoretical framework of this research was designed based on literature review. Thereon, the study undertook a comparative analysis of the SDGs agreed by the UN member states and the MDGs and other proposed development goals/programmes initiated in Ecuador. In doing so, it has analysed the compliance of the MDGs at national and regional (Ecuadorian Amazon) levels; identified the actors who were directly engaged in the MDG implementation process at the local level; and finally, provides an assessment on the applicability of the SDGs in the Amazon region, based on structured interviews with the identified implementing stakeholders of MDGs in one province (as pilot), and also with those who had been involved in the follow-up process of the SDGs. Finally, the paper draws a conclusion and some recommendations based on the gleaned findings.

Theoretical framework[1]

In order to analyse whether the proposal for a post-2015 agenda is applicable to different regions, it is important to understand first where the differences among regions lie. The rationale for this analysis is that the way the concept of development is understood is the underlying cause of the differences. Thus, the study now provides a brief overview of the definition of development and its variations throughout history.

Alternatives for development

The concept of development conceived as economic prosperity, per capita income growth, production, mass consumption and modernity emerged after World War II. Its main objective was that all countries follow the same path as the 'developed' countries, and as a result, grow economically and overcome problems such as poverty, hunger, illiteracy and inequality. From the 1970s, critics of this model observed that economic growth did not necessarily lead to the reduction of poverty. Questions then were raised on the issue of redistribution as the goal for social development. The consensus was "to consider the satisfaction of the basic needs of people a priority of development" (Dubois, n.d., 5). In the 1980s, economic growth again became the priority of development, using the market as the key instrument and the private sector as the main actor, reducing the state's role and creating serious social and environmental costs.

These changes in the concept of development and the tools to achieve it were challenged by concepts such as *limits to growth* that emerged from the Club of Rome in 1972, as well as the *Our Common Future* report in 1989 which laid the foundation for the Conference on Environment and Development in Rio de Janeiro in 1992. From here, the concept of *sustainable development* emerged, which emphasised "the need for solidarity among different populations [current and future] to use natural resources in a way that allows all to reach satisfactory levels of welfare" (Dubois, n.d., 6).

While this model also failed, it laid the foundations for the promotion of the human development approach, launched in the late 1980s by the United Nations Development Programme (UNDP). The UNDP changed "the vision of development focused on the production of goods for another focused on extending the capabilities of the people" (Dubois, n.d., 10).

However, despite various attempts to conceptualise, build upon and implement the different models of development, the contemporary development notion is understood "as [a] linear, modernizing, base material progress essentially based on the appropriation of Nature, mediated by science and technology, and guided by economic growth as a key generator of welfare. From this perspective, welfare is achieved by monetary incomes and consumption" (Gudynas, 2013a, 138) and "[a] political and cultural construction like the image of the industrialized countries" (Gudynas, 2013b, 190).

The MDGs and the currently initiated SDGs are part of a global effort to tackle social, economic and environmental problems such as poverty, hunger, inequality and deforestation, among others.

Alternatives to development

As noted above, the planet's ability to generate the resources needed to achieve 'development' are limited. Environmental degradation, social and even economic problems are leading to a 'civilization crisis', which threatens the survival of the human species. Biodiversity loss, natural resource scarcity and global warming challenge the bases of life. Modern human ambition for accumulation has set the development standards mainly in terms of monetary and individualistic criteria. This type of development is causing serious social, economic and environmental impacts, which exacerbate problems connected to poverty, exclusion and violence (Lander, 2013, 27–30). This has forced a reconsideration of ways to better understand and improve human welfare, urging us to think and imagine *alternatives to development* that might lead to new types of social, cultural, economic, political and environmental systems.

Since the 1990s onwards, groups in the Andean Region (notably in Ecuador and Bolivia) started to challenge the global definition of development and argued the need for a new paradigm. Those groups (government, civil society, indigenous groups, feminists and others) started talking about alternatives to development not necessarily linked to the traditional concept of development. Some authors note that these alternatives to development must focus on key concepts such as

- Conviviality
- Strong sustainable development, biocentric, deep ecology
- Economy dematerialisation, degrowth
- Interculturality, pluralism, related ontologies, expanded citizenship
- *Buen Vivir* or Good Living (Gudynas, 2011, 47)

In South America, the paradigm of Buen Vivir or Good Living is taking greater strength. For example, Ecuador and Bolivia enrol in their constitutions the decision to build states aligned to Good Living, recognising diversity, interculturality and national diversity as fundamental axioms for the development of their populations. Principles of Good Living arise from the interpretation of the worldview of ancient Andean groups, in which the human being is part of the cosmos. As such, it is essential to maintain harmony with nature through new methods of production and social and cultural rights based on equality, cooperation and respect (Acosta, Martínez and Sacher, 2013, 310–311).

The intrinsic characteristics of these nations, considering their histories of marginalisation, oppression and poverty, have led to the construction of an alternative paradigm based on the understanding of life and in the struggle for equal rights and opportunities for every inhabitant of this planet, as the main basis to confront the crisis mentioned previously:

> Any alternative to the current civilization crisis and the effects of the destruction of the conditions that make life possible, should be incorporated as a core dimension of the fight against [the] obscene inequality; otherwise, it is doomed to failure.
>
> (Lander, 2013, 36)

In Ecuador, Good Living or *Sumak Kawsay* (in the Kichwa language) emerged as political discourse in the last decade of the 20th century. It is an epistemological paradigm that breaks with the occidental notion of development, the base of which is the human being and its harmonious coexistence with the individual, communal and collective environment (Guandinango, 2013, 18–19).

In order to bring the concept of Good Living to practice, the Ecuadorian government established the 'National Plan for Good Living 2009–2013', and later the 'National Plan for Good Living and 2013–2017'. These became official instruments to guide the new policies that allow the implementation of Good Living in Ecuador. The Ecuadorian experience leads the country to realise new visions of development emphasising the need to promote structural changes on designing and articulating their own politics, according to their social and economic features to benefit the national population.

Instruments for the concepts of development and Good Living

Context and definition of the MDGs and the proposal for the SDGs

In September 2000 at the Millennium Summit, world leaders adopted the UN Millennium Declaration, through which they committed their nations to a new global partnership known as the MDGs. The main goal was to "reduce extreme poverty in its many dimensions: income poverty, hunger, disease, lack of adequate shelter, and exclusion – while promoting gender equality, education, and environmental sustainability" (UN Millennium Project, 2006).

According to the 2013 UN report, the MDGs have been the most successful global anti-poverty push in history. Significant and substantial progress has been made in meeting many of the targets including halving the number of people living in extreme poverty and the proportion of people without sustainable access to improved sources of drinking water. Remarkable gains have been made in the fight against malaria and tuberculosis. There have been visible improvements in all health areas as well as primary education (UNDP, 2014, 3).

However, as stated in several reports, progress has not been uniform across the world or across the goals. There are still disparities across and within countries.

Accordingly, the 2030 Agenda for Sustainable Development suggests that the post-2015 agenda should be supported by dynamic partnerships to ensure compliance with the goals and with the aim to shift the world onto a sustainable and resilient path. The agenda follows the guiding principles proposed by the members of the HLP, which were built upon meetings and consultations all around the world:

- Leave no one behind
- Put sustainable development at the core
- Transform economies for jobs and inclusive growth
- Build peace and effective, open and accountable institutions for all
- Forge a new global partnership

The 2030 Agenda for Sustainable Development states that

> all countries and all stakeholders, acting in collaborative partnership, will implement this plan. We are resolved to free the human race from the tyranny of poverty and want and to heal and secure our planet. We are determined

> to take the bold and transformative steps which are urgently needed to shift the world onto a sustainable and resilient path. As we embark on this collective journey, we pledge that no one will be left behind. The 17 Sustainable Development Goals and 169 targets which we are announcing today demonstrate the scale and ambition of this new universal Agenda. They seek to build on the Millennium Development Goals and complete what these did not achieve. They seek to realize the human rights of all and to achieve gender equality and the empowerment of all women and girls. They are integrated and indivisible and balance the three dimensions of sustainable development: the economic, social and environmental.
>
> (United Nations, 2015, 4)

(The 17 new SDGs are included in the volume as an Appendix.)

Context and definition of the National Plan for Good Living in Ecuador

In 2008, Ecuador made deep constitutional reforms, starting with the recognition of ethnic and cultural population diversity, as well as the Rights of Nature. Additionally, the country proposed to change the theoretical, political and philosophical foundations of its development model to a new paradigm known as Buen Vivir or Sumak Kawsay (Good Living). This proposal represents the ideological foundations for ensuring the welfare and quality of life of the population in harmony with nature.

In order to materialise the concept of Good Living, the Ecuadorian government established a national policy known as *Plan Nacional del Buen Vivir* (PNBV) or the National Plan for Good Living (2009–2013 and 2013–2017), which contains the official instruments that establish the goals, outcomes and outputs expected for the country.

Analysis

Among the goals stated in the PNBV are the consolidation of a democratic state; equality, cohesion, inclusion and social and territorial equity and diversity; improvement of the quality of life of the population; strengthening the capacities and potential of citizens; establishing common meeting spaces; building and strengthening national identity, plurinational and intercultural; respect for human rights; guaranteeing the rights of nature; the promotion of regional and global environmental sustainability; consolidation of social solidarity and economic systems; ensuring jobs for all; promotion of the transformation of the productive matrix and industrial and technological transformation; sovereignty and peace in the world; and Latin American integration.

Therefore, Ecuador absorbs the eight MDGs proposed by the United Nations as a convention signatory country, as well as the 17 goals proposed in the 2030 Agenda for Sustainable Development. However, this country recognises that for its context, these goals are not enough to achieve Buen Vivir. The PNBV proposes "high social levels" to improve human rights and universal values as well as the rights of nature. Poverty reduction is not the only principal goal, but also the capability to reduce social, territorial, economic, environmental and cultural inequalities. This paper offers an initial comparison of the MDGs, SDGs and the PNBV to show how these three frameworks differ in various dimensions.

From the analysis, it can be concluded that the MDGs and the new 2030 Sustainable Development Agenda are *alternatives for development* because the improvement of quality of life is essentially linked with economic growth and progress. On the other hand, the proposal made in Ecuador for Good Living, intended as an *alternative to traditional development*, promotes a new paradigm which includes interculturality, solidarity, social inclusion and the rights of nature and explicitly addresses the decrease of inequities. However, there is no black-and-white answer; it is unrealistic to think that one country alone can have its own unique system that will work aside from the global model. Therefore, although the contribution of these new alternatives is undeniable, it is still based on the traditional concept of development. Furthermore, there are still challenges to prove whether these policies are having a real impact on society and whether they are applicable to different regions within and among countries.

The next section presents the results of an analysis that examined the compliance between MDGs and the PNBV in Ecuador and in the Amazon region. In conducting the analysis, it took only those indicators for which information was available. It also provides a brief summary of the information gathered from interviews. Topics that were identified to be the most significant by the interviewees have been presented below in descending order of importance.

From theory to practice

An analysis published by Amazonian Regional Articulation (Articulación Regional Amazónica) – ARA (Celentano and Vedoveto 2011, 10) regarding compliance with the MDGs in the Amazon region shows that poverty, inequality and some serious health problems, such as malaria and tuberculosis, still prevail. People's access to basic sanitation is inadequate. Maternal mortality and the incidence of HIV/AIDS have increased in recent years. In relation to gender equality, progress is still slow. Women have little involvement in politics and are disadvantaged in the labour market. A great challenge is the disparity in indicators between urban and rural areas and among indigenous peoples.

On the other hand, since the issuance of the 2008 Constitution, Ecuador has entered a new planning process and political organisation with the aim of ensuring a better quality of life for the population in harmony with nature and its resources. The introduction of the National Plan for Good Living (PNBV) 2009–2013 marks a 'before and after' in the planning of political, economic and social development of the country. The PNBV is the main planning tool at national and local levels. Therefore, the parishes, municipalities and provincial governments have to base and align their local plans to the goals in the PNBV (Interview MCAR02, 2014).

This new framework allows Ecuador to comply and even exceed the minimum targets set by the MDGs worldwide, marking a milestone in the region. However, the challenges at the local level, mainly in the Amazon region, fail to comply with the goals. The results of the Ecuadorian state planning under a theoretical and epistemological principle, based on Sumak Kawsay, suggest a political environment that does not necessarily meet the needs and aspirations of the Amazon population.

The PNBV comprises 89 targets, which are part of the strategies that serve different areas of priority needs in the political, economic, social and environmental arenas. At present, these targets, prioritised by the Ecuadorian state, show varied levels of progress and compliance. Likewise, there are some targets whose fulfilment are delayed and/or suggested to be rethought from the central government.

These 89 targets are composed of 96 indicators. Of these, 42 have been accomplished; 21 have been delayed in fulfilment; 19 are deficient; and 14 have not changed at all.

Additionally, through interviews with the National Secretary of Planning and Development, both in Quito and in the city of Tena, it can be said that many implementation challenges persist. For this reason, the state has worked to develop zonal agendas, trying to localise the objectives of the PNBV to the particular characteristics of each area.

The construction of these local agendas, according to the government, was participatory. The objective of these agendas is to apply the PNBV at the local level:

> [W]e are establishing what we were lacking, which is territorial-local goals; once we have the local agendas we will see which will be the responsibilities of actors such as ministries and local governments, for the fulfillment of the goals that are outlined in the PNBV and some that are also articulated to the MDGs. The construction of the agendas started the previous year, we have done several workshops in all the provinces that correspond to zone 2 (Pichincha, Napo and Orellana) where we have been collecting input from the public, mostly in terms of defining local policies, that is what they expect from the state.
>
> (Interview GCAP03, 2014)

With this information, it can be inferred that Ecuador has a mandatory tool for ministries and local governments which are in charge of local activities in the territory. Thus, the Ecuadorian government proposes a tool to address the particular needs of areas with lower population density, such as the Amazon (Interview GCAP03, 2014). However, it will be necessary to evaluate whether these zonal agendas manage to beat one of the biggest obstacles that exist locally within the Amazon, the lack of intra- and inter-institutional joint efforts:

> The problem has been that many of the activities we are doing are different and are not related to the great goals we have set nationally and internationally.
>
> (Interview MCAR02, 2014).

Poverty

The respondents highlighted two main challenges that will have to be addressed while tackling poverty: first, coordination between institutions and fostering the active and informed participation of the population; and second, implementation of local policies based on recognition and respect of diversity.

> For us poverty means not having a territory, without land there is no life. That is not the problem in our province, the problem here is that there are no opportunities, no access to credit, no participation.
>
> (Interview DGRE10, 2014)

> Poverty means lack of involvement in decision-making. There is a lot of racism still in the province. Only a few communities have running water, but no safe water. Perhaps in the city things are different, but not all is well in communities.
>
> (Interview GTAN12, 2014)

> Poverty is lack of education, lack of ability to work, to make loans. What people earn in agriculture is not enough, the prices they receive for their products are insignificant. We entered a house during the campaign and saw a bunch of green rotting bananas, when we asked why bananas where there, a woman said she was told that a truck was coming but it has not arrived in a week, and when asked how much she sells bananas for, she said that a large cluster will cost USD 1.50. Therefore, why would farmers pay intermediaries? That is why people do not want to work on agriculture.
>
> (Interview CSHI09, 2014)

Education

The invisibility of the differences is a challenge that has not yet been overcome in Ecuador. Neither has there been effective, real and concrete actions to respond to the policies outlined in the PNBV regarding intercultural education.

Access to education according to people's worldviews and culture is still the demand of the Amazonian community leaders; they ask for education, which can revitalise the identity, traditions and worldviews of indigenous peoples.

> The problem is the coverage of services in rural areas because the Amazon has a high level of dispersed populations, the cost for the provision of services is quite high, the problem is with the communities within which access is by rivers, by air, or in border where the situation is critical.
>
> (Interview GCAP03, 2014)

Additionally, ethnic diversity is an essential factor that has not been completely visualised in an intercultural education; the efforts done by the state to unify the Hispanic bilingual education hampers education in native languages:

> Children are not taught in Kichwa only in Spanish. According to the Constitution is understood that the State respects plurinationality, multiculturalism but in practice it does not happen.
>
> (Interview MILL06, 2014)

> The Kichwa in our region is not like that of the Andes, but the latter is the one that prevails and is taught in schools, that is why in Napo we are losing our identity.
>
> (Interview MTAN11, 2014)

Health

As with education, health at the local level requires different treatment. While the population and local institutions recognise that there has been progress, they also state that many national policies do not apply at the local level. These include issues related with access to services and satisfaction with the system:

> Although there have been policies that are working on this, they are not being effective in the territory, I speak from the most remote communities, for example the women said that they walk two or three hours to the health center and when they arrive they cannot get appointments anymore because the phone system is not working or because they have no access to a telephone. We always try to point these apparently irrelevant issues to the Health Ministry in order to make some way to the problem.
>
> (Interview MCAB01, 2014)

> We need a certificate to be treated at the hospital, it is a critical issue because before we went directly to the hospital and had the attention but now with this new management model implemented by the State the problem is that if you live in Chontapunta you must have a certificate to transfer to the hospital otherwise the hospital will not attend you unless it is an emergency. Mostly poor people do not have access to these services.
>
> (Interview MILL06, 2014)

The issue of multiculturalism and respect for traditional medicine is also relevant; people state that there should be greater coordination and transfer of knowledge, a kind of nexus with Western medicine so that indigenous communities do not lose their knowledge in health:

> Midwives, shamans and other traditional medicine should work with health centers and hospitals. Like education, there must be transition of power, knowledge . . . the yachaks, midwives, shamans must be in the classroom.
>
> (Interview MTAN11, 2014)

Gender

The gender dimension in the Amazon is conceptualised mainly from the defence of women's rights, a topic in which various CSOs have been working, due to the high rates of domestic violence in the territory. The influence of a macho culture in Ecuadorian society represents a permanent obstacle to a deconstruction of social paradigms rooted in the society. Particularly among the Amazonian indigenous people, these difficulties are very evident, which has demanded continuous and gradual work for a few decades.

> The Kichwa culture is too complex; it is difficult to talk about family planning. We had a fellow once by Morona Santiago province almost lynched when he spoke of family planning, worse if you are giving or promoting condoms, Copper T. We like a Users' Committee did workshops with the support of the Municipality in 2009 in three parishes, we had assistance, but is very difficult to involve women, the macho culture do not let you. Getting women to get into the topic of leadership training picture is quite difficult.
>
> (Interview MILL06, 2014)

However, it is important to remember that gender includes not only the claim to the rights of women, but other genders which are not included and accepted in Ecuadorian Amazon provinces.

> We have not worked with other genders, it is an issue that is still a taboo in our society. The other day I was talking to some journalists and they told me "do not bring those ideas from Quito, you leave them there, here we are men and women, the bible does not recognise anything else." We also have to see that these people are facing discrimination. Before it was terrible, now they are accepted, but it is still difficult to talk about these topics locally.
>
> (Interview MCAB01, 2014)

While there has been progress in terms of gender equality, the goal of inclusion and respect for diversity of gender is far from being achieved, understood and accepted by Ecuadorian society and less in the Amazon area.

Environmental sustainability

The issue of the environment is represented in the area as a recurring problem whose solutions mostly have meant short-range attention with few results. There are several barriers to addressing environmental issues in Tena, both in urban and rural areas.

The main problems are the processing of solid waste and liquid waste in urban areas. There are no suitable landfills, the discharge of liquid wastes ends up in rivers and there are constant cuts in the provision of potable water.

Another problem in this area is the exploitation of natural resources, such as timber extraction and sand mining. With international cooperation since the 1990s, the actors of the area have established spaces of dialogues and coordination. It was possible with this support to encourage state cooperation and to promote good governance of natural resources. All the institutions responsible for monitoring environmental and land management agree that the main purpose is to achieve the aim of Good Living. However, this is not necessarily perceived by the population:

> We want to be able to use the resources we have in our communities in a sustainable manner, we want to be able to hunt and fish, but now we have restrictions.
>
> (Interview MTAN11, 2014)

Generally speaking, the fulfilment of goals recognising the rights of nature still appears as a work in progress at the national and local levels. The most significant progress seems to be the conservation and reforestation projects. However, much remains to be done.

Conclusions

Throughout history, the meaning of 'development' has evolved to meet humanity's political, social, economic and environmental needs. However, the premise of achieving a society more just and equitable still persists as an unfinished challenge. Paradigms of sustainability and Good Living, among others, have not materialised into tangible results yet, which demonstrate a less-than-expected improvement in the quality of human life. The interest of achieving higher income and keeping the traditional concept of 'growth and progress' exceeds the number of international proposals designed to tackle them and which seek agreement at the economic, environmental and social levels.

However, global efforts remain. The civilizational crisis that humankind confronts requires states and civil society to rethink its way of development, in which economic and political objectives should not prevail over social, cultural and environmental needs. Thus, the objectives proposed in the new post-2015 agenda should generate further discussion for their implementation at national and regional levels, but especially locally.

Ecuador, through its 'alternative' proposal of Good Living, offers new epistemological bases and structural policies for development. Through the National Plan for Good Living or PNBV, innovative goals seek maximum social benefits, depending on the recognition of national diversity, human rights and rights of nature, poverty eradication and greater social inclusion.

However, so far according to the results obtained, only 44 per cent of these goals have been met nationally (Buen Vivir, 2014). This represents a significant improvement, but national averages tend to hide local disparities, a situation that was found in this research in the city of Tena, in Ecuadorian Amazonia.

In Ecuador, the lack of information about the Amazon in different aspects and levels represents a significant barrier for the effectiveness of local agendas that the state has built to fulfil the goals of the PNBV. In this sense, it is urgent to formalise a database to be validated by the civil society, to help build development indicators which reflect an authentic quality of life for the Amazonian population.

This must also be adapted to its geographical, biological, ecosystem, social and cultural characteristics.

It is also important to emphasise the need to build qualitative indicators that demonstrate the diversity of this region. In the case of the SDGs, the objectives proposed do not reveal this diversity, and in the case of the PNBV goals, they have not yet materialised in the Amazon region, its provinces, cities and mainly rural parishes.

Finally, and as already been noted, there are neither unique nor standardised solutions. Although theoretically Ecuador proposes an alternative to development, until now the fulfilment of its goals reflects changes that are more quantitative than qualitative. For this reason, the state must continually think about the epistemes of Good Living beyond a political speech, and as a representative example that exposes the bases of the new post-2015 agenda.

Note

1 The quotations used in this document were taken from texts in Spanish; these have been translated by the authors.

References

Acosta, A., Martínez, E. and Sacher, W. (2013) Salir del Extractivismo: Una Condición Para el Sumak Kawsay: Propuestas Sobre Petróleo, Minería y Energía en el Ecuador. In Ortiz, C. and Ojeda, S. (eds.) *Alternativas al Capitalismo/Colonialismo del Siglo XXI* (pp. 307–380). Ecuador: Grupo Permanente de Trabajo sobre Alternativas al Desarrollo.

Buen Vivir. (2014) Available from: http://www.buenvivir.gob.ec/inicio [Accessed: 10 May 2014].

Celentano, D. and Vedoveto, M. (eds.) (2011) *La Amazonía y los Objetivos del Milenio*. Quito: ARA Regional.

Dubois, A. (n.d.) Un concepto de desarrollo para el siglo XXI. *Lumina Magazine*. Available from: http://www.umanizales.edu.co/publicaciones/campos/economicas/lumina1/html/8/concepdesar.pdf [Accessed: 20 April 2014].

Guandinango, Y. A. (2013) *Sumak Kawsay – Buen Vivir: Comprensión teórica y práctica vivencial comunitaria: Aportes para el Ranti de conocimientos*. Unpublished M.Sc. thesis, Department of Socio-Environmental Studies. Facultad Latinoamericana de Ciencias Sociales FLACSO-Sede Ecuador.

Gudynas, E. (2011) Debates sobre el Desarrollo y sus alternativas en América Latina: Una Breve Guía Heterodoxa. In Jarrín, S. (ed.) *Más Allá del Desarrollo* (pp.21–53). Ecuador: Grupo Permanente de Trabajo sobre Alternativas al Desarrollo.

Gudynas, E. (2013a) Transiciones Hacia un Nuevo Regionalismo Autónomo. In Ortiz, C. and Ojeda, S. (eds.) *Alternativas al Capitalismo/Colonialismo del Siglo XXI* (pp.129–160). Ecuador: Grupo Permanente de Trabajo sobre Alternativas al Desarrollo.

Gudynas, E. (2013b). Postextractivismo y Alternativas al Desarrollo Desde la Sociedad Civil. In Ortiz, C. and Ojeda, S. (eds.) *Alternativas al Capitalismo/Colonialismo del Siglo XXI* (pp.189–221). Ecuador: Grupo Permanente de Trabajo sobre Alternativas al Desarrollo.

Lander, E. (2013) Con el Tiempo Contado: Crisis Civilizatoria, Límites del Planeta, Asaltos a la Democracia y Pueblos en Resistencia. In Ortiz, C. and Ojeda, S. (eds.) *Alternativas al Capitalismo/Colonialismo del Siglo XXI* (pp.27–61). Ecuador: Grupo Permanente de Trabajo sobre Alternativas al Desarrollo.

Onofa, M., Rodríguez, F. and Ponce, J. (eds.) (2012). *Avance de los Objetivos de Desarrollo del Milenio en la Amazonía Ecuatoriana.* Quito: EcoCiencia.

UNDP. (2014) *The Millennium Development Goals Report 2013.* New York: United Nations Development Programme (UNDP). Available from: http://www.undp.org/content/undp/en/home/librarypage/mdg/the-millennium-development-goals-report-2013.html [Accessed: 10 May 2014].

United Nations. (2013) *A New Global Partnership: Eradicate Poverty and Transform Economies through Sustainable Development.* Report of the High-Level Panel of Eminent Persons on the Post-2015 Development Agenda. New York: United Nations. Available from: http://www.post2015hlp.org/the-report/ [Accessed: 5 May 2014].

United Nations. (2015) *Transforming Our World: The 2030 Agenda for Sustainable Development.* New York: United Nations. Available from: https://sustainabledevelopment.un.org/post2015/transformingourworld [Accessed: 19 August 2015].

UN Millennium Project. (2006) *About MDGs.* Available from: http://www.unmillenniumproject.org/goals/index.htm [Accessed: 5 May 2014].

Sustainability and growth

4 Growth within natural limits

The debates, propositions and possibilities

Karin Fernando and Prasanthi Gunawardena

Introduction

Nearing the end of the Millennium Development Goals (MDGs), the global development community has conceded that current economic growth models have to be revamped, even transformed, to eradicate poverty, with due consideration to addressing inequalities and climate change. In parallel, the Conference on Sustainable Development, widely known as Rio+20, proposed to establish Sustainable Development Goals (SDGs), with greater emphasis on environmental sustainability. The SDGs acknowledge the necessity of dealing with climate change, mitigating greenhouse gases (GHGs), living in harmony with nature, and protecting biodiversity (OWG, 2015). After more than two years of discussions and negotiations, in September 2015, the SDGs that build on and take over from the MDGs will be adopted. It is a more ambitious and universal set of goals that calls for a change the trajectory of the planet's future by transforming economies and relationships between people as well as with the planet. This is a vital global call for those who have been raising the alarm about the environmental consequences of current pathways and lobbying for sustainable development for more than 50 years. However, the proposed SDGs (and their implementation) still raise questions: Do they go the distance? Are they transformative enough to protect the earth's ecological functions, distribute development benefits more equitably and create a more just society? Do they align with a sustainable development model, where economic growth is controlled and managed within natural limits? Will they allow a metric for ecological processes to be developed and used?

This paper analyses the overarching SDG objectives and the goals in terms of how they conform to the principles of sustainability, which stem theoretically from the basis that natural resources are finite and ecosystems have a threshold capacity to absorb waste. This paper describes a conceptual framework derived from the growth within natural limits ideology and concludes with a discussion on the alignment of the SDGs to this framework.

The need for transformation and a new development model

Advancements in reducing poverty are attributed to economic growth, which has generated jobs, investments and incomes and enabled fiscal space for social spending for the poor. Economic growth, measured largely in terms of gross domestic product (GDP), remains the key indicator for economic development and social well-being. However, current growth models – based on rapid, monetised, material development – have also created immense inequalities with increasing gaps between the rich and the poor, both within and among countries. A study by Credit Suisse Research Institute shows that the richest 0.5 per cent hold well over one-third of the world's wealth (CSRI, 2010).

South Asia has experienced some of the fastest economic growth spurts in the new millennium but has yet to meet the needs of the poor (World Bank, 2015b). While economic growth has reduced poverty, there are still 507 million people, or 33 per cent of the developing world's poor, living in South Asia. From 1981 to 2010, the number of people living on less than USD 1.25 per day declined, but the number of those living on less than USD 2.00 per day increased (World Bank, 2015b). It is also debatable if a meagre amount such as USD 1.25 per day allows people to live a decent life. When other indicators of social well-being are surveyed, South Asia continues to lag behind. The region still has 400 million illiterate adults, 300 million people facing hunger, 700 million people living without access to standard sanitation services and some of the highest malnutrition rates in the world (SDSN, 2012). Multidimensional inequality[1] remains high within South Asia at 28 per cent, with only Sub-Saharan Africa (SSA) having higher inequality at 35.5 per cent (UNDP, 2014). Figure 4.1 shows disparities in the accumulation of wealth in various South Asian countries. Current models of growth and development appear to have created a dichotomous South Asia, where on the one hand, growth and progress have led to a 'Shining Asia', but deep disparities

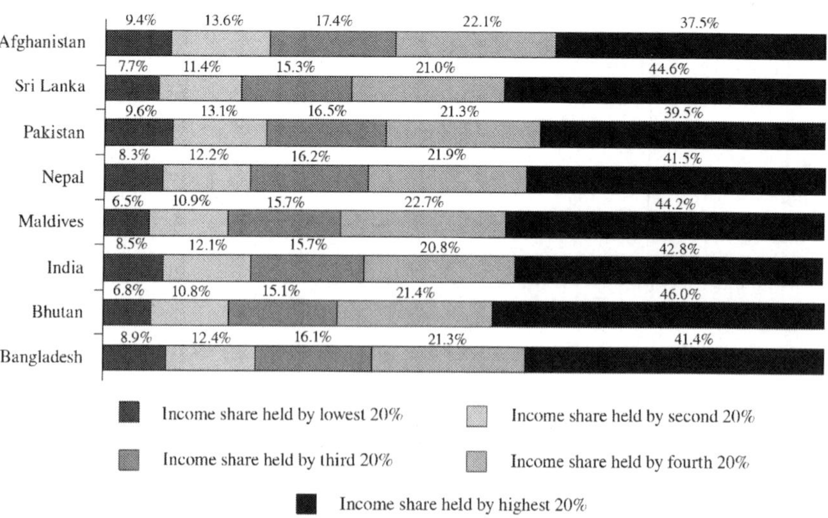

Figure 4.1 Distribution of income or consumption by quintile

Source: Derived from the data available on PovcalNet (World Bank, 2015a).

in how benefits are accrued and distributed have also created a 'Suffering Asia', which is developmentally and morally unacceptable (Gunasekera, 2013).

Another consequence of the hegemony of current growth models is that the degradation and pollution of natural systems is seen as an unavoidable, even acceptable, part of economic growth. Ever-growing populations, increased life expectancy and intense consumption-based lifestyles mean that more natural resources, particularly energy resources, are needed to meet the demand.

The dangers of population growth without a concomitant increase in the means of subsistence were anticipated by Malthus in the early 1800s. More recently, the growth within limits ideology was delineated and popularised by the Club of Rome (Meadows et al., 1972). This ideology is based on the overarching theoretical concept that the size of the economy, as well as the scale and growth trajectory of any economic activity, should not violate the biophysical limits of ecosystems, which refer to the abilities of ecosystems to continuously perform their regulatory functions and availability of non-renewable natural resources (Meadows et al., 1972; Daly, 2005). Daly (2005) argues that violating these limits leads to 'uneconomic' growth, where the degraded environment and indirect social costs (for health, disaster response, etc.) outweigh economic gains.

The Ecological Footprint metric developed by the Global Footprint Network (Ewing et al., 2010) takes into account the natural resources of a geographic area, or 'biocapacity', in its estimation of development. Calculations show that greater human development has resulted in the greater extraction and use of resources (see Figure 4.2, where developed countries are in the upper right quadrant). A micro-level

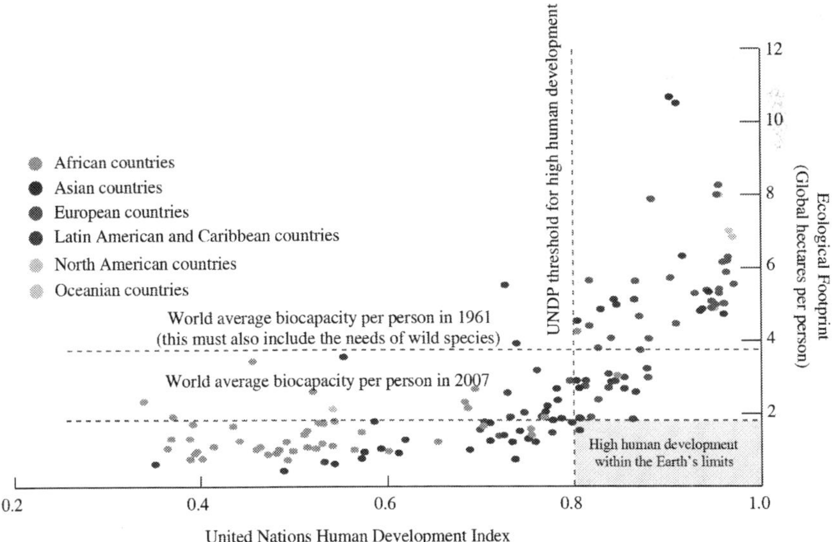

Figure 4.2 Human development and ecological footprint

Source: Ewing et al. (2010).

Note: © 2010 Global Footprint Network.

illustration using Rees's (1992) ecological footprint methodology shows that the fossil fuel and food needs of the 1.7 million inhabitants of Canada's Fraser Valley, a 400,000 hectare region, require 8.3 million hectares of land for continuous production. This population is living well beyond its own natural resources, but also exhausting the natural capital of other people and places. According to the Global Footprint Network, no developed country reached its 'developed' status without exceeding its natural capital base.

The dominant economic growth model is built on the assumption that there are enough natural resources to grow the economy, which is essential for human development, and if the economy stagnates or declines, like many did during the 2008–09 global financial crisis, then more people fall or sink deeper into poverty. However, scientists and economists continue to produce convincing proof that such an economy is extracting natural resources faster than they can be replenished and increasing pollution to levels that are affecting the regulatory functions of the earth and leading to climate change (Millennium Ecosystem Assessment, 2003).

Climate change is a vicious cycle aggravated by human activity, which has and will have serious consequences on human well-being. Increased incidences of disasters, rising surface and ocean temperatures, as well as higher sea levels, melting ice caps and weather variability will affect cities, homes and businesses and reverse advancements made in human development thus far. The Intergovernmental Panel on Climate Change (IPCC) warns that "warming of the climate system is unequivocal, and since the 1950s, many of the observed changes are unprecedented over decades to millennia" (IPCC, 2013). It also states that risks and vulnerabilities to sectors of the economy, human health, food security, livelihoods and poverty increase as temperatures rise (exponentially, in some places, at the level of 3^{0}C). The World Bank states that South Asia will be one of the most severely affected regions, and the poor and vulnerable, unable to recover easily from such external shocks, will be the worst affected (World Bank, 2015b). This sums up the reality and challenge confronting governments in negotiations on the post-2015 development goals.

Growth models vs. growth within natural limits

The field of economics deals with the production, distribution and consumption of goods and services for the fulfilment of human needs. The foundation of these economic processes is the use of natural resources, such as raw materials and ecosystem services, defined broadly as benefits people obtain from ecosystems, such as erosion control and pollination. Natural resources are part and parcel of economic activities as raw materials. They are entwined with economic activities as both resources and by products or waste. Hence unlimited growth is only possible if resources and waste assimilation is unlimited (Gunawardena, 2013). This latter point has fuelled debate between neoclassical and ecological economists over the role of growth and the ways in which the development of countries, communities and individuals should move ahead. At the core of this debate is the concept of sustainability (Gunawardena, 2013).

Neoclassical economics involves an abstract belief in the substitutability of natural and human-made capital. The depletion of natural capital is justified by the increasing wealth of current and future generations that is sustainable due to the assumed substitution of natural resources and their synthetic equivalents (Gunawardena, 2013). Technological innovation, efficiency in processes and substitution of one scarce resource with another are prescribed as the ways to keep growing and developing, tackling environmental challenges including climate change, and overcoming scarcity. It can be argued that environmental economics was introduced to the neoclassical economic model to internalise environmental 'externalities' and ascribe monetary values to natural resources and ecosystem services through mathematical formulations. The field fixes a market price on the environment that encourages greater efficiency and better use of natural resources (Beder 2011). The economy then continues to function according to the neoclassical logic of consumer willingness to pay for 'green' products and services. However, the field does not question the overall principle that growth can be limitless and market forces will adjust accordingly.

Conversely, ecological economics recognise the necessity of maintaining a critical minimum of natural resources, which is linked to the non-substitutability of some resources, the uniqueness of some environmental components and the criticality of certain environmental processes essential to supporting life, such as climate control, nutrient cycling and pollution management (Gunawardena, 2013). These considerations lead ecological economists to espouse three strong sustainability rules based on biophysical limits and Earth sciences (Farley and Daly, 2006, as quoted in Gunawardena (2013)):

1. For renewable resources, consumption (or the rate of use) should not exceed the rate of regeneration. Use should be determined by the quantity that can be produced using renewable resources.
2. For consumption of non-renewable resources, the rate of use should not exceed the investment into renewable resources that can be substituted for that use (e.g. an oil deposit can only be used at the rate at which some funds are set aside and invested in an equivalent renewable energy source that could replace it).
3. The rate of waste emission must remain within the assimilative capacity of the environment. Moreover, waste that cannot be assimilated should not be emitted (e.g. heavy metals, persistent organic pollutants, nuclear waste and emissions from burning fossil fuels).

Above all, ecological functions that maintain life must not be compromised.

Working within biophysical limits questions consumption-based well-being that, under the dominant economic growth model's logic of "more is better," has led to exploitation and overuse of natural resources as well as skewing toward creating affluence rather than meeting basic needs. As the global population continues to grow, and indeed poorer countries quicken development, consumption rates will increase, and with them, ecological footprints. The Global Footprint

Network estimates that if each person on the planet consumed like the average American did in 2007, the global population would need the biocapacity of 4.5 earths, though if people lived like the average Indian, the population would use only half of the current earth's biocapacity (Ewing et al., 2010). These estimates raise questions about what type of development, what kind of lifestyles and for whose benefit governments should strive. Increasing sustainability is a complex exercise, which forces people to consider socio-ethical aspects with future generations in mind and their likely diminished natural capital, as well as the conditions for other living species. Dealing with consumption and consumerism requires tackling *prosperity* as well as poverty and dealing with rights, choices, ethics and aspirations, which are subjective issues but which can be revolutionary for the cause of saving the planet in the interest of humanity. The ecological approach evidently has a stronger sustainability base that considers the Earth sciences and a stronger orientation toward managing natural resources in the pursuit of economic growth.

Building a conceptual framework

To develop a conceptual framework for comparing SDGs, various sustainability frameworks were reviewed, including those by Munasinghe (2010), Daly (described in (Gjoksi and Sedlacko, 2010), the Millennium Ecosystem Assessment (2003), Raworth (2014) and Nilsson, Lucas and Yoshida (2013). All these frameworks largely agree on the ecological domain – human activities must not exceed or destroy the earth's regulatory and assimilation capacities. However, they differ on how the other two domains, especially the economic domain, are perceived. An economic domain explicitly framed according to the principles of sustainability appears to be necessary to measure progress within the domain. Based on these existing models, the principles of sustainability and needed transformative shifts in world order that the SDGs strive to catalyse, this paper proposes the framework in Figure 4.3 as an integrated sustainability analysis tool.

The inner circle is the core of sustainable development – the three integrated, equally important facets that drive development. They are part of a loop, where each facet influences the other in a non-linear dynamic system. The outer circle is the enabling environment, the means of implementation needed to support the integrity of the inner circle. Each facet and its orientation are described below.

Circular economy

The logic of a circular economy is to keep economic activities within the bounds of natural resource limits and the assimilative capacity of the environment. The circular economy is a 'materials balance model', with the environment having three economic functions – resource supplier, waste assimilator and direct source of utility (e.g. aesthetic benefits). They are economic functions because they each have a positive economic value (i.e. if they were bought and sold in the

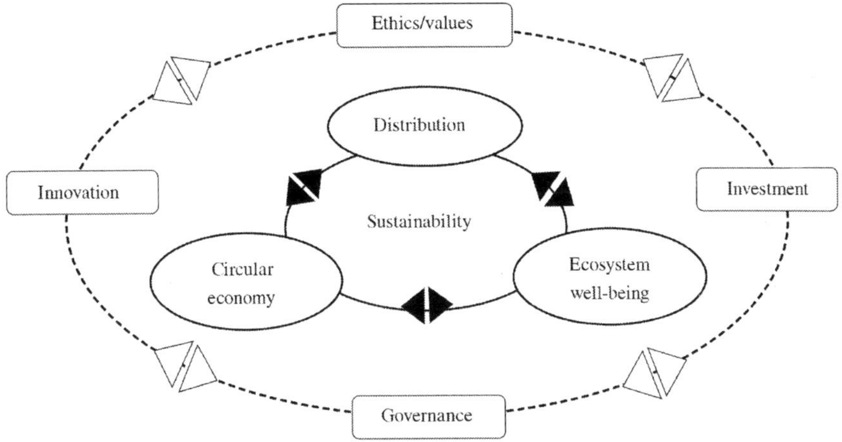

Figure 4.3 Conceptual framework for comparing SDGs

Source: Prepared by the authors.

marketplace, they would all have positive prices). Dangers arise from the mistreatment of the environment, stemming from the lack of recognition of the positive prices for these economic functions.

As described by Pearce and Turner (1990), resources (R) can be disaggregated into two types of natural resources: Exhaustible Resources (ER), which cannot renew themselves and include coal, oil, gas and minerals, and Renewable Resources (RR), which can renew themselves. For instance, a forest produces a 'sustainable yield', so that if *x* cubic metres of timber are cut in any year, the stock of trees will stay the same as long as the trees have grown by *x* cubic metres. The same is true for stocks of fish. Some resources, such as soil, are mixes of exhaustible and renewable resources. Some renewable resources renew quickly, while others take a longer time. If a renewable resource is harvested at a faster rate than it regenerates, the stock will be reduced. In this way, a renewable resource can be 'mined', and is essentially treated like an exhaustible resource. If the choice is to sustain renewable resources, care must be taken to harvest them at a rate no greater than their natural regenerative capacity (Pearce and Turner, 1990). In terms of waste (W), so long as waste is disposed of in quantities (and qualities) that are commensurate with the environment's assimilative capacity, the circular economic system will function just like a natural system (Pearce and Turner, 1990). What a circular economy model strives to do is extend the life and use of raw materials and reduce the amount of waste at every point – it seeks to be restorative based on material flows from design to planning to implementation. The use of renewable energy, energy efficiency, 3R principles (Reduce, Reuse, Recycle) and clean technologies is embedded in the processes of the circular economy.

Distribution

The neoclassical economic model perpetuates wealth based on market demand. For example, if a metal is a limited resource, using it to make luxury items leads to less availability of the metal for more necessary basic items, such as agricultural implements. Additionally, a few controlling the bulk of a resource marginalises others, while the poor rely on degraded resources or fewer value-added jobs linked to natural resources (e.g. small-scale fisheries and farming), which reduces their opportunity to move out of poverty. Widespread asymmetries in incomes and access to services, decent jobs, healthcare, education and mediums of expression need to be addressed. If poverty and inequality are to be addressed, given the realities of finite resources and widespread environmental degradation, it is necessary to prioritise the basic needs of all in society over wealth accumulation and more equitable distribution of economic benefits. It also requires addressing gross inequalities both within and among countries, among individuals and groups (e.g. minorities, women, and groups based on caste, ethnicity, disability and sexual orientation), and the privileging of some actors (e.g. companies) over others (e.g. citizens) in the distribution of development benefits (CEPA, 2013). Better distribution can be achieved through a combination of progressive taxes, which are set aside for the poor and do not replace safety nets, affirmative action, just governance, improvements in service quality and quantity for poor people, and regulation and non-discrimination in applying laws and regulations (CEPA, 2013). Using tools (such as cost–benefit analysis) that account for specific costs and benefits – economic, social and environmental, as well as the impact on future generations, can assist in making choices on what projects/policies or initiatives should be selected, and for whose benefit.

Ecological well-being

The earth provides a series of ecosystem services – water and air purification, flood and erosion control, generation of fertile soils, detoxification of waste, climate regulation, pollination, and aesthetic and cultural benefits – without which life cannot exist (Millennium Ecosystem Assessment, 2003). The earth also has the capacity to tolerate changes and absorb shocks within a certain threshold without collapsing or transforming its state (Millennium Ecosystem Assessment, 2003). However, failures in current economic growth models and consumer lifestyles to take into account ecosystems' functions are causing these functions to collapse rapidly. Some of the 'planetary boundaries', or the levels of change that the earth can withstand before it starts to collapse, are being violated (Rockström et al., 2009). Three of these boundaries have already been crossed in the pursuit of economic growth – climate change, rate of biodiversity loss and biogeochemical flows – and crossing more of these boundaries will have catastrophic effects on the earth's life-support functions.

A considerable part of the problem is that in current economic growth models, many environmental and well-being deficits are considered to be market externalities. Essential ecosystem services have no direct market value, and thus, no price signals through which to channel the so-called supply and demand feedback that communicates the need to maintain them. In fact, markets cannot produce such services, but some valuation methods (such as the cost–benefit analysis, green accounting) can assign values and can be used to make decisions. Meanwhile, environmental costs are often not shown in national accounts (e.g. health expenditure due to pollution). Notably, economic growth clearly benefits the exploiters and polluters, at the expense of the poorest strata of the current generation, future generations and other species, whose well-being is disproportionately affected by the costs of environmental degradation (Gunawardena, 2010).

The global commons and the trans-boundary nature of ecological well-being also pose challenges for individual countries. Many of the aforementioned planetary boundaries and the protection of earth's ecological functions are covered by multilateral environmental treaties, but suffer from lack of implementation and buy-in from world leaders. Another global commitment without the support of all countries will suffer the same fate. The onus to address overuse of the world's biocapacity has to be on developed countries. Developing countries must be supported to build in the planetary boundaries or earth's limits as a part of national development frameworks, so that overextraction is not repeated.

Enabling factors

As visualised in the conceptual framework (Figure 4.3), it is not just the inner circle of facets of sustainability that has to be adhered to – these facets are very much influenced by the enabling factors that surround the core. A short description of each enabling factor is given below.

Innovation

Human ingenuity and ambition coupled with technology and innovation have propelled economic growth forward while pushing natural limits back due to substitution and increasing efficiency. The dominant rationale is that technology or innovation will overcome biophysical limits and perpetuate current economic growth models. However, this approach would most likely only extend the timeframe for reaching limits, rather than overcome the limits. Using Ehrlich's equation, Jackson (2009) shows how the pace of technological advancement cannot keep up with carbon dioxide (CO_2) emissions that are influenced by affluence and population growth. Given these conditions, economic growth will inevitably lead to a slowdown of production with consequences for some people and technology will not be enough to avoid it. A major consequence of technological advancement is that it has fostered a culture of well-being that is dependent on material wealth and physical assets. For a real transformation, it is necessary to recognise and prioritise innovation that supports the ideals of 'strong sustainability'. Such innovation is not merely a technological fix for the status quo, but a behavioural and conceptual shift to gear technology and creativity to build systems and products that maintain the well-being of all on a planet with finite resources.

Governance

Natural resources and ecosystems' functions are global public goods. For instance, a breathable atmosphere, clean water, a stable climate and vibrant biodiversity belong to no one person and benefit us all. However, some resources can be diminished or controlled by some at a cost to others at many scales in society, which violates the concept of the global commons and leads to discrimination and suppression of the well-being of some people. Given this predicament, good governance and strong institutions must be responsive to people's needs. There must be accountable political institutions that allow public participation in decision-making and oversight. They must promote non-violent modes of conflict resolution that lead to safety, security and respect of separate identities. They need to ensure transparency, accountability and access to information. They should also respect the interdependence of the individual and collective dimensions of social existence (CEPA 2013). These principles also need to apply to the private sector and civil society in both developed and developing countries as well as global governance institutions (i.e. multilateral organisations that are responsible for trade, investment, technology, etc.). Sustainable development requires transboundary cooperation and collaboration to build a single shared society.

Investment

This enabling factor encompasses monetary and fiscal support and investments in knowledge and capacity to orchestrate a true shift toward sustainable development. Investments must be made in an integrated manner with the intention to achieve all facets of sustainable development. They must be targeted and earmarked to develop specific processes, such as clean energy and low-carbon development processes, sustainable technology and infrastructure, ecological protection, and the achievement of rights, equality and well-being for all. Investments must also spur the ideological momentum and capacity increases for change. This enabling factor is crucial since most attempts to catalyse sustainable development have been faced with limited buy-in along with a lack of finance, capacity and knowledge.

Ethics and values

Sustainability ideology dictates that the current generation has an obligation to conserve natural resources for future generations and ensure them a planet that does not diminish their rights and opportunities. This ideology also states that people have an obligation to meet the needs of the poorest and protect the integrity of earth's ecosystems. To achieve these objectives, the current generation needs to increase the prominence of intergenerational rights, value nature beyond its utilitarian uses and not overexploit natural resources that are shared, limited and interconnected and that must meet the needs of all, even the unborn. Consumerism and materialistic well-being, along with the waste they generate, and the growing human population, whose needs have to be met, are at the core of the environmental and social debacle. Shifting from consumerist lifestyles and living within the means of this planet require challenging our ethics, values and ambitions – if we are to achieve well-being for all.

The SDGs against the growth within natural limits framework

The conceptual framework described above was designed to assess the sustainability of the proposed SDGs with the logic that if each facet is covered adequately, the SDG upholds the criteria of sustainability. The analysis is done against the chapeau section of the 2030 Agenda for Sustainable Development, against each goal and target, and provides overall conclusions on the sustainability of the SDGs.

Overall, the language in the SDGs[2] is supportive of 'sustainable development' and reiterates several times the integrated and balanced manner in which the three dimensions – economic, social and environmental – must be met and the universal and indivisible nature of achieving all the goals. It attempts to push for the stabilisation of ecosystem services, calls for action against "dangerous anthropogenic interference with the climate system" and emphasises the need to tackle inequality and address human rights. It also advocates a shift from unsustainable economic processes to one that is aligned to sustainable consumption and production (SCP). While it calls for a transformative economy, it does not openly state that there are limitations in the current economic system to address such a course of action. It also does not critique the consumption-based prosperity ideals that we aspire to. While growing within nature's means, using resources sustainably, combating climate change and the degradation of ecosystems and protecting the earth for the next generation are highlighted, it does not specifically acknowledge that resources are limited. The priority and purpose of sustainable development is clearly poverty eradication – in all forms.

The social domain, particularly the addressing of the distribution facet, prevails in all of the proposed goals. There is a concerted effort across the SDGs to achieve equity through the tenets of better distribution and better sharing of benefits. There are several explicit goals that address the social domain, specifically multidimensional basic needs (Goals 1 to 7), better access to economic resources, infrastructure, and economic opportunities (Goals 8, 9 and 12), as well as rights, non-discrimination and rule of law (Goals 5, 10 and 16). Goals more geared toward the economic and ecological domains also address the needs of poor people (i.e. addressing decent jobs, child labour, youth unemployment in Goal 8; access to technology and infrastructure for small and medium enterprises in Goal 9; access to resources to small-scale and artisanal fishers in Goal 14). Evidently, there is much elaboration on the distribution facet. Some targets are specific, such as bringing the number of people living in extreme poverty down to zero (Goal

1), ending all forms of hunger and malnutrition (Goal 2), and sustaining income growth of the bottom 40 per cent at a rate that is higher than the national average (Goal 10). Nevertheless, critics maintain that some bars are too low (e.g. that the USD 1.25 per day as an inadequate poverty threshold) and that language has been diluted (e.g. the word 'promote' replacing 'ensure' in relation to access and sharing of benefits of genetic resources in Goal 2 and Goal 15 [Targets 2.5 and 15.6] and the revision of paragraph 19 on human rights that reduces its progressive and expansive underpinnings). The inadequate explicit emphasis on issues of gender-based violence, rights of migrants, elders and people of different sexual orientation have also been highlighted by the submissions made to the UN sessions.

In contrast, the proposed SDGs align far less with ecological well-being facets. In terms of ecological well-being, there are two specific goals for marine and terrestrial systems (Goals 14 and 15), which means that a huge range of biodiversity issues and ecosystem functions are generalised. For example, Target 14.5 asks for conservation of at least 10 per cent of coastal and marine areas, but what type of ecosystems on what basis are not specified. The tone of these two goals and indeed most other goals addressing social needs (e.g. Goal 2 on hunger and Goal 6 on water) all indicate alignment with sustainable use rather than ecological balance or biophysical functions. Some targets such as Goal 7 on energy and Goal 13 that have an overall impact on achieving the SDGs do not set strong quantitative targets for managing human impacts. For instance, the renewable energy target is set ambiguously as increasing renewable energy 'substantially' and does not call for phasing out of fossil fuels. The temperature target is specifically mentioned in the preamble (paragraph 31), but Goal 13 has no quantitative targets and only provides broad statements for adaptation and mitigation. Both Goals 7 and 13 weigh in on the responsibility and support needed for developing countries, but do not stipulate the onus on developed countries – who can and need to make the most significant changes – to take stronger measures.

The goals directly addressing the economic domain do not show a clear path toward a circular economy. While transforming the economy is vital for sustainable development, only a few goals are geared towards this domain. Goal 12 on SCP, by definition (see Box 4.1), shares an orientation towards the principles of a circular economy.

Some of the economic goals (i.e. 8 and 12) are mindful of the need for efficient use of resources and managing wastes and gearing science and technology towards this cause. However, there is only one reference to wasteful consumption, and although referred to in the preamble, responsible consumption is not embedded adequately into the economic goals or targets. It is production that is dominant. In addition, these three goals make no reference to managing scarce/non-renewable resources within biophysical limits or changing the limitless growth mind-set. Tweaking the existing system to improve its efficiency and manage both resources and waste is the general orientation. In Goal 8, the specific GDP target of 7 per cent also goes against the need to plot a growth trajectory based on ecological and social needs. GDP itself is an inadequate measure of better distribution of economic benefits. This is further confused, as Goal 8 touches on decoupling but

Box 4.1 The United Nations Environment Programme (UNEP) definitions of 'Sustainable Consumption and Production (SCP)' and 'Decoupling'

SCP is the use of services and products to provide basic needs to improve the quality of life, while minimising both the use of natural materials and wastes produced over the life cycle of the service/product without jeopardising the needs of future generations (UNDESA, 2015).

Decoupling has several definitions: *Resource decoupling* means reducing the rate of use of resources per unit of economic activity. *Impact decoupling* refers to maintaining economic output while reducing negative environmental impact. *Relative decoupling* of resources or impacts means that the growth rate of resources used or environmental impacts are lower than the economic growth rate; therefore resource productivity is rising (UNEP, 2011).

not with enough substance or ambition to make it more meaningful – as given the definition in Box 4.1, the objective will differ based on the type of decoupling is intended.

Compared against the enabling factors, the proposed SDGs have some positives but also notable gaps. Science, technology and innovation are mentioned in some goals and specifically discussed in Goal 17. Targets encourage more research and development, capacity building and financing for the development of clean technologies and industrial processes. However, the emphasis on technology as a means to transform current economic growth models based on consumerism into a sustainability model is not clearly emphasised. The shift to a sustainable development orientation has come from a moral obligation to alleviate poverty and suffering. This point is acknowledged in the preamble and appears across the goals. However, there is a distinct lack of focus on consumerism and intergenerational responsibility in all the targets. The concentration is clearly on raising the bottom, rather than managing the top, where the problems of high consumption at the cost to biocapacity are rife. Given that the SDGs are envisioned as a universal set of goals and targets, all types of countries must assume certain roles. Better cooperation, moving beyond country ambitions/boundaries, sourcing finances and reforming trade and tax regimes are prescribed in some goals, while Goal 17 concentrates solely on these means of implementation. Yet, here too is some disjuncture in conceptualising these roles in consideration of all three facets of sustainability, especially those of the circular economy and ecological well-being.

The compartmentalisation of the goals, and insufficient and explicit integration of all three facets, can lead to the sub-optimal performance of sustainability. It has been agreed that the goals will be indivisible and not mutually exclusive. Some reinforce each other (poverty, hunger and inequality goals), others are dependent (the energy goal with most other goals along with the goal on peaceful societies) and some can be constraints on other goals (ending hunger and sustaining economic growth may come at a cost to protecting terrestrial and marine ecosystems). However, if the facets of sustainability prevail and an integrated framework is adopted, sustainable food systems can also lead to the protection of terrestrial and marine ecosystems. Such inter-linkages are less obvious when the goals, targets and indicators are compartmentalised, while each of the goals do not adequately consider the complexity of the interrelationships between the three facets of sustainability in a balanced way.

Conclusions

The SDGs have emerged as an attempt to 'transform' the world's development trajectory with the acknowledgement that current economic models based on unlimited growth and consumerism have not solved the problems of poverty and inequality for millions of people and have led to a state of crisis for the planet.

The social domain is explicitly evident in the SDGs' intentions to eradicate poverty, improve well-being and create a more equal global society. The targets related to the social domain have a high degree of ambition and clarity. However, the economic and ecological domains are far less ambitious and require greater attention in the SDGs. The interface between economic and ecological facets is inadequate to be transformative and does not subscribe to the fundamentals of biophysical limits.

For a sustainable development approach to work, the integration of different theoretical approaches and knowledge tracks is required– conceptually drawing from economics, social sciences and Earth sciences. The 'sustainability science' still requires further refinement. The SDGs, despite their limitations, should spur on greater debate and assessment on how development is perceived and measured.

Notes

1 In this instance, inequality is measured by the "coefficient of human inequality", as developed in the most recent Human Development Report (see UNDP, 2014), based on an unweighted average of inequalities in health, education and income.

2 The August 2015 version of the SDGs has been used (OWG, 2015).

References

Beder, S. (2011) Environmental economics and ecological economics: The contribution of interdisciplinarity to understanding, influence and effectiveness. *Environmental Conservation*. 38 (2). pp.140–150.

CEPA. (2013) Making sustainability the next metric: The outcome of the South Asian consultation. *Economic Review*. 39, August–November. pp.4–6. Colombo: Centre for Poverty Analysis (CEPA).

CSRI. (2010) *Global Wealth Report*. Zurich: Credit Suisse Research Institute (CSRI).

Daly, H. E. (2005) Economics in a full world. *Scientific American*. 293 (3). pp.100–107.

Ewing, B., Moore, D., Goldfinger, S., Oursler, A., Reed, A. and Wackernagel, M. (2010) *The Ecological Footprint Atlas 2010*. Oakland: Global Footprint Network.

Farley, J. and Daly, H. (2006) Natural capital: The limiting factor – a reply to Aronson, Blignaut, Milton and Clewell. *Ecological Engineering*. 28 (1). pp.6–10.

Gjoksi, N. and Sedlacko, M. (2010) *The 'Beyond GDP' Debate and Measuring Societal Progress in the Context of Sustainable Development*. ESDN Quarterly Report, December 2010. Vienna: European Sustainable Development Network (ESDN). Available from: http://www.sd-network.eu/?k=quarterly%20reports&report_id=19 [Accessed: 19 January 2015].

Gunasekera, V. (2013) Life on the margins: Putting inequality at the heart of the post-2015 development agenda. *Economic Review*. 39, August–November. pp.26–28.

Gunawardena, U. A. D. P. (2010) Inequalities and externalities of power sector: A case of Broadlands Hydropower Project in Sri Lanka. *Energy Policy*. 38 (2). pp.726–734.

Gunawardena, U. A. D. P. (2013) Economic growth within nature's limits: The need and the issues. *Economic Review*. 39, August–November. pp.15–17.

IPCC. (2013) *Climate Change 2013: The Physical Science Basis*. Contribution of Working Group I to the Fifth Assessment Report of the Intergovernmental Panel on Climate Change (IPCC). New York: Cambridge University Press.

Jackson, T. (2009) *Prosperity without Growth: Economics for a Finite Planet*. London: Earthscan.

Meadows, D. H., Meadows, D. L., Randers, J. and Behrens III, W. W. (1972) *The Limits to Growth*. New York: Universe Books.

Millennium Ecosystem Assessment. (2003) *Ecosystems and Human Well-being: A Framework for Assessment*. Washington, DC: Island Press.

Munasinghe, M. (2010) *Making Development More Sustainable: Sustainomics Framework and Practical Applications*. Colombo: MIND Press.

Nilsson, M., Lucas, P. and Yoshida, T. (2013) Towards an integrated framework for SDGs: Ultimate and enabling goals for the case of energy. *Sustainability*. 5 (10). pp.4124–4151.

OWG. (2015) *Transforming Our World: The 2030 Agenda for Sustainable Development*. New York: Open Working Group on SDGs, United Nations. Available from: https://sustainabledevelopment.un.org/content/documents/7891Transforming%20Our%20World.pdf [Accessed: 10 September 2015].

Pearce, D. W. and Turner, R. K. (1990) *Economics of Natural Resources and the Environment*. London: Harvester Wheatsheaf.

Raworth, K. (2014) Will these Sustainable Development Goals get us into the doughnut (aka a safe and just space for humanity)? *Oxfam Blogs*. Available from: http://oxfamblogs.org/fp2p/will-these-sustainable-development-goals-get-us-into-the-doughnut-aka-a-safe-and-just-space-for-humanity-guest-post-from-kate-raworth [Accessed: 16 January 2014].

Rees, W. E. (1992) Ecological footprints and appropriated carrying capacity: What urban economics leaves out. *Environment and Urbanization*. 4 (2). pp.121–130.

Rockström, J., Steffen, W., Noone, K., Persson, A., Chapin III, F. S., Lambin, E., Lenton, T. M., Scheffer, M., Folke, C., Schellnhuber, H., Nykvist, B., De Wit, C. A., Hughes, T., Van der Leeuw, S., Rodhe, H., Sörlin, S., Snyder, P. K., Costanza, R., Svedin, U., Falkenmark, M., Karlberg, L., Corell, R. W., Fabry, V. J., Hansen, J., Walker, B., Liverman, D., Richardson, K., Crutzen, P. and Foley, J. (2009) Planetary boundaries: Exploring the safe operating space for humanity. *Ecology and Society*. 14 (2). p.32. Available from: http://www.ecologyandsociety.org/vol14/iss2/art32/ [Accessed: 6 August 2014].

SDSN. (2012) *Global Profile of Extreme Poverty*. Background paper for the High-Level Panel of Eminent Persons on the Post-2015 Development Agenda. New York: Sustainable Development Solutions Network (SDSN). Available from: http://unsdsn.org/wp-content/uploads/2014/02/121015-Profile-of-Extreme-Poverty.pdf [Accessed: 19 January 2015].

UNDESA. (2015) *Sustainable Consumption and Production*. New York: United Nations Department of Economic and Social Affairs (UNDESA). Available from: https://sustainabledevelopment.un.org/topics/sustainableconsumptionandproduction [Accessed: 19 January 2015].

UNDP. (2014) *Human Development Report 2014 – Sustaining Human Progress: Reducing Vulnerabilities and Building Resilience*. New York: United Nations Development Programme (UNDP).

UNEP. (2011) *Decoupling Natural Resource Use and Environmental Impacts from Economic Growth*. New York: United Nations Environment Programme (UNEP). Available from: http://www.unep.org/resourcepanel/decoupling/files/pdf/Decoupling_Factsheet_English.pdf [Accessed: 19 January 2015].

World Bank. (2015a) *PovcalNet*. Available from: http://iresearch.worldbank.org/PovcalNet [Accessed: 13 August 2015].

World Bank. (2015b) *South Asia Overview*. Washington, DC: The World Bank. Available from: http://www.worldbank.org/en/region/sar/overview [Accessed: 13 August 2015].

5 Sustainable energy access for all

Building sustainability into universal energy access

Mohd. Sahil Ali, Nihit Goyal and Shweta Srinivasan

Introduction

Although the Millennium Development Goals (MDGs) did not include access to energy, subsequent work has emphasised its importance for human development. UN-Energy (2005) highlighted that energy services – lighting, heating, cooking and mechanical power – are essential for alleviating poverty and achieving the MDGs. While the direct impacts of access to modern energy on economic development may be contested, studies suggest that such access plays a critical role in improving quality of life, health, communication, education, access to information and development outcomes for women (Modi et al., 2005; UNDP, 2012). Deficient access implies poor resilience to socio-economic and climate variability and change. For example, energy services for use by health centres and communities are essential for disaster management (O'Brien and Hope, 2010; UNDP, 2012). Energy access is therefore crucial to resilience and adaptive capabilities.

The lack of universal energy access has been a chronic problem in developing countries. Many of the 1.7 billion people without access to electricity and nearly all of the 2.7 billion people without access to modern cooking fuels reside in the developing world (Jewell, 2011; Banerjee et al., 2013). With this in mind, United Nations (UN) Secretary-General Ban Ki-moon identified *Sustainable Energy for All* (SE4ALL) as a top priority in his five-year action agenda on Sustainable Development Goals (SDGs) that aims to secure "The Future We Want" plan adopted during the 2012 UN Conference on Sustainable Development, widely known as Rio+20 (HLG, 2012). The SE4ALL framework proposes a robust structure to address energy poverty reduction and environment sustainability through its three main objectives:

i Ensure universal access to modern energy services;[1]
ii Double the global rate of improvement of energy efficiency;
iii Double the share of renewable energy in the global energy mix by 2030.

The SE4ALL framework also offers some key insights on how to measure and track multiple dimensions of energy access.

The action agenda of the UN Sustainable Development Solutions Network (SDSN) seeks to inform the Open Working Group (OWG) on SDGs and integrates the objectives of 'curbing human-induced climate change' and 'clean energy for all' into a single goal. Additionally, it emphasises two challenges that are relevant to an energy goal: (i) inequality and social exclusion are widening within many rich and poor countries and (ii) current patterns of energy use and their impacts on the global climate are unsustainable (SDSN, 2013).

The UN High-Level Panel of Eminent Persons on the Post-2015 Development Agenda (HLP) identified energy as one of the 12 goals in the ongoing post-MDG dialogue (UN, 2013). Its suggestion for a goal to secure sustainable energy in the post-2015 period resonates with the idea of SE4ALL. In fact, the HLP relies on the Global Tracking Framework in SE4ALL for the overlapping objectives – universal access, energy efficiency and renewable energy – between the two.

Given the importance of energy access for development and climate adaptation and mitigation strategies, this paper reviews the post-MDGs dialogue on energy access in the context of challenges faced by energy sectors in Southern countries. It argues that the electrical energy system is susceptible to several disruptions that can affect long-term continuity of access. At present, the dialogue does not take a dynamic view of these systems and, consequently, of access.

By operationalising the definition of sustainability[2] proposed by Ian Scoones et al. (2007), this paper posits that the post-MDG dialogue could be broadened to capture the *sustainability* of energy access. An approach to assess and track sustainability of access as part of the objective to ensure universal access to modern energy services is also proposed. This approach may be particularly important given that energy systems involve long lock-in periods, and infrastructure built over the post-MDG timeframe is likely to determine energy pathways beyond 2050.

The paper is organised as follows. It begins with a review and analysis of the SE4ALL framework from the perspective of Southern countries. In particular, the Global Tracking Framework for universal access is reviewed.[3] The challenges faced by electrical energy systems and their implications for these systems' sustainability are then highlighted using the 'dynamic sustainabilities' framework (Scoones et al., 2007). Finally, an approach to incorporate and track sustainability of access within the objective of universal energy access is proposed.

Universal energy access in the SE4ALL framework

The overarching goal of sustainable energy is part of each of the three main objectives in the SE4ALL framework. The first objective deals specifically with universal access to modern energy. The second and third objectives – doubling the global rate of improvement of energy efficiency and doubling the share of renewable energy in the global energy mix by 2030 – are aimed at shaping global energy trajectories with due consideration for climate change mitigation (Nakićenović, Kammen and Jewell, 2012).[4] These objectives are tracked separately by the SE4ALL Global Tracking Framework. SE4ALL acknowledges that Southern countries' focus is likely to be on universal access rather than improving energy efficiency and decarbonising energy systems. Country-level tracking offers countries flexibility to set their own targets for all three objectives.

In most Southern countries, existing indicators on electricity access have been defined and measured in terms of grid connection alone. Bazilian et al. (2010) aptly point to this being a binary measure for evaluating energy access. The problems of access, however, go beyond this simple categorisation in most Southern countries. Poor electrification rates, poorly energised grids, irregular supply of electricity, frequent breakdowns, problems of quality (such as low or fluctuating voltage) and high losses due to theft are common. Electricity planning is also characterised by supply-based approaches rather than emphasis on services (Practical Action, 2013).

Power in rural areas is often supplied at odd hours (such as midnight or midday), which restricts its usefulness and does not cater to the needs of vulnerable people (Practical Action, 2013). At the household level, connection costs and electricity charges are considerable and hence not affordable for poorer households. Many are served by illegal and secondary connections (Udupa, 2011), which not only result in losses for utilities but also pose a safety hazard. Further, the way that energy is produced, distributed and consumed affects the local, regional and global environment through land degradation, local air pollution and greenhouse gas (GHG) emissions (HLG, 2012).

In addressing several of these challenges to energy access, the Global Tracking Framework moves beyond binary measures to a multi-tier approach that captures the quantity and quality of electricity supply and services more comprehensively (Banerjee et al., 2013). The framework defines access to electricity supply on the basis of attributes of electricity supply, such as peak available capacity, duration, evening hours, affordability, legality and quality, as well as access to electricity services on the basis of appliance ownership categorised by tiers.

To determine the extent of access, the Global Tracking Framework suggests the use of household-level data[5] to apportion the number of households into each of the six tiers. This takes care of tracking distributional aspects and inequity across households. As commonly used indicators of consumption fail to capture access to energy services, the framework proposes to track the use of electricity services as well (Banerjee et al., 2013). Thus, the tracking framework is cognisant of measuring both the supply and demand perspectives of access.

Scholars have argued that in opting to use household surveys to enable tracking, SE4ALL would not address subnational, urban–rural and gendered disparities in access that are masked in such data. The need to track these disparities using indicative frameworks has been identified by several researchers (Barnes and Foley, 2004; Bazilian et al., 2010; Khandker, Douglas and Samad, 2010; Nussbaumer et al., 2011). Observers, however, have not yet elaborated on the limited conceptualisation of sustainability in SE4ALL.

SE4ALL seems to associate sustainability primarily with environmental sustainability and does not discuss the sustainability of energy access. While the dimensions of energy access considered within the Global Tracking Framework, such as duration, affordability and quality of supply, help in determining past and current levels of access, they may not provide insight into future levels of access. Hence, the framework offers a static conceptualisation of access. In other words, the framework implicitly considers energy access as a variable that can be maintained at its current level over time. In reality, access is a dynamic variable that depends on several factors and could follow one of several probable trajectories.

Subsequently, based on the OWG's proposal on the SDGs, the UN Summit (2015) added the dimension of reliability within the energy goal; however, the proposed tracking of this dimension is not discussed. As the outcome document with 17 goals and 169 targets are adopted by the UN General Assembly in September 2015 and would come into effect from 1 January 2016, an attempt has been made in the following sections to demonstrate a framework to assess reliability of access.

Sustainability of an electrical energy system

The electrical energy system of a country, illustrated in Figure 5.1, involves the provision of electricity using various fossil and non-fossil sources and infrastructure for electricity generation, transmission and distribution. It is comprised of interactions among many actors, such as electricity producers and consumers, tempered by policies and regulations. Different aspects of this system are affected by climate change, international energy markets, economic development and natural exigencies such as hydrometeorological and geophysical events. In turn, the system affects other systems such as water, transportation and climate systems, as well as energy markets.

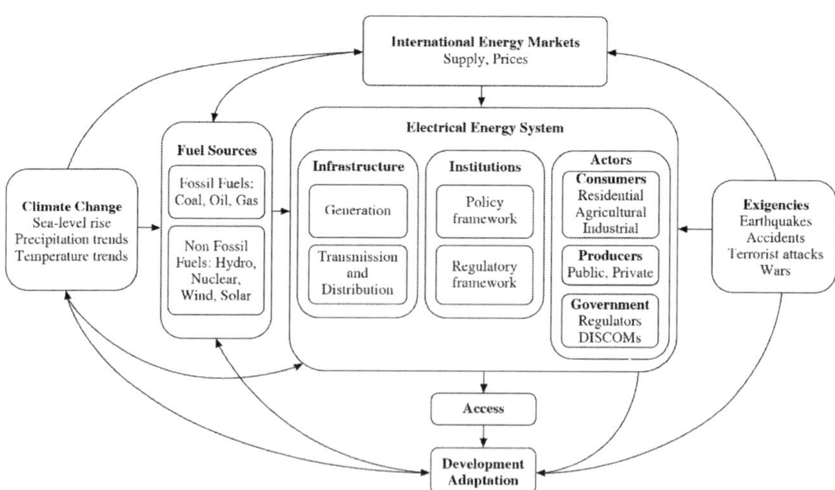

Figure 5.1 Electrical energy system in a complex, dynamic environment

Source: Prepared by the authors.

The electrical energy system is evidently complex and dynamic, with non-linear relationships and outcomes and strong path dependencies. These complexities arise from design, co-dependencies and unpredictable interactions (Lovins and Lovins, 2001). The system interacts with wider socio-political and ecological environments, directly influencing and being influenced by them. Moreover, outcomes of planning and operations in the system may impact other systems with an indeterminate time lag. These systems then attempt to adjust to new conditions. Amory Lovins and L. Hunter Lovins (2001, 19) summarise this nature of the system: "Considering the energy system as a mere collection of components . . . ignores the crux of the problem: interactions, combinations, feedback loops, higher-order consequences, and links across the system boundary."

A simple illustration of the complexities follows. Coal has been a cheap and trusted source of electric power since the Industrial Revolution. Decades later, implications of open fossil-fuel combustion for climate change came into scrutiny. These are manifested not only through temperature rises, but also with an increase in the frequency and intensity of extreme events and shifts in precipitation patterns that may be temporary or lasting. These implications can:

1 Increase demand for agricultural water pumping, while simultaneously increasing demand for air conditioning in residential and commercial buildings.
2 Reduce availability of hydroelectric power due to adverse impacts on hydrological flows and threaten coal-based electricity generation (especially in rural areas) due to water constraints (FICCI and HSBC, 2013).

Together, these consequences imply that energy access can be compromised despite no fundamental changes occurring within the energy system. From a long-term perspective, assessing the predictability of demand during energy planning becomes difficult and energy infrastructure, especially along coastal lines, could be adversely impacted.

Hence, the Brundtland Commission's definition of sustainability,[6] commonly understood as the ability of a system to maintain a certain level of functioning, is limiting in the context of such a system (Cary, 1998, 12; Scoones et al., 2007, 34). J. Cary (1998, 12) highlighted the reflexive and adaptive properties of a complex system in arguing that sustainability is "not a fixed ideal, but an evolutionary process of improving the management of systems, through improved understanding and knowledge." Scoones et al. (2007, 40) posited that a system should be able to withstand shocks and stresses for it to be considered sustainable. Sustainability may then be defined as "long-term maintenance of system functions with respect to equity, well-being and environmental quality."

The "dynamic sustainabilities" framework helps in identifying disruptions that an energy system is likely to face and resolves ambiguities through precise characterisation (Scoones et al., 2007, 39). The temporality of change determines whether a disruption is a shock (short-term) or stress (long-term). Further, shocks and stresses may originate and persist within the boundaries of an energy system or outside of it.

History is replete with events that caused disruptions due to such complexities. For instance, the 1986 Chernobyl nuclear disaster could be categorised as an *internal shock* in the former Union of Soviet Socialist Republics, where a power spike led to explosions in the core of a nuclear reactor, dispersing large particles of radioactive fuel and core materials into the atmosphere. An example of *internal stress* is the lack of skilled personnel and physical infrastructure to help undertake expansion and diversification in a climate-vulnerable, energy-constrained (less than 20 per cent of people have access to electricity) and energy-dependent, and natural resource-rich Sub-Saharan Africa (SSA) (Williamson, Connor and Moezzi, 2009). The oil shock in the wake of the 1979 Iranian Revolution and Iran–Iraq War that began the following year originated outside the energy systems (*external shock*) of the United States, Italy, France, Brazil and India, which were particularly affected and had their energy vulnerabilities pronounced. Also in the 1970s, the US state of California received 60 per cent less rainfall for three consecutive years, reducing hydroelectric output by 40 per cent and causing a 30 per cent increase in the operating costs of Pacific Gas and Electric Company, since 50 million extra barrels of oil had to be burned (*external stress*), which resulted in much stress on the people of the state (Lovins and Lovins, 2001, 12).

This characterisation of disruptions helps in identifying appropriate coping strategies. Shocks may involve engineered approaches to overcome temporary barriers, while stresses may call for long-term overhauls and realignments of strategies.[7] The properties that sustainable energy systems must demonstrate in the wake of such disruptions are illustrated in Figure 5.2. The system must exhibit

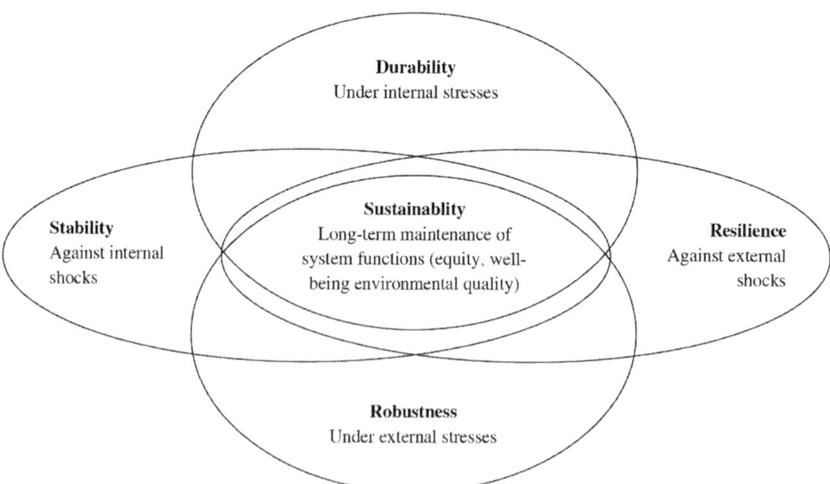

Figure 5.2 Sustainability and its properties

Source: Scoones et al. (2007).

stability (against internal shocks), *durability* (under internal stresses), *resilience* (against external shocks) and *robustness* (under external stresses).

Stability is required when an electrical energy system is exposed to *temporary internal* disruptions, such as miscalculations of peak power requirements in the short-term, to which having adequate peak reserves is a solution. Durability is required to successfully meet *stresses* originating *within* the system, such as chronic technical and commercial losses that affect most Southern countries' grids. Technological innovations like smart grids and feeder separation for different consumer categories help in this respect. But in cases of events occurring *outside* the energy system, such as extreme climatic events like floods or sustained sea-level rise, the system will nevertheless need to adjust either by withstanding *shocks* (resilience) or transforming itself in the *longer term* (robustness). In case of the former, having an adequate number of skilled personnel on the ground to quickly restore energy services could improve the resilience of the system. On the other hand, locating key power projects so that they are not affected by sea-level rise could make the system more robust.

Sustainable access for the global South

A majority of the world's vulnerable population resides in the global South. Even in Northern countries, low-income groups are threatened by the impacts of climate change. The UN Intergovernmental Panel on Climate Change noted that among the regions and people especially at risk of climate change impacts, Africa (particularly SSA), small islands, Asian mega-deltas, and the poor in Northern countries will be particularly vulnerable due to low adaptive capacities and high exposure of populations and infrastructure (Parry et al., 2007, 64). As mentioned above, access to energy is crucial for alleviating poverty and building adaptive capacities. Thus, vulnerable populations could be affected by the lack of sustainable access when they need it most.

Several Southern countries are in high-risk regions and their energy systems may be compromised by natural disasters if not properly safeguarded. In the event of natural disasters, the resilience of these populations, among other things, will be determined by the efficacy with which health, communication and other crucial services are provided for relief and rehabilitation; all of these services require energy (Jewell, 2011; Banerjee et al., 2013).

Even in the absence of natural disasters, the health and livelihoods of vulnerable populations are affected by energy insecurity. Bhowmick (2012) noted how the blackout experienced in North India in 2012 asymmetrically impacted vulnerable groups that received electricity subsidies. Others have also argued that internal system failures invariably produce more unfavourable outcomes for the vulnerable by disrupting their livelihoods (Williamson, Connor and Moezzi, 2009). For example, the majority of the rural population in the developing world still relies on electricity subsidies for irrigation pumping, and any decline in energy availability in a system impacts subsidised sectors first.[8] Notably, in regions where water availability is already low, the uncertainty of electricity supply pronounces the income vulnerability of farmers.

Energy systems that already lack capacities, such as financial or institutional capacities, seem to take longer to respond to shocks. Illustratively, Arpana Udupa (2011) noted that the supply-deficient Indian states of Uttar Pradesh and Bihar recorded higher repair times and greater irregularity of supply compared to Andhra Pradesh, a more developed state where the supply deficit was much less and grievance redressal mechanisms were much better organised. Thus, energy systems in Southern countries with low capacities are at greater risk of being unsustainable.

Energy investments are characterised by large gestation lags and lock-in periods that limit long-term energy pathways. Southern countries' energy demand is rapidly growing and so they are in the process of building large-scale energy infrastructure and networks. This provides opportunities to account for systems' vulnerabilities based on geopolitical, environmental and other factors and to develop specific approaches to mitigate or overcome the most pressing challenges. To build sustainability into the energy system now could be cheaper than to constantly redesign or repair it in response to failures. This may be especially true when one considers the costs of resulting failures in other systems (such as water, transport, and information and communication technologies (ICTs)) that depend on energy (ADB, 2012).

Incorporating sustainability into universal energy access

The post-MDG dialogue provides an appropriate opportunity to highlight the importance of sustainable access and expand the discourse on the sustainability of energy systems. As an international and consensus-driven process, it enjoys the support of many developing and developed country governments. It also includes actors from the private, non-profit and philanthropic sectors. Consequently, the financing likely to be channelled through the post-MDG framework is expected to be over USD 600 billion annually (Banerjee et al., 2013). In addition, the post-MDG dialogue presents an opportunity to emphasise important issues for dealing with uncertainties, such as capacity building in climate science and disaster management, technology transfer and financing. The learning from this dialogue can feed into the final discussions on the post-MDG framework.

It may be more desirable to embed the notion of sustainable access into the goal of universal access rather than incorporating the idea into a separate goal, such as one on improving disaster management and resilience. There are two reasons for this:

- As this paper attempts to demonstrate, the concept of sustainability goes beyond disaster management or climate adaptation and requires a wider perspective of not only energy systems but also relevant properties and conditions necessary for sustainability.
- Treatment of sustainability outside the goal of energy access may reduce the problems with energy systems to infrastructure, ignoring complex dynamics.

To incorporate sustainability of access into the post-MDGs/SDGs, a framework to assess it would be required. Loucks and Gladwell (1999) argued that the sustainability of water systems can be measured as a combination of reliability, resilience and vulnerability. Various studies have defined indicators involving aspects of reliability, resilience and vulnerability in the context of energy (Hirschberg et al., 2008; Williamson, Connor and Moezzi, 2009; Ebinger and Vergara, 2011). The literature on energy security also deals with the question of ensuring the availability of energy at an affordable price (Jewell, 2011). A sustainability indicator for energy systems or access could build on the indicators and approaches proposed by these studies.

However, anticipation of what may go wrong in the future is complicated by a wide range of uncertainties. In the context of national energy security, Amory Lovins and L. Hunter Lovins (2001, 177) contended that "for the most serious and unacceptable types of failure, the probability cannot be calculated." To some extent, this argument holds for complex events such as natural disasters, as seen in the case of the recent Fukushima nuclear disaster in Japan. Further, Scoones et al. (2007) suggested that the tendency to focus on disruptions for which knowledge is complete – in other words, likelihoods and outcomes that can be easily estimated – may result in "closing down" the system to alternate pathways. This could lead to an overemphasis on stability at the cost of durability, resilience and robustness. Thus, this paper proposes a sustainability assessment framework that allows for the flexibility to capture disruptions about which knowledge may be limited. Conceptualising such a framework requires following steps to be taken:

a Identify disruptions
b Estimate likelihoods of occurrence
c Consider vulnerabilities
d Assess impact on access

Adapted from the literature on risk assessment (ISO/IEC, 2009), the framework enables systematic analysis of disruptions that may affect an energy system and their likely impact on access. The first step involves identifying disruptions that may affect the system. The assessor should list short- and long-term disruptions during this step. Also, a broad categorisation of events could be used so that factors both within and outside the energy system are considered. One possible categorisation is shown in Table 5.1.

Once disruptions are identified, the likelihood of occurrence for each should be estimated, either quantitatively or qualitatively. The probability of an event could be estimated by way of quantitative evaluation. If qualitative assessment is used, the likelihood could be rated as high, medium, low or negligible. When an event has a significant impact on access and the knowledge of likelihood is highly problematic, then the rating 'unknown' could be used. This would allow the assessor to capture the current state of knowledge more accurately and keep alternate pathways open. Further, a transparent representation of the current knowledge could draw more people into the exercise and facilitate crowd-sourcing of data and information.

Table 5.1 Categorising disruptions

Nature of disruption	*Temporality*	*Example*
Environmental	Shock	Disruptions by earthquakes
	Stress	Sustained sea-level rise
Economic	Shock	Costly short-term purchases in times of peaking deficit
	Stress	Chronic commercial losses due to theft, non-payment
Organisational	Shock	Corruption in implementation of a major scheme
	Stress	Lack of technical and administrative capacities
Security	Shock	Terrorist attacks on strategic facilities
	Stress	Protracted wars in fuel-exporting regions
Fuel supply	Shock	Short-term drop in oil supply in the global oil market
	Stress	Discovery of large shale reserves
Socio-political	Shock	Political opposition to nuclear power
	Stress	Chronic end-use inefficiency of subsidised sectors
Technical	Shock	Grid failure caused by overdrawal of electricity
	Stress	Chronically high transmission and distribution losses

Source: Authors' elaboration.

Next, the vulnerability of the energy system to each disruption should be considered. This involves examining factors such as the sub-sector(s) exposed (supply, transmission and distribution, demand), the region disrupted, and the communities affected. The impact of the disruption on access can then be assessed in terms of its magnitude (how many people affected), extent (geographical area affected), and temporality (for how long effects are felt). This assessment should go beyond just electrification and duration of supply to analyse all dimensions of access included in SE4ALL to the extent possible. The assessor could choose to quantify the impact on access into a metric or evaluate it qualitatively as high, medium, low or negligible. As in the case of estimation of likelihood, the rating "unknown" could be used to indicate insufficient knowledge of the impact.

The likelihoods of disruptions in combination with the impacts on access give an indication of the sustainability of access or lack thereof. Quantitatively, the overall threat to sustainability could be gauged by aggregating the expected impacts on access for various disruptions identified. A smaller result would indicate a more sustainable system, while a larger result would indicate a relatively unsustainable system. In qualitative assessment, sustainability of access can be gauged using the matrix in Figure 5.3. As sustainability increases, the overall threat to the energy system would be reduced and disruptions would move toward the bottom left of the matrix. Thus, sustainability can be improved by lowering the likelihoods of disruptions, where possible, and by reducing their impacts on access.

An illustration of this framework is shown in Table 5.2.

The adoption of such a sustainability assessment framework alongside the goal of universal access would complement the Global Tracking Framework by adding

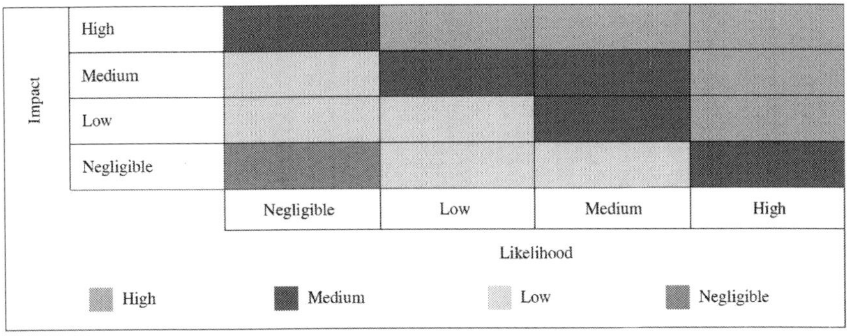

Figure 5.3 Matrix to assess threats to sustainability of access

Source: Prepared by the authors.

Table 5.2 An illustration of the sustainability assessment exercise

Disruption	*Likelihood*	*Vulnerability*	*Impact on access*
Sustained sea-level rise	Medium	Electricity supply as well as transmission and distribution network are both vulnerable; coastal regions would be affected	Medium
Costly short-term purchases in times of peaking deficit	High	Price of electricity would increase; affordability may be impacted	Low
Terrorist attacks on strategic facilities	Unknown	Electricity supply would be affected for the entire grid; surrounding areas may require evacuation	High
Discovery of large shale reserves	Low	Electricity supply sector may be affected; impact on affordability would depend on cost of extraction	Unknown

Source: Authors' elaboration.

the dimension of sustainability of access and also raise the objective so far discussed during the post-MDGs dialogue to sustainable access for all.

Conclusion

Access to energy has been recognised as a precondition for facilitating human development and building the adaptive capacities of vulnerable populations. At the same time, the production and consumption of energy need to be consistent with the global goal of climate change mitigation.

The post-MDG dialogue on energy strives for a balance between these objectives. The HLP proposed the following goals: achieving universal access to modern energy services, increasing the share of clean energy, improving energy efficiency and phasing out subsidies for fossil fuels. This is broadly in line with the objectives proposed under the SE4ALL initiative. Notably, the HLP recommends using the Global Tracking Framework in SE4ALL for monitoring progress on the goal of achieving universal access.

While the dialogue considers access in a static context, energy systems operate in a complex, dynamic environment. The sustainability of such a system is best defined as its ability to maintain long-term functionality – to withstand and recover from shocks and stresses – without compromising well-being, equity or the environment. The energy system, thus, needs to possess stability, resilience, durability and robustness to be sustainable. The failure to exhibit these properties could compromise the goal of energy access. The costs of ensuring sustainability when energy infrastructure is being built may be much lower than the costs of incorporating these properties in the system at a later date.

The post-MDGs dialogue on energy, therefore, should include the dimension of sustainability within its goal on universal access. Though it may be possible to define a metric to track sustainability of access, such an approach may overemphasise the easily quantifiable – stability, or reliability. Consequently, resilience, durability and robustness of the system may not receive sufficient consideration. This paper proposes the adoption of a flexible sustainability assessment framework to complement the Global Tracking Framework for energy access.

The sustainability assessment framework permits assessment of threats to sustainability through a quantitative or qualitative evaluation of likelihoods of disruptions and their impacts on access. A systematic assessment of sustainability of access could encourage planning and designing for sustainability and reduce the vulnerabilities of energy systems over time. Low-hanging fruits – actions that have significant benefits for relatively small costs – for sustainable access may also be identified through such assessments. Assessments could detect significant gaps in current knowledge and highlight areas for further research.

Finally, the choice of sustainability in the post-2015 dialogue may involve trade-offs with efficiency and the pace of universalisation of access. Not all countries may possess the capabilities to translate the findings of an assessment into sustainable access. Some may need support in areas such as climate science, capacity building, financing and access to technology. In order for this exercise to be effective, governments in developing countries would also need to work across silos and take a holistic view of the issue. By creating the space to bring these challenges to the fore, the post-MDGs dialogue could facilitate international learning and make 'the future we want' more *sustainable*.

Notes

1 The goal for universal energy access is that every person has access to modern energy services provided through electricity, clean cooking fuels, and clean heating fuels and energy for productive use and community services (Banerjee et al., 2013).

2 Defined as "long-term maintenance of system functions with respect to equity, well-being and environmental quality" (Scoones et al., 2007, 40).

3 Though the need to evaluate the sustainability of access is equally relevant for both electricity and cooking fuels, this paper focuses on the provision of electricity services, which faces more perceivable challenges and inherent complexities.
4 For instance, the New Policies Scenario of the International Energy Agency (IEA) took into account the relevant policy commitments and plans announced or adopted by governments to model global energy trajectories. It found that total energy consumption would rise by 29 per cent and fossil fuels will remain the dominant source of energy. In this scenario, the world will not be on track to achieve the agreed objective of maintaining a global temperature increase under 2°C. The IEA estimated that meeting this objective would require renewables to make up 50 per cent of electricity generation by 2030 (Jewell, 2011).
5 This data is proposed to be obtained through detailed surveys that will be piloted in the medium-term.
6 The Brundtland Commission defined sustainable development as "development that meets the needs of the present without compromising the ability of future generations to meet their own needs" (Brundtland, 1987).
7 In this framework, shocks and stresses denote the temporality of the disruption and are not considered to have a negative connotation.
8 In the event of supply shortfall in developing countries such as India, higher-paying customers such as firms and industries are served first, while poorer rural and agricultural customers are served last.

References

ADB. (2012) *Climate Risk and Adaptation in the Electric Power Sector*. Manila: Asian Development Bank (ADB).

Banerjee, S. G., Bhatia, M., Azuela, G. E., Jaques, I., Sarkar, A., Portale, E., Bushueva, I., Angelou, N. and Inon, J. G. (2013) *Global Tracking Framework Vol. 3 – Sustainable Energy for All*. Washington, DC: The World Bank.

Barnes, D. and Foley, G. (2004) *Rural Electrification in the Developing World: A Summary of Lessons from Successful Programs*. Washington, DC: The World Bank.

Bazilian, M., Nussbaumer, P., Cabraal, A., Centurelli, R., Detchon, R., Gielen, D. and Rogner, H. (2010) *Measuring Energy Access: Supporting a Global Target*. New York: The Earth Institute, Columbia University.

Bhowmick, N. (2012) After the blackout: How India's planners failed its people. *Time*, 2 August. Available from: http://world.time.com/2012/08/02/after-the-blackout-how-indias-planners-failed-its-people [Accessed: 6 June 2013].

Brundtland, G. H. (1987) *Our Common Future: Report of the World Commission on Environment and Development*. Oxford: Oxford University Press.

Cary, J. (1998) Institutional Innovation in Natural Resource Management in Australia: The Triumph of Creativity over Adversity. In Wolf, S. A. and Zilberman, D. (eds.) *Abstracts of the Conference "Knowledge Generation and Transfer: Implications for Agriculture in the 21st Century"* (pp.125–150). Berkeley: University of California.

Ebinger, J. and Vergara, W. (2011) *Climate Impacts on Energy Systems: Key Issues for Energy Sector Adaptation*. Washington, DC: The World Bank.

FICCI and HSBC. (2013) *Water Use and Efficiency in Thermal Power Plants*. New Delhi: Federation of Indian Chambers of Commerce and Industry (FICCI).

Hirschberg, S., Bauer, C., Burgherr, P., Dones, R., Simons, A., Schenler, W., Bachmann, T. and Carrera, D. G. (2008) *Final Set of Sustainability Criteria and Indicators for Assessment of Electricity Supply Options*. Zurich: Paul Scherrer Institut (PSI).

HLG. (2012) *A Global Action Agenda: Pathways for Concerted Action toward Sustainable Energy for All*. New York: Secretary-General's High-Level Group on Sustainable Energy for All (HLG), United Nations.

ISO/IEC. (2009) *Risk Management – Risk Assessment Techniques*. Geneva: International Organization for Standardization (ISO) and International Electrotechnical Commission (IEC) 31010:2009.

Jewell, J. (2011) *The IEA Model of Short-term Energy Security (MOSES): Primary Energy Sources and Secondary Fuels*. IEA Energy Papers 2011/17. Paris: Organisation for Economic Co-operation and Development (OECD) and International Energy Agency.

Khandker, S. R., Douglas, F. B. and Samad, H. A. (2010) *Energy Poverty in Rural and Urban India: Are the Energy Poor Also Income Poor?* Policy Research Working Paper 5463. Washington, DC: The World Bank.

Loucks, D. P. and Gladwell, J. S. (1999) *Sustainability Criteria for Water Resource Systems*. Cambridge: Cambridge University Press.

Lovins, A. B. and Lovins, L. H. (2001) *Brittle Power: Energy Strategy for National Security*. Andover: Brick House.

Modi, V., McDade, S., Lallement, D. and Saghir, J. (2005) *Energy Services for the Millennium Development Goals*. New York: United Nations Development Programme (UNDP) and The World Bank.

Nakićenović, N., Kammen, D. and Jewell, J. (2012) *Sustainable Energy for All: Technical Report of Task Force 2 in Support of Doubling the Global Rate of Energy Efficiency Improvement and Doubling the Share of Renewable Energy in the Global Energy Mix by 2030*. New York: United Nations.

Nussbaumer, P., Bazilian, M., Modi, V. and Yumkella, K. K. (2011) *Measuring Energy Poverty: Focusing on What Matters*. OPHI Working Paper 42. Oxford: University of Oxford.

O'Brien, G. and Hope, A. (2010) Localism and energy: Negotiating approaches to embedding resilience in energy systems. *Energy Policy*. 38 (12). pp.7550–7558.

Parry, M. L., Canziani, O. F., Palutikof, J. P., van der Linden, P. J. and Hanson, C. E. (eds.) (2007) *Climate Change 2007: Impacts, Adaptation and Vulnerability*. Contribution of Working Group II to the Fourth Assessment Report of the Intergovernmental Panel on Climate Change. Cambridge: Cambridge University Press.

Practical Action. (2013) *Poor People's Energy Outlook 2013: Energy for Community Services*. Rugby: Practical Action Publishing.

Scoones, I., Leach, M., Smith, A., Stagl, S., Stirling, A. and Thompson, J. (2007) *Dynamic Systems and the Challenge of Sustainability*. STEPS Working Paper 1. Brighton: STEPS Centre (Social, Technological and Environmental Pathways to Sustainability).

SDSN. (2013) *An Action Agenda for Sustainable Development*. Report for the UN Secretary-General. New York: Sustainable Development Solutions Network (SDSN) of the United Nations.

Udupa, A. (2011) *Failed Aspirations: An Inside View of the RGGVY*. Bengaluru: Greenpeace India Society.

UNDP. (2012) *Towards an 'Energy Plus' Approach for the Poor: A Review of Good Practices and Lessons Learned from Asia and the Pacific*. Bangkok: United Nations Development Programme (UNDP).

UN-Energy. (2005) *The Energy Challenge for Achieving the Millennium Development Goals*. New York: UN-Energy.

United Nations. (2013) *A New Global Partnership: Eradicate Poverty and Transform Economies through Sustainable Development*. Report of the High-Level Panel of Eminent Persons on the Post-2015 Development Agenda. New York: United Nations.
UN Summit. (2015) *Transforming Our World: The 2030 Agenda for Sustainable Development*. New York: United Nations.
Williamson, L. E., Connor, H. and Moezzi, M. (2009) *Climate-proofing Energy Systems*. Paris: HELIO International.

6 Carbon emission, energy consumption, deforestation and agricultural income in LDCs

Lessons for post-2015 development agenda

Fahmida Khatun and Muhammad Al Amin

Introduction

The world is getting warmer at an increasing pace, with each of the last three decades being warmer than the preceding decade since 1850 (IPCC, 2013). Greenhouse gas (GHG) emissions are considered one of the most important causes of global warming. Among the GHGs, carbon dioxide (CO_2) is the most prevalent in the atmosphere. Most of the CO_2 emissions come from the consumption of fossil fuels such as coal, oil and gas. Driving the acceleration of economic growth across the world requires intensive use of fossil fuels, which eventually leads to huge CO_2 emissions in the atmosphere. Economic activities such as manufacturing, agriculture and transportation necessitate the intensive use of coal, oil and gas, which consequently generates significant amounts of CO_2 each year. CO_2 emissions and economic growth are thereby intrinsically linked.

Least developed countries (LDCs) have been identified as the most vulnerable to the effects of climate change. Greater dependence on rain-fed agriculture and forestry as sources of income and employment make many LDCs vulnerable to climatic changes. Many LDCs are already subject to climatic stress. CO_2 emissions in LDCs are also increasing at an alarming pace. During the 1980s, CO_2 emissions increased in LDCs by an average of 0.22 per cent, by 1.04 per cent in the 1990s and by 4.38 per cent during the 2000s (WDI, 2013). This acceleration in CO_2 emissions is making LDCs more vulnerable to the adverse effects of climate change. Rising levels of energy consumption are considered one of the main contributors to the continuously increasing CO_2 emissions. Between 1981 and 2010, per capita energy use in LDCs increased by 15.66 per cent. Besides rapid growth in energy consumption, LDCs are also experiencing rapid deforestation.

Deforestation is considered to be the second largest contributor towards rising global CO_2 emissions, and it contributes between 12 per cent and 17 per cent of annual global GHG emissions (Van der Werf et al., 2009). Trees capture CO_2 by absorbing it into their cells through photosynthesis. However, when trees are destroyed, they release their carbon back into the atmosphere. In a forest, the ground can hold 50 per cent of CO_2, and the loss of trees generates degradation of the ground. Rapid reduction in trees therefore leads to a huge quantity of CO_2

emissions in the atmosphere. Between 1990 and 2011, LDCs lost about 3.87 per cent of forest area. Thus, deforestation is considered the other key reason behind higher CO_2 emissions in LDCs.

Agriculture represents one quarter of gross domestic product (GDP) in LDCs and is another key source of CO_2 emissions (WDI, 2013). Tubiello et al. (2014) estimate that over the past 50 years, CO_2 emissions from agriculture have nearly doubled. Intensive use of chemical fertilisers and pesticides and the mismanagement of agricultural residues generate and release high levels of CO_2 into the atmosphere of LDCs. Deposited manure and leftover pastures also emit CO_2, further exacerbating the problem. Therefore, it is apparent that there are numerous factors leading to rapid increases in CO_2 in the atmosphere of LDCs. However, the relationship among the variables has not yet been statistically investigated. Statistical evidence, which can definitively demonstrate the causes behind increasing CO_2 emissions, can assist LDCs in reducing their CO_2 emissions in a more knowledgeable way.

A new international development framework will be put forward after 2015, and the global community has now finalised the post-2015 Sustainable Development Goals (SDGs). The knowledge about how energy consumption, deforestation and agricultural income contribute to CO_2 emissions in LDCs can provide valuable inputs for global leaders in shaping the post-2015 SDGs in a more informed manner. Therefore, the objectives of this study are to

(i) Examine how CO_2 emissions, energy consumption, deforestation and agricultural production are related in the long run.
(ii) Estimate the long-term elasticity of energy consumption, deforestation and agricultural production with respect to CO_2 emissions.
(iii) Investigate the causal relationship between CO_2 emissions and energy consumption, CO_2 emissions and deforestation, and CO_2 emissions and agricultural production.

The rest of the paper is organised as follows. The next section provides a brief review of the most relevant existing literature. The section after that describes the model, data and estimation methodology. The empirical results are presented in the following section. The final section presents a few implications for shaping the post-2015 SDGs.

Review of literature

A significant body of literature in ecological economics has investigated the relationship between economic activities and the emissions of pollutants. It finds that increases in per capita income, energy consumption, deforestation and trade liberalisation lead to higher levels of CO_2 emissions. The following is a short overview of the existing literature relevant to the present study.

Halicioglu (2009) examines the dynamic causal relationships between income, energy consumption, CO_2 emissions and foreign trade in Turkey by using time series data for the period 1960–2005. He applies the bounds testing and the co-integration procedure to find an interrelationship between the variables. The bounds test results indicate that two forms of long-run relationships exist between the variables. Case in the first, income, CO_2 emissions and foreign trade determine energy consumption. In the second, income is determined by energy consumption, CO_2 emissions and foreign trade. The author concludes that in Turkey, income is the most significant variable in explaining CO_2 emissions, while energy consumption and foreign trade are the next most significant.

Mozumder and Marathe (2006) examine the causal relationship between per capita GDP (PCGDP) and per capita electricity consumption (PCEC) in Bangladesh using techniques of co-integration and vector error correction model (VECM). They find evidence of unidirectional causality running from per capita GDP to per capita electricity consumption. However, the inverse is not true in the case of Bangladesh, i.e. per capita electricity consumption does not cause per capita GDP. They also investigate the co-integrating relationship between the variables by employing the Johansen co-integration test and use the Granger causality framework which allows for the testing of the existence and the direction of causality between the variables. The results indicate that per capita GDP Granger causes per capita electricity consumption at a 5 per cent level of significance. However, the reverse causality, i.e. PCEC Granger causes PCGDP, was not found to be significant even at a 10 per cent significance level.

Ang (2007) examines the dynamic causal relationships between energy consumption, pollutant emissions and output in France for the period 1960 to 2000. The author applies co-integration and VECM techniques to investigate the relationship. The study finds the existence of a strong long-term relationship between the variables. The causality test results indicate that economic growth exerts a causal influence on pollution and energy use in the long-term. The study also finds that in the short-term, there is unidirectional causality running from energy use to output growth.

Soytas and Sari (2009) examine the causal relationship between energy use, environmental pollution and income in the Turkish economy. They also apply the Toda-Yamamoto (T-Y) procedure to test for Granger causality. The study finds that CO_2 emissions cause energy consumption, but energy consumption does not cause CO_2 emissions. The study also finds a long-term causal relationship between CO_2 emissions, energy consumption and economic growth in Turkey, controlling for labour and gross fixed capital formation.

Ang (2008) investigates the dynamic causal relationship between energy consumption, output and CO_2 emissions in Malaysia for the period 1971–1999. The study applies the procedure of co-integration and the trivariate VECM for examining the relationship. The study finds that pollution and energy use are positively related to output in the long-term. The study also finds a strong causal relationship running from economic growth to energy consumption in both the long- and short-terms.

Zhang and Cheng (2009) investigate the existence and direction of Granger causality between energy consumption, CO_2 emissions and economic growth in China for the period of 1960 to 2007. The study finds evidence of long run unidirectional Granger causality running from energy consumption to CO_2 emissions. The study also finds a unidirectional Granger causality running from GDP to energy consumption for the same period. Moreover, the study indicates that neither energy consumption nor CO_2 emissions lead to economic growth. Therefore, the study suggests that in the long-term, the government of China can pursue a CO_2 emissions reduction policy and a conservative energy policy without impeding economic growth.

Jalil and Mahmud (2009) examine the long-term relationship between foreign trade, income, energy consumption and CO_2 emissions in China for the period 1975 to 2005. They also investigate whether or not the environmental Kuznets curve (EKC) relationship exists between per capita real GDP and CO_2 emissions in the long run in China. In order to conduct the analysis, they employ the autoregressive distributed lag (ARDL) bound test method. The study finds a quadratic relationship between CO_2 emissions and income for the sample period, which supports the EKC relationship. The Granger causality test results suggest that one-way causality runs through economic growth to CO_2 emissions. The study also finds that in the long run, CO_2 emissions are mainly determined by energy consumption and income. However, the study finds that foreign trade does not relate to CO_2 emissions in China.

Lean and Smyth (2010) examine the causal relationship between economic growth, electricity consumption and CO_2 emissions, using a panel VECM for five ASEAN (Association of Southeast Asian Nations) countries for the period 1980 to 2006. The study finds evidence of the environmental Kuznets curve for these countries. The study also finds a positive association between electricity consumption and emissions and a non-linear relationship between real output and emissions. However, the long-term estimates do not indicate the direction of causality between the variables. The authors also examine for Granger causality among the variables. The Granger causality tests suggest that in the long-term, there is unidirectional causality running from emissions to economic growth and electricity consumption. However, in the short-term, the Granger causality runs from emissions to electricity consumption only.

Ghosh (2010) investigates the causality and co-integration between economic growth and CO_2 emissions for India by using the ARDL bounds testing approach and the Johansen-Juselius maximum likelihood procedure for the period 1971–2006. The study results indicate a unidirectional short-term causality running from energy supply to CO_2 emissions and economic growth to energy supply. However, the study fails to establish any long-term causality or any long-term equilibrium relationship between economic growth and CO_2 emissions.

Sharma (2011) investigates the determinants of CO_2 emissions in a global panel consisting of 69 countries in the period 1985–2005. The study makes the panel data more homogenous by constructing a number of sub-panels, such as the high-income country panel, the middle-income country panel and the low-income country panel. The study finds that increases in per capita GDP, trade openness, per capita electric power consumption and energy consumption (using per capita total primary energy consumption as a proxy variable) lead to increased levels of CO_2 emissions. It also finds that urbanisation leads to lower levels of CO_2 emissions in the high-income, middle-income and low-income panels. In the context of the global panel, only per capita total primary energy consumption and GDP per capita are found to be statistically significant determinants of CO_2 emissions.

However, per capita electric power consumption, urbanisation and trade openness have a negative impact on CO_2 emissions.

Yousefi-Sahzabi et al. (2011) investigate the relationship between Iran's economic growth and CO_2 emissions for the period 1994 to 2007 using a national panel data set. They construct the Pearson product-moment correlation coefficients (PPMCC) matrix to test the relationships between GDP and CO_2 emissions. The study finds evidence of correlation between economic development and CO_2 emissions in Iran. The study also conducts a sector-wise analysis for Iran. They find that there is a strong positive correlation between economic growth and CO_2 emissions across all sectors (excluding agriculture). However, in most sectors it is observed that absolute emission rapidly increases with economic growth, while CO_2 emission intensity (the emission per unit of GDP) does not necessarily show increasing trends.

Alam et al. (2012) investigate the likely existence of dynamic causality between electricity consumption, CO_2 emissions, energy consumption and economic growth in Bangladesh. The study used the Johansen bivariate co-integration model to check for co-integrating relationships. An analysis of an autoregressive distributed lag model was carried out to check for robustness. Next, the VECM framework tests were carried out to test for Granger short-term, long-term and strong causality. The results indicate that a bidirectional long run causality exists between electricity consumption and economic growth, while unidirectional causality exists from energy consumption to economic growth both in the short- and the long-terms. However, no causal relationship exists in the short-term. The strong causality results indicate bidirectional causality in both cases. The study also finds that a feedback causality exists in the long-term from energy consumption to CO_2 emission while unidirectional causality runs in the short-term. Moreover, CO_2 Granger causes economic growth both in the short- and in the long-terms.

Hossain (2012) examines the dynamic causal relationship between energy consumption, CO_2 emissions, foreign trade, economic growth and urbanisation in Japan for the period 1960–2009. The study finds short-term unidirectional causality from trade openness to energy consumption, from CO_2 emissions to economic growth, from economic growth to trade openness and from energy consumption and trade openness to CO_2 emissions. The study also finds that CO_2 emissions, energy consumption, economic growth, foreign trade and urbanisation are co-integrated. This implies that despite of having deviations in the short-term, the explanatory variables merge with CO_2 emissions in the long-term to achieve steady-state equilibrium. It is found that both in the long-term and in the short-term, energy consumption has a significant positive impact on CO_2 emissions, which implies that due to the expansion of industrial output for economic development, more and more energy is being consumed in Japan. The study also finds that given there is unidirectional causality from CO_2 emissions to economic growth in Japan, any policy in respect of reduction of CO_2 emissions will be harmful for further economic development.

Even though a significant number of studies have been carried out to explore how energy consumption and economic activities affect CO_2 emissions, there has been no study in the context of LDCs as a whole. This study addresses this particular gap in the existing literature. Moreover, the study examines how deforestation is related to CO_2 emissions in both the short- and long-terms, which is also a unique initiative in the literature of ecological economics.

Model, data and econometric methodology

Model

In order to find the long-term relationship between CO_2 emissions, energy consumption, deforestation and agricultural income, utilising Hossain (2012), the following logarithmic functional form is estimated:

$$lnCO_{2_t} = \beta_0 + \beta_1 lnENC_t + \beta_2 lnDFRST_t + \beta_3 lnPCAGY_t + \varepsilon_t \quad (1)$$

where CO_{2t} is the per capita CO_2 emission in LDCs in year t; ENC_t is the per capita energy consumption in LDCs in year t; $DFRST_t$ is net forest depletion as percentage of gross national income (GNI)[1] in LDCs in year t; $PCAGY_t$ is the per capita agricultural income in LDCs in year t; βs are the parameters to be estimated; ln is natural logarithm; and ε_t is an error term. Following Ang (2007 and 2008); Jalil and Mahmud (2009); Soytas, Sari and Ewing (2007); Alam et al. (2012); and Hossain (2012), we use CO_2 emissions as the proxy for the level of environmental degradation.

Generally, it is expected that higher levels of energy consumption lead to higher levels of economic activity and generate more CO_2 emissions, therefore we expect $\beta_1 > 0$. Since deforestation is considered one of the leading contributors of CO_2 worldwide, we assume $\beta_2 > 0$. Agricultural activities, such as the use of chemical fertilisers in farming and agricultural residues, emit CO_2. Therefore, we also assume $\beta_3 > 0$, i.e. if per capita agricultural income increases, CO_2 emissions are also likely to increase.

Data

The present study covers the period 1981 to 2010 and uses annual aggregated time series data for 48 LDCs[2] as defined by the United Nations (UN). A detailed description of the variables used in this study and the summary statistics is provided in Table 6.1 and Table 6.2. Data used in this study are collated from the World Development Indicators (WDI), released by the World Bank in 2013. WDI measures per capita CO_2 emissions in metric tonnes, per capita energy consumption in kg of oil equivalent and net forest depletion as percentage of GNI. For per capita real value added in agriculture, the total value addition in agriculture (in constant 2005 USD) is divided by the total population in LDCs. Population data has also been obtained from the WDI. Finally, for the ease of modelling, data are defined as follows: CO_2 is per capita CO_2 emissions, ENC is per capita energy consumption, DFRST is net forest depletion as percentage of GNI and PCAGY is per capita real value added in agriculture. Time series plots of the variables are presented in Figure 6.1, which will provide a snapshot on the features of the data used in this study.

Table 6.1 Description of variables

Variable	*Description*
CO_2	CO_2 emissions (metric tonnes per capita)
ENC	Energy use (kg of oil equivalent per capita)
DFRST	Net forest depletion (% of GNI)
PCAGY	Per capita real value added in agriculture (Constant: 2005 USD)

Source: Authors.

Table 6.2 Summary statistics

	CO_2	*ENC*	*DFRST*	*PCAGY*
Mean	0.17	298	2.98	97.61
Median	0.16	291	2.84	96.99
Maximum (Year)	0.256 (2010)	338.8 (2010)	4.96 (1996)	114 (2010)
Minimum (Year)	0.138 (1993)	277.52 (1993)	2.18 (1985)	88 (1994)
Std. Dev.	0.04	17.34	0.63	5.88
Skewness	1.06	0.99	1.05	1.22
Kurtosis	2.69	2.72	4.35	4.37
Jarque-Bera	5.72*	4.98*	7.84***	9.80***
Sum	5.24	8953	89	
Observations	30	30	30	

Source: Authors.

Note: ***, ** and * indicate that Jarque-Bera statistics are significant at 1 per cent, 5 per cent and 10 per cent levels.

Econometric methodology

The dynamic causal relationship between CO_2 emissions, energy consumption, deforestation and agricultural income in LDCs are tested by using standard time series techniques. The testing procedure involves three steps: (i) explore whether each variable contains a unit root, (ii) examine whether there is a long-term co-integrating relationship between the variables and, finally, (iii) estimate a VECM.

Time series data may produce spurious results if the variables under consideration are linked to common factors. Therefore, to identify the correct model, the presence of stochastic terms in the variables needs to be examined. A series is said to be non-stationary if the mean and variance of the variable are not constant over time, i.e. it follows a time trend. Two non-stationary variables may seem to be related, simply because of the common nature of their time trends when in fact they are not. This motivates us to perform the Augmented Dickey Fuller (ADF) and the Phillips-Perron (PP) unit root test to check for data stationarity.

When time series data are characterised by non-stationarity, co-integration is a particularly appropriate statistical technique (Engle and Granger, 1987). Consequently, Johansen's method is used, which is capable of determining the number of co-integrating vectors for any given number of non-stationary series of the same order. However, before applying the Johansen approach, it is important to determine the lag length or order of the vector autoregression (VAR). This is a key element in the

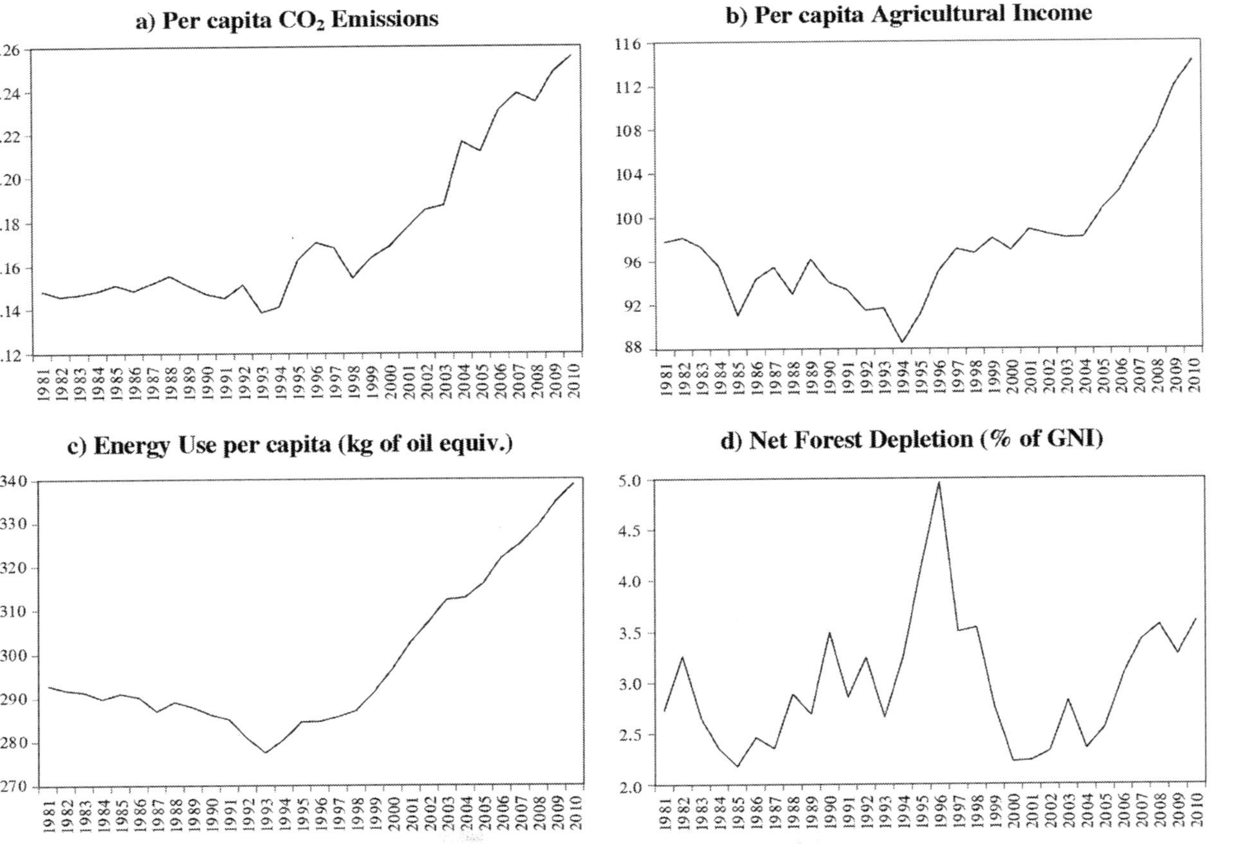

Figure 6.1 Time series plots of the variables

Source: Authors.

specification of the VAR and forms the basis for co-integrating ranks. In order to identify the number of co-integrating ranks, i.e. the number of co-integrating equations, trace tests and maximum eigenvalue tests are applied. The hypothesis that is tested is that there are 'r' co-integrating vectors against the alternative of 'r or more' (trace statistic) or 'r + 1' (maximum eigenvalue statistic) co-integrating vectors.

If the Johansen test indicates a co-integrating relationship between the variables, estimation of an error correction model (ECM) can be performed. The ECM has an advantage of combining both the short-term properties of economic relationships in the first difference form, as well as the long-term information in the level form. It should be noted that an ECM enables estimation of the speed of adjustment back to the long-term condition among the variables. If variables are found to be co-integrated, then there must exist an associated error correction mechanism (Engle and Granger, 1987). Therefore, for the four variable cases, assuming that there is only one co-integrated relationship, the VECMs can be expressed as follows:

$$\Delta lnCO_{2_t} = \alpha_1 + \alpha_{11} ECT_{t-1} + \sum_{j=1}^{p-1} \phi_{1j} \Delta lnCO_{2_{t-j}} + \sum_{j=1}^{p-1} \theta_{1j} \Delta lnENC_{t-j} + \sum_{j=1}^{p-1} \psi_{1j} \Delta lnDFRST_{t-j} + \sum_{j=1}^{p-1} \delta_{1j} \Delta lnPCAGY_{t-j} + \varepsilon_{1t} \quad (2)$$

$$\Delta lnENC_t = \alpha_2 + \alpha_{21} ECT_{t-1} + \sum_{j=1}^{p-1} \phi_{2j} \Delta lnCO_{2_{t-j}} + \sum_{j=1}^{p-1} \theta_{2j} \Delta lnENC_{t-j} + \sum_{j=1}^{p-1} \psi_{2j} \Delta lnDFRST_{t-j} + \sum_{j=1}^{p-1} \delta_{2j} \Delta lnPCAGY_{t-j} + \varepsilon_{2t} \quad (3)$$

$$\Delta lnDFRST_t = \alpha_3 + \alpha_{31} ECT_{t-1} + \sum_{j=1}^{p-1} \phi_{3j} \Delta lnCO_{2_{t-j}} + \sum_{j=1}^{p-1} \theta_{3j} \Delta lnENC_{t-j} + \sum_{j=1}^{p-1} \psi_{3j} \Delta lnDFRST_{t-j} + \sum_{j=1}^{p-1} \delta_{3j} \Delta lnPCAGY_{t-j} + \varepsilon_{3t} \quad (4)$$

$$\Delta lnPCAGY_t = \alpha_4 + \alpha_{41} ECT_{t-1} + \sum_{j=1}^{p-1} \phi_{4j} \Delta lnCO_{2_{t-j}} + \sum_{j=1}^{p-1} \theta_{4j} \Delta lnENC_{t-j} + \sum_{j=1}^{p-1} \psi_{4j} \Delta lnDFRST_{t-j} + \sum_{j=1}^{p-1} \delta_{4j} \Delta lnPCAGY_{t-j} + \varepsilon_{4t} \quad (5)$$

where $ECT_{t-1} = CO_{2_{t-1}} + \left(\frac{\beta_{21}}{\beta_{11}}\right) ENC_{t-1} + \left(\frac{\beta_{31}}{\beta_{11}}\right) DFRST_{t-1} + \left(\frac{\beta_{41}}{\beta_{11}}\right) PCAGY_{t-1}$ is the normalised co-integrated equation. The ECT measures the long-term equilibrium relationship while the coefficients on lagged difference terms indicate the short-term dynamics.

Empirical results

Both the ADF and PP tests indicate that all of our variables are non-stationary at their levels but stationary at their first difference, irrespective of using the random walk model with drift or random walk model with slope (Table 6.3). Hence, it can be concluded that all series are $I(1)$ at the 1 per cent level of significance.

Before undertaking the co-integration test, the relevant order of lengths of the VAR model should be specified. Given the sample size, a maximum lag length of three is considered. However, based on the log likelihood ratio (LR), final prediction error (FPE), Akaike information criterion (AIC) and HQ test, an optimal lag length of two is found. This lag structure for the rest of the estimations is followed in this study (Table 6.4).

Table 6.3 Unit root test

Variable	*Augmented Dickey Fuller*		*Philip-Perron*		*I*(d)
	Intercept	*Trend and Intercept*	*Intercept*	*Trend and Intercept*	
CO_2	0.664268	−1.519475	1.337769	−1.246172	*I*(1)
ΔCO_2	−5.479409***	−5.8994***	−5.52239***	−12.26926***	
ENC	0.774427	−0.848385	1.650792	−0.533538	*I*(1)
ΔENC	−2.530724	−3.783686**	−2.383999	−3.783686**	
DFRST	−2.324915	−2.394247	−2.474022	−2.532756	*I*(1)
ΔDFRST	−6.190929***	−6.133407***	−6.179343***	−6.122296***	
PCAGY	0.8557	−0.843285	0.900821	−0.624628	*I*(1)
ΔPCAGY	−4.739478***	−5.935609***	−4.757812***	−5.975266***	

Source: Authors.

Note: The lag length for ADF test is decided based on Schwarz information criteria (SIC); and the maximum bandwidth for PP test is decided based on Newey and West (1994). *, ** and *** indicate 10 per cent, 5 per cent and 1 per cent levels of significance, respectively.

Table 6.4 VAR lag order selection criteria

Lag	*LR*	*FPE*	*AIC*	*SIC*	*HQ*
0	n/a	0.00	−11.21	−11.02	−11.15
1	131.60	0.00	−16.01	−15.05*	−15.72
2	27.75*	0.00*	−16.36*	−14.64	−15.85*
3	13.51	0.00	−16.14	−13.65	−15.40

Source: Authors.

Note: * indicates lag order selected by the criterion.

Table 6.5 Johansen co-integration test

Null Hypothesis: no co-integration						
No. of co-integrated equation(s)	*Trace statistic*	*Critical value at 95%*	*Probability***	*Max-Eigen statistic*	*Critical value at 95%*	*Probability***
r = 0***	57.1948	47.8561	0.0052	28.0789	27.5843	0.0432
r ≤ 1	29.1159	29.7971	0.0598	15.2310	21.1316	0.2730
r ≤ 2	13.8849	15.4947	0.0862	13.6183	14.2646	0.0631
r ≤ 3	0.2667	3.8415	0.6056	0.2667	3.8415	0.6056

Source: Authors.

Note: *** denotes rejection of the null hypothesis at the 1 per cent level.
** MacKinnon, Haug and Michelis (1998) values.

As we understand that our variables are stationary at first difference, we proceed to carry out the Johansen co-integration test to determine whether any combinations of variables are co-integrated. Both the trace tests and maximum eigenvalue tests indicate that there is one co-integrating equation among the selected variables at the 1 per cent level of significance (Table 6.5). It implies that our variables are co-integrated and that in the long-term, CO_2 emissions, energy consumption, deforestation and agricultural income move together.

Then, for estimating the long-run co-integrated equation, the following can be written:

$$\ln CO_2 = 20.69 + 6.10 \ln ENC_{t-1} + 0.26 \ln DFRST_{t-1} - 3.51 \ln PCAGY_{t-1}$$
$$R^2 = 0.67 \qquad F = 3.84^{***}$$
$$\alpha_{11} = -0.97961^{***}$$

All coefficients in the long-term co-integrated equation have the expected signs except for agricultural income. It is found that energy consumption and deforestation are positively related to CO_2 emissions. However, CO_2 emissions are negatively related with agricultural income. Since a double logarithmic functional form is used, the β coefficients are interpreted as long-term elasticities. Energy consumption and deforestation have positive elasticity coefficients of 6.10 and 0.26. It means a 1 per cent increase in energy consumption and deforestation leads to 6.1 per cent and 0.26 per cent CO_2 emissions in LDCs. However, agricultural income elasticity is negative and 3.51, which implies that in the long-term if agricultural income increases by 1 per cent, it is likely to reduce CO_2 emissions by 3.51 per cent. The finding of the study that increased energy consumption affects CO_2 emissions is consistent with the existing literature. For example, Saboori and Soleymani (2011) found that energy consumption leads to CO_2 emissions in the long-term in Iran. Zhang and Cheng (2009) found that energy consumption and CO_2 emissions are related in the long-term in China. Baek and Kim (2011) found that energy consumption causes environmental degradation in developed and developing countries, while Menyah and Wolde-Rufael (2010) found a relationship between energy consumption and CO_2 emissions in South Africa.

The error correction coefficient (α_{11}) is −0.97961, and is correctly signed (negative) and significant at 1 per cent level. The error correction term indicates how the variables will adjust once they deviate from the equilibrium. The term should have negative sign and the magnitude should be less than unity. Results of the study imply that the variables adjust at the speed of 98 per cent every year, or it takes about 1.02 years to restore equilibrium when there is shock on the steady-state relationship.

ECM-based short-term causality tests are also performed in this study and reported in Table 6.6. It shows that no short-term causality exists between CO_2 emissions and energy consumption. However, in the short-term, both deforestation and agricultural income cause CO_2 emissions. This implies that, for a given growth in real agricultural income and deforestation, CO_2 emissions are likely to increase in LDCs in the short-term.

The model of this study is sound and robust. The F statistic is significant at the 1 per cent level and the R square value is 67 per cent, which indicates that the model is correctly specified and fits the data well. The residual diagnostic is also tested here. The Breusch-Godfrey serial correlation LM test indicates that there is no serial correlation in residuals in the model (Table 6.7). The Breusch-Pagan-Godfrey test for heteroskedasticity indicates that this model does not have any heteroskedasticity (Table 6.7). The test for normality indicates that the residuals are normally distributed (Table 6.7).

Table 6.6 Short-run causality test

Dependent variable: Co_2			
	Chi-square statistic	*Probability*	*Decision*
Testing for the null hypothesis that coefficient of ENC_{t-1} and ENC_{t-2} is equal to 0	1.339	0.512	No SR causality
Testing for the null hypothesis that coefficient of $DFRST_{t-1}$ and $DFRST_{t-2}$ is equal to 0	5.655958	0.0591*	SR causality
Testing for the null hypothesis that coefficient of $PCAGY_{t-1}$ and $PCAGY_{t-2}$ is equal to 0	7.970717	0.0186**	SR causality

Source: Authors.

Note:*, ** and *** indicate 10 per cent, 5 per cent and 1 per cent levels of significance, respectively.

Table 6.7 Diagnostic test results

Test	*Statistic*	*Probability*
Breusch-Godfrey serial correlation LM test	3.838	0.1467
Breusch-Pagan-Godfrey test of heteroskedasticity	12.378	0.4158
JB test for normality	1.533	0.4645

Source: Authors.

Lessons for shaping the post-2015 agenda

The findings of the study have a number of implications for both LDCs in terms of pursuing their development path, and for the global development communities in terms of setting development agendas. These are as follows:

(i) No relationship was found between higher CO_2 emissions and higher energy consumption in the short-term. This implies that, for the time being, higher energy use may not affect the environment of LDCs adversely. Therefore, LDCs could pursue a development path requiring a higher use of non-renewable fossil fuels, such as coal, gas and oil, in the short-term. This would help them achieve higher growth, eradicate poverty and improve the quality of lives of their populations. Since the post-2015 agenda aims to be inclusive and not leave anyone behind, access to energy for all is a pre-requisite. Thus, the findings on the relationship between energy consumption and carbon emission have significance for LDCs.

(ii) The study finds that in the long-term higher energy consumption leads to higher CO_2 emissions. Therefore, LDCs have to follow a development strategy which will help them reduce their energy consumption in the long-term so that development can be sustainable. They will also have to follow the strategy to use clean energy to control CO_2 emissions.

(iii) It is found that deforestation contributes to increased CO_2 emissions in LDCs in both the short- and long-terms. Deforestation has been identified as the second largest contributor to global CO_2 emissions. As results of this study are consistent with the observed phenomena, LDCs need to take the initiative for preservation and restoration of forests. Conversion of forestland to agricultural and industrial uses needs to be limited. Moreover, reclamation of land for jungles, woodlands and sustainable forestry industry should be given priority. The specific focus of the post-2015 development agenda should be to set a target to maintain a specific level of forest cover in each country. To achieve this, a baseline standard for forest covers should be established, which can be achieved by each country within a specific timeline.

(iv) The study finds that in the short-term, increases in agricultural income (production) leads to higher CO_2 emissions in LDCs. The intensive use of chemical fertilisers and pesticides in farming leads to CO_2 emissions in the atmosphere. Therefore, LDCs need to engage in agricultural activities from which CO_2 emissions are low. They should pursue a balanced and efficient use of chemical fertilisers and pesticides. Furthermore, agricultural residues such as straw and animal slurry also cause CO_2 emissions. LDCs could focus on environmentally friendly use of these residues. For example, animal slurry can widely be used for soil nutrient recycling. Therefore, in the post-2015 SDGs, attention should be placed on developing a goal for the practice of sustainable agriculture. This should be achieved by, for example, the balanced and efficient use of chemical fertilisers and pesticides and by the proper management of agricultural wastes and residues.

Notes

1 "GNI per capita (formerly GNP per capita) is the gross national income, converted to U.S. dollars using the World Bank Atlas method, divided by the midyear population. GNI is the sum of value added by all resident producers plus any product taxes (less subsidies) not included in the valuation of output plus net receipts of primary income (compensation of employees and property income) from abroad" (WDI, 2013).

2 LDCs include Afghanistan, Angola, Bangladesh, Benin, Bhutan, Burkina Faso, Burundi, Cambodia, Central African Republic, Chad, Comoros, Democratic Republic of the Congo, Djibouti, Equatorial Guinea, Eritrea, Ethiopia, Gambia, Guinea, Guinea-Bissau, Haiti, Kiribati, Lao People's Democratic Republic, Lesotho, Liberia, Madagascar, Malawi, Mali, Mauritania, Mozambique, Myanmar, Nepal, Niger, Rwanda, Samoa, Sao Tome and Principe, Senegal, Sierra Leone, Solomon Islands, Somalia, Sudan, Timor-Leste, Togo, Tuvalu, Uganda, United Republic of Tanzania, Vanuatu, Yemen and Zambia (United Nations, 2014).

References

Alam, J. M., Begum, I. A., Buysse, J. and Huylenbroeck, G. V. (2012) Energy consumption, carbon emissions and economic growth nexus in Bangladesh: Cointegration and dynamic causality analysis. *Energy Policy*. 45. pp.217–225.

Ang, J. B. (2007) CO_2 emissions, energy consumption, and output in France. *Energy Policy*. 35 (10). pp.4772–4778.

Ang, J. B. (2008) Economic development, pollutant emissions and energy consumption in Malaysia. *Journal of Policy Modeling*. 30 (2). pp.271–278.

Baek, J. and Kim, H. S. (2011) Trade liberalization, economic growth, energy consumption and the environment: Time series evidence from G-20 economies. *Journal of East Asian Economic Integration*. 15 (1). pp.3–32.

Engle, R. F. and Granger, C. W. (1987) Co-integration and error correction: Representation, estimation, and testing. *Econometrica: Journal of the Econometric Society*. 55 (2). pp.251–276.

Ghosh, S. (2010) Examining carbon emissions economic growth nexus for India: A multivariate cointegration approach. *Energy Policy*. 38 (6). pp.3008–3014.

Halicioglu, F. (2009) An econometric study of CO_2 emissions, energy consumption, income and foreign trade in Turkey. *Energy Policy*. 37 (3). pp.1156–1164.

Hossain, S. (2012) An econometric analysis for CO_2 emissions, energy consumption, economic growth, foreign trade and urbanization of Japan. *Low Carbon Economy*. 3 (3A). pp.92–105.

IPCC. (2013) *Climate Change 2013: The Physical Science Basis*. Contribution of Working Group I to the Fifth Assessment Report of the Intergovernmental Panel on Climate Change (IPCC). New York: Cambridge University Press.

Jalil, A. and Mahmud, F. S. (2009) Environment Kuznets curve for CO2 emissions: A cointegration analysis for China. *Energy Policy*. 37 (12). pp.5167–5172.

Lean, H. H. and Smyth, R. (2010) CO_2 emissions, electricity consumption and output in ASEAN. *Applied Energy*. 87 (6). pp.1858–1864.

MacKinnon, J. G., Haug, A. A. and Michelis, L. (1998) *Numerical Distribution Functions of Likelihood Ratio Tests for Cointegration* (No. 9803). Canterbury, UK: Department of Economics, University of Canterbury.

Menyah, K. and Wolde-Rufael, Y. (2010) Energy consumption, pollutant emissions and economic growth in South Africa. *Energy Economics*. 32 (6). pp.1374–1382.

Mozumder, P. and Marathe, A. (2006) Causality relationship between electricity consumption and GDP in Bangladesh. *Energy Policy*. 35 (1). pp.395–402.

Newey, W. K. and West, K. D. (1994) Automatic lag selection in covariance matrix estimation. *The Review of Economic Studies*. 61 (4). pp.631–653.

Saboori, B. and Soleymani, A. (2011) CO_2 emissions, economic growth and energy consumption in Iran: A co-integration approach. *International Journal of Environmental Sciences*. 2 (1). p.44.

Sharma, S. S. (2011) Determinants of carbon dioxide emissions: Empirical evidence from 69 countries. *Applied Energy*. 88 (1). pp.376–382.

Soytas, U. and Sari, R. (2009) Energy consumption, economic growth, and carbon emissions: Challenges faced by an EU candidate member. *Ecological Economics*. 68 (6). pp.1667–1675.

Soytas, U., Sari, R. and Ewing, B. T. (2007) Energy consumption, income, and carbon emissions in the United States. *Ecological Economics*. 62 (3). pp.482–489.

Tubiello, F. N., Salvatore, M., Golec, R. C., Ferrara, A., Rossi, S., Biancalani, R., Federici, S., Jacobs, H. and Flammini, A. (2014) *Agriculture, Forestry and Other Land Use Emissions by Sources and Removals by Sinks*. Rome: Statistics Division, Food and Agriculture Organization (FAO).

United Nations. (2014) *List of Least Developed Countries*. Available from: http://www.un.org/en/development/desa/policy/cdp/ldc/ldc_list.pdf [Accessed: 24 July 2014].

Van der Werf, G. R., Morton, D. C., DeFries, R. S., Olivier, J. G. J., Kasibhatla, P. S., Jackson, R. B., Collatz, G. J. and Randerson, J. T. (2009) CO_2 emissions from forest loss. *Nature Geoscience*. 2. pp.737–738.

WDI. (2013) *World Development Indicators*. Washington, DC: The World Bank. Available from: http://data.worldbank.org/data-catalog/world-development-indicators [Accessed: 15 March 2014].

Yousefi-Sahzabi, A., Sasaki, K., Yousefi, H. and Sugai, Y. (2011) CO_2 emission and economic growth of Iran. *Migration and Adaptation for Global Change*. 16 (1). pp.63–82.

Zhang, X. P. and Cheng, X. M. (2009) Energy consumption, carbon emissions, and economic growth in China. *Ecological Economics*. 68 (10). pp.2706–2712.

7 Is the current booming growth in Africa worth celebrating?

Some evidence from Tanzania

Bitrina Diyamett and Musambya Mutambala

Introduction

The aim of any well-meaning government is to ensure a decent standard of living for its citizens. This is also at the heart of the Sustainable Development Goals (SDGs). Many of the SDGs, whether social or economic, finally boil down to ensuring secure life for all the world's population, and this to a large extent can be achieved by eradicating extreme poverty, hunger and ensure healthy lives (Goals 1, 2 and 3) (United Nations, 2015).

In addition to the statements in the SDGs, most poor countries have their social and economic policies focusing largely on poverty alleviation. An important factor here is economic growth (since the SDGs, unlike previous Millennium Development Goals (MDGs), thankfully recognise the role of growth in achieving the envisaged goals), which to a large extent explains why the current high growth rate in some of the African countries is being celebrated. A key question, however, has to be, is this growth worth celebrating? More specifically, is African economic growth positioned to eradicate poverty?

Largely focusing on Tanzania, this paper attempts to answer this crucial question by analysing this growth and looking beyond the aggregate figures. To set the context, following a short methodological note in the second section, the paper examines the theoretical construct of the relationship between growth and poverty in the third section, where issues on structural transformation are introduced. Sources of growth for most African countries are detailed in the fourth section; applying the theoretical construct provided in the previous section to the case of Tanzania, this section assesses the extent to which Africa's current growth is reducing poverty. The fifth section, on the analysis of the current state of the manufacturing sector in Tanzania and associated technological capabilities, further confirms arguments made earlier, but also brings in a proposal for an appropriate move towards more desirable growth that comes from normal structural transformation. The last section provides some concluding remarks and suggests ways forward for Tanzania and other African countries for the achievement of the SDGs.

Methodology

The empirical materials used in this paper are largely drawn from secondary sources. A number of items from the literature, including the World Economic

Outlook, have provided insights into the growth status of economies in Africa. In the case of Tanzania, this information has provided a base to establish a relationship between poverty levels and growth. Above all, the recently published Tanzania Industrial Competitiveness Report 2012, to which the Science, Technology and Innovation Policy Research Organization (STIPRO) contributed, was used to analyse the state of the science, technology and innovation environment, especially for the Tanzanian manufacturing sector. A number of research reports carried out by STIPRO have also enriched this analysis.

Growth and poverty: a theoretical construct

The concept of 'poverty' is multidimensional in character. It is commonly defined with reference to income (the economic aspects), such as the less than 1 USD/day measure, and to non-income measures (the social aspects), such as low educational attainment and poor health (World Bank, 2001). It is perhaps income, over all other aspects, which has the greatest implications for poverty. As noted by Mejer (1999, 1) for example, "the poor shall be taken to mean persons, families and groups of persons where resources are so limited as to exclude them from a minimum acceptable way of life in the countries in which they live." Of course, income poverty is also easy to measure and monitor. In fact, the MDGs have placed an emphasis on this form of poverty, and it is also the way poverty is understood in this paper.

Methods to reduce poverty are debated in both policy and academic arenas. One very important debate surrounds the growth of the economies. It is now universally accepted that economic growth is a necessary condition for poverty alleviation. Growth in general facilitates poverty alleviation; an observation from the World Development Report 2000–01 tells us that as countries become richer, on average the incidence of income poverty falls. Other indicators of well-being, such as average levels of education and health, also tend to improve (World Bank, 2001). This happens because growth encourages increase in incomes, which in turn pushes people out of poverty (Dollar and Kraay, 2002).

However, this does not seem to be an automatic process, because others have observed the converse and argue that growth is a necessary but not a sufficient condition for poverty reduction. Osmani (2003), for example, argues that there is no invariant relationship between the rate of growth and the rate of poverty reduction, i.e. faster growth is not always accompanied by faster poverty reduction, just as slower growth does not always entail slower rates of poverty reduction. According to Osmani, three factors affect the incomes of the poor in growing economies. The first is the growth factor (a necessary condition), which is the rate at which the production potential of the economy expands. The second is the elasticity factor, which is the extent to which growth enhances employment potential. Third is the integratability factor, which is the extent to which the poor are able to integrate into economic processes in such a way that when growth occurs and the employment potential expands, they can take advantage of the improving quality and quantity of employment.

For this reason, sustainable and poverty-reducing growth, as well as employment generation, will ultimately depend on positive structural transformation in countries. This means the movement of resources from low-productivity to high-productivity employment, while at the same time generating more employment that is inclusive. It also entails a transition of the economy from a reliance on low to higher value-added sectors. The process starts with a successful structural transformation where agriculture, through higher productivity, provides food, labour, and even savings to the process of urbanisation and industrialisation; as economies move up the ladder of development, services sectors would gain importance (Timmer, 2007).

Overall, observations of the process by many scholars and practitioners have revealed the critical importance of the manufacturing sector in growth and development because of its unique multiplier effect. The US Manufacturing Institute, in its book *The Facts About Modern Manufacturing*, for instance, has shown that manufacturing has a 'pull effect' on other sectors of the economy. Its multiplier effect is stronger than other sectors due to its potential in creating employment (Manufacturing Institute, 2009). The development of the manufacturing sector stimulates demand for more and better services, including banking, insurance, communication and transport, and leads to job creation.

To a large extent, the above has been demonstrated by the recent Malaysian development processes. Malaysia underwent a structural shift associated with a transition from an agrarian to industrial society. This can be seen in the changing shares of the agriculture and manufacturing sectors in their respective contributions to gross domestic product (GDP), the total value of exports and total employment. With an agrarian economy, Malaysia in the late 1980s experienced high export-oriented and manufacturing-led growth, averaging over 8 per cent annually. This helped in transforming Malaysia into a newly industrialising economy. Between 1960 and 2000, the agriculture sector's share of GDP declined from 40.5 per cent to 12.8 per cent, while the contribution from manufacturing rose from 8.2 per cent to 34.7 per cent (Khoo, 2010). As explained in the process of structural transformation, the process has to start with productivity growth in agriculture, and Malaysia did not ignore this sector but rather strengthened its link with the manufacturing sector. Skill development and worker redeployment gradually brought about labour shifts from agriculture to industry. Employment in Malay manufacturing increased from 17 per cent in 1990 to 26.3 per cent in 2000, while it decreased in agriculture from 36.7 per cent to 18.2 per cent. In services, the proportion of labour slightly increased from 21.2 per cent to 25 per cent in the respective years (World Bank, 2004).

Alongside the structural transformation was a dramatic reduction of poverty. At the beginning of the Five Year Economic Plan (the Sixth Malaysia Plan of 1991–1995), statistics indicated an official poverty rate of 17.1 per cent (Government of Malaysia, 1991a, 32). By 2004, according to the Ninth Malaysia Plan, 2006–2010, the incidence of poverty had fallen to 5.7 per cent for all households (Government of Malaysia, 2006, 329). A related example is the salmon-growing regions of Chile. Typically, Chile was successful in adding value to her agricultural products, namely fish (salmon), grape fruits, berries and fresh fruits. The development of the salmon industry led to the development of other local manufacturing industries, such as fish farming, which gained cages and nets, the construction of floating warehouses, the manufacture of feed, vaccines and antibiotics, transportation and infrastructure maintenance. Consequently, the poverty rates in salmon-producing regions dropped from over 40 per cent in 1990 to 24 per cent in 2000 (Montero, 2004; cited in URT and UNIDO, 2012).

Booming growth in Africa and poverty: the case of Tanzania

Like many African countries, Tanzania is growing fast. Her GDP increased from 4.9 per cent in 2000 to 6.9 per cent in 2012 (UNDP and URT, 2015). This economic growth places Tanzania among the 17 fastest growing economies alongside other African countries such as Ethiopia (7 per cent GDP growth), Mozambique (7.5 per cent), Democratic Republic of Congo (7.1 per cent), Ghana (7 per cent), Zambia (6.9 per cent), Angola (8.4 per cent), Cote d'Ivoire (9.8 per cent) and Nigeria (6.3 per cent) (IMF, 2013). Indeed, the World Bank recently released its list of 29 fastest growing economies in the world in its semi-annual Global Economic Prospect. Sixteen countries from the list are from Africa, including those cited above. On the back of rapid growth, many African countries could have markedly reduced their numbers of poor people. This is not the case for most, however.

In Tanzania, for instance, despite high economic growth, household income poverty has remained virtually unchanged; the national poverty headcount fell from 33.3 per cent in 2007 to 28.2 per cent in 2012 (UNDP and URT, 2015); and as correctly predicted by URT (2014), Tanzania could not decrease the proportion of her population which earns below USD 1 per day to 19.5 per cent by 2015 as was targeted in the previous MDGs. In addition, household surveys have found that income inequality did not change significantly during 2001–2007 (URT, 2001; URT, 2007), and that it is not likely to change (World Bank, 2009). This paradox is even more obvious if one looks at the trends in the purchasing power of Tanzanians, which has drastically declined at a time of consistent GDP growth over the past decade, as indicated in Figure 7.1, whereby increase in the retail price index implies increase in costs of goods or inflation that also reduces the purchasing power of the population.

The failure of current economic growth to translate into a corresponding reduction of poverty, and the dramatic decrease in purchasing power witnessed in Tanzania, indicates that such a growth has not been pro-poor. It is not coming from sectors that are employment-generating, and the poor have not fully been involved in both the production and consumption in the national economy. This is indicated in Figure 7.2, which shows the structure of the Tanzanian economy, indicating that growth is coming from the service sectors that are less knowledge-intensive and less employment-generating; the figure also shows that there has been a premature structural transformation, where there was a sharp decline of agriculture contribution to GDP and an increase of services from 1992, while manufacturing has lagged far behind.

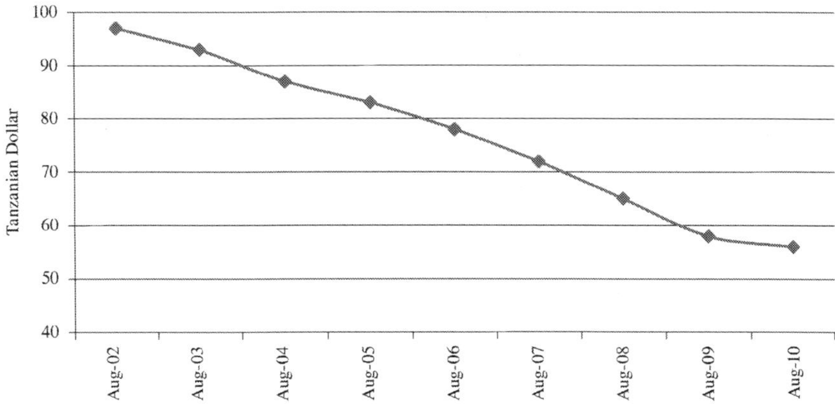

Figure 7.1 Trend in purchasing power of Tanzania

Source: URT (2011).

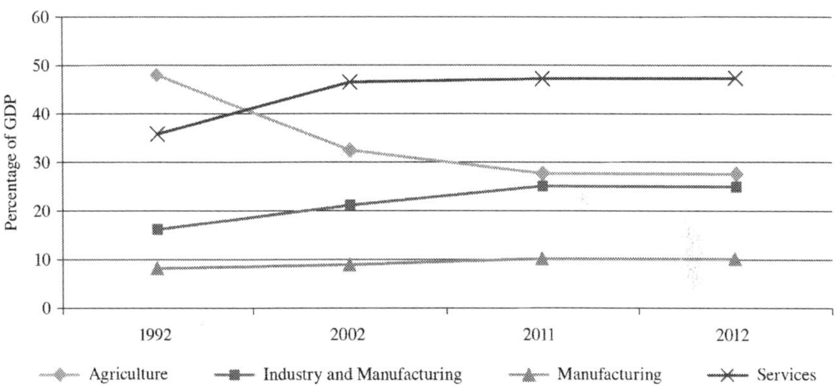

Figure 7.2 Share of productive sectors in Tanzanian GDP

Source: Prepared by the authors based on World Bank (2015).

There are two possible explanations for the above paradox. First, services grew abruptly because of increased informal activities which arose from labour being displaced from formal employment during the privatisation of the early 1990s. It can also partly be explained by people abandoning agriculture due to falling productivity and prices. This fall in prices of traditional export crops is said to be a contributing factor to a reduction in export earnings by the agriculture sector from 50 per cent in the mid-1990s to 23 per cent in 2002 (Amani, 2005). It is also important to note that industry (particularly mining and construction) experienced a modest growth around the same time. This could again be attributed to privatisation which was associated with increased foreign investments, particularly in the mining sector. Generally, however, and important for this paper, this brought about an increase in capital-intensive investments that were not employment-generating.

As indicated in Figure 7.2, the Tanzanian economy is now service-oriented. We call this a premature transformation because there was no prior productivity increase in either agriculture or manufacturing (as indicated in the theoretical framework section). As already indicated, conventional transformation starts with agricultural transformation, leading to growth in the industrial and then the services sectors. Every territory in the world has followed this pattern with the exception of those who had no agriculture to begin with (such as Hong Kong and Singapore) (Timmer, 2007). In addition, much of the contribution of the services sector in Tanzania is from less skill- and employment-intensive sub-sectors of trade (mostly retail in the informal) and repair. According to URT (2013), the leading sub-sectors of the services sector are trade and repair (12.3 per cent), real estates and business services (8.5 per cent) and public administration (7.8 per cent), with very little contribution from knowledge-intensive sub-sectors of information technology (IT) services, research and development, financial, as well as the logistics and communications industries.

Tanzania is not alone in this way: we believe it is the case for most of the countries in Africa. According to the World Bank, for example, services is the leading contributing sector to the GDPs of Mozambique, Zambia and Ghana, with figures of 47.2 per cent, 43.2 per cent and 48.5 per cent respectively (World Bank, 2013). In countries like Democratic Republic of Congo and Ethiopia, services follow agriculture with contributions of 32.6 per cent and 43.1 per cent of GDP respectively, leaving behind manufacturing sectors that are still at an infant stage. McMillan and Rodrik (2012) have observed the same trend for Africa as well as Latin America that globalisation appears not to have fostered the desirable kind of structural change in these regions; rather, labour has moved in the wrong direction, from more productive to less productive activities, and most notably, informal employment has spurred up to a great extent.

The above-mentioned dominance of low productivity and low employment in the services sectors in the economies must have – to a significant extent – accounted for much of the poverty in poor countries. If conventional transformation is followed, a services orientation tends to be accompanied by high income and high quality of life. Singh (2006), for instance, argues that the transformation process which follows the standard pattern is considered superior because along with raising productivity and standards of living also comes institutional, organisational and cultural changes, which make society as a whole more capable, productive, innovative and peaceful.

The empirical evidence for structural transformation and growth that enhance employment and reduce poverty is highly mixed between Tanzania and Malaysia. Malaysia primarily selected strategies that could provide opportunities for the poor to be involved in the production and consumption functions or gain employment in higher-paying jobs, which would allow them to become self-supporting. The country implemented a variety of innovative programmes that were aimed at increasing productivity and diversifying sources of income. Since poor households were mostly in the agriculture sector, the focus was on providing them with the support and opportunities to be involved in modern farming and the value-added processing of agricultural products, as well as non-farm or off-farm activities that generated additional employment. This way, Malaysia managed to drastically reduce the incidence of poverty within the context of rapid and continuous economic growth (World Bank, 2004). The role of technology, innovation and structural transformation here is critical; the Malaysian case of poverty reduction shows that some of the gains in rural incomes came from productivity increases brought about by modernisation, commercialisation and technological improvement of smallholder agriculture and from more intensive farming. But above all, significant gains came from structural changes in rural employment, resulting in the diversification of income sources with non-agricultural activities accounting for more than half of the income of rural households. In addition, the growth in the demand for non-agricultural labour encouraged large numbers of self-employed and unpaid family workers to enter the wage-labour market, making wage income a more important determinant of rural household income (The Government of Malaysia, 1991b, 43). Unlike in Malaysia, the high incidence of poverty in Tanzania corresponds to a failure to implement and support programmes that create productive employment and raise incomes of the poor, most notably, failure to promote the manufacturing sector as indicated in the next section.

State of the manufacturing sector in Tanzania: looking beyond the slow growth

Having established that increasing productivity in the manufacturing sector is the way towards more employment-enhancing and poverty-reducing growth, we now closely examine this sector in Tanzania. The main purpose is to further explain the reasons why Tanzanian economic growth is failing to alleviate poverty and to explore the best way forward not only for Tanzania, but also for many other African countries. We start with the structure of the sector, before discussing its technology readiness and innovation.

Structure of the sector

As indicated by the structure of the national economy (Figure 7.3) and in the Tanzania Industrial Competitiveness Report 2012, the performance of Tanzania's manufacturing sector is not impressive. The technology intensity of the sector is very low, and even in the medium- and high-technology sectors, the products are at the lower end of the technology spectrum (URT and UNIDO, 2012). Furthermore,

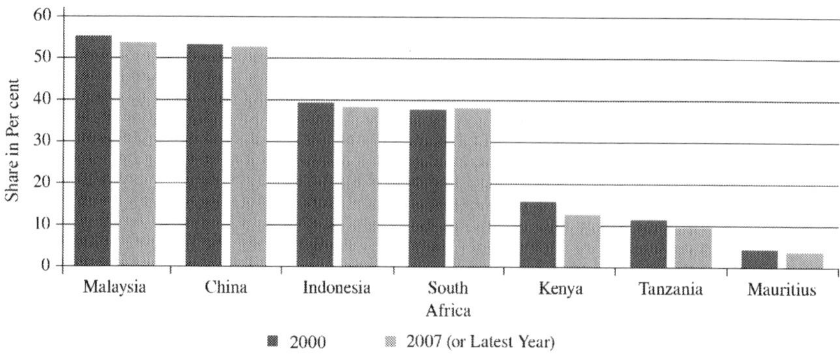

Figure 7.3 Share of manufactured value addition in medium and high technology

Source: URT and UNIDO (2012).

Tanzania appears to be de-industrialising as the share of manufactured value addition in medium and high technology is falling rather than increasing. That is, the level of sophistication is lower compared to other countries, and as the Figure 7.3 shows, Tanzania has in fact become less sophisticated over the period.

The manufacturing sector is dominated by resource-based sectors, which constitutes around two-thirds of manufactured exports (Figure 7.4). Much of the resource-based industry is dominated by low value addition (Figure 7.5), and therefore very limited employment potential. A resource base is not necessarily a bad thing to start with if correct policies are implemented to quickly move up the value chain. It should be recognised, however, that opening up to the world economy, as occurs through globalisation, reduces incentives to diversify towards modern manufactures and reinforces traditional specialisation patterns for countries that have comparative advantage in natural resources (McMillan and Rodrik, 2012). This fact should be taken into account when devising strategies for moving up the value chain.

The major problem for Tanzanian manufacturing sector is not only the very low value addition to its resource-based industries, but also a very thin, labour-intensive and low technology sector that would have provided ample employment if appropriate policies had been put in place, which is something that could very easily be achieved. According to the World Bank (2015), there is a negative gap between the Tanzanian imports and exports, with imports rising very sharply. Many of the imported goods are those that can easily be manufactured locally, generating significant employment in the low-tech sectors such as agro-processing, while at the same time contributing to productivity growth in the agriculture sector. A recent study carried out in Tanzania indicates that much of the low performance of the agriculture sector is to a large extent attributed to the underperformance in the manufacturing sector (Diyamett et al., 2013).

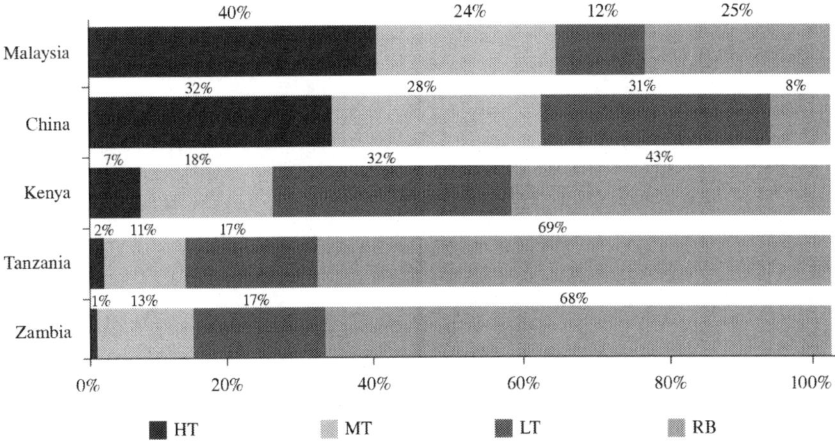

Figure 7.4 Structure of manufactured exports by technology classification

Source: URT and UNIDO (2012).

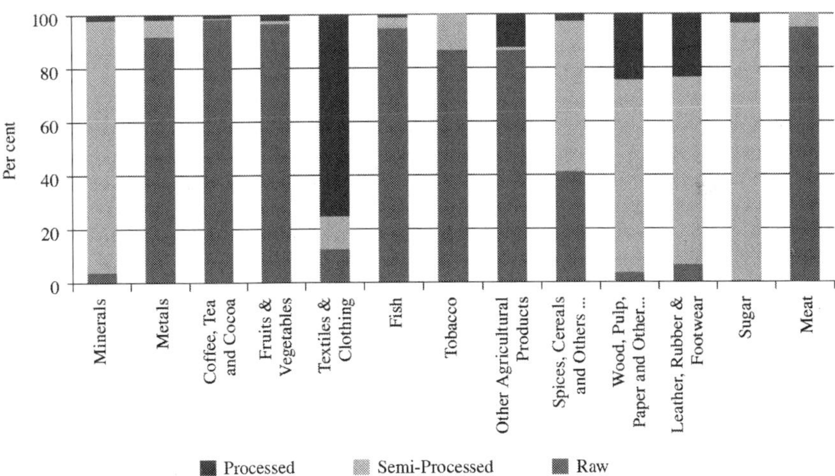

Figure 7.5 Processing degree of resource-based exports

Source: URT and UNIDO (2012).

Technology readiness and innovation

Technological change and innovation are essential to productivity growth, proper structural transformation and employment generation. It is unfortunate that Tanzania and other growing economies in Africa have low capacities to harness the benefits of existing technologies, from either home or abroad, to enhance the productivity of their industries. Furthermore, they fail to strengthen enabling factors for innovative activities. In the Global Competitiveness Report 2014–2015 by the World Economic Forum (WEF), the fastest growing economies in Africa rank very low in technology readiness and innovation.

The Global Competitiveness Report indicates that of the 144 countries, Tanzania ranked 131st, with 2.5 of value scored for technology readiness. For innovation, she ranked 98th, with 3.1 score values (WEF, 2014). The ranking confirms that Tanzania has low capacities in technologies and innovation. The report has also revealed similar levels of capacities in technology readiness and innovation in other fastest growing economies in Africa. For example, Ethiopia has ranked 133rd and 109th for technology readiness and innovation respectively, and Mozambique ranked 122nd for both technology readiness and innovation.

Looking ahead, important reforms will be needed to solve the competitiveness challenges, particularly in all the factors that enable industries to harness technologies. While in general these economies seem to provide favourable environments for foreign direct investment (FDI) and technology transfer – given the size of the flow of FDI to these countries – they need to attract the right kind of FDIs and forge linkages with local firms, while strengthening the absorptive capacity of local firms for effective transfer and adoption of technologies (Diyamett and Mutambala, 2014).

Additionally, according to WEF (2014), enabling factors for innovative activities in these economies receive low scored values compared to those of other countries. Poor assessment that needs improvement appears largely across areas such as patents applications and availability of scientists and engineers. These factors indicate that the booming growth in Africa is not coming from improvement in technological capabilities and areas that are skill-intensive, and therefore, the sustainability of such growth is questionable.

Conclusion and recommendations

The current economic growth in Tanzania is not worth celebrating because it is not set to reduce poverty, which is the major concern of governments and the SDGs. The findings of this report show that growth is coming from low productivity- and low employment-potential sectors. To make matters worse, instead of moving up the value chain, Tanzania seems to be de-industrialising with very low performances in regards to technological and innovation capability indicators. In addition, the manufacturing sector has not yet been given the priority it deserves in terms of a concrete industrial development strategy with adequate financial commitments (URT and UNIDO, 2012). Unless important steps are immediately taken, the situation is likely to get worse. To be competitive and support the SDGs, the Tanzanian manufacturing sector must undergo structural transformation within itself to ensure movement up the value chain and expand the low technology and employment-intensive sub-sectors. This also has the potential to increase productivity in agriculture through forward and backward linkages and therefore address Goal 2 of the SDGs on eradicating hunger. These processes should be implemented carefully following short-, medium- and long-term strategies:

a) In the short-term, there is need to promote investment in low technology and labour-intensive sub-sectors. These sectors do not require a lot of investment in terms of capital and human skills, thus providing an opportunity to expand the manufacturing industry. Labour-intensive and low-tech manufacturing provides jobs to the unemployed and the poor, decreasing unemployment and poverty levels in this group. This strategy should start with the identification of firms within these sectors which are capable of involving the poor widely and whose growth must effectively create opportunities for generating income among the poor. Here, agro-processing and associated non-farm activities in the rural areas should be given top priority because of their potential to increase agricultural productivity and improve incomes of the rural poor.
b) In the medium-term, new technological and investment capabilities are needed. This requires strategies to help low-tech and labour-intensive sectors gradually move up the innovation capability ladder by deepening their technological capabilities. In addition to the above, there is a need to develop innovative clusters around mining sites. Increased FDI has helped Tanzania make substantial investments, particularly in the gold-mining sector, but with no or very little value addition. If the current rapid expansion of the mining sector in Tanzania can be combined with mineral processing activities, the sector will experience a substantial multiplier effect for the benefit of the national economy. The most effective strategy is to provide incentives to attract FDI towards mineral processing activities and develop innovative clusters that also include local companies around mining sites. Such clusters, which could be anchored around existing foreign mining companies, have the potential to enable local enterprises to overcome many binding constraints in the areas of capital, skills, technology and markets as they learn from foreign investors. It is important to note, however, the necessity of developing physical and knowledge infrastructure around mineral exploitation and processing. The same applies to the recently emerging gas and oil sectors in Tanzania.
c) In the long-term, the target should be to move towards a more diversified and sophisticated and internationally competitive national manufacturing sector. It is important to recognise Tanzania's comparative advantage in this and to achieve a competitive advantage around it by building a secure physical and knowledge infrastructure.

In addition, efforts should be made to increase productivity in Tanzania's agriculture sector, because it is this sector which currently employs the majority of the Tanzania's poor, and therefore it has the potential to play a key role in eradicating hunger and poverty. This can only happen, however, if forward and backward linkages with the manufacturing sector are enhanced.

References

Amani, H. R. (2005) *Making Agriculture Impact on Poverty in Tanzania: The Case on Non-Traditional Export Crops*. Dar es Salaam: Economic and Social Research Foundation (ESRF).

Diyamett, B., Mneney, E., Komba, A. and Liberio, J. (2013) *Science, Technology and Innovation for Poverty Reduction in Tanzania: An Analysis of the Sectoral Systems of Innovation*. A Research Report for Manufacturing and Agriculture – Part II. Dar es Salaam: Research for Poverty Alleviation (REPOA).

Diyamett, B. and Mutambala, M. (2014) Foreign direct investment and local technological capability in least developed countries: Some evidence from the Tanzanian manufacturing sector. *African Journal of Science, Technology, Innovation and Development*. 6 (5). pp.401–414.

Dollar, D. and Kraay, A. (2002) Growth is good for the poor. *Journal of Economic Growth*. 7 (3). pp.195–225.

IMF. (2013) *World Economic Outlook Database*. Washington, DC: International Monetary Fund (IMF). Available from: https://www.imf.org/external/pubs/ft/weo/2013/02/weodata/weorept.aspx?pr.x=42&pr.y=6&sy=2011&ey=2016&scsm=1&ssd=1&sort=country&ds=.&br=1&c=738&s=NGDP_RPCH&grp=0&a= [Accessed: 8 August 2015].

Khoo, B. (2010) *Policy Regimes and the Political Economy of Poverty Reduction in Malaysia*. New York: United Nation Research Institute for Social Development (UNRISD).

Malaysia, Government of. (1991a) *The Sixth Malaysia Plan, 1991–95*. Kuala Lumpur: Economic Planning Unit, Prime Minister's Department, Government of Malaysia.

Malaysia, Government of. (1991b) *The Second Outline Perspective Plan, 1991–2000*. Kuala Lumpur: Government of Malaysia.

Malaysia, Government of. (2006) *The Ninth Malaysia Plan, 2006–2010*. Putrajaya: Economic Planning Unit Prime Minister's Department, Government of Malaysia.

Manufacturing Institute. (2009) *The Facts About Modern Manufacturing* (8th ed.). Washington, DC: Manufacturing Institute. Available from: www.nist.gov/mep/upload/FINAL_NAM_REPORT_PAGES.pdf [Accessed: 28 August 2013].

McMillan, M. and Rodrik, D. (2012) *Globalization, Structural Change and Productivity Growth*. IFPRI Discussion Paper 01160. Washington, DC: International Food Policy Research Institute (IFPRI).

Mejer, L. (1999) *Statistics on Social Exclusion: The EU Methodological Approach*. Luxembourg: EUROSTAT. Mimeo.

Montero, C. (2004) Formación y desarrollo de un cluster globalizado: el casodelaindustria del salmón en Chile. *Serie Desarrollo Productivo*. 145, January. Santiago: United Nations Economic Commission for Latin America and the Caribbean (UNECLAC).

Osmani, S. (2003) *Exploring the Employment Nexus: Topics in Employment and Poverty*. Report Prepared for the Task Force on the Joint ILO-UNDP Programme on Employment and Poverty. Geneva and New York: International Labour Organization (ILO) and United Nations Development Programme (UNDP).

Singh, L. (2006) *Innovation and Economic Growth in a Fast Changing Global Economy: Comparative Experience of South East Asian Countries*. Paper Presented at the conference on *Korea and the World Economy V*. Korea University, 7–8 July, Seoul, South Korea.

Timmer, P. (2007) *The Structural Transformation and the Changing Role of Agriculture in Economic Development*. Washington, DC: Wendt Lecture, American Enterprise Institute.

UNDP and URT. (2015) *Tanzania Human Development Report 2014: Economic Transformation for Human Development*. Dar es Salaam: United Nations Development Programme (UNDP) and Government of Tanzania (URT).

United Nations. (2015) *Transforming Our World: The 2030 Agenda for Sustainable Development*. New York: United Nations.

URT. (2001) *The Integrated Labour Force Survey 2000*. Dar es Salam: National Bureau of Statistics, Government of Tanzania (URT).

URT. (2007) *The Integrated Labour Force Survey 2006*. Dar es Salam: National Bureau of Statistics, Government of Tanzania (URT).

URT. (2011) *Economic Survey 2010*. Dar es Salaam: Ministry of Finance, Government of Tanzania (URT).

URT. (2013) *National Accounts of Tanzania Mainland 2001–2012*. Dar es Salam: National Bureau of Statistics, Government of Tanzania (URT).

URT. (2014) *Country Report on the Millennium Development Goals 2014: Entering 2015 with better MDG scores*. Dar es Salaam: Ministry of Finance, Government of Tanzania (URT).

URT and UNIDO. (2012) *Tanzania Industrial Competitiveness Report 2012*. Dar es Salam: Ministry of Industry and Trade (MIT) and President's Office Planning Commission (POPC), Government of Tanzania (URT) and United Nations Industrial Development Organization (UNIDO).

WEF. (2014) *The Global Competitiveness Report 2014–2015*. Geneva: World Economic Forum (WEF). Available from: http://www3.weforum.org/docs/WEF_GlobalCompetitivenessReport_2014–15.pdf [Accessed: 8 October 2015].

World Bank. (2001) *World Development Report 2000–01: Attacking Poverty*. New York: Oxford University Press. Available from: http://wdronline.worldbank.org//worldbank/bookpdfdownload/24 [Accessed: 3 September 2013].

World Bank. (2004) *Malaysia: 30 Years of Poverty Reduction, Growth and Racial Harmony*. Kuala Lumpur: The World Bank.

World Bank. (2009) *Lost in Transition: Income Poverty Reduction since 2001*. Paper prepared for the Research and Analysis Working Group. Mimeo.

World Bank. (2013) *Tanzania at a glance*. Available from: http://data.worldbank.org/data-catalog/at-a-glance-table [Accessed: 10 September 2013].

World Bank. (2015) *At-a-glance table*. Available from: http://data.worldbank.org/data-catalog/at-a-glance-table [Accessed: 18 May 2015].

Inclusion and social policies

8 Role of social exclusion in human development of excluded groups

Nidhi S. Sabharwal

Introduction

The South Asian experience with respect to changes in poverty and hunger in the Millennium Development Goals (MDGs) is positive. Notably, it is forecasted that extreme poverty and hunger will halve by 2015 (World Bank, 2011). The Sustainable Development Goals (SDGs) follow and expand on the MDGs. The goals and principles embodied in the MDGs and the SDGs have been reflected in India's development priorities, which are inculcated in the 11th and 12th Five Year Plans. The 11th Five Year Plan (2006–11) and the 12th Five Year Plan (2012–17) have adopted several monitorable targets as key features of an inclusive growth strategy. These targets are designed to capture the economic and social objectives of an inclusive approach to growth. In all, 25 targets have been identified at the national level which have been placed in six major categories: (1) income and poverty, (2) education, (3) health, (4) women and children, (5) infrastructure and (6) environment.

Now, as we approach 2015, we come closer to the committed year of meeting the MDGs' targets, the experiences of numerous countries including India indicate that achieving the target for the indigenous and excluded groups remains an urgent challenge. Indigenous, ethnic and other excluded groups tend to suffer from high poverty, malnutrition, illiteracy and poor health outcomes compared to the general population. Large disparities in poverty and nutritional levels exist across gender, economic, social, ethnic and religious groups. Within indigenous and ethnic groups, poverty is often persistent and chronic in nature and is passed on to consecutive generations. In some growing economies, such as India and China, these groups have experienced reductions in poverty and improvements in indicators of human development. However, the pace of poverty reduction and malnutrition is invariably lower than the non-excluded groups, and therefore, group disparities persist, as they continue to lag behind the remainder of the population.

The central argument of this paper is that a part of group disparities in poverty and malnutrition is attributed to social exclusion and discrimination associated with group identity such as gender, caste, ethnicity and religious background (Thorat and Sabharwal, 2015). Social exclusion and discrimination is embedded in relational aspects and processes that underpin poverty (de Haan, 1997). Discrimination associated with the group identity results in denial of equal access to rights and entitlements in various spheres of economy and society. Therefore, social exclusion and discrimination make marginalised groups more vulnerable to poverty than their counterparts from the general population. The new set of global goals (SDGs) for poverty reduction and sustainable development reflects commitment to dealing with inequality, with the clear intent of putting the needs of marginalised groups at the heart of the policy guidance (HLP on Global Sustainability, 2012). It is important to recognise that group characteristics of exclusion are based on social and cultural identity, which results in the denial of equal rights and entitlements and are irrespective of individual attributes. Hence, we can ensure that 'no one is left behind' by

a) Making non-discriminatory access and participation a right; and
b) Combining universal policies with affirmative action policies to address group-specific causes of human poverty.

The objective of the paper is to examine the performance of the excluded groups in India with respect to some of the goals in the SDGs related to the status of poverty and hunger, malnutrition, reproductive health of women, education and access to housing, water and sanitation. First, it discusses the changes and disparities in these among both excluded groups and the general population since the early 1990s. Then, it discusses the reasons for relatively slower progress in the dimensions of human development for excluded groups and persistent disparities between them and the 'rest' of the population. An attempt is then made to highlight the structural causes of poverty related to societal interrelations and the institution of exclusion, the prevalent forms of exclusion and discrimination, and their consequences on deprivation of the excluded groups. Finally, it proposes a way to bridge the gap and addresses the issues of exclusion-induced poverty and deprivation with regard to human development of excluded groups in India.

Progress in human development in India: positive improvement for all, but at lower rate for excluded groups

In India, social exclusion is generated by institutions that exclude, discriminate, isolate and deprive some groups based on their identities defined, for example, by caste, ethnicity and religion. Excluded groups include the scheduled castes (SCs), other backward classes (OBCs), scheduled tribes (STs), nomadic and de-notified tribes (NTs and DNTs), and religious minorities such as Muslims. The SCs, STs and OBCs account for around half of India's population. If we add minorities like Muslims, the proportion goes up to 64 per cent. So it is deduced that almost three-fifths of India's population suffers from one or the other form of social exclusion and isolation.

The groups that suffer from social exclusion and discrimination associated with the institution of caste include former untouchables (SCs) and socially and educationally backward sections of OBCs. The groups that suffer from exclusion and isolation associated with ethnic background include STs and nomadic and de-notified tribes. The de-notified tribes also suffer from the stigma of criminality. The groups that suffer exclusion and discrimination because of religious identity are mainly Muslims. Women from all religious backgrounds face discrimination in various forms, although the nature of discrimination differs depending on their caste, ethnicity and religious background. The nature of social exclusion and discrimination of each of these groups differs in term of spheres and forms.

The Indian government has recognised the unique problems of these groups and developed group-specific policies as early as 1930. The government has developed affirmative action policies for SCs, STs and OBCs. The policies for these three groups are legal in nature. However, in the case of religious minorities (the Muslims), it takes the form of informal affirmative action policy. The government has also developed policies along the lines of affirmative action for women.

In this section, the paper assesses indicators of human poverty and human development in India. These indicators include incidence of poverty, malnutrition, lack of access to safe drinking water, lack of access to sanitation and literacy rates at the aggregate level and by social groups, namely the SCs and the STs in comparison to the rest of the population. We limit our exercise to the SCs and the STs, due to the paucity of official data available for other excluded groups. Together, SCs and STs constitute around a quarter of India's population. In order to gain a comparative picture, we take the 'rest' of the population as others or non-excluded groups (the non-SC/ST/OBC population). The focus is on the period 1990s and 2000s. Changes in poverty, monthly per capita expenditure, malnutrition, health indicators and literacy by gender, caste and ethnic groups of SCs, STs and the 'rest' are based on the data for the 1990s and 2000s from official sources, National Family and Health Surveys (1992–93, 1998–99, 2005–06), Census of India 2011 and National Sample Survey. The changes are studied for the relevant years in this period depending on the availability of the data.

The specific variables studied are as follows:

- Proportion of poor below the poverty line in India (poverty ratio)
- Income (monthly per capita expenditure – MPCE)
- Prevalence of underweight children under 5 years of age
- Infant mortality rates (IMR)
- Access to safe drinking water
- Access to sanitation
- Literacy rates of those aged 7 years and above

Changes in incidence of poverty

The paper has examined the changes in the incidence of poverty, the Head Count Ratio (HCR) at the national level in India by caste and ethnic groups in the rural and urban sectors. The change in the incidence of poverty (measured as HCR) is reported in Table 8.1.

Table 8.1 Incidence, change and rate of change (annual) in HCR for socio-religious groups

Socio-religious groups	*Poverty incidence (HCR) (%)*					
	1993–94			*2009–10*		
	Rural	*Urban*	*Total*	*Rural*	*Urban*	*Total*
All	36.9	32.8	35.9	21.9	20.8	21.6
STs	50.2	42.9	49.6	33.0	28.6	32.5
SCs	48.3	49.7	48.6	29.6	32.8	30.3
Others	31.2	29.6	30.7	17.5	18.2	17.7
Socio-religious groups	*Net change in HCR (Percentage Point) (1993–94 to 2009–10)*			*Rate of change (Annual %) 1993–94 to 2009–10*		
	Rural	*Urban*	*Total*	*Rural*	*Urban*	*Total*
All	−15.0	−12.0	−14.3	−2.5	−2.3	−2.5
STs	−17.2	−14.3	−17.0	−2.1	−2.1	−2.1
SCs	−18.7	−16.9	−18.3	−2.4	−2.1	−2.4
Others	−13.7	−11.4	−13.0	−2.7	−2.4	−2.6

Source: Thorat and Dubey (2012).

Table 8.1 shows that the HCR is 30 per cent for SCs and 33 per cent for STs, while the total poverty incidence is close to 22 per cent in 2009–10. Between 1993–94 and 2009–10, rural poverty declined at a per annum rate of 2.5 per cent, which is equivalent to a 15 percentage points decline (Table 8.1). Across social groups, the rate of decline in poverty for the 'others' (i.e. non-SCs/STs), has been 2.7 per cent, followed by 2.4 per cent among SCs and 2.1 per cent among STs.

Changes in urban poverty

The urban poverty level was 20.8 per cent in 2009–10, which is only marginally lower than that in the rural sector discussed above (Table 8.1). The incidence of poverty in urban India was highest among the SCs in 2009–10, followed by STs and 'others'. It is the change in the incidence of poverty across social groups that presents an interesting picture (Table 8.1). Between 1993–94 and 2009–10, the rate of decline has been highest among 'others' at 2.4 per cent annually, while for SCs and STs it has been uniformly at 2.1 per cent.

Changes in income: monthly per capita expenditure (MPCE) as a proxy for income

A study by Thorat and Dubey (2012), based on the National Sample Survey data, reported that during 1993–94 to 2009–10, the MPCE in India increased at per annum rate of 1.9 per cent. The per annum rate of increase in MPCE varied among the groups. The rate of increase in MPCE was the higher (2 per cent) as compared to the SCs and STs (1.7 per cent per annum for both the groups). Therefore, we find that all households showed a positive change, but at relatively higher rate for households from the non-excluded groups as compared to the excluded groups such as the SCs and the STs.

Changes in proportion of underweight children

According to National Family Health Survey (NFHS), during 2005–06 (the latest years for which the data are available), nearly 45 per cent of India's children were underweight. The proportion of underweight children declined over the years, from 47.1 per cent in 1998–99 to 45 per cent in 2005–06 at an annual rate of change of −0.9 per cent at the aggregate level. The decline of child malnutrition levels in SCs and STs over the three rounds of NFHS (1992 to 2006) has been slower than that is seen in the case of the 'others' category (Figure 8.1). The rate of decline in malnourishment was slower among children in SCs (0.9 per cent) and STs (0.8 per cent) compared to children from the 'others' category (2.3 per cent).

Change in the IMR

At the national level in India, the infant mortality was 57 per 100,000 in 2005–06, a decline from 73 per 100,000 in 1998–99 (NFHS, 1998–99; NFHS, 2005–06). The annual rate of change was negative at 3.7, indicating a decline in IMR. The IMR declined in the period 1999 to 2005 across social groups. The annual rate of change was highest for STs at −4.4, followed by OBCs (−4.3), 'others' (−3.5), and the least for the SCs (−3.3).

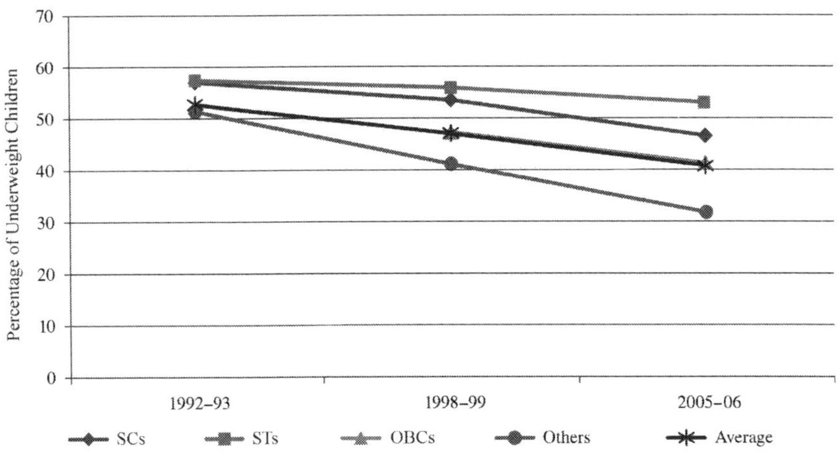

Figure 8.1 Malnutrition levels by social groups

Source: IIPS (1995); IIPS and ORC Macro (2000, 2007).

Access to safe drinking water: proportion of houses in rural areas without drinking water facilities

At the national level in India, the proportion of houses in rural areas which lack drinking water facilities was 56.8 per cent in 2008. This level declined steadily between 1993 and 2008, from 73.2 per cent 65.6 per cent (Thorat and Sabharwal, 2014a). The rate of change from 1993 to 2008–09 was −1.6, indicating a positive change, as the proportion of houses in rural areas with no drinking water facilities has gone down over the years. Across social groups, the proportion of houses in rural areas which lack drinking water facilities also declined gradually over the years. The rate of change from 1993 to 2008–09 was −0.6 for STs, −0.9 for SCs and −2.1 for 'others'. However, the improvement has been slower for the SC and ST groups compared to others.

Access to sanitation: proportion of houses in rural areas having no latrine facility

At the national level in India, the proportion of houses in rural areas with no latrine facilities has gone down over the years. That is, from 87.2 per cent in 1993 to 78.3 per cent in 2002 and to 66.4 per cent in 2008–09 (Thorat and Sabharwal, 2014a). The rate of change from 1993 to 2008–09 was −1.72, indicating a positive change. Across social groups, the proportion of houses with no latrine facilities also declined in the period from 1993 to 2008. The rate of change from 1993 to 2008 was −1.1 for STs, −1 for SCs, and −2.1 for 'others'. This further indicates a positive change as the proportion of houses with no latrine facilities declined across all social groups. However, for this indicator of development as well the rate of improvement was higher for 'others' as compared to the SCs and the STs.

Changes in literacy rates of those aged 7 years and above

As Figure 8.2 shows, in 2011, at the aggregate level, 73 per cent of India's population were literate (Census of India, 2011a). In the period 2001 and 2011, the rate of increase was the highest among STs (2.3 per cent), followed by SCs (1.9 per cent), and non-SCs/STs (1 per cent). The data thus indicate an improvement in literacy rates for the SCs and the STs, which has been more than for the rest of the population.

Thus, the analysis above provides us with two specific findings. First, there has been an improvement in the human development dimensions, such as income, education, health, drinking water and sanitation for all, including for the excluded groups of SCs and STs. Second, the rate of improvement in most (if not all) of these dimensions for SCs and STs has been lower compared to the 'rest' of the population, which also means that SCs and STs have benefited from development less than others. Since progress towards the human development indicators for SCs and STs has been slower, disparities continue to persist between the SC/ST groups and the 'rest' of the population. The next section of the paper presents the analysis on group disparities in poverty and human development indicators.

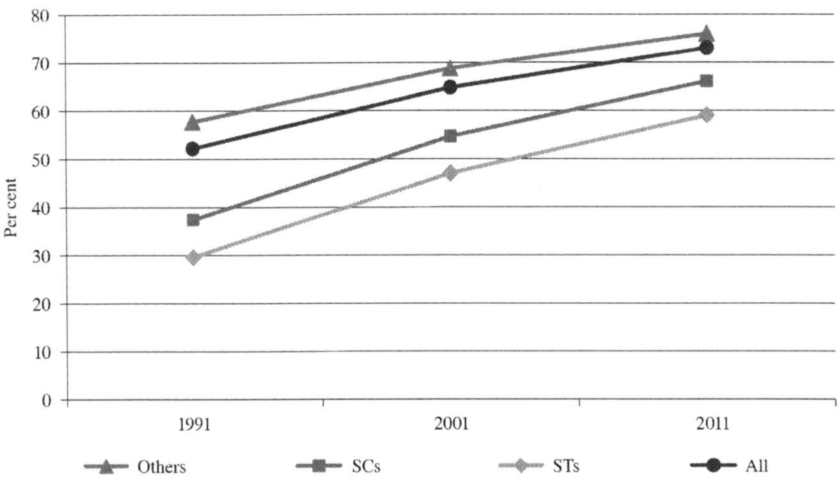

Figure 8.2 Literacy rates across social groups: 1991, 2001 and 2011

Source: Census of India (2011a).

Higher levels of human poverty and inter-group disparities persist in human development

While indicators towards human development have improved in India, as is seen above, the rate of improvement for excluded groups, SCs and STs, has been lower than for the rest of the population, resulting in the persistence of gap between them. For example, in 2009–10, we find a 15 percentage point gap in the incidence of poverty between STs and 'others' and 12 percentage point between SCs and 'others' (Table 8.1). The incidence of poverty was thus higher in case of the SCs and the STs, 30 per cent and 33 per cent for STs respectively as compared to 'others' (17.7 per cent). Similarly, in case of underweight children (less than 5 years of age), 56 per cent of children from the ST group and 51 per cent in SC group were underweight as compared to 'others' (36 per cent) in 2005–06 – still disturbingly high, but significantly better than rates among children in SCs and STs (IIPS and ORC Macro, 2007).

In case of adults, according to NFHS, in 2005–06, the proportion of women suffering from malnutrition with a BMI (body mass index) below 18.5 kg/m2 was particularly high amongst STs (almost 49 per cent) and amongst SCs (45 per cent) as compared to 36 per cent amongst others. Moreover, around 69 per cent of ST and 58 per cent of SC women suffered from anaemia, compared to 51 per cent 'others' category (non-SC/ST/OBC) women. Low nutritional status impacts their children's nutritional status and chances of surviving. IMR was highest among SCs (66.4), followed by STs (62.1) and 'others' (48.9).

The gap in the literacy rates between the SCs, STs and others is another feature that becomes evident from the data. Data from Census of India (2011a) indicates that literacy rates were lower among SCs and STs (65 per cent for both) compared to 'others' (82 per cent respectively). In terms of access to safe drinking water and sanitation, there are wide gaps across social groups. For example, according to the Census of India (2011b), the proportion of houses in rural areas without drinking water facilities was found to be highest among STs (86 per cent), followed by those among SCs (72 per cent), and then 'others' (59.3 per cent). Among social groups, the proportion of houses in rural areas without latrine facilities was highest among SCs (77.2 per cent), followed by STs (84.2 per cent), compared to 'others' (64.4 per cent) in 2011.

The above analysis thus brings out two features of human development dimensions of the excluded groups. First, the level of attainment of human development is lower amongst the excluded groups such as the SCs and STs as compared to the non-excluded. Two disparities in attainment of human development between the social groups, which has also been the feature in the past, continue to persist. Studies (Thorat, Sabharwal and Thorat, 2014) indicate that reasons for high poverty and low human development amongst the SCs and the STs is due to lower access to capital assets, like agricultural land, and non-land assets (and/or low productivity of those assets), exceptionally high dependence on casual wage labour, high underemployment, lower daily wages and low levels of literacy and education, compared with non-SC/ST groups in Indian society.

Analysis in studies, however, also indicates that lower access for the excluded groups to income-generating resources and inter-group inequalities is linked with the processes of exclusion and discrimination (Sabharwal, 2011a; Thorat, Sabharwal and Thorat, 2014; Thorat and Sabharwal, 2014b; Borooah et al., 2015). What forms does group-based exclusion take and yield outcomes which induce high level of deprivation? Although this an under-researched area, we have some empirical evidence which provide us with the processes and forms of discrimination in access to social protection programmes which provide food security, nutrition, maternal and child health. These are discussed in the next section.

Causes of slow progress in human development among the excluded groups

As stated above, there is now empirical evidence that indicates that among other factors, the deprivation of excluded groups like women and ethnic, social, religious and other minorities generally occurs through the process of exclusion and discrimination.

Borooah et al. (2015) examine whether there is a 'caste/religion basis' to inequality and poverty in India or whether distributional and deprivation outcomes are 'caste/religion blind' so that they are entirely determined by the attributes of the individual households. The analysis is based on the India Human Development Survey (IHDS) (2004–05) of over 41,000 households spread over India (University of Maryland and NCAER, 2006). The study found that households' outcomes with respect to their position on the distributional ladder, or with respect to their chances of being poor, were dependent in large measure on their caste or religion. So SCs, STs and Muslim households were more likely to be in the lowest quintile of consumption than high-caste Hindu households. For a rural SC household, the probability of being poor was increased by 9 percentage points over that for a rural high-caste household. For an urban SC household, the probability of being poor was increased by 13 percentage points over that for an urban high-caste household, *after controlling other factors.* These factors were mother's education, household income, main source of household income, age, region of residence and rural/urban location.

Similarly, using the national data, Sabharwal (2011a), while studying key factors impacting child malnutrition, found that income levels, educational attainment of the mother, access to antenatal care (as an indicator for access to health services) and social belonging emerged as important determinants of nutrition levels (Table 8.2). The author found that even after controlling factors such as income, education level and access to health services, the likelihood of children in SCs and STs being malnourished was still 1.4 times higher than among children from the 'others' category.

Such analysis captures the indirect influence of caste and ethnic background on the incidence of malnutrition, which shows that even when the wealth index, education, access to health services and other factors are held constant, the likelihood of children from these groups being malnourished is higher as compared to the rest. The econometric findings demonstrate that there are constraints associated with their social belongings. A lack of data means it is not possible to include

Table 8.2 Logistic regression results of factors affecting child malnutrition

Explanatory variables		*Exp (B)*
Wealth Index	Poorest	1.000
	Poorer	.856*
	Middle	.681*
	Richer	.538*
	Richest	.342*
Education of Mother	No education	1.000
	Primary	0.828*
	Secondary	0.799*
	Higher	0.463*
Mother's Antenatal Care	No antenatal care	1.000
	Taken antenatal care	.669*
Social Group	Others	1.000
	SC	1.350*
	ST	1.418*
	OBC	1.218*
Religious Group	Others	1.000
	Hindu	1.092
	Muslim	1.065

Source: Computed from NFHS-3, Unit-Level Data.

Note: *denotes significant at 1 per cent level; Exp (B) is the Odds ratio.

such constraints in the regression equation. However, some field-based studies indicate group-specific factors for high malnutrition levels. These factors generally relate to the discriminations that these communities face in accessing income earning assets, education and government schemes providing services like food and health. There is some evidence for the SCs. The SCs face discrimination in accessing employment and government programmes to provide food security (Public Distribution System (PDS), Integrated Child Development Programme) and maternal health services for safe motherhood (*Janani Suraksha Yojana*).

The empirical evidence from the limited studies indicates that discrimination associated with caste and untouchability faced by the excluded group, namely SC, takes various forms in the market access, such as in seeking employment in farm and non-farm operations, in seeking inputs and services necessary to undertake farm and non-farm production including business, and in sale and purchase of products and consumer goods. This indicates that even when SCs have access to various markets, it is constrained by restrictions and discriminatory behaviour on the part of the higher-caste persons (Shah et al., 2006; Thorat and Lee, 2010; Thorat, Mahamallik and Sabharwal, 2010; Sabharwal et al., 2014a).

These studies find that the SC labourers face discrimination in being hired in some particular farm and non-farm sectors, for example, in the harvesting of fruit and vegetables. Because of the notion of impurity and pollution, women from the SC are excluded from household employment, and in particular, they are hardly ever allowed to cook or to clean food grains. This notion of purity also affects the implementation of government programmes: SC women are not taken on as cooks and helpers in the Mid Day Meal Programme. In the market, sellers from the SC of edible products like milk, fruit, vegetables and cooked food find it difficult to find buyers. In case of land, sales of land are generally confined to persons of the seller's caste (or higher), and this restricts the entry of lower-caste households into the land-owning class. Furthermore, even if they do get to buy land, lower-caste households do not get higher-valued land: for example, land that is adjacent to irrigation project command areas or near to the village or main road, or near to any farm of high-caste cultivators.

Empirical studies also throw selective evidence on discrimination in non-market transactions, that is, goods and services supplied by government and its agencies and the schemes runs by the government in some spheres. From the PDS, the SCs receive less food and other services; the dealers inflict preferential service to the higher-caste customers and segregated timings for the lower caste (Thorat and Lee, 2010). The study further observed that this discriminatory practice varies considerably from state to state. It was observed that where the owners of PDS were from SCs (such as in Andhra Pradesh), the access of SCs to PDS was satisfactory and non-discriminatory in its functioning as compared to the situation where the owners happens to be from higher caste (such as in Rajasthan, Uttar Pradesh and Bihar). In the kindergarten centres (*anganwadi* centres), discrimination takes place in the form of provision of less food and less frequent visits to lower-caste neighbourhoods for counselling service on child care issues; these also lead to lack of information on the services available at the anganwadi centre (Borooah et al., 2015). In addition, the location of the anganwadi centres in 'main' parts of the villages, where the upper caste live, contributes to difficulty in accessing for the mothers and children from the SC social groups (FOCUS, 2009; Borooah, Diwakar and Sabharwal, 2014).

In the Mid Day Meal Programme in schools, SC children are seated separately, served last, served insufficient quantities, selectively denied meals and given separate plates marked for different categories of students due to notion of pollution and purity (Thorat and Lee, 2010; Sabharwal et al., 2014a). Such discriminatory forms in accessing mid-day meals in schools and anganwadi centres are humiliating and adversely affect the food intake of scheduled caste, and thereby, their level of nutrition. These forms of discrimination are not uniformly practiced nationwide and the practices vary considerably across states, but their incidence is enough to affect people's access to food and nutritional level.

In case of health services, Acharya (2010) and Sabharwal et al. (2014b) provide evidence on the discriminatory access faced by SC women and children. Table 8.3 captures the forms and spheres of discrimination faced by SC women from the doctors, nurses and village health nurses in the government hospitals and outside the hospitals. The evidence from the field data suggests that high-caste service

Table 8.3 Spheres and indicators of caste-based discrimination faced by women from scheduled castes in public health services

Spheres of discrimination	*Identifiers of discrimination*	*Consequences of discrimination*
Treatment at the time of antenatal check-up	Face rude verbal response from health workers, without check-up the nurse gives medicines and send away	Lack of care leads to requirement of private medical attention
Treatment by auxiliary nurse for family planning operations	Indifferent verbal response and coerced into taking decisions, e.g. prospect of ration card being withdrawn if refused to have tubectomy, do not receive appropriate post-operative care	Lack of post-operative care leads to requirement of private medical attention
Treatment at the time of delivery	Ignored and kept waiting for long, the staff directs to go to a distant district headquarters hospital for the delivery	The delay complicates delivery which leads to requirement of private medical attention Take loan for delivery in private hospital
Treatment after assault by men in authority (police and dominant caste landlord-employer)	Refusal of treatment by doctors in the local government hospital in order to avoid being involved in a police case	Lack of care leads to requirement of private medical attention

Source: Sabharwal (2011b, 159).

providers towards the low-caste users are still governed by customary notions of their social status and notion of 'purity and pollution'.

For example, health workers avoid visits to 'untouchable' hamlets to offer health information and services; SC mothers are not informed/aware of the auxiliary mid-wife timings and village health and nutrition meetings; often, these meetings take place in higher-caste neighbourhoods, and the lower-caste groups are reluctant to attend these meetings. Further, healthcare services which require contact between the medical professionals and the patient/recipient are impacted negatively, e.g. tablets would simply be dropped into the hands of a lower-caste person from a 'contact-safe distance'. SC mothers indicated that they receive less post-natal check-ups and advice – service providers (anganwadi workers) avoid holding newborn children to weigh them and instead ask mothers to do it; auxiliary nurses avoid holding children's hands for immunisation, and they also ask someone from the SC community to dispense polio drops to the SC children. Discrimination at home during the visit by the health workers occur by avoiding entering the house, avoiding touching the user and avoiding sitting or drinking/eating in the user's house.

In primary health centres, SC women sometimes face discrimination in the dispensing of medicines or during the diagnosis stage itself, where the medical professional may be reluctant to engage adequately with the patient. Discrimination during diagnosis may take the form of less time spent in asking about the problem, or may manifest in avoiding to touch the user. Discrimination during dispensing the medicine may be practiced in the way the medicine is given to the user – not kept on the palm, but on the window sill/floor, or when someone else is asked to give the medicine to avoid physical touch. Such discriminatory access faced by SC women and children to primary health services lead to lower utilisation of health services. This is in addition to its immense implications on their human rights and human dignity.

Indeed, the NFHS data for 2005–06 reveals that SC mothers and children have relatively poorer access to public health services than others do. For example, the immunisation rates for SC children are about 20 per cent lower than for the others. Access to health services at the time of delivery is also lower for SC mothers compared with others. Thus, discrimination resulting in limited access appears to be an additional pervasive factor contributing to lower levels of progress towards MDGs among SCs compared to others. The issue of discrimination-induced deprivation has been neglected in the literature, and more research is needed.

In sum, lower levels of human development are directly affected not only by factors such as income levels, education, public health and other services, but also indirectly by discriminatory access to income opportunities and publicly supplied goods. Thus income level, education and access to public services in health and sanitation are important factors in reducing human poverty and increasing levels of human development for all, including in the SCs and the STs. So, in the case of the excluded groups, additional affirmative action measures and safeguards are necessary to tackle the socially inherent discriminations.

Policy implications

The trend analysis of human development progress in India between the 1990s and 2010 indicates that:

- There has been an improvement across the dimensions of human development for all social groups, including for the most excluded groups of SCs and STs. Poverty, which is an aggregate indicator of well-being, has declined in both rural and urban areas. Similarly, the incidence of underweight children, IMR, maternal mortality and literacy rates and the proportion of those without housing, drinking water and sanitation facilities have also declined at the national level. To that extent, there was progress towards the MDGs in India between the early 1990s and 2010 (the latest years for which the data are available).
- However, the rate of improvement among SCs and STs has been lower than that in the 'others' category. The gains of development seem to have been shared unequally across groups. With isolated exceptions, the rate of improvement in SCs and STs has been lower compared to the rest of the population ('others'), which means that others have benefited more than the excluded groups.
- The disparities between the SCs and STs and the rest of the population – which had been a feature in the past – continue to persist, since reduction in disparities across social groups would require relatively higher rate of improvement among the backward groups, which has not occurred in this instance.

The approach by Indian policymakers to overcoming the problems suffered by SCs and STs includes two types of measures:

- Measures against discrimination, including legal safeguards such as an anti-untouchability law; fair access policy in the form of reservation in government institutions, such as politics, employment in public sector enterprises, education and other spheres; legal mandates for corporate spending on social welfare; and affirmative action policies for the private sector focused on the capacity enhancement and promotion.
- General measures for economic and social empowerment, which are part of anti-poverty and other welfare programmes, including focused government interventions in food, nutrition, health and education.

These policies have brought about positive changes, but the gap in deprivation levels between SCs, STs and non-SC/STs remains wide. General economic and educational empowerment, although a necessary precondition for human development, is not enough. Like other economically and educationally backward sections from the non-excluded groups, the excluded groups require income-earning opportunities and education and skill development to raise employability and improve access to capital assets. But unlike others, they face discrimination in economic and social spheres, and hence require affirmative action policies to ensure non-discriminatory access to market institutions and services supplied by non-market institutions engaged in the implementation of government programmes in food, nutrition, health and education. The discrimination faced by the excluded groups of SCs and STs is one of the reasons for slower improvement in the indicators of human development compared with their counterparts from non-excluded groups and the persistence of disparities between them.

A reduction in disparities across social groups would require a relatively higher rate of improvement among the excluded groups through a combination of universal and targeted or affirmative action policies. For example, Malaysia has developed comprehensive affirmative action policy covering multiple economic spheres. It has developed policies to enable the minorities to have greater shares of the capital in private companies. In India, legal methods have been recently implemented for economic empowerment and as a safeguard against discrimination in market space for the SC producers. In 2012, the Centre's Public Procurement Policy made it mandatory for the Central Ministries, Departments, Public Sector Undertakings and States to procure 4 per cent of its goods and services from micro and small enterprises (MSEs) owned by SCs and STs (Government of India, 2012). In 2014, the State enacted the Corporate Social Responsibility Policy, under which every company (private limited or public limited with a net worth of Rs 500 crore/a turnover of Rs 1,000 crore/net profit of Rs 5 crore), needs to spend at least 2 per cent of its average net profit (of the last three financial years) on corporate social responsibility (CSR) activities (Government of India, 2014). The CSR activities in this policy include measures for reducing inequalities faced by socially and economically backward groups. As well as back in 2008, the private sector in India accepted an affirmative action policy, voluntary in nature, to address the challenges of the SCs and the STs in education, employability, entrepreneurship and employment (Confederation of Indian Industry, 2008).

However, affirmative action policies, including those in India, are mostly confined to a very small state sector, and the vast private sector that accounts for the bulk of employment and economic activities is free from any affirmative action. The existing affirmative action policy in India in the private sector is on a voluntary and self-regulatory basis with no legally binding responsibility on the part of the private sector. In other countries, as well, the affirmative action policy is narrow and selective in nature and excludes many sectors where excluded groups face discrimination (Thorat and Sabharwal, 2014b). The absence of broad-based affirmative action policies in multiple market and non-market transactions, including a focus on non-discriminatory access to the excluded groups, is an important missing element towards reducing inter-group inequalities. The absence of such complementary policies results in slower improvement in the human development indicators and persistent disparities between excluded and non-excluded groups.

References

Acharya, S. S. (2010) Caste and Patterns of Discrimination in Rural Public Health Care Services. In Thorat, S. and Newman, K. S. (eds.) *Blocked by Caste: Economic Discrimination in Modern India* (pp.208–229). New Delhi: Oxford University Press.

Borooah, V. K., Diwakar, D. and Sabharwal, N. S. (2014) Evaluating the social orientation of the integrated child development services programme. *Economic and Political Weekly*. 49 (12). pp.52–62.

Borooah, V. K., Sabharwal, N. S., Diwakar, D., Mishra, K. V. and Naik A. K. (2015) *Caste, Discrimination, and Exclusion in Modern India*. New Delhi: Sage Publications India.

Census of India. (2011a) *Status of Literacy*. New Delhi: Registrar General and Census Commissioner of India.

Census of India. (2011b) *H – Series: Tables on Houses, Household Amenities and Assets*. New Delhi: Registrar General and Census Commissioner of India.

Confederation of Indian Industry. (2008) *Affirmative Action for the Scheduled Castes and Scheduled Tribes*. New Delhi: Confederation of Indian Industry. Available from: http://www.ciiaffirmativeaction.in/ [Accessed: 13 September 2015].

de Haan, A. (1997) *Poverty and Social Exclusion: A Comparative of Debates on Deprivation*. Working Paper No. 2. Brighton: Poverty Research Unit, University of Sussex.

FOCUS. (2009) *Focus on Children under Six*. New Delhi: Citizens' Initiatives for the Rights of Children under Six.

Government of India. (2012) *Procurement Policy for Micro and Small Enterprises, 2012*. New Delhi: Ministry of Micro, Small and Medium Enterprise, Government of India. Available from: http://pib.nic.in/newsite/erelease.aspx?relid=77047 [Accessed: 13 September 2015].

Government of India. (2014) *Companies (Corporate Social Responsibility Policy) Rules 2014*. New Delhi: Ministry of Corporate Affairs, Government of India. Available from: http://www.mca.gov.in/Ministry/pdf/CompaniesActNotification2_2014.pdf [Accessed: 13 September 2015].

HLP on Global Sustainability. (2012) *Resilient People, Resilient Planet: A Future Worth Choosing*. New York: United Nations Secretary General High Level Panel on Global Sustainability.

IIPS. (1995) *National Family Health Survey (1992–93)*. Mumbai: International Institute for Population Sciences (IIPS).

IIPS and ORC Macro. (2000) *National Family Health Survey (NFHS-2), 1998–99*. Mumbai: International Institute for Population Sciences (IIPS).

IIPS and ORC Macro. (2007) *National Family Health Survey (NFHS), 2005–06*. Mumbai: International Institute for Population Sciences (IIPS).

Sabharwal, N. S. (2011a) Caste, religion and malnutrition linkages. *Economic and Political Weekly*. 46 (50). pp.16–18.

Sabharwal, N. S. (2011b) Dalit Women in Political Space: Status and Issues Related to Their Participation. In Wakahara, Y., Nagasaki, N. and Shiga, M. (eds.) *Voices for Equity Minority and Majority in South Asia* (pp.154–174). Rindas International Symposium Series 1. Kyoto, Japan: The Centre for the Study of Contemporary India, Ryukoku University.

Sabharwal, N. S., Diwakar, D., Naik, A. K. and Sharma, S. (2014a) Swallowing the humiliation: The mid-day meal and excluded groups. *Journal of Inclusion Studies*. 1 (1). pp.169–182.

Sabharwal, N. S., Diwakar, D., Sharma, S. and Naik, A. K. (2014b) Caste discrimination as a factor in poor access to public health service system: A case study of *Janani Suraksha Yojana*. *Journal of Inclusion Studies*. 1 (1). pp.148–168.

Shah, G., Mander, H., Thorat, S. K., Deshpande, S. and Baviskar, A. (2006) *Untouchability in Rural India*. New Delhi: Sage Publications India.

Thorat, S. and Dubey, A. (2012) Has growth been socially inclusive during 1993–94/2009–10? *Economic and Political Weekly*. 47 (12). pp.43–54.

Thorat, S. and Lee, J. (2010) Food Security Schemes and Caste Discrimination. In Thorat, S. and Newman, K. S. (eds.) *Blocked by Caste: Economic Discrimination in Modern India* (pp.287–307). New Delhi: Oxford University Press.

Thorat, S. K. and Sabharwal, N. S. (2014a) *Affirmative Action Policy for Post-2015 Million Development Goals Strategy*. Background Paper for the Report on *Strengthening Social Justice to Address Intersecting Inequalities Post-2015 of Overseas Development Institute (ODI), London*. New Delhi: Indian Institute of Dalit Studies (IIDS).

Thorat, S. K. and Sabharwal, N. S. (eds.) (2014b) *Bridging the Social Gap: Perspectives on Dalit Empowerment*. New Delhi: Sage Publications India.

Thorat, S. K. and Sabharwal, N. S. (2015) Caste and Social Exclusion: Concept, Indicators and Measurement. In Kumar, A. K. S., Rustagi, P. and Subrahmania, R. (eds.) *India's Children: Essays on Social Policy* (pp.374–392). New Delhi: Oxford University Press.

Thorat, S. K., Mahamallik, M. and Sabharwal, N. S. (2010) Caste System and Pattern of Discrimination in Rural Markets. In Thorat, S. and Newman K. S. (eds.) *Blocked by Caste: Economic Discrimination and Social Exclusion in Modern India* (pp.148–176). New Delhi: Oxford University Press.

Thorat, S. K., Sabharwal, N. S. and Thorat, A. (2014) The Role of Social Exclusion in Explaining Poverty in Income – Poor States of India. In Ramachandran, V. K. and Swaminathan, M. (eds.) *Dalit Households in Village Economies* (pp.24–52). New Delhi: Tulika Books.

University of Maryland and NCAER. (2006) *India Human Development Survey (2004–05)*. New Delhi: University of Maryland and National Council of Applied Economic Research (NCAER).

World Bank. (2011) *Global Monitoring Report: Improving the Odds of Achieving the MDGs*. Washington, DC: The World Bank.

9 Social protection and the MDGs in Sri Lanka

Implications for the post-2015 agenda

Ganga Tilakaratna

Introduction

Social protection has been increasingly viewed as an important tool for addressing poverty, vulnerability, inequality and social exclusion. It can play a vital role in accelerating progress on the Millennium Development Goals (MDGs) by ensuring access to quality education, healthcare services, nutrition and income security. Evidence from several countries, such as Mexico and Brazil, has shown that social protection programmes like cash transfers have contributed to the achievement of the MDGs (UNICEF, 2010; Fiszbein, Kanbur and Yemtsov, 2013). Social protection has also been recognised as a key element that needs to be included in the post-2015 development agenda (UNICEF, 2010; ECA et al., 2012; HLP, 2013). Yet, approximately 80 per cent of the world's population lack access to comprehensive social protection (ECA et al., 2012).

Sri Lanka has a long history of providing social protection, particularly in free education and healthcare, pensions, and food subsidy and cash transfers to various segments of its population including the poor, the elderly, children and women. Social protection policies and programmes implemented by successive Sri Lankan governments over the past six decades have helped the country to make remarkable progress with regard to social indicators such as literacy ratio, primary school enrolment ratio, child and maternal mortality ratio and life expectancy at birth – well before the declaration of the MDGs. The country's contemporary social protection system has contributed to achieving a number of MDGs. Sri Lanka has already achieved or is on track to achieve the MDGs on reducing poverty, achieving universal primary education, promoting gender equality, reducing child mortality and improving maternal health (IPS, 2010).

Given this context, this paper reviews the social protection system in Sri Lanka and analyses the country's progress on achieving the MDGs and the role of social protection in attaining them. It is based on a body of research on social protection carried out by the author, as well as other recent secondary sources. The following section provides an overview of Sri Lanka's social protection system and highlights some of the gaps and weaknesses in it. The next section analyses the country's progress on the MDGs and the importance of social protection policies and programmes in attaining them. The final section discusses conclusions and policy implications for the post-2015 development agenda.

The social protection system in Sri Lanka

The Sri Lankan social protection system consists of a range of policies and programmes (see Figure 9.1) that are implemented by the government, specifically ministries and provincial councils, and non-governmental sectors and targeted toward various vulnerable segments of the population, such as the poor, the elderly, the disabled, internally displaced persons, children and women. Social protection programmes vary from cash and in-kind transfers to education programmes, pensions and other retirement benefits, healthcare assistance, micro-insurance and livelihood development programmes. They can be broadly categorised as (i) social insurance, (ii) social assistance and (iii) active labour market programmes (ADB, 2011; Galappattige et al., 2012; Tilakaratna, 2012).

Social insurance

Social insurance programmes generally cover against contingencies such as old-age-related problems, permanent disability, death and other life cycle events. They are largely employment-related and involve the provision of old-age retirement

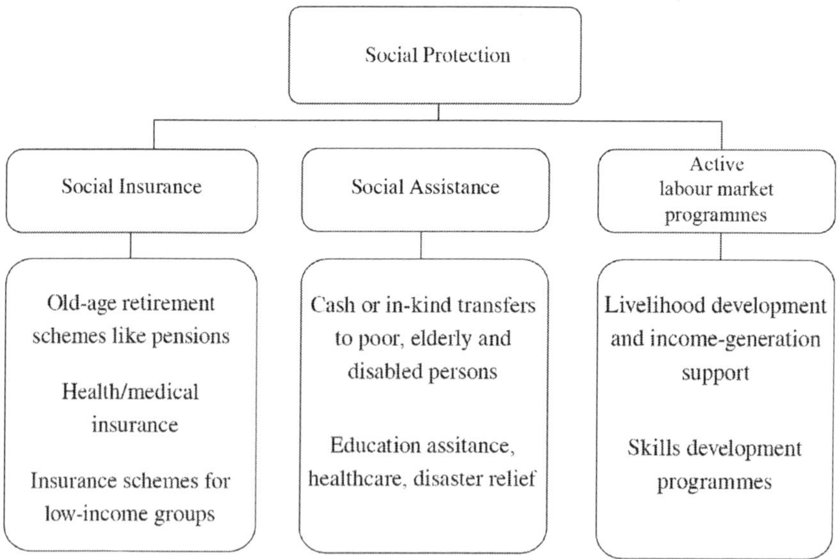

Figure 9.1 Social protection system in Sri Lanka

Source: Prepared by the author.

benefit schemes (e.g. pensions). The social insurance programmes available for different segments of the population are briefly discussed below.

For public sector workers, the Public Service Pension Scheme (PSPS) is a non-contributory pension scheme managed by the Department of Pensions. It covers all permanent public sector employees, and the entitlement for a pension arises after 10 years of service in a permanent post. Under the PSPS, employees are also covered against work injuries, disability and death. In the event of the death of a public servant, his/her dependents are entitled to the pension under the Widows'/ Widowers' and Orphans' Pension Scheme (W&OP) – a mandatory contributory scheme under the PSPS. In addition, there is a Public Service Provident Fund, a contributory old-age benefit scheme for public servants who are not eligible for the PSPS. In 2012, there were 510,343 beneficiaries of the PSPS and 130,416 beneficiaries of the W&OP.[1] The annual expenditure for public sector pensions accounts for nearly 2 per cent of gross domestic product (GDP).

Regarding private sector workers, all are mandated to contribute toward the Employees' Provident Fund and Employment Trust Fund. Currently, the Employees' Provident Fund has a membership of over 2 million people (covering about 25 per cent of the labour force). It provides old-age, permanent disability and survivor's benefits to its members in the form of a lump sum based on the total contributions made by the employee and the employer(s).

Despite the considerable share of employment in the informal sector, social security programmes available to informal sector workers are limited. These workers often lack maternity and medical benefits, retirement benefits like those in the Employees' Provident Fund and Employment Trust Fund, and pensions. There are a handful of contributory pension schemes (and insurance schemes) designed for specific groups of informal sector workers, such as farmers and fishermen. These are voluntary contributory schemes where benefit amounts are based on the contributions of individual members. In 2010, farmers' and fishermen's schemes had gross enrolments of around 959,000 and 67,000, respectively, but their active membership numbers remain much lower. Low coverage, inactive membership, low old-age benefit amounts, high administration costs and weak financial sustainability are the major challenges that these schemes face.

Regarding social insurance schemes for low-income groups, there are a number of micro-insurance programmes, such as the government's *Samurdhi* social security programme[2] and programmes carried out by non-governmental or private organisations. The Samurdhi social security programme is the largest insurance programme for low-income groups, covering over 1 million families (who are beneficiaries of the government's cash transfer programme) and providing insurance related to life-cycle events such as marriage, childbirth, sickness and death. This programme also includes a scholarship component aimed at providing benefits for children of beneficiary families who pass the General Certificate of Education (Ordinary Level) examination in Grade 5. Social insurance benefits are provided from the Samurdhi Social Security Fund formed from a monthly deduction of Rs. 45 from the monthly cash transfer given to these families (see Table 9.1).

Table 9.1 Benefits of the Samurdhi subsidy programme: 2012 (in Rs.)

Category of Samurdhi beneficiary family	*Total monthly subsidy*	*Net subsidy allowed for withdrawal*	*Compulsory savings*	*Contribution to social security fund*	*Contribution to housing fund*
1–2 member family	750	595	100	45	10
3–5 member family	1,200	945	200	45	10
6 or more member family	1,500	1,145	300	45	10
Empowered family	210	155	n/a	45	10

Source: Tilakaratna, Galappattige and Jayaweera (2013).

Social assistance

In Sri Lanka, there are many social assistance programmes targeted toward the poor and other vulnerable groups such as the disabled, the elderly, internally displaced persons, children and women. These programmes are primarily funded by the government.

With regard to assistance for the poor, the Samurdhi programme is the main social assistance initiative in Sri Lanka. It is designed with dual objectives: the short-term objective of reducing vulnerability to various risks, such as consumption shortfalls and sicknesses, and the long-term objective of poverty reduction through livelihood development and empowerment. It is comprised of multiple components, including the subsidy (or cash transfer), social security and nutrition programmes, which are designed to achieve its short-term objective, and the microfinance and livelihood development programmes that are geared toward the long-term objective. Under the Samurdhi subsidy component, identified families receive a monthly cash transfer valued between Rs. 210 and Rs. 1,500, depending on family size (see Table 9.1). The Samurdhi subsidy is currently received by approximately 1.5 million families. Despite its substantial coverage, the subsidy programme suffers from a number of weaknesses, such as targeting errors and the relatively low value of the cash transfer.

As for assistance for the disabled, the National Secretariat for Persons with Disabilities has a disability assistance programme that provides a monthly allowance of Rs. 3,000 for identified low-income families with disabled members. In 2011, this programme covered 11,216 families. The secretariat also implements programmes offering medical assistance for surgeries, housing assistance and financial assistance for disabled persons engaged in self-employment activities. The low coverage of eligible persons, which is related to budgetary constraints, is the main weakness of the disability assistance programme.

Regarding assistance for the elderly, in addition to the old-age retirement benefit schemes discussed in the previous section, a number of programmes for the elderly are carried out by the National Secretariat for Elders (NSE) of the Ministry of Social Services. With the elderly assistance programme, identified persons above 70 years of age who are without any source of income are given a monthly allowance of Rs. 1,000. This is a relatively new programme that began to be implemented in 2012. Other programmes cover the establishment of day centres for the elderly, financial assistance for elders' homes and elders' committees, medical assistance and financial assistance for medical clinics. Moreover, elders (persons above the age of 60) who do not qualify for the monthly allowance of Rs. 1,000 provided by the NSE and do not have any source of income are often eligible for the Samurdhi programme or assistance under the public assistance monthly allowance programme.

In terms of assistance for internally displaced persons (including those affected by natural disasters) and resettling families, programmes such as the Vulnerable Group Feeding, Food for Work and Food for Training programmes are carried out by the Ministry of Economic Development and the Ministry of Disaster Management. In 2011, the beneficiaries of the first programme totalled nearly 600,000 persons, while those benefitting from the second and third programmes together totalled nearly 200,000.

With regard to assistance for schoolchildren, the universal free education policy that was introduced in 1945 is designed to provide education free of charge to all students from kindergarten to university and is the most far-reaching measure taken by the Sri Lankan government to improve school enrolment and attendance among children. Moreover, the compulsory education policy for all children aged 5–14 years, which ensures a minimum of nine years of education for all children, was implemented in 1998. In addition, successive governments over the past few decades have implemented various programmes to increase educational opportunities for children from low-income families. These include the free textbooks programme started in 1980 under which all students in Grades 1–11 in the government school system are provided with relevant textbooks for free, the free school uniform programme introduced in 1993 under which all students in the government school system are provided with free school uniform materials on an annual basis, the school and higher education bus season tickets programme that provides a transportation subsidy to all students, and the scholarship programme that awards scholarships to students from low-income families. Moreover, a Mid-day meal programme is carried out in selected schools, where students from Grades 1 to 5 are covered with the aim of improving the nutritional status of schoolchildren from low-income groups. The details of some of the social assistance programmes for schoolchildren are provided in Table 9.2.

In terms of health assistance, public healthcare is provided free of charge in government hospitals and dispensaries. By 2012, there were 593 government hospitals with 73,437 beds, which amount to 3.6 beds per 1,000 persons, excluding beds in private hospitals. By the end of 2012, there were 17,129 qualified doctors in the state health sector, or a doctor for every 1,187 persons, and 29,781 qualified nurses, or a nurse for every 683 persons (CBSL, 2013). However, the public health service has not been adequate in meeting the demand for health care and, consequently, private expenditure on health care has been increasing in Sri Lanka.

Table 9.2 Major social protection programmes for children

Programme	*Institution*	*Beneficiary type*	*Benefit level*	*Number of beneficiaries in 2011*	*Expenditure in 2011 (Rs. million)*
School textbooks	Ministry of Education	All students in government schools and *Pirivens* (Grades 1–11)	Free textbooks each year	3,410,280 (students)	2,200*
School uniforms	Ministry of Education	All students in government schools	Free uniform material each year	3,994,813 (students)	1,260*
School and higher education bus season tickets	Sri Lanka Transport Board, Ministry of Transport	All students in government schools, *Pirivens* and universities	Subsidised bus tickets at 10 per cent of the cost per ticket	2,373,120 (students)	2,436*
Grade 5 scholarship	Ministry of Education	Students from low-income households who pass the Grade 5 scholarship exam	Rs. 5,000 per year until end of senior secondary education	45,019 (students)	225*
Mid-day meal	Ministry of Education	Students of primary and secondary schools in Grades 1–5 in selected rural areas and students in special education	Mid-day meal	1,117,219	2,486*
Thriposha	Ministry of Health	All pregnant and lactating mothers for first six months as well as infants and children aged 6–59 months deviating from the normal weight and those whose growth is faltering	Two take-home packs of Thriposha (cereal) once a month	873,509	980*
Food for education	Ministry of Economic Development	Students in Grades 1–9 in selected schools	Cooked meals at school	170,433	457

Mother and child health nutrition	Ministry of Economic Development	Pregnant and lactating mothers as well as children under 5 years of age in selected areas	Corn soya blend ration per person per month	197,762	230
Fresh milk for nursery children	Ministry of Child Development and Women's Affairs	Children aged 2–5 years in the low-nutrition areas	Rs. 200 per child for 25 days a month in selected nurseries	78,329	191*

Source: Tilakaratna, Galappattige and Jayaweera (2013).

Note: * denotes that data is for 2010.

Currently, government expenditure on health care accounts for about 1.3 per cent of GDP. Total expenditure on health care is typically much higher – it was 4.15 per cent of GDP in 2008 (UNDP, 2012).

Nutrition programmes for children and pregnant and lactating mothers are carried out by various ministries. The largest programme is the *Thriposha* programme implemented by the Ministry of Economic Development. Under this national supplementary food programme, Thriposha (cereal) packs are provided to the identified pregnant and lactating mothers, infants and children aged 6–59 months. This programme recorded a total of 873,509 beneficiaries in 2010. The Ministry of Economic Development carries out the Food for Education programme with the objective of promoting education and reducing hunger among children. Under this programme, cooked meals are provided for students in Grades 1–9 in selected schools in the Northern Province. The ministry also carries out the Mother and Child Health Nutrition programme for pregnant and lactating mothers and children under 5 years of age. In addition, the Ministry of Child Development and Women's Affairs carries out nutrition programme for nursery children (children aged 2–5 years) in low-nutrition areas, as shown in Table 9.2.

Active labour market programmes

Two types of programmes can be identified under this category: livelihood development programmes and skills development programmes. The major livelihood development programmes targeted toward low-income families include the Samurdhi programme and *Divi Neguma* programme implemented by the Ministry of Economic Development, under which selected families are provided with support (grants, loans, inputs and technical assistance) to start or expand livelihood activities in the areas of agriculture, livestock, fisheries and cottage industries. In addition, livelihood development programmes to help single mothers and women-headed households are carried out by the Ministry of Social Services and Ministry of Child Development and Women's Affairs.

The Ministry of Youth Affairs and Skills Development, through a number of training institutes that come under the purview of the ministry and training centres located across the island, offers vocational training to youth and school leavers (both male and female) with the aim of enhancing their entrepreneurial skills and employability. Training covers a range of areas such as carpentry, agri-business, hotel management, and information and communications technology (ICT). Vocational training programmes are also offered by a number of other ministries and the provincial councils.

Gaps and weaknesses of Sri Lanka's social protection system

Despite the multitude of social protection programmes ranging from cash and in-kind transfers, insurance, old-age retirement benefits like pensions, education welfare programmes, nutrition programmes and livelihood development programmes, a number of gaps and weaknesses exist in Sri Lanka's social protection system.

Low coverage and poor targeting are the two most common weaknesses in many social protection programmes. With the exception of some welfare programmes for schoolchildren (the free school textbooks, free school uniforms and subsidised transportation programmes) that are almost universal in coverage, many programmes designed for the poor, the elderly, the disabled and other vulnerable groups cover only a small share of eligible persons. Limited coverage is largely a result of budgetary constraints. Moreover, many programmes suffer from targeting problems. Tilakaratna, Galappattige and Jayaweera (2013) find that less than half of households (47.4 per cent in 2009–10) in the poorest decile receive Samurdhi benefits, while 3–15 per cent of households in each of the top four deciles also receive these benefits. Targeting errors in other social protection programmes are difficult to measure owing to the lack of data. Many programmes also lack clearly defined eligibility criteria and entry and exit mechanisms that have contributed to targeting errors in some programmes.

The inadequacy of benefit amount is another limitation in many social protection programmes, particularly cash transfer programmes such as the Samurdhi, elderly assistance and public assistance monthly allowance programmes. The PSPS is perhaps the only exception, given that benefit amounts are quite substantial in order to protect against old-age poverty. Under the Samurdhi subsidy programme, the maximum subsidy received by a family is Rs. 1,500 per month, which is far below the minimum amount required to meet a family's basic needs. According to the national poverty line, one person requires around Rs. 3,700 per month to cover his/her minimum consumption expenditure.[3] Moreover, the net cash value received by a family is much lower than the aforementioned amount since there are deductions for compulsory savings, social security fund and housing fund (see Table 9.1). The monthly allowances provided under the elderly assistance programme (Rs. 1,000) and the public assistance monthly allowance programme (between Rs. 250 and Rs. 500) are also far from adequate to cover basic expenses such as food and medical costs.

Lack of coordination among institutions involved in the provision of social protection and duplication of programmes targeted toward certain vulnerable groups are two gaps in Sri Lanka's social protection system. Currently there are several ministries, departments and provincial councils carrying out different social programmes for various vulnerable groups. Lack of coordination among institutions and programmes also leads to overlaps in beneficiaries served by programmes.

Many programmes suffer from budgetary constraints, which restrict the expansion of coverage and improvement of benefit amounts. For instance, the present number of beneficiaries of the disability assistance programme is far below the number of total eligible persons who have applied for this programme. Furthermore, the unsustainability of programmes such as the PSPS and the inadequacy of pensions for informal sector workers are issues of concern. The unsustainability of the PSPS is primarily due to its fully funded (non-contributory) nature, while the inadequacy of pensions in the informal sector is a result of small and irregular contributions from beneficiaries alongside inadequate funding from the government.

MDGs and social protection in Sri Lanka

Sri Lanka has made significant progress toward achieving the majority of the MDGs. It has already achieved the target of halving extreme poverty between 1990 and 2015. The poverty head count ratio (HCR) declined from 26.1 per cent in 1990 to 6.7 per cent by 2012–13, as is shown in Table 9.3, indicating that the MDG poverty target at the national level had been met well before the target year. This MDG target has already been met in both rural and urban sectors of the country, while the estate sector (plantation sector) is on track to meet it by 2015 (UNDP, 2012; UN, 2015). Sri Lanka has also already met the target of halving the proportion of the population without sustainable access to water and sanitation. Furthermore, the country is on track to meet many MDG targets such as achieving universal primary education, eliminating gender disparity in education at all levels, reducing child mortality, reducing maternal mortality and combating diseases including malaria (UN, 2015).

Despite these achievements, progress has been slow on a handful of MDGs and their targets. Sri Lanka's progress on halving the proportion of the population below the minimum level of dietary energy consumption has been inadequate to meet the MDG target by 2015. Approximately 48 per cent of the population was recorded as below the minimum level of dietary energy consumption in 2012–13, a figure that has to be brought down to 25 per cent by 2015 if the country is to meet the target. Moreover, over one-fifth of the children under 5 years of age remain underweight (UN, 2015).

Social protection policies, including the universal free education and healthcare policies, and various welfare programmes, particularly subsidy and food ration programmes, implemented by successive governments over many decades have contributed to the achievement of numerous MDGs and many targets being met.

The universal free education policy and the compulsory education policy that followed are two key government efforts that have contributed to Sri Lanka's achievement of near universal primary school enrolment and primary completion ratios and near gender parity in education at all levels – primary, secondary and tertiary. The free school textbook, free school uniform, mid-day meal and subsidised transportation programmes for students have also helped improve school enrolment and attendance among children, particularly among those from remote areas and from low-income groups (Tilakaratna et al., 2008).

It is noteworthy that many of the policies and programmes that have been instrumental in Sri Lanka's progress on MDGs 2 and 3 were initiated well before the declaration of the MDGs in 2000, and even before the 1990 base year, as is demonstrated in Table 9.4. Efforts by successive governments have helped the country to achieve high levels of school enrolment and high literacy rates at a relatively early stage. By 1990, Sri Lanka had already achieved a net primary school enrolment ratio of 88 per cent, with over 64 per cent of those who start Grade 1 reaching Grade 5. By the mid-1990s, the country had a net primary school enrolment ratio of over 95 per cent, youth literacy rate of 92.7 per cent, and girl-to-boy

Table 9.3 Summary statistics on selected MDGs and indicators

Goal/Indicator	*1990*	*2002**	*Latest*	*2015*
Goal 1: Eradicate extreme poverty and hunger				
Proportion of population below the national poverty line	26.1	22.7	6.7 (2012–13)	13.1
Poverty gap ratio	5.6	5.1	1.2 (2012–13)	2.8
Share of poorest quintile in the national consumption	8.9	7.0	7.2 (2012–13)	No target
Prevalence of underweight children under 5 years	38.0	29.0	21.6 (2006–07)	19.0
Proportion of population below the minimum level of dietary energy consumption	50.9	51.3	47.8 (2012–13)	25.0
Goal 2 : Achieve universal primary education				
Net primary school enrolment ratio	88.0	96.3	99.7 (2012–13)	100.0
Proportion of children starting Grade 1 who reach Grade 5	64.1	95.6	99.6 (2006–07)	100.0
Literacy rate in the age group 15–24	92.7 (1994)	95.6 (2001)	97.8 (2012)	100.0
Goal 3: Promote gender equality and empower women				
Ratio of girls to boys enrolled in primary school	94.2 (1995–96)	94.6	99.4 (2012)	100.0
Ratio of girls to boys enrolled at lower secondary level	91.2 (1995–96)	94.8	105.7 (2006–07)	100.0
Ratio of girls to boys enrolled at upper secondary level	107.7 (1995–96)	101.8	n/a	100.0
Ratio of girls to boys enrolled at tertiary level	75.4 (1995–96)	113.8	n/a	100.0
Goal 4: Reduce child mortality				
Under 5 mortality rate	22.2	13.5 (2003)	11.3 (2009)	8.0
Infant mortality rate (IMR)	17.7	11.3 (2003)	9.4 (2009)	6.0
Proportion of 1-year-old children immunised against measles	84.0	n/a	95.0 (2012)	100.0
Goal 5 : Improve maternal health				
Maternal mortality ratio	42.0	14.0 (2003)	7.4** (2009)	10.6
Proportion of births attended by a skilled birth attendant	94.1 (1993)	n/a	99.8 (2010)	100.0

Source: IPS (2010); UNDP (2012); UN (2015).

Note: All figures are percentages; * denotes that data in this column are for 2002 unless otherwise specified; n/a indicates that data are not available; ** figures of the Registrar General's Department.

Table 9.4 MDGs and social protection programmes and policies

MDG	*Key social protection programmes and policies*	*Year(s)*
Goal 1: Eradicate extreme poverty and hunger	• Food subsidy schemes (universal programme)	1948–77
	• Food stamp programme (targeted)	1977–94
	• *Janasaviya* Poverty Alleviation Programme	1989–94
	• Samurdhi programme	1994-present
	• Monthly assistance for disabled persons and elders	Post-2000
	• National supplementary food programme (Thriposha)	1973
	• Mother and Child Health Nutrition	Post-2000
	• Nutrition programme for pregnant and lactating mothers	Post-2000
Goal 2: Achieve universal primary education	• Universal free education policy	1945
	• Compulsory education for all aged 5–14 years	1998
	• Free school textbook programme for students	1980
	• Free school uniform programme	1993
	• Mid-day meal programme for students	Pre-1990
	• Grade 5 scholarship programme	Pre-1990
	• Subsidised transport (bus season tickets) for students	Pre-1990
Goal 3: Promote gender equality and empower women	• Universal free education policy	1945
	• Compulsory education for all between aged 5–14	1998
	• Free school textbook programme for students	1980
	• Free school uniform programme	1993
	• Mid-day meal programme for students	Pre-1990
	• Grade 5 scholarship programme	Pre-1990
	• Subsidised transport (bus season tickets) for students	Pre-1990
Goal 4: Reduce child mortality	• Universal free health policy	1940s
	• National supplementary food programme (Thriposha)	1973
	• Mother and Child Health Nutrition	Post-2000
	• Nutrition programme for pregnant and lactating mothers	Post-2000

Source: Compiled by the author.

ratios of over 90 at both the primary and secondary levels. Various policies and programmes in the post-1990 period, such as the compulsory education policy, have helped accelerate progress on MDGs 2 and 3. By 2012–13, the net primary school enrolment ratio had increased to 99.7 per cent, with almost 100 per cent of those who start Grade 1 reaching Grade 5, while the ratio of girls to boys was almost 100 per cent at the primary level and 105.7 per cent at the secondary level. The youth literacy rate had increased to 97.8 per cent by 2012, with a higher level of literacy among female youth.

Sri Lanka's progress on MDGs 4 and 5 can be to a large extent attributed to the universal 'free' health policy that was introduced over six decades ago, under which public healthcare and services are provided free of charge through government hospitals and dispensaries to all citizens throughout the country. Alongside free healthcare provision and improvement in the coverage of health services, the universal free education policy that resulted in higher literacy rates and educational attainment in the country, particularly among women, has also contributed to the significant reduction in infant, under-5 and maternal mortality rates since the 1950s. By 1990, the infant mortality rate had fallen to 17.7 per 1,000 live births from a rate of around 141 per 1,000 live births in 1946, while the under-5 mortality rate had declined to 22.2 per 1,000 live births. The under-5 mortality rate declined further to 11.3 per 1,000 live births by 2009 and the infant mortality rate (IMR) declined to 9.4 per 1,000 live births by 2009 (IPS, 2010; UN, 2015). The maternal mortality rate also saw a remarkable decline over many decades – by 1990, it was 42 per 100,000 live births, a rate much lower than those in many developing countries, and it declined further to 14 per 100,000 live births by 2003 and 7.4 per 100,000 live births by 2009, indicating that the country is well on track to achieve MDG 5 by 2015.

Despite the significant reductions in the poverty HCR and improved child and maternal health, under-nutrition remains an issue of great concern. About 48 per cent of the population was below the minimum level of dietary energy consumption in 2012–13, and figures have shown only marginal improvement since 1990. Moreover, around one-fifth of children under the age of 5 were underweight in 2006–07. The share of underweight (low weight for age) and stunted (low height for age) children is particularly higher in the estate sector and among low-income groups (IPS, 2010). Successive governments have attempted to improve nutritional levels among low-income groups, children and mothers through the Thriposha programme, Mid-day meal programme, Mother and Child Health Nutrition programme and Samurdhi subsidy and nutrition programmes. These programmes seem to have been inadequate to make substantial progress on meeting the MDG target on nutrition. As discussed in the previous section, some programmes like the Samurdhi subsidy programme suffer from weaknesses such as poor targeting, inadequacy of benefits, lack of clearly defined eligibility criteria and lack of entry and exit mechanisms.

Conclusions, emerging issues and implications for the post-2015 agenda

Sri Lanka has made substantial progress on many MDGs and targets that include achieving universal primary education, promoting gender parity in education, reducing extreme poverty and reducing child and maternal mortality. Various social protection policies and programmes carried out by successive governments over the past six decades, such as the universal free education and health policies and food subsidy and cash transfer programmes, have immensely contributed to this progress. Investments in the social sector – specifically education and health – since the 1940s has helped the country to make remarkable progress on literacy rates, school enrolment and reducing mortality rates at a much earlier stage than many other developing countries.

Despite this progress, further efforts are required in areas such as improving nutritional status in order to achieve the MDGs by 2015. Although significant progress has been made on the MDGs at the national level, further measures are needed to reduce existing disparities across regions and among income groups. Alongside universal measures, there is a need for more targeted programmes and policies focusing on vulnerable groups and lagging regions. The gaps and weaknesses in the current social protection system and existing programmes, such as low coverage, targeting errors, inadequate benefits and lack of coordination among institutions and programmes must be addressed.

A number of emerging issues beyond the MDGs and their associated targets stress the need for a more comprehensive social protection system in Sri Lanka. Despite the steady decline in the poverty HCR over the past decade and the attainment of the MDG target on poverty at the national level, a significant share of the population is clustered just above the official poverty line, facing the risk of slipping into poverty due to various shocks like economic stresses, vagaries of weather and life-cycle events. The country's estate sector, where the poverty HCR is the highest, has the largest proportion of this vulnerable population (Tilakaratna and Galappattige, 2013). Furthermore, over 60 per cent of employed persons are in the informal sector with little or no social security benefits (retirement and maternity benefits, sick leave and so on). The share of informal sector workers is particularly high in the agriculture sector (85 per cent), the construction, mining and quarrying sector (about 79 per cent) and the manufacturing sector (about 47 per cent) (DCS, 2012). Increasing informalisation of work is being seen in many formal sectors primarily due to the weaknesses of current regulations governing the labour market. The continuing low female labour force participation rate, currently 30–35 per cent, and high youth unemployment rate are other issues in the labour market that highlight the need to strengthen the social protection system.

Population aging is another emerging issue that challenges Sri Lanka's social protection system. By 2041, the share of the population over the age of 60 will double, meaning that around one-fourth of the population will be above 60 years of age (De Silva, 2012). Population aging raises concerns about the ability of the social protection system to cater to the needs of the growing number of elderly persons. Moreover, since the longevity of women is expected to increase further relative to that of men, there will be a larger share of women in the 60 years and above age group. This adds to the concerns because many women are less likely to have adequate social protection, specifically old-age retirement benefits, due to the continuing low female labour force participation rate in the country. In addition, old-age retirement benefit schemes are at present largely confined to the formal sector. Only a small share of informal sector workers have access to pension schemes. Many of these emerging issues are not unique to Sri Lanka, but rather are currently faced by many developing countries.

The role of social protection in achieving the MDGs has been widely recognised (UNICEF, 2010; UNDP, 2012). The Sri Lankan experience demonstrates that a variety of social protection policies and programmes carried out by successive governments over decades can help a country make substantial progress on many development goals and targets. Nevertheless, the importance of social protection goes beyond the current MDGs. Social protection can also play an important role in reducing inequality, reducing social exclusion and building resilience against risks and vulnerabilities. Emerging issues – vulnerabilities to various shocks, the increasing informalisation of work, continuing low female labour force participation and population aging – that are faced by many developing countries stress the need for more comprehensive social protection systems to ensure at least a minimum level of social protection for all. Thus, social protection has to be a key element of the post-2015 development agenda – either as a goal/target or as several targets under different goals, in particular those related to poverty and productive employment.

Notes

1 Department of Pensions of Sri Lanka.
2 This is a component of the government's largest poverty alleviation programme known as the Samurdhi programme.
3 The official poverty line at the national level for August 2013 was Rs. 3,774 (DCS, 2014).

References

ADB. (2011) *The Revised Social Protection Index: Methodology and Handbook*. Mandaluyong: Asian Development Bank (ADB).

CBSL. (2013) *Annual Report 2012*. Colombo: Central Bank of Sri Lanka (CBSL).

DCS. (2012) *Sri Lanka Labour Force Survey: Annual Report – 2011*. Colombo: Department of Census and Statistics (DCS), Sri Lanka.

DCS. (2014) *District Official Poverty Lines*. Colombo: Department of Census and Statistics (DCS), Sri Lanka. Available from: http://www.statistics.gov.lk/poverty/monthly_poverty/index.htm [Accessed: 10 April 2014].

De Silva, W. I. (2012) The age structure transition and the demographic dividend: An opportunity for rapid economic take-off in Sri Lanka. *Sri Lanka Journal of Advanced Social Studies*. 2 (1). pp.3–46.

Economic Commission for Africa (ECA), International Labour Organization (ILO), United Nations Conference on Trade and Development (UNCTAD), United Nations Department of Economic and Social Affairs (UNDESA) and United Nations Children's Fund (UNICEF). (2012) *Social Protection: A Development Priority in the Post-2015 UN Development Agenda*. New York: United Nations System Task Team on the Post-2015 UN Development Agenda.

Fiszbein, A., Kanbur, R. and Yemtsov, R. (2013) *Social Protection, Poverty and the Post-2015 Agenda*. Policy Research Working Paper 6469. Washington, DC: The World Bank.

Galappattige, A., Jayaweera, R., Perera, N. and Buhari, R. (2012) *The Democratic Socialist Republic of Sri Lanka: Updating and Improving the Social Protection Index*. Technical Assistance Consultant's Report, Project Number 44152. Mandaluyong: Asian Development Bank (ADB).

HLP. (2013) *A New Global Partnership: Eradicate Poverty and Transform Economies through Sustainable Development*. New York: High-Level Panel of Eminent Persons on the Post-2015 Development Agenda, United Nations.

IPS. (2010) *Millennium Development Goals Country Report 2008/09*. Colombo: Institute of Policy Studies of Sri Lanka (IPS).

Tilakaratna, G. (2012) *Universalisation of Social Security in Sri Lanka*. Paper Presented at the Regional Symposium on *Universalisation of Social Security in South Asia*, Co-organised by the South Asia Centre for Policy Studies (SACEPS) and Friedrich-Ebert-Stiftung, 3–4 October, Kathmandu, Nepal.

Tilakaratna, G. and Galappattige, A. (2013) Emerging Challenges for Social Protection in Sri Lanka. In *Sri Lanka: State of the Economy 2013 – The Transition to a Middle-Income Economy*. Colombo: Institute of Policy Studies of Sri Lanka (IPS).

Tilakaratna, G., Galappattige, A., Jayathilaka, R. and Perera, R. (2008) *Educational Opportunities for the Poor in Sri Lanka: Assessing Spatial Disparities*. Human Resource Development Series No. 6. Colombo: Institute of Policy Studies of Sri Lanka (IPS).

Tilakaratna, G., Galappattige, A. and Jayaweera, R. (2013) *Safety Nets in Sri Lanka: An Overview: Prepared for The World Bank*. Colombo: Institute of Policy Studies of Sri Lanka (IPS). Mimeo.

UN. (2015) *Millennium Development Goals Country Report 2014 – Sri Lanka*. Colombo: United Nations (UN), Sri Lanka.

UNDP. (2012) *Sri Lanka Human Development Report 2012: Bridging Regional Disparities for Human Development*. Colombo: United Nations Development Programme (UNDP) Sri Lanka Country Office.

UNICEF. (2010) *Social Protection: Accelerating the MDGs with Equity*. Social and Economic Policy Working Brief. New York: United Nations Children's Fund (UNICEF).

10 Measuring of progress of decent work to support the MDGs and post-MDGs

Luis Linares and Julio Prado

The purpose of this paper is to assess the contribution of progress on decent work to the achievement of the Millennium Development Goals (MDGs) in Guatemala. The study is based on indicators outlined in the System of Decent Work Indicators for Guatemala (SITDG in Spanish; see Coyoy (2013)), which was developed by the Association for Research and Social Studies (ASIES in Spanish) of Guatemala. Data were processed from Guatemala's 2012 National Survey of Employment and Income (INE, 2012).

With the United Nations Millennium Declaration, countries committed to "spare no effort to free our fellow men, women and children from the abject and dehumanizing conditions of extreme poverty, to which more than a billion of them are currently subjected" and "to making the right to development a reality for everyone and to freeing the entire human race from want" (UNGA, 2000, 4). To establish the right to development, they identified the eight MDGs, and the year 2015 as their target for achieving these goals.

As pointed out in *An Action Agenda for Sustainable Development*, the Sustainable Development Solutions Network (SDSN): "The Millennium Declaration and the Millennium Development Goals have successfully focused world attention and action on ending extreme poverty in all its forms and reducing gender inequality" (SDSN, 2013, 1). Nevertheless, not all countries will achieve all the goals by the end of 2015. Hence, the outcome document of the 2012 United Nations (UN) Conference on Sustainable Development, widely known as Rio+20, stated the need to continue with the task of ending extreme poverty and hunger, emphasising poverty eradication to be "the greatest global challenge facing the world today and an indispensable requirement for sustainable development" (United Nations, 2012, 1).

This link between poverty eradication and sustainable development is undoubtedly a major breakthrough. As pointed out by the SDSN, sustainable development is a holistic concept that addresses four dimensions of society: economic development, social inclusion, environmental sustainability and good governance (SDSN, 2013, 1). The holistic nature of the concept implies the need to take action on all four of these dimensions.

An important aspect highlighted by the SDSN is that the world has experienced changes between 2000 and 2015 that have resulted in the need to reconsider the focus of the MDGs. The SDSN suggests that the post-MDGs need to be relevant for the real world of 2015–2030, taking into account five major global shifts: "(i) the feasibility of ending extreme poverty in all its forms, (ii) a drastically higher human impact on the physical Earth, (iii) rapid technological change, (iv) increasing inequality, and (v) a growing diffusion and complexity of governance" (SDSN, 2013, 2).

The Millennium Declaration also states countries' commitment to "develop and implement strategies that give young people everywhere a real chance to find decent and productive work" (UNGA, 2000, 5). This commitment should be extended to the entire world population, regardless of age.

The link between decent work and the MDGs is easily demonstrated. According to the International Labour Organization (ILO), the objective of decent work helps to accomplish the eight MDGs within the context of the global fight against poverty. Full and productive employment must be the centre of economic and social policies and should be based on the four equally important strategic pillars of the Decent Work Agenda (ILO, 2010b). MDG 1 (eradicate extreme poverty and hunger), MDG 7 (ensure environmental sustainability) and MDG 8 (develop a global partnership for development) are priorities for reducing poverty that are inextricably linked to the concept of decent work, since dignified paid work is a key factor in improving family income, and thereby overcoming poverty.

Moreover, MDG 3 (promote gender equality and empower women) is a condition that must be met to achieve all the MDGs, and equality in employment and remuneration is one of the fundamental aspects of equality between men and women. MDG 2 (achieve universal primary education) depends largely on decent work for parents, a comfortable transition from school to working life and the elimination of child labour. Decent work is key to achieving both goals. Progress on MDGs 4, 5 and 6, each relating to health, can be accelerated if there is good coverage by social security programmes.

The MDGs should be addressed in concert, since together they form a comprehensive development vision (Maurás, 2005). This paper will focus on MDG 1: eradicate extreme poverty and hunger; MDG 2: achieve universal primary education; and MDG 3: promote gender equality and empower women.

The precise indicators included in the SITDG make it an exceptional instrument to measure progress on decent work. Such progress contributes directly to the achievement of MDGs 1, 2 and 3 and indirectly to the rest. As evidenced by ASIES's experience in the study published in 2013, the system is easy to implement and keep updated, insofar that periodic surveys on employment and incomes, or proxy indicators, are available.

On Sunday 2 August 2015, the United Nations Summit adopted the draft output document of the 2015 Development Agenda – *Transforming Our World: The 2030 Agenda for Sustainable Development*. Among others, it seeks to end poverty and hunger, achieve equality and foster peaceful, just and inclusive societies. It encompasses 17 Sustainable Development Goals (SDGs).

Goal 8 is directly linked to the topic of this paper: "Promote sustained, inclusive and sustainable economic growth, full and productive employment and decent work for all." Following are the targets, out of the 10 of this goal, that are related with the objective of decent work:

8.1 Sustain per capita economic growth and at least 7 per cent gross domestic product growth per annum in the least developed countries.
8.2 Promote development-oriented policies that support productive activities, decent job creation and entrepreneurship, encouraging the formalization of growth of micro, small and medium-size enterprises, including access to financial services.
8.5 Achieve full and productive employment and decent work for all women and men, young people and persons with disabilities and equal pay for work of equal value.
8.6 By 2020, substantially reduce the proportion of youth not in employment, education or training.
8.7 Eradicate forced labour, end modern slavery and human trafficking and eliminate the worst forms of child labour, including recruitment and use of child soldiers, and by 2025 end child labour in all its forms.
8.8 Protect labour rights, and promote safe and secure working environments for all workers, including migrant workers, in particular women, migrants and those in precarious employment.

Conceptual framework

The conceptual framework of this paper is built upon the three key concepts of sustainable development – human development and decent work – approached from a human rights perspective, as developed by the UN Office of the High Commissioner for Human Rights (UN-OHCHR), United Nations Development Programme (UNDP) and the ILO.

The traditional view of human rights is based on the three generations of rights. The rights of the first generation – individual and political – were classified as essential, immediately applicable and enforced by the state. Those of the second generation – economic, social and cultural – and the third generation, collective rights, were only regarded as desirable goals and their realisation was not a state obligation.

The human rights approach employed in this paper finds its basis in the principles contained in the 1993 Vienna Declaration of the World Conference on Human Rights, which states on Article 5, among others, that human rights are universal, indivisible, interdependent and interrelated, all individuals should be treated equally and that their rights bear the same weight (United Nations, 1993). This means that the fulfilment of a right is related to the satisfaction of other right(s) (Jiménez, 2007, 4).

Sustainable development, according to the prioritisation of the following definition in the Rio+20 outcome document, may be defined in the post-2015 development framework as:

> promoting sustained, inclusive and equitable economic growth, creating greater opportunities for all, reducing inequalities, raising basic standards of

> living, fostering equitable social development and inclusion, and promoting the integrated and sustainable management of natural resources and ecosystems that supports, inter alia, economic, social and human development while facilitating ecosystem conservation, regeneration and restoration and resilience in the face of new and emerging challenges.
>
> (United Nations, 2012, 1)

This definition acknowledges that democracy, good governance and the rule of law at the national and international levels are essential for sustainable development.

A complementary concept is that of human development, formulated by the United Nations Development Programme, which consists of "The expansion of people's freedoms to live long, healthy and creative lives; to advance other goals they have reason to value; and to engage actively in shaping development equitably and sustainably on a shared planet." Such expansion empowers people to actively participate in developing a shared planet and focuses on essential freedoms. According to this concept, development goals should focus on the real freedoms of people and promote positive social contexts for those freedoms (UNDP, 2010, 22).

The concept of decent work is understood as promoting "opportunities for women and men to obtain decent and productive work, in conditions of freedom, equity, security and human dignity" (ILO, 1999, 3), and is directly linked to the human rights approach. Rights at work – necessary conditions to work in an environment of freedom and fairness, especially those recognised as fundamental rights and the achievement of decent work – are essential for attaining a decent standard of living by the majority of people. The achievement of decent work involves four key pillars:

a Promoting work within a sustainable institutional and economic environment;
b Respecting, supporting and implementing fundamental core labour standards and rights;
c Embracing and broadening the scope of social protection;
d Encouraging social dialogue and tripartite activities.

The aforementioned dimensions of sustainable development complete the conceptual framework that guides this paper. These dimensions are essential for realising the three key concepts using a human rights approach.

This conceptual framework is consistent with the ideas typically mentioned during discussions on the post-2015 development framework that was largely outlined by countries at Rio+20. The outcome document reiterates that "eradicating poverty is the greatest global challenge facing the world today and an indispensable requirement for sustainable development" (United Nations, 2012, 1).

The outcome document comprises 26 thematic areas and intersectional issues. Under the area 'Promoting full and productive employment, decent work for all and social protection' there is concern about the conditions of the labour market and shortage of decent work opportunities, especially for women and youth.

It recognises that "workers should have access to education, skills, health care, social security, fundamental rights at work, social and legal protections, including occupational safety and health," a reference to the rights contained in the International Covenant on Economic, Social and Cultural Rights. It also highlights the roles that governments, unions, workers and employers should play in the dialogue on the concept of decent work (United Nations, 2012, 28–30).

In a communication titled *A Decent Life for All: Ending Poverty and Giving the World a Sustainable Future*, the European Commission (EC) implies that there is a fundamental link between poverty eradication and global environmental sustainability. In the preparation for Rio+20, the European Union proposals emphasised the need to "focus on resources which represent public goods and basic 'pillars of life', such as energy, water, food security, oceans, sustainable consumption and production, as well as social inclusion and *decent work*" (EC, 2013, 8; emphasis added).

Measurement of decent work in Guatemala

Since the ILO endorsed the concept of decent work, attempts have been made to address the difficulties of measuring the multidimensional nature of decent work. The ILO Declaration on Social Justice for a Fair Globalization stressed the importance of national and regional strategies for decent work and "the establishment of appropriate indicators or statistics, if necessary with the help of the ILO, to monitor and evaluate progress made" (ILO, 2008, 14). The ILO has made numerous efforts to measure decent work, including pilot projects to develop a system of indicators that can be applied by all countries. In the 2003 issue of *International Labour Magazine*, a group of experts from the ILO published an article on measuring decent work with statistical indicators, in which they suggest a set of categories for measuring the various dimensions of decent work (Anker et al., 2003). The concept of decent work is disaggregated into 10 categories, with an 11th on the economic and social context for decent work.

Since 2011, ASIES, with support from the European Union, has been implementing the project 'Strategic Dialogue on Decent Work and Informal Economy', with the objective of building the capacities of civil society to monitor public policies that aim to formalise the informal sector under a decent work framework. Project activities include the elaboration of a 'Proposal of National Decent Work Agenda'.

As recommended by the aforementioned ILO experts, ASIES developed the SITDG, which includes the following categories related to decent work:

- i Employment opportunities
- ii Unacceptable work
- iii Adequate earnings and productive work
- iv Decent hours
- v Stability and security of work
- vi Fair treatment in employment and at work
- vii Safe work environment

viii Social protection
ix Combining work and family life
x Social dialogue and workplace relations
xi Economic and social context of decent work

The database generated by the National Survey of Employment and Income (ENEI, 2012), executed by Guatemala's National Institute of Statistics, was used to develop the indicators, complemented with information from the Ministry of Labour and Social Welfare and the Guatemalan Institute for Social Security.

To further develop the Strategic Dialogue on Decent Work and Informal Economy project, this paper directly applies the data provided by the National Survey of Employment and Income and database generated by the SITDG.

Promoting work within a sustainable institutional and economic environment

The economically active population (EAP) in Guatemala is 6.24 million people, 64 per cent of whom are men and 36 per cent women (INE, 2012). Figure 10.1 shows that the unemployed population represents only a minimal share of the EAP. It also shows that nearly one-fifth of the population is visibly underemployed (individuals working fewer hours than they desire or need).

It becomes obvious from this data that, unlike developed countries, which have unemployment insurance, the most important variable in our environment is underemployment, which results in the underutilisation of labour and an income

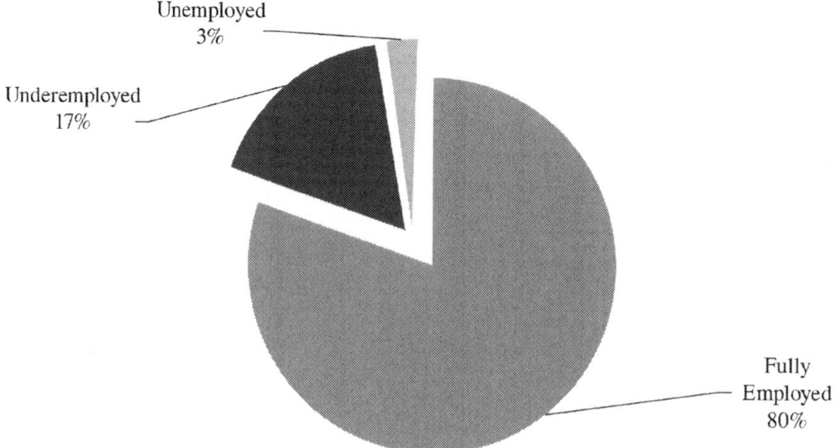

Figure 10.1 Distribution of EAP by employment

Source: Prepared by the authors based on the data from INE (2012).

lower than what the occupied workers expect to earn. The main reason behind this is that, in the absence of unemployment insurance, a person who becomes unemployed or cannot get a job has to engage in order to survive in any available economic activity, most of the time becoming self-employed or an unpaid worker in a family-operated business.

In relation to the hours worked per week by the EAP, the SITDG (2013) indicates that 14.5 per cent work less than 20 hours per week; 33.3 per cent work between 20 and 40 hours per week; 24.8 per cent work between 41 and 48 hours per week; and 27.4 per cent work over 48 hours per week.

The duration of the workday is a useful indicator for determining the quality of work. According to ILO, in industrial undertakings, decent work hours correspond to the working hours being lawfully admitted, which are set at a maximum of 8 hours a day and 48 hours in a week. The constitution of Guatemala, on the other hand, maintains a limit of 8 hours of work a day, but 44 hours in a week. Besides, a not-decent workday may involve excessive hours of work per day, which can be detrimental to both physical and emotional well-being. Overworking can be a sign of low wages, while underworking can signal to a lack of job opportunities (Anker et al., 2003).

Agriculture, farming, forestry and fishing industries continue to be the principal source of work in Guatemala, but according to the SITDG (2013), gross domestic product (GDP) per worker in 2011 amounted to USD 4,416, while the GDP per worker in agriculture reached only USD 1,506. The next most important area of economic activity is wholesale and retail trade, which also includes industries such as transport, storage, lodging and restaurants, and other food-related activities. Agriculture, farming, forestry and fishing industries, and wholesale and retail trade activities also have the higher number of underemployed individuals.

The first four occupational categories of the EAP, which are made up of salaried workers, include public sector employees, private sector employees, farm hands and labourers, and domestic employees and together account for 48 per cent of the EAP. Employers and partners account for less than 3 per cent, therefore the other half of the EAP is made up of self-employed and unpaid workers.

Youth aged 15–24 (3,091,422) represent 32 per cent of the 9,531,370 individuals in the Working-Age Population (WAP). Of those, 23.7 per cent (732,667) do not work or study, forming the group known as 'who neither work nor study'. People of the WAP aged 15–64 who are employed represent 65.4 per cent.

Surprisingly, in respect to education, the group of individuals without any education and the group with complete superior education are the groups that have the least percentages of unemployed, with the former group having the smallest percentage. Three groups with some education show high levels of unemployment. The largest unemployed is the group with complete secondary education. Overall, the groups with some and complete primary and secondary education account for 83.6 per cent of the unemployed.

For the employed, salaries are affected by laws and additional instructions. Guatemala has enforced minimum monthly salaries for a range of activities. As indicated by the SITDG (2013), professional instruction appears to be a positive factor on improving the salaries of individuals.

- Median real salary (affected by the consumer price index): GTQ 1,782.5[1]
- Employed with less income than two-thirds of the median (GTQ 1,140.8): 31.1 per cent
- Minimal salary as a percentage of the median salary: 152.7 per cent
- Salaried employees who received professional instruction in the past year: 4.9 per cent

Figure 10.2 divides the EAP by ranges of income. It clearly illustrates pervasive precarious conditions, with 52.2 per cent of individuals having an income less than or equal to the enforced minimum monthly salary for agricultural activities (GTQ 2,012, equivalent to USD 251.5) and an additional 3.2 per cent earning less than or equal to the enforced minimum monthly salary for non-agricultural activities (GTQ 2,290, equivalent to USD 286.3). This results in an approximate total of 55 per cent of individuals earning less or equal to the enforced minimum monthly salaries. Only 0.4 per cent of the EAP earn over GTQ 20,000, which is equivalent to USD 2,500 per month. The figure shows that a considerable number of respondents (18.6 per cent) did not provide data about their income (system missing), which accounts mainly for the non-remunerated family workers.

The monthly salary between men and women are nearly the same for those with salaries up to GTQ 10,000; the proportion of men to women is nearly the same.

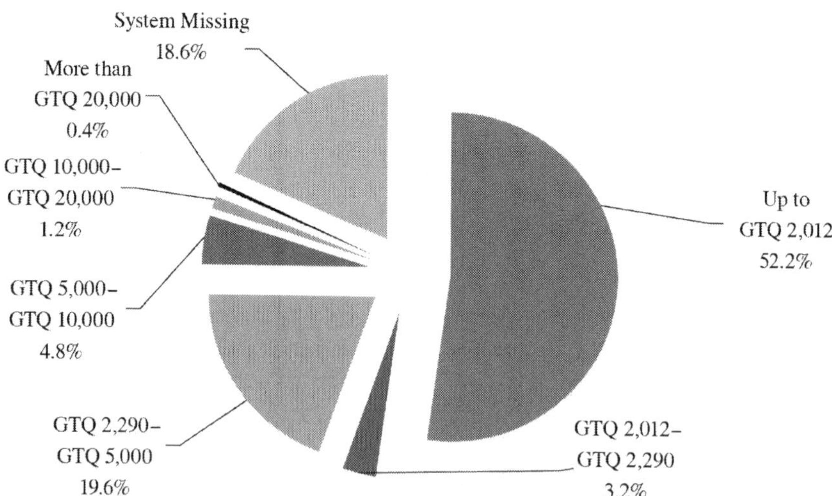

Figure 10.2 Distribution of EAP by income

Source: Prepared by the authors based on the data from INE (2012).

Above GTQ 10,000 per month, however, there is a decline in the proportion of women, reaching 8 per cent when it comes to monthly salaries of GTQ 20,000 or greater, which is equivalent to USD 2,500 or more.

Women have a high presence at the director and manager level, where they show a participation rate of only 5 per cent less than men do. They surpass men at the scientific and intellectual professional level by 4 per cent and are almost in equal proportion to men in administrative support. They have the highest participation rate in jobs related to selling in commercial and farmers markets (60.8 per cent), but salaries at this level are lower than at other levels.

Respecting, supporting, and implementing the core labour standards and rights

The ILO Declaration on Fundamental Principles and Rights at Work adopted by the International Labour Conference in 1998 states that there are four fundamental principles and rights at work that are recognised as fundamental both inside and outside of the ILO. They are:

- Freedom of association and the effective recognition of the right to collective bargaining
- The elimination of all forms of forced or compulsory labour
- The effective abolition of child labour
- The elimination of discrimination in respect of employment and occupation (ILO, 2010a).

Guatemala has ratified the associated conventions, which have been integrated into the Guatemalan Political Constitution, making the promotion and protection of the four fundamental principles and rights a government responsibility.

From the perspective of human rights, the exercise of human rights at work, as well as other economic and social rights such as the right to education, health and housing, are considered as a guarantee for the exercise of civil and political rights, since the former creates minimum material conditions for the exercise of the latter (Jiménez, 2007, 35).

The percentage of the EAP in Guatemala that holds a job at a private company or public institution with an existing or functioning labour union is 4.1, and 31.5 per cent of those are associated with a union. The SITDG (2013) indicates that the total union membership in Guatemala is 1.4 per cent of the EAP.

The only situation highlighted by the ILO with respect to the elimination of all forms of forced or compulsory labour has been the imposed obligation on the employees of some companies to work overtime in Guatemala. The ILO indicates that employees are only obligated to work overtime during the legal ordinary workday and that any overtime work must be a result of a mutual agreement between employers and employees.

Considering the effective abolition of child labour in Guatemala, 19 per cent of children aged 7–14 are involved in some kind of economic activity. This percentage goes up to 25 per cent for this age group in rural areas, with male children representing 71 per cent and females 29 per cent. Ethnicity can be a great disadvantage. Indigenous children represent 60 per cent of the child labour force. Notably, 81 per cent of working children are classified as unpaid workers. By economic activity, 67 per cent are employed in the agricultural sector. By type of occupation, 79 per cent work in non-skilled labour occupations (INE, 2012).

Regarding the elimination of discrimination in respect of employment and occupation, discriminatory practices have been observed at some companies in Guatemala, especially in relation to opportunities for women to access the job market.

All of the above statistics and considerations are clear evidence that working conditions in Guatemala are precarious. Precarious labour is defined as labour activities that deviate from the legal standards of formal employment. These standards include access to social security and employment benefits; a continuous, normal salary; uncontrolled labour union association; and a safe and secure workplace.

Embracing and broadening the scope of social protection

Social protection in Guatemala is determined primarily by affiliation to the health and pension system administered by the Guatemalan Institute for Social Security. At the time of writing, coverage by the institute is limited to employees in the public and private sectors who work on a relation of dependency for an employer who is affiliated to the system. But even for those employees in a dependency relation – 48 per cent of the EAP (approximately 3 million people) – only about 33 per cent are covered by social security. In accordance with the affiliated population reported by the Guatemalan Institute for Social Security (IGSS by its initials in Spanish) for the year 2012, the report shows the number of beneficiaries to be 1,185,866, which is actually equivalent to 19 per cent of the EAP (IGSS, 2013, 3).

In Guatemala, 65 years is the eligibility age for a government pension. The SITDG (2013) reports that 353,064 individuals (48 per cent) of those over 65 years of age receive a pension, but of that total 32 per cent receive income from the National Programme for Older Persons, which assigns only a minimal non-contributory monthly pension of GTQ 500, which is equivalent to USD 62.5.

Employment vulnerability is an aspect that helps identify the level of social protection for workers. The INE understands vulnerability to be the situation where employees are not covered by social security or do not enjoy the advantages of salaried workers such as public and private employees and, in some instances, even farm hands and labourers. Estimates show that 48 per cent of the EAP is in a vulnerable circumstance.

Regarding health and occupational safety, the SITDG (2013) reports a rate of 2,281 work accidents for every 100,000 employees covered by social security. There is no information on the accident rate for the rest of the population not covered by social security.

Encouraging social dialogue and tripartite activities

ILO is the only tripartite UN agency where upper management bodies (governing body and International Labour Conference) participate in social dialogues as equal representatives along with workers' organisations, employers and the representatives of the governments of the member states. A social dialogue, according to the ILO, promotes the permanent relation between government, employers and employees for consultation and negotiation on issues related to work and the regulation of labour relations. It is seen as the most adequate way to create rigorous standards and policies that contribute to democratic governance, stability and social cohesion (Ghai et al., 2006).

Due to low union membership and fragmentation suffered by labour unions in Guatemala, collective negotiations between employers and employees are limited. In 2012, only 35 collective agreements on working conditions were registered – 10 of those were for private companies and 25 for public institutions. Limited collective negotiations in the country indicate the importance of tripartite dialogue on agreements that prevent and solve labour disputes and accords on themes of common interest.

The main space for tripartite dialogue in Guatemala is the Tripartite Commission on International Labour Affairs. Established in 1995, it brings together the Ministry of Labour and Social Welfare, employers and employees. In 2012, the Guatemalan National Congress created the Economic and Social Council (CES in Spanish), conceived according to the model of councils existing in various European countries, a model that has also been adopted by councils in Honduras and El Salvador. The CES is a permanent consulting body that provides support to government on economic and social public policies. It includes eight representatives from each of the following sectors: cooperatives, employers and employees, and its primary purpose is to provide space for ongoing social dialogue.

MDG advancements in Guatemala

As mentioned, the concept of decent work is integral to the achievement of MDGs 1, 2 and 3. In Guatemala, progress on these goals has been fraught by difficulties related to labour. Issues affecting the achievement of each of these goals will be analysed in turn.

MDG 1: Eradicate extreme poverty and hunger

The UN uses two indicators on poverty for this goal – extreme and general poverty – that necessarily relate to hunger. Changes in poverty in Guatemala over time are illustrated in Table 10.1. Table 10.2 compiles a number of evident trends related to labour since the base year of 1989.

Conditional cash transfers are one of the preferred instruments used by Latin American governments to reduce extreme poverty. Guatemala started a programme

Table 10.1 Poverty indicators for MDG 1

Poverty	*Base year*	*Subsequent evolution*			*Goal*	*BREACH*
	1989	*2000*	*2006*	*2011*	*2015*	
Extreme poverty (%)	18.1	15.7	15.2	13.3	9.1	4.2
Population (millions)	n/a	1.8	2.0	1.9	–	–
General poverty (%)	62.8	56.2	51.0	53.7	31.4	22.3
Population (millions)	n/a	6.4	6.6	7.9		

Source: SEGEPLAN (2010).

Table 10.2 Labour-related trends relevant to MDG 1 (in per cent)

Description	*1989*	*2000*	*2006*	*2012*
Contribution from the lowest quintile of the population to national income	n/a	2.8	2.9	–
Contribution from the highest quintile of the population to the national income	n/a	61.8	60.3	–
Growth rate of labour productivity	<0.1	−1.7	−0.8	–
Relation employment/population	48.7	57.4	57.7	64.5
EAP living in extreme poverty	n/a	12.7	12.4	–
EAP self-employed or working in a family business	49.9	45.7	47.4	–

Source: SEGEPLAN (2010).

called *Mi Familia Progresa* (My Family Makes Progress) in 2008 that provides conditional targeted cash transfers to help families living in extreme poverty conditions and ensure children's health and education. The programme has reached 302 out of 334 municipalities, covering 862,000 families with a total of 4.8 million beneficiaries (33 per cent of the country's population), which includes 2.3 million children. The transfer is GTQ 300 (USD 37), divided into a health bonus for women with children aged 0–6 and an education bonus for families with preschool and primary school children aged 6–15 years. In 2011, these transfers totalled GTQ 1.2 billion, equivalent to USD 150 million. With respect to eradicating hunger, bags of food under the name *bolsa solidaria* (solidarity bag) were delivered to poor families in urban areas within the department of Guatemala. These bags include 33 pounds of diverse food essentials, such as rice, beans and cooking oil.

The conditional cash transfers programme is currently the responsibility of the Ministry of Social Development (created in 2012). The government in 2013 reported covering 308 municipalities and 776,390 beneficiaries. Funding of GTQ 783 million, equivalent to USD 98 million, was allocated to the programme.

MDG 2: Achieve universal primary education

The effective abolition of child labour is a significant goal that will effectively allow children to gain a primary education and develop their potential as envisioned in

MDG 2. As mentioned, the problem of child labour is concentrated in rural areas. According to the ENEI (2012), child employment rate in rural areas of Guatemala is 25 per cent, while in the metropolitan area (capital and surrounding), the prevalence of children involved in an economic activity is only 7 per cent. SISCA (2013) underlines the fact that primary school attendance has indeed improved in Guatemala. The net rate of schooling at the primary level reached 98 per cent in 2009, with the percentage of students who start and finish primary school increasing from 48 per cent to 78 per cent and the ratio of girls to boys in enrolment at the primary level reaching 93 per cent and 90 per cent at the secondary school level.

MDG 3: Promote gender equality and empower women

A useful indicator for the achievement of MDG 3 is the share of women in wage employment in the non-agricultural sector. In Guatemala, women represented 35 per cent of salaried workers in this sector in 1989, 37.6 per cent in 2006 (SEGEPLAN, 2010), and 47 per cent in 2012 (INE, 2012). Another important indicator for gender equality is the percentage of women covered by social security. In 2011, women represented 37 per cent of the EAP, which is problematic when only 18.9 per cent per cent of the total population (IGSS, 2011, 36) in Guatemala is covered by social security and a dependency relation in formal employment is required for coverage.

Conclusions

Progress on decent work is essential to achieving the MDGs, with measurement of such progress remaining a challenge moving into 2015. A commitment to provide opportunities for decent work alongside a progress measurement framework should be a part of the post-MDGs. Nine conclusions are evident from this study that would be valuable in discussions on such a commitment and framework during the ongoing dialogue on the post-2015 development framework.

First, the human rights approach emphasises the universality, indivisibility and interdependence of the various categories of human rights and the responsibility of the state to promote and protect them. This approach leads to the understanding that sustainable development is a result of the effective realisation of individual, political, economic, social and cultural rights. The human rights approach deserves a place in formulating the post-MDGs.

Second, it has become increasingly clear that the achievement of decent work, poverty eradication and sustainable development are inextricably linked. The Rio+20 outcome document identifies ‘promotion of decent work for all’ as one of the most important catalysts for the eradication of poverty. The implementation of the post-2015 development framework should recognise these things.

Third, given that decent work is an essential element in the achievement of poverty eradication, the development of the SITDG in Guatemala is an important step that allows the assessment of the various categories comprising the concept of decent work according to a set of indicators that can be applied by all countries.

Fourth, in Guatemala, there is a lag in the participation of women in the labour market, which influences the incomes of families, particularly affecting the earning capacities of households headed by women. Such lags must be addressed there and worldwide.

Fifth, Guatemala's low unemployment rate can be explained by the absence of unemployment insurance, and this weakness forces people who cannot get salaried jobs to join the informal economy either as independent workers or through self-employment. Extending social security must be a priority for developing countries during the post-MDGs period.

Sixth, in Guatemala, only one out of four workers are employed within the ordinary hours of the legal workday, while one out of four workers works more hours than the legal workday. About 17 per cent of the EAP are underemployed and are working fewer hours than they would like. Enforcing a legal workday should be a focus in the post-2015 development framework.

Seventh, the agricultural sector remains the largest employer in Guatemala, despite the agriculture, farming, forestry and fishing industries together contributing only 10.9 per cent to the GDP. This indicates low labour productivity, which fell between 1989 and 2006, according to the latest data available. Specific attention must be given to decent work in the agricultural sector and labour productivity both in and outside the sector in the post-MDGs period.

Eighth, in Guatemala, the high degree of informality in the labour market remains a problem. Self-employed workers in agricultural and non-agricultural activities account for just over 27 per cent of the total labour force, while unpaid workers (usually working in family businesses) represent almost 20 per cent. These workers are part of the two-thirds of Guatemala's working population who are not covered by social security. Informal labour must be urgently addressed alongside the extension of social security in the post-MDGs period.

Ninth, the low rate of union membership in Guatemala and consequently reduced presence of collective bargaining, especially in the private sector, affects the ability of workers to effectively participate in social dialogue processes, especially in direct dialogue with employers in the field of business or the different branches of economic activity. This highlights the need to strengthen social dialogue spaces existing at the macro level, including the Tripartite Commission on International Labour Affairs and the Economic and Social Council. These platforms can help reach agreements to advance the goal of decent work, especially in relation to fundamental rights of workers.

Note

1 GTQ denotes Guatemalan Quetzal.

References

Anker, R., Chernyshe, I., Egger, P., Mehran, F. and Ritter, J. (2003) La medición del trabajo decente con indicadores estadísticos. *Revista Internacional del Trabajo*. 122 (2). pp.125–160.

Coyoy, E. (2013) *Desarrollo del Sistema de Indicadores de Trabajo Decente para Guatemala*. Ciudad de Guatemala: Asociación de Investigación y Estudios Sociales.

EC. (2013) *A Decent Life for All: Ending Poverty and Giving the World a Sustainable Future*. Brussels: European Commission (EC).

Ghai, D., Godfrey, M., Hepple, B., Kuruvilla, S. and Saith, A. (2006) *Material Pedagógico sobre el Trabajo Decente*. Ginebra: Instituto Internacional de Estudios Laborales.

IGSS. (2011) *Informe Anual de Labores 2011*. Guatemala City: Instituto Guatemalteco de Seguridad Social (IGSS).

IGSS. (2013) *Resumen del Informe Anual de Labores 2012*. Guatemala City: Instituto Guatemalteco de Seguridad Social (IGSS). Available from: http://www.igssgt.org/07_informes_estadisticas/documentos/resumen_ial2012.pdf [Accessed: 15 January 2014].

ILO. (1999) *Decent Work*. Geneva: International Labour Organization (ILO).

ILO. (2008) *ILO Declaration on Social Justice for a Fair Globalization*. Geneva: International Labour Organization (ILO).

ILO. (2010a) *ILO Declaration on Fundamental Principles and Rights at Work and Its Follow-up*. Geneva: International Labour Organization (ILO). Available from: http://www.ilo.org/declaration/thedeclaration/textdeclaration/lang/en/index.htm [Accessed: 8 February 2014].

ILO. (2010b) *The Millennium Declaration, the MDGs and the ILO's Decent Work Agenda*. Geneva: International Labour Organization (ILO).

INE. (2012) *Encuesta Nacional del Empleo e Ingresos (ENEI)*. Guatemala City: Instituto Nacional de Estadística Guatemala (INE).

Jiménez, W. (2007) *Enfoque de los Derechos Humanos y las Políticas Públicas*. Bogotá: Universidad Sergio Arboleda.

Maurás, M. (2005) *Presentación del documento interinstitucional sobre el cumplimiento de los objetivos de desarrollo del Milenio en la región*. Discurso de la señora Marta Maurás, Secretaria de la Comisión para CEPAL. Mar del Plata: América Latina y el Caribe de las Naciones Unidas (CEPAL).

SDSN. (2013) *An Action Agenda for Sustainable Development*. New York: Sustainable Development Solutions Network (SDSN).

SEGEPLAN. (2010) *Tercer Informe de Avances en el Cumplimiento de los Objetivos de Desarrollo del Milenio*. Guatemala: Secretaría de Planificación y Programación de la Presidencia de la República de Guatemala (SEGEPLAN).

SISCA. (2013) *Los Objetivos de Desarrollo del Milenio en Centroamérica y República Dominicana: Estado de Avance*. San Salvador: Secretaría de la Integración Social Centroamericana (SISCA).

SITDG. (2013) *Desarrollo del Sistema de Indicadores de Trabajo Decente para Guatemala*. Ciudad de Guatemala: Asociación de Investigación y Estudios Sociales.

UNDP. (2010) *Human Development Report 2010 – The Real Wealth of Nations: Pathways to Human Development*. New York: United Nations Development Programme (UNDP).

UNGA. (2000) *United Nations Millennium Declaration*. A/RES/55/2. New York: United Nations General Assembly (UNGA).

United Nations. (1993) *Vienna Declaration and Programme of Action Adopted at the World Conference on Human Rights*. Vienna: United Nations (UN).

United Nations. (2012) *The Future We Want*. A/CONF.216/L.1. Rio de Janeiro: United Nations (UN).

11 Unpacking the middle

A class-based analysis of the labour market in Sri Lanka

Vagisha Gunasekara

Introduction

Middle-income countries (MICs), the homes to the 'global middle class', are also currently homes to two billion other people – 80 per cent of the world's poor who live on under USD 2 per day (World Bank, 2013). Two-thirds of the world's population, who live on under USD 1.25 per day, live in MICs. Although above the global poverty line (and even national poverty lines), many of the people who are classified as part of the new middle class may, in fact, hover just above the poverty line and remain vulnerable to poverty. Moreover, a significant proportion of this 'middle' may engage in informal, precarious work that exacerbates multiple vulnerabilities. As such, many in the middle may face realities that are similar to those of their poor counterparts. It is too soon to celebrate the growth of this middle as the motor of growth and domestic demand. The fleeting gains made on one score, poverty reduction, often get lost because of unabated or worsened unemployment and inequalities that token policies often fail to address in meaningful ways.

A lot has been written about the benefits of the middle class (Easterly, 2001; Amoranto, Chun and Deolalikar, 2010; Birdsall, 2010; Chun, 2010; Kharas, 2010; AfDB, 2011; Loyaza, Rigolini and Llorente, 2012). Many scholars have focused on estimates of the size of middle classes in various countries and others have examined trends in working poverty. Less is known about the specific job-related features of different economic classes and the extent that labour markets are inclusive of poor and near-poor workers vis-à-vis middle-class workers (Kapsos, 2004; ILO, 2011). It is generally understood that ensuring adequate and secured livelihoods for each individual and inclusivity in the labour market is an important prerequisite for social mobility and the emergence of a stable middle class. However, country-level studies examining employment of workers from various economic classes are few. This paper presents new measurements of workers by economic class and their distinguishing employment characteristics in Sri Lanka, a brand-new entrant to the MIC category.

Approach and methodology

This paper takes a closer look at the links between economic class and different labour market variables related to economic participation and employment in Sri

Lanka. It highlights the features that distinguish the poor from the middle class in terms of education, access to better quality jobs, working conditions and opportunities for young people.

Adopting past practice, a cross-tabulation of employment status and economic class status are presented as the estimates of employment by economic class. Employment status is defined at the individual level (whether or not an individual is employed), and economic class is determined by per capita household consumption of the household in which the individual lives. Total employment in a given class is equal to the number of individuals of working age who are employed and living in a household with per capita consumption or income between the upper and lower bounds of per capita consumption for a particular economic class.

The methodology adopted for this paper requires primary household-level data on Sri Lanka. The primary data source used in this paper is the Sri Lanka Household Income and Expenditure Survey (HIES) for 2009–10. This survey was conducted by the Department of Census and Statistics of Sri Lanka. The survey is cross-sectional in nature and adopts a two-stage stratified sampling frame (DCS, 2009–10). The HIES includes information on income and expenditure as well as the demographic and other socio-economic characteristics of household members. The 2009–10 survey covers 25,000 housing units. It is important to note that the analysis of economic class and employment as presented in this paper is primarily descriptive and does not examine longitudinal trends or assess causality. Therefore, inferences about whether higher economic class leads to better access to wage employment, or conversely if holding a salaried job leads to higher economic class status, are not attempted. In addition to academic and policy literature, supplementary data sources, such as desk reviews of surveys, evaluation studies and grey literature covering a wide range of low-income countries (LICs) and MICs, are utilised in this study.

Defining economic class

There is little consensus in the literature on an absolute definition of economic 'class'. This study adopts the economic class definitions established in Kapsos and Bourmpoula (2013) and Huynh and Kapsos (2013), which classify working individuals with incomes below USD 1.25 per day (at purchasing power parity) as the 'extreme working poor' (Class 1), those living on between USD 1.25 and USD 2 per day as the 'moderate working poor' (Class 2) and those living on between USD 2 and USD 4 per day as 'near-poor workers' (Class 3). Given the relatively small cohort of workers with incomes above USD 13 per day in Sri Lanka, the two 'middle class' categories as stated in Kapsos and Bourmpoula (2013) – comprising of workers living on from USD 4 to USD 13 per day and USD 13 and above – have been combined to form the 'developing middle class and above' (Class 4).

The application of a class-based framework, albeit rigid (and arguably arbitrary),[1] provides a slightly more nuanced understanding of employment challenges that must be addressed in the post-2015 agenda. Further disaggregation by sex and age helps emphasise key concerns for poor women and youth and policy measures that can improve their positions in the labour force. The class-based framework was employed solely to question the assumptions about MICs and the new middle class in the developing world, and thereby caution policymakers not to dilute the notion of inclusive growth by merely implementing the standard variety of poverty-alleviation programmes. Failure to reform the processes that assure continued enrichment of the relatively small upper crust of society, enjoying both direct and indirect support and use of public exchequer as ordained by the logic of market-determined economic processes, will only worsen the social exclusion of billions of people.

Economic growth and the right to full, productive and decent employment

Work is one of the most defining aspects of a person's life. Having a job is not merely a means to receive a wage and survive – it provides a way to become a part of societal processes. As such, the notion of work is a conscious activity, purposive and fulfilling in that it allows human beings to be *someone*. Unemployment and underemployment have direct economic costs such as the loss of potential output and income, deterioration of labour skills and productivity, lower tax revenues and serious social costs such as poverty, inequality, malnutrition and injustice. Schokkaert and van Ootegem (1990), as quoted in Sen (1997, 156), say that unemployment is an injustice since "the unemployed may feel deprived because of the lack of freedom in their lives, and this goes well beyond just the lowness of income." For these reasons, it is important that governments design and implement policies to achieve full employment of the labour force as a way of ensuring inclusive growth.

According to Felipe (2010), full employment refers to zero involuntary unemployment and zero involuntary part-time employment. The latter is particularly important in developing countries, where underemployment is a much more serious problem than open unemployment. While policymakers often show interest in implementing policies that reduce unemployment, there is a general sense of ignorance about the actual places of individuals on the economic and social playing field, their relative and absolute positions, and the levels, growth and sustainability of their well-being and contributions to national-level economic variables and hence to development (Kabra, 2012). The stark reality in most developing countries is that large segments of their populations are forced to live without consistent or adequate means of income due to exclusion from mainstream market activities. Palliatives such as social protection schemes are not lasting solutions to fulfil the needs, rights and aspirations of people at the lower rungs of society. As such, the objective of policymaking must also be to generate decent employment that provides a living wage, employee benefits, reasonable job security and a sound work environment.

Although hardly any policymaker would protest policies that generate full, productive and decent employment, there is reason to emphasise the importance of such policies. An assumption made by mainstream proponents of economic growth is that rapid economic growth resulting from open markets and globalisation of market processes in turn creates employment in developing countries. But the realities in many developing countries falsify this assumption. In those countries, there is broad consensus that creating adequate and assured livelihood opportunities for all working-age individuals is one of the most daunting challenges. Contemporary theories of economic growth that stem from the experiences of Western industrialised democracies understand unemployment to be a cyclical issue, not an endemic structural problem as it is understood in developing countries (Kabra, 2012). Thus, these theories do not assign the level of priority to employment as needed in the contexts of developing countries. Rather, employment occupies a secondary place and is regarded as a by-product of economic growth, capital accumulation, technological progress and macroeconomic balance (Kabra, 2012). This is not to disregard the importance of economic growth, but to point out that it will not, by itself, deliver full, productive and decent employment for all.

Employment in neoliberalised Sri Lanka

The structural adjustment process and internal and external liberalisation that began in 1977 in the country was expected to boost growth in agriculture, industry and services by removing the barriers stipulated by protectionist policies, a higher rate of employment growth and a higher growth rate of the incomes of workers engaged in these labour-intensive sectors (Jayasuriya, 2010).

In the years following liberalisation and despite a civil war that spanned nearly three decades, Sri Lanka has maintained a healthy rate of economic growth over time, registering an average annual growth rate of 6.53 per cent from 2003 to 2014 and recording an all-time high of 8.6 per cent in the fourth quarter of 2010 (Trading Economics, 2014). This favourable trend has been premised on structural transformation that steered the economy away from agricultural production to value-added service-oriented activities. Changes in the Sri Lankan labour market, however, have not been commensurate with the gains in economic growth.

In 1980, the agriculture sector absorbed 46 per cent of all employed persons, but by 2012, this share had dropped to 30 per cent. The manufacturing sector now accounts for one-fourth of all employed persons, while the services sector accounts for roughly half (DCS, 2012). Unemployment rates declined to 3.9 per cent for males and 10.2 per cent for females in 2012, but the nature of available employment options remains a matter of concern. Job creation in the formal private sector is relatively low, and roughly two-thirds of the Sri Lankan labour force is employed in the informal sector (DCS, 2006). This is a particularly worrying observation since economic growth in recent years has not managed to create decent jobs for the growing and educated labour force (Gunatilaka, 2008).

One explanation for the growth of informal employment is the slow pace of formal job creation in Sri Lanka. A 2005 assessment conducted by the World Bank and the Asian Development Bank (ADB) noted that Sri Lanka has very low job flows relative to other countries (World Bank and ADB, 2005). Moreover, firms at or below 14 workers are less likely to increase employment compared with firms above the threshold (Gunatilaka and Vodopivec, 2010). These observations are largely attributed to Sri Lanka's restrictive labour regulations, particularly the Termination of Employment of Workers Act of 1971, which makes it very difficult for firms to fire or lay off employees (Gunatilaka and Vodopivec, 2010). Interestingly, however, evidence from India questions whether slow job creation in the formal sector is entirely dependent on the nature of labour regulations (Kabra, 2012). In the absence of an equivalent to Sri Lanka's act, India faces similar challenges in the area of job growth in the formal sector. Thus, the changing nature of production (in favour of high-value consumption goods as opposed to mass consumption products) and lack of incentives for the growth of small and medium-sized enterprises (e.g. high unofficial 'fees' and charges by public officials when obtaining permits, licenses and registrations, lack of information and knowledge on core business activities, and a general lack of a business-friendly environment) may serve as plausible alternative explanations for the negative trends observed in both countries (Kabra, 2012).

Findings

This study presents a number of key findings that warrant further discussion. First, as indicated in Figure 11.1, individuals from higher economic classes have higher labour force participation rates in comparison to those from lower classes.

Despite reaching MIC status, Sri Lanka has a disproportionately high proportion of economically inactive and unemployed individuals among the extremely poor. Economic inactivity could be due to old age, physical or mental disabilities that make it difficult for individuals to gain employment in a country that offers

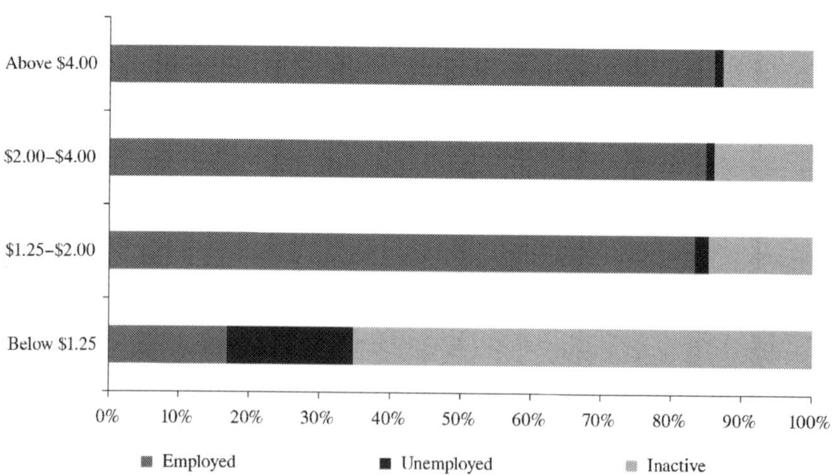

Figure 11.1 Distribution of employed, unemployed and economically inactive in total population aged 15+ by economic class

Source: Author's calculation based on DCS (2009–10).

limited options for the differently abled, or a lack of motivation to participate in the labour force. Aside from the old aged, the economic inactivity of these other two groups is a matter of concern because it suggests labour market exclusion. What this means is that Sri Lanka's economy has not grown on a sufficient scale to absorb the expanding labour force, which in turn has resulted in adverse employment outcomes. This situation is inherently tied to the pattern of economic growth in the recent past. As such, achieving desired employment outcomes for the lower classes will be contingent upon reversing some aspects of the prevailing pattern of production that enables retrenched workers to get back into the labour force and simultaneously benefit from social assistance.

Second, as indicated in Figure 11.2, this study finds that educational attainment is positively related to economic class with tertiary education being elusive for many living under or just above the poverty line.

Young extremely poor, moderately poor and near-poor workers have significant difficulties in accessing higher education opportunities and gainful employment options. In the Sri Lankan context, access to primary and secondary education is less of an obstacle than access to higher education, particularly for low-income groups, although it is the quality of public education that is the matter of greater concern.[2] The diminishing quality of public education is invariably associated with the marketisation of education and the lack of government spending on higher education.[3] The sharp rise of 'private tuition' by teachers (who are part of the public school system) and increasing competition for university admission push students to 'purchase' market-offered education as a ticket to higher education (de Silva et al., 1991; de Silva, 1994; Gunawardena, 1994; Nanayakkara and Ranaweera, 1994; Aturupane, Glewwe and Wisniewski, 2013). This trend leaves

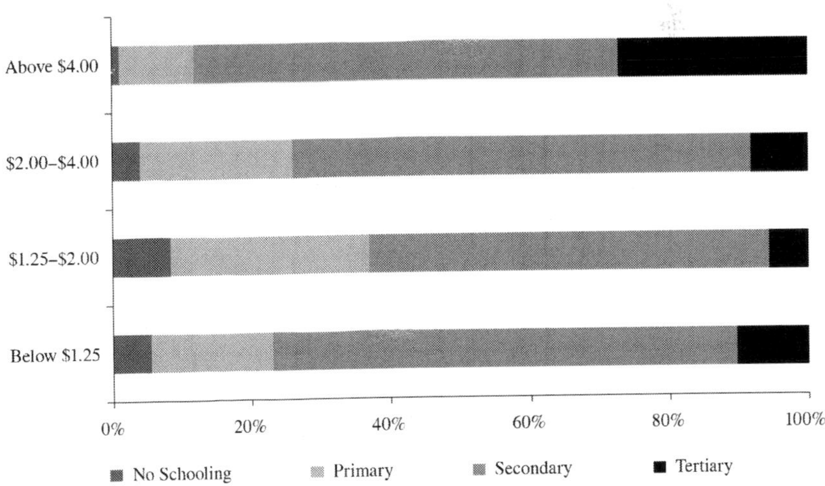

Figure 11.2 Distribution of labour force aged 15+ by education and economic class

Source: Author's calculation based on DCS (2009–10).

behind students from low-income groups who are unable to afford the extra help that is offered by the market. Moreover, the emergence of private higher education institutions, which boast affiliations with prestigious foreign universities, charge exorbitant fees for degree programmes and offer alternatives to individuals from wealthier families who are either unable or unwilling to attend local universities. Given the wide assortment of education options at their disposal and social networks that open avenues for employment, youth from relatively affluent families get a head start in the labour force, whereas their poor counterparts are gradually robbed of their rights to education and work. Thus, measures that improve the quality of education and access to higher education and skills training for the poor and near-poor must be supplemented with structural reforms concerning public spending for education and the marketisation of education.

Youth, particularly young females, face considerable obstacles in accessing employment. Sri Lanka's national labour force participation rates for youth aged 20–24 years and 25–29 years are 56 per cent and 65.9 per cent, respectively, compared to around 70 per cent for older age groups (UNDP, 2014). Among youth are the currently unemployed and the 40 million estimated first entrants into the job market (UNDP, 2014). The latest Youth and Development report (National Human Development Report 2014) finds that around 19 per cent of young workers are unsatisfied with their current jobs, and a further 15.5 per cent engage exclusively in unpaid household work. Prior studies find a mismatch between the supply of job-seekers with higher education levels and job aspirations and the demand for workers with those levels of educational attainment (Arunatilake and Jayawardena, 2010). Evidence points to the inability of the Sri Lankan education system to teach general skills (e.g. command over the English language and computer skills) essential for securing 'good' jobs (Arunatilake and Jayawardena, 2010), which is a reflection of the quality of education highlighted earlier in this discussion. The lack of formal employment opportunities for youth is generally explained by the slow rate of job creation, skills mismatch and queuing[4] (Arunatilake and Jayawardena, 2010). There is intense competition for a limited number of desirable jobs and most vacancies are in low-skill occupational categories. Available jobs that require few skills may not meet the expectations of many young workers with higher education who aspire to sophisticated white-collar jobs, which in turn results in high levels of underemployment.

However, fixating on supply-side interventions – higher education, vocational training and enhancement of skills – all of which increase an individual's 'employability', is only one part of the solution. The presence of a sizable population of unemployed educated youth in Sri Lanka indicates that the benefits of supply-side interventions are unlikely to be commensurate with related outlays. While the importance of long-term policy focus on improving the quality of education is crucial for MICs, recalibrating economic growth models to become inclusive and create decent jobs that can absorb the growing labour force is equally important. There is an urgent need to create jobs at the middle and higher ends of the occupational hierarchy and improve working conditions of low-skill occupations so that the job market appeals to job-seekers with diverse skill sets.

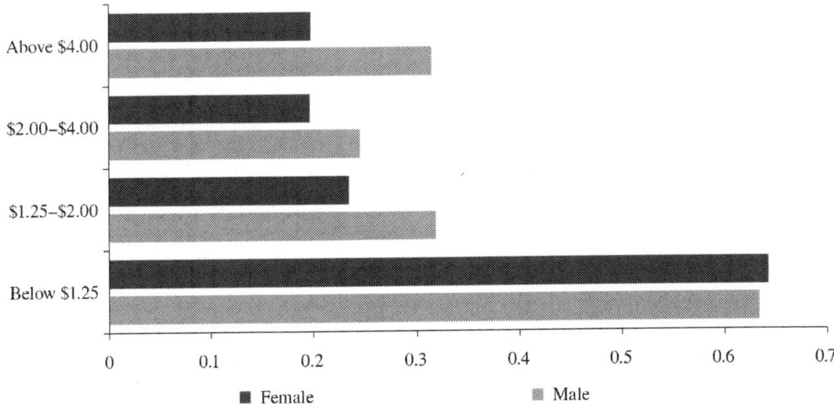

Figure 11.3 Share of vulnerable employment (own-account and contributing family workers) in total employed population aged 15+ by sex and economic class

Source: Author's calculation based on DCS (2009–10).

Third, as indicated in Figure 11.3, vulnerable employment – jobs in the agricultural sector, casual wage labour, own-account work and contributions to family activities – is significantly linked to lower economic classes.

In South Asia, the poor and the near poor vis-à-vis middle-class workers face notable disadvantages in accessing better quality jobs. Although the size of the services sector has increased at the expense of the agriculture sector, this change cannot be viewed as 'employment-friendly'. While this situation may be viewed by mainstream proponents of economic growth as 'normal', a large population of agricultural workers is denied full, productive and decent employment as they face difficulties in gaining access to decent work. Moreover, whether low-quality informal and irregular employment or own-account work with harsh conditions, low productivity and low and uncertain remuneration can even be considered 'employment' in an inclusive growth model is a matter that requires further discussion and reflection. This situation must be addressed in a systematic manner with investment in infrastructure and by striking a balance during sectoral transition from agriculture to the production of value-added goods and services (in a way that maintains agricultural output and consistent food production).

Finally, as indicated in Figure 11.4, gender disparities in labour force participation and job quality are prevalent across all economic classes in Sri Lanka.

Higher household affluence is associated with relatively widening gender gaps in economic activity, which signal institutional discrimination that is sharpened by the patriarchal biases of employers, or reflect women's choices not to engage in paid labour. This finding questions the generally accepted positive association between education and employment as Sri Lanka boasts high educational attainment levels for women relative to their male counterparts. The narrow range of skills typically acquired by women, gender segregation by occupation, demand

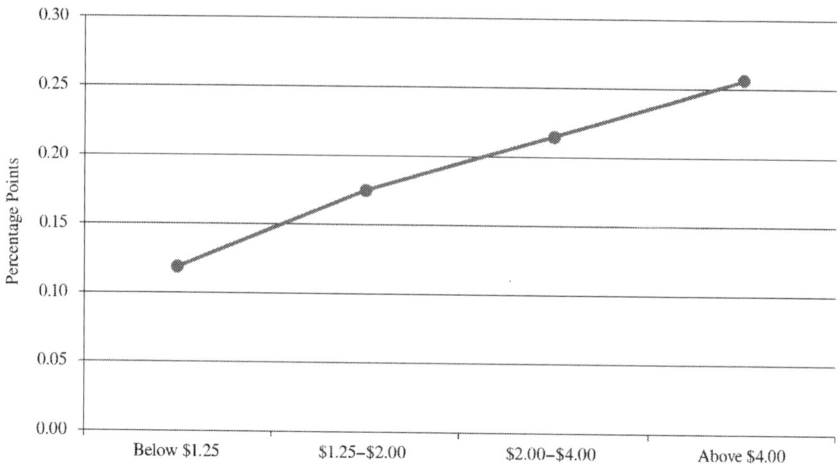

Figure 11.4 Male–female gap in labour force participation rates aged 15+ by economic class

Source: Author's calculation based on DCS (2009–10).

for low-cost female labour and the dual/multiple roles of women – paid work and unpaid reproductive and family responsibilities – are considered obstacles to women's participation in paid employment (Wijayaweera, 2012). The finding from Sri Lanka also challenges the widely accepted notion that 'middle-class values' facilitate the removal of barriers faced by women in entering the labour force, suggesting that affirmative action measures, family-friendly employment benefits and gender sensitisation of employees in both public and private sectors should be adopted to encourage women's participation in the labour force regardless of their economic class.

Previous studies that examine the gender wage differential for Sri Lanka find that discrimination in the labour market, rather than differences in productive characteristics, account for a large fraction of the gender wage gap (Aturupane, 1993; Ajwad and Kurukulasuriya, 2002). Gunewardena (2003) finds that although the rates of return to education in employment are higher for women, occupational segregation of men and women has a negative impact on women's wages, since wages are depressed in the predominantly female professions of teaching and nursing (Gunewardena, 2003). Moreover, while the high levels of educational attainment by females indicate a rational response to the higher rates of return to education in employment, a bias against women still persists at the level of unskilled labour (Gunewardena, 2003). In addition to gender wage gaps, there are also noticeable differences in wages along ethnic lines, particularly among young workers. Young Tamil men living outside the North and East are underpaid in comparison to Sinhala men in the same regions (Gunewardena, 2010).

Larger unexplained wage differentials in the public sector relative to the private or agricultural sectors may reflect language constraints or patronage politics. Ethnic wage gaps among young females are largely explained by productive characteristics (i.e. low levels of education among minority women). This observation indicates a need for policymakers to redress gender bias in the labour market, especially for young and unskilled women, while continuing investment in the education of both women and men.

Conclusions and recommendations for the post-2015 agenda

This paper has discussed characteristics that distinguish the poor from the middle class in terms of education, access to better quality jobs, working conditions and opportunities for young people and women. Since "ending poverty" ranks high among the proposed goals for the post-2015 development agenda, it is important to reinforce the well-established link between poverty reduction and gainful employment and push for development goals and targets that foster inclusive growth in a meaningful way.

The proposed goals and targets of the post-2015 agenda tackle the issues of employment in proposed Goal 8: "promote sustained, inclusive and sustainable economic growth, full and productive employment and decent work for all" (United Nations, 2015). The above analysis suggests that the economic growth models of developing countries need to be recalibrated in a way that enables individuals from lower economic classes to access gainful employment, which in turn will facilitate poverty reduction and social mobility of low-income groups. While Target 8.2 under the proposed goal advocates to "achieve higher levels of economic productivity of economies through diversification, technological upgrading and innovation, including through a focus on high value added and labour-intensive sectors" (United Nations, 2015), evidence from Sri Lanka suggests that the lower classes need an extra boost during their participation in this transition. Felipe (2010) suggests a strategy of carefully approaching the transition to value-added production without compromising the well-established importance of a thriving agricultural sector. The policy recommendation, then, is to redress the neglect of agriculture or renew efforts to revive the sector.

Agriculture has been considered the most important pursuit of Sri Lankan people. It has greatly conditioned the socio-economic environment of the country and continues to dominate every sphere of the economy. Although agriculture's contribution to gross domestic product (GDP) has declined over the decades, it must be noted that more than 30 per cent of the labour force still make their livelihoods directly or indirectly based on this sector (DCS, 2013a). However, for decades, agriculture has been neglected in Sri Lanka as well as in many other developing countries that have been attempting to emulate the growth track of East Asian countries. While the prospect of achieving fast economic growth via export orientation is attractive, the neglect of agriculture in favour of industrialisation may lead to food crises that are otherwise preventable. If growth in Sri Lanka is to be inclusive, then agriculture will have to be made a policy priority.

Although it could be argued that a better strategy might be to reallocate the agricultural labour force (mostly low-paid workers) from the agriculture sector to more productive sectors such as construction, manufacturing and services, an increase in employment outside of agriculture without a concomitant increase in food production may cause real wages to decrease. For this reason, reviving the agriculture sector, creating productive and decent employment opportunities in this sector, alongside stimulating sectoral transformation is a careful balancing act that policymakers should aim to strike. Relatedly, developing countries must increase public investment in basic infrastructure – energy, transport and urban facilities and services – targeted at high-employment projects and supply-side interventions (i.e. higher education, skills training, health, etc.) that would enable the labour market to be more inclusive.

The discussion above suggests that production choices must be reconsidered in tandem with the design of more employment-friendly policies. Such changes challenge the neoliberal model of economic growth and the choice of production that is associated with comparative advantage. The growth–employment link will likely get eroded owing to the policy of opening up the domestic market to imports. In 2007–08, for every one rupee of domestic manufactured goods, Sri Lanka imported Rs. 1.94 worth of foreign manufactured goods (Department of Commerce, 2012). This is a classic scenario in which imports disrupt the domestic economy in terms of production output, employment and their inter-linkages. In order to address this likely scenario, macro-level changes must be supplemented by support mechanisms that allow the growth of micro, small and medium-sized enterprises (e.g. credit opportunities, investment, business development, training, etc.) that tend to be overlooked in the current paradigm of economic growth. Maintaining demand to be filled by enterprises by means of stimulation packages seem crucial for many MICs that have employment challenges owing to labour market exclusion.

In a series of papers, Rodrik (2004, 2006) argues that a country's structural transformation requires 'strategic collaboration' between the public and private sectors to arrive at areas in which the country has a comparative advantage. The reason for such collaboration is that governments and entrepreneurs may have different sets of information and there may be a lack of communication between them. As such, the process of structural transformation, which is integral to the industrialisation of a country, should be a joint initiative between the public and private sectors to determine new economic activities. The question then is not whether to protect, but *how* to protect and promote industry in order to guarantee technological progress leading to higher labour productivity. These efforts require a private sector that is ready to invest in mutually agreed upon initiatives.

Also required is a sound macroeconomic environment at the national, regional and international levels. Governments, more often than not, are obsessed with deficits. 'Deficit fetishism' does not allow governments to address the difference between the saving desire of the private sector and the required government expenditure on an economy to run at full employment (Stiglitz et al., 2006). However, when analysing deficits, whether or not a country is operating at full employment should be factored in (Felipe, 2010). For instance, if a country is at full employment, deficits are likely to crowd out private investment given high interest rates accompanied by high inflation. If the country is not at full employment, the aforementioned adverse effects may not arise. As such, governments should exogenously increase aggregated demand (i.e. increase expenditure) when private sector spending falls short of the full-employment level of effective demand, but reduce aggregate demand (i.e. increase taxation) if this spending exceeds the full-employment level (Felipe, 2010). The balancing act of maintaining government expenditure at a level that induces neither inflation nor deflation is a difficult though achievable feat.

Target 8.5 under proposed Goal 8 for the post-2015 agenda, "by 2030 achieving full and productive employment and decent work for all women and men, including for young people and persons with disabilities, and equal pay for work of equal value" (United Nations, 2015), is supported by the evidence in this study. The findings in this study advocate targeted assistance to retrenched workers in lower economic classes that allows them to access gainful employment. The analysis above highlights the indispensable function played by the informal economy in Sri Lanka, providing means of livelihood to those who are excluded from the formal sector. Although precarious in nature, accessing informal employment serves as a survival and coping strategy for the majority of workers in developing countries who are cut off from regular wage employment due to a lack of productive characteristics and discriminatory social and institutional norms. This situation requires action – public, private or mixed – that enables informal workers to acquire secure and adequate livelihoods that provide a level of reward for work consistent with a minimum standard of basic needs. This minimum standard should be re-evaluated periodically to reflect realistic and current standards of living.

Target 4.4 under proposed Goal 4 for the post-2015 agenda, which advocates the provision of "relevant skills, including technical and vocational skills, for employment, decent jobs and entrepreneurship" (United Nations, 2015), is also supported by the evidence in this study. In the context of MICs, this target must be further qualified to specifically assist excluded low-income groups within the population who lack access to good-quality education that provides general and specialised skills required in the evolving labour market. Without targeting excluded groups, governments will only give lip service to the blanket priority of "improving access to education," rather than have real and effective impacts on the ground.

Finally, the findings of this study suggest that there is a need for high-quality and timely disaggregated data on employment. While most developing countries currently collect data according to internationally accepted standards and definitions, diverse labour market realities need to be captured as well. For example, most South Asian countries have informal economies that are proportionally larger than their formal economies. However, data on the informal sector lack contextual depth. Labour in both the formal and informal sectors is not captured in consistent and robust ways. Additionally, relevant authorities in countries must revisit their definitions of employment in order to ensure accurate representation of the total labour force. For instance, while the official unemployment rate in Sri Lanka was only 4.4 per cent in 2013, the official definition of employment is very broad. It includes those individuals working a minimum of one hour during the reference week, indicating that there is a strong possibility that widespread underemployment could be undermining prospects for many workers (DCS, 2013b). Apparently, more than 20 per cent of employed individuals who are willing to work 35 hours or more in a week do not have the opportunity to do so (Karunatilake, 2006). The availability of high-quality, context-sensitive data that provide an accurate picture of unemployment and underemployment will assist in the process of restructuring required in most labour markets in developing countries to achieve full employment.

The recommendations of this study are either superficially or substantially included in the United Nations' *Sustainable Development Goals* (see United Nations, 2015). While this is a positive sign, the post-2015 agenda must respond adequately to the accumulated evidence for and increasing challenge of immense livelihood insecurity in MICs. The time has come for governments to finally address the reality that achieving full, productive and decent employment must be deliberately and unequivocally integrated into the economic growth models of developing countries.

Notes

1 When factoring in the cost of survival in Sri Lanka, even USD 4 a day cannot be considered a living wage. According to the DCS (2012–13), the monthly average household expenditure of an urban household is estimated to be LKR 59,001 (relative to USD 15 per day per household or roughly USD 4 per day per person), and the monthly average expenditure of a rural household is estimated to be LKR 37,561 (relative to USD 9.5 per day or roughly USD 2.5 per day per person). The 2014 national poverty line is LKR 3,924 per person per month, which is almost USD 1 a day.

2 Arunatilake (2006) examined the factors that determine unequitable rates of education participation among students aged 5–14 years, finding that demand-side problems such as poverty, direct and indirect costs of schooling, and cultural factors as well as supply-side shortcomings, such as the quality of education, affect the schooling of the observed group.

3 Sri Lanka's public spending on education has remained at 2–3 per cent of gross domestic product (GDP) during the past decade and a half, compared to a 3.5 per cent average across the rest of South Asia. General education, which includes primary and secondary levels, absorbs the largest share of total education expenditure. In 2005, higher education received a meager 14 per cent of the education budget, whereas technical training was granted an abysmal 3 per cent (World Bank, 2008).

4 The idea of a labour/employment queue refers to the sets of individuals that compete for job openings at the same time and are rank ordered by the employer. Understanding the rank orderings that employers impose on candidates for job vacancies becomes a high priority for accounts of the determinants of inequality.

References

AfDB. (2011) *The Middle of the Pyramid: Dynamics of the Middle Class in Africa*. Market Brief, April. Tunis: African Development Bank (AfDB).

Ajwad, M. I. and Kurukulasuriya, P. (2002) Ethnic and gender wage disparities in Sri Lanka. *Sri Lanka Economic Journal*. 3 (1). pp.1–26.

Amoranto, G., Chun, N. and Deolalikar, A. (2010) *Who Are the Middle Class and What Values Do They Hold? Evidence from the World Values Survey*. Working Paper No. 229. Manila: Asian Development Bank. (ADB).

Arunatilake, N. (2006) Education participation in Sri Lanka: Why all are not in school. *International Journal of Educational Research*. 45 (3). pp.137–152.

Arunatilake, N. and Jayawardena, P. (2010) Explaining Labor Market Imbalance in Sri Lanka: Evidence from Jobsnet Data. In Gunatilaka, R., Mayer, M. and Vodopivec, M. (eds.) *The Challenges of Youth Employment in Sri Lanka* (pp.19–48). Washington, DC: The World Bank.

Aturupane, H. (1993) *Is education beneficial? A microeconomic analysis of the impact of education on economic welfare of a developing country*. Ph.D. thesis. University of Cambridge, Cambridge, UK.

Aturupane, H., Glewwe, P. and Wisniewski, S. (2013) The impact of school quality, socio-economic factors and child health on students' academic performance: Evidence from Sri Lankan primary schools. *Education Economics*. 21 (1). pp.2–37.

Birdsall, N. (2010) *The (Indispensable) Middle Class in Developing Countries; Or, the Rich and the Rest, Not the Poor and the Rest*. Working Paper 207. Washington, DC: Center for Global Development (CGD).

Chun, N. (2010) *Middle Class Size in the Past, Present, and Future: A Description of Trends in Asia*. Working Paper No. 217. Manila: Asian Development Bank (ADB).

DCS. (2006) *Additional Bulletin of Labour Force Statistics in Sri Lanka*. Colombo: Department of Census and Statistics (DCS), Government of Sri Lanka.

DCS. (2009–10) *Household Income and Expenditure Survey*. Colombo: Department of Census and Statistics (DCS), Government of Sri Lanka.

DCS. (2012) *Sri Lanka Labour Force Survey: Annual Report – 2012*. Colombo: Department of Census and Statistics (DCS), Government of Sri Lanka.

DCS. (2012–13) *Sri Lanka Household Income and Expenditure Survey 2012–13*. Colombo: Department of Census and Statistics (DCS), Government of Sri Lanka.

DCS. (2013a) *Gross Domestic Product 2013 – Annual*. Colombo: Department of Census and Statistics (DCS), Government of Sri Lanka.

DCS. (2013b) *Quarterly Report (Second Quarter): Sri Lanka Labour Force Survey*. Colombo: Department of Census and Statistics (DCS), Government of Sri Lanka.

Department of Commerce. (2012) *Total Imports, Exports and Balance of Trade in Sri Lanka 2005–2012*. Colombo: Department of Commerce, Government of Sri Lanka.

de Silva, W. A. (1994) The present status of private tutoring in Sri Lanka. *Economics Review*. 20 (2, 3). pp.4–7, pp.20–24.

de Silva, W. A., Gunawardane, C., Jayaweera, S., Perera, L. and Rupasinghe, S. (1991) *Extra School Instruction, Social Equity and Educational Quality (Sri Lanka)*. Report prepared for the International Development Research Centre, Singapore.

Easterly, W. (2001) The middle class consensus and economic development. *Journal of Economic Growth*. 6 (4). pp.317–335.

Felipe, J. (2010) *Inclusive Growth, Full Employment, and Structural Change: Implications and Policies for Development Asia*. London: Anthem Press.

Gunatilaka, R. (2008) *Informal Employment in Sri Lanka: Nature, Probability of Employment and Determinants of Wages*. New Delhi: International Labour Organization (ILO).

Gunatilaka, R. and Vodopivec, M. (2010) Labour Market Institutions and Labour Market Segmentation in Sri Lanka. In Gunatilaka, R., Mayer, M. and Vodopivec, M. (eds.) *The Challenges of Youth Employment in Sri Lanka* (pp.49–68). Washington, DC: The World Bank.

Gunawardena, C. (1994) The emergence of private tuition in Sri Lanka. *Economics Review*. 20 (2, 3). pp.8–10.

Gunewardena, D. (2003) Reducing the gender wage gap in Sri Lanka: Is education enough? *Sri Lanka Economic Journal*. 3 (2). pp.177–207.

Gunewardena, D. (2010) An Analysis of Gender and Ethnic Wage Differentials among Youth in Sri Lanka. In Gunatilaka, R., Mayer, M. and Vodopivec, M. (eds.) *The Challenges of Youth Employment in Sri Lanka* (pp.217–241). Washington, DC: The World Bank.

Huynh, P. and Kapsos, S. (2013) *Economic Class and Labour Market Inclusion: Poor and Middle Class Workers in Developing Asia and the Pacific*. Geneva: International Labour Organization (ILO).

ILO. (2011) *Key Indicators of the Labour Market*. Geneva: International Labour Organization (ILO).

Jayasuriya, L. (2010) *Taking Social Development Seriously: The Experience of Sri Lanka*. New Delhi: Sage Publications India.

Kabra, K. N. (2012) Employment in Neoliberal India. In Alternative Survey Group (ed.) *Alternative Economic Survey, India: Two Decades of Neoliberalism* (pp.419–450). Delhi: Daanish Books.

Kapsos, S. (2004) *Estimating Growth Requirements for Reducing Working Poverty: Can the World Halve Working Poverty by 2015?* Employment Strategy Paper 14. Geneva: International Labour Organization (ILO).

Kapsos, S., and Bourmpoula, E. (2013) *Employment and Economic Class in the Developing World*. ILO Research Paper No. 6. Geneva: International Labour Organization (ILO).

Karunatilake, C. P. A. (2006) *Trends in Labour Markets and Future Challenges: The Experience of Sri Lanka*. Colombo: Centre for Banking Studies, Central Bank of Sri Lanka (CBS).

Kharas, H. and Gertz, G. (2010) The New Global Middle Class: A Cross-Over from West to East. In Li, C. (ed.) *China's Emerging Middle Class: Beyond Economic Transformation* (pp.32–54). Washington, DC: Brookings Institution.

Loyaza, N., Rigolini, J. and Llorente, G. (2012) Do middle classes bring about institutional reforms? *Economic Letters*. 116 (3). pp.440–444.

Nanayakkara, G. L. S. and Ranaweera, M. (1994) Impact of private tuition and the educational challenges of the 21st century. *Economics Review*. 20 (2, 3). pp.11–17.

Rodrik, D. (2004) *Industrial Policy for the Twenty-First Century*. Paper prepared for the United Nations Industrial Development Organization (UNIDO). John F. Kennedy School of Government, Harvard University, Cambridge, MA.

Rodrik, D. (2006) *Industrial Development: Stylized Facts and Policies*. Paper prepared for United Nations Department of Economic and Social Affairs (UNDESA). John F. Kennedy School of Government, Harvard University, Cambridge, MA.

Schokkaert, E. and Van Ootegem, L. (1990) Sen's concept of the living standard applied to the Belgian unemployed. *Recherches Economiques de Louvain (Louvain)*. 56. pp.429–450.

Sen, A. (1997) Inequality, unemployment and contemporary Europe. *International Labour Review*. 136 (2). pp.155–172.

Stiglitz, J. E., Ocampo, J. A., Spiegel, S., French-Davis, R. and Nayyar, D. (2006) *Stability with Growth: Macroeconomics, Liberalization and Development*. New York: Oxford University Press.

Trading Economics. (2014) *Sri Lanka GDP Annual Growth Rate*. Available from: http://www.tradingeconomics.com/sri-lanka/gdp-growth-annual. [Accessed: 15 August 2014].

UNDP. (2014) *Sri Lanka National Human Development Report: Youth and Development.* Colombo: United Nations Development Programme (UNDP), Sri Lanka.

United Nations. (2015) *Sustainable Development: Knowledge Platform*. Available from: https://sustainabledevelopment.un.org/topics [Accessed: 18 September 2015].

Wijayaweera, U. (2012) *Female Employment Challenges and Opportunities for Inclusive Growth.* Colombo: Institute of Policy Studies of Sri Lanka (IPS).

World Bank. (2008) *Building the Sri Lankan knowledge economy*. Available from: http://siteresources.worldbank.org/SOUTHASIAEXT/Resources/223546–1206318727118/4808502–1206318753312/slknowledgeeconomy.pdf [Accessed: 10 July 2014].

World Bank. (2013) *World Development Indicators 2013.* Washington, DC: The World Bank. Available from: http://databank.worldbank.org/data/download/WDI-2013-ebook.pdf [Accessed: 11 July 2014]

World Bank and ADB. (2005) *Sri Lanka: Improving the Rural and Urban Investment Climate*. Washington, DC: The World Bank.

12 Social institutions and gender inequality in fragile states

Are they relevant for the post-MDG debate?[1]

Boris Branisa and Carolina Cardona

Introduction

The UN High-Level Panel of Eminent Persons on the Post-2015 Development Agenda (HLP), while advising on the global development framework beyond 2015, established the need for a new development paradigm and urged for five transformative shifts (UN High-Level Panel, 2013). The fifth required shift (to forge a new global partnership) articulates the need to build a new global partnership towards a new spirit of solidarity, cooperation and mutual accountability that must underpin the post-2015 agenda. The first required shift (to leave no one behind) asserts that the international community should ensure that no person – regardless of ethnicity, gender, geography, disability, race or other status – is denied of the universal human rights and basic economic opportunities. If the idea of 'leaving no one behind' is taken seriously, it is evident that there are countries in the world that deserve special attention: the so-called fragile states. The OECD (2013), for example, argues that we must ensure that fragile states are not left behind and warns that fragility remains one of the biggest obstacles to global peace and development.

It has been estimated that one billion of the world's population in 2006, including the 340 million of the world's extreme poor, were living in fragile states, and that 70 per cent of these states were located in Africa (Collier, 2008). Fragile states have consistently experienced slower economic growth than other low-income countries (LICs) with a rise in the rate of extreme poverty. Over the period 1990–2006, fragile states performed worse than other stable developing countries in terms of attaining the Millennium Development Goals (MDG) targets (Harttgen and Klasen, 2010). It is believed that many fragile states will not achieve the MDGs by 2015, as they have 50 per cent higher levels of malnutrition, 20 per cent higher levels of child mortality and 18 per cent lower primary education completion rates than other LICs (World Bank, 2007).

Following the reasoning of Baranyi and Powell (2005), who claim that gender inequality is a "central feature of state fragility," this paper focuses on an issue that appears particularly relevant for fragile states and which has not received enough attention in the literature: social institutions related to gender inequality. These are defined as societal practices and legal norms that frame gender roles and the distribution of power between men and women in the family, the market, and social and political life (de Soysa and Jütting, 2007; Branisa et al., 2014). We show that fragile states perform worse than non-fragile developing countries in terms of social institutions related to gender inequality.

The paper takes into account the empirical results from Branisa, Klasen and Ziegler (2013), who, using a sample of more than 100 developing countries, suggest that apart from geography, political system, level of economic development and religion, one should also consider gender inequality related to social institutions for a better account of disparities in critical developmental impacts. The present paper argues that it is important for the post-2015 development agenda to take into cognisance the view championed by Amartya Sen (Sen, 1999) that freedom is intrinsic and instrumental to development.

Trying to address the institutional gender constraints in fragile states should be high on the priority agenda in promoting development in those countries. On the one hand, from an *intrinsic* point of view, it should be clear that fragile states should take into account the inequalities in social institutions as relevant constraints while designing policies for gender-oriented development outcomes. This is an issue that should be addressed outright to eliminate the deprivation against women; it is crucial for the balanced 'sustainable development' which is a promise of the post-2015 era.

On the other hand, we should keep in mind that different kinds of freedom interrelate with one another, and freedom of one type may to a great extent help in advancing freedom of other types (Sen, 1999). From this *instrumental* point of view, we should consider the studies at the cross-country level that show that social institutions related to gender inequality are associated with, and appear to be relevant for, several development outcomes such as female education, child mortality, fertility and governance in developing countries (e.g. Branisa, Klasen and Ziegler, 2013). Reducing gender inequality does not benefit women only, but the society as well, in the long run.

Therefore, one could think of including a special set of indicators to measure the persisting gender inequalities in the social institutions in both fragile and non-fragile states as part of the post-MDG agenda. It is also important to think of special measures to help fragile states improve their situation and reduce gender inequality, as part of the new global partnership towards a new spirit of solidarity, cooperation and mutual accountability.

In recent years, there have been some attempts to define fragile states. Regrettably, a consensus does not exist for classifying 'fragile states' due to a lack of information and a common framework. It is also important to note that the term 'fragile state' has empirical and normative shortcomings; hence, some agencies use the terms 'fragility' or 'situations of fragility' (OECD, 2012). The OECD (Organisation for Economic Co-operation and Development) identifies five types of state fragility that reflect different vulnerabilities to violent conflict or humanitarian crisis: (i) weak states, (ii) divided states, (iii) post-war states, (iv) semi-authoritarian states and (v) collapsed states (Jones et al., 2008).

This paper follows the classification proposed by the OECD (2013), which establishes 47 'fragile states' that can be used for quantitative analyses. The 47 countries are from the World Bank/African Development Bank/Asian Development

Bank–harmonised list of fragile and post-conflict countries for 2012 and the 2011 Failed State Index (FSI). The list includes all countries rated 'alert' (FSI above 90) or 'critical' (FSI between 80 and 90) on the FSI index (OECD, 2013).[2] These countries are all defined as 'fragile', but they are not an entirely homogenous group. In 2012, 26 of the 47 fragile states were low-income fragile states (LIFS), and 21 were middle-income fragile states (MIFS). A decade before, all 47 were considered LIFS.

We consider that the classification proposed by the OECD (2013) is practical and based on a reasonable framework. Nevertheless, and as a robustness check for the empirical part of this paper, we use additional classifications of fragile states. These are (i) the FSI 2013 definition (FFP, 2014); (ii) the CPIA 2008 definition (Klasen, 2013); and (iii) the DFID definition (Klasen, 2013).[3] Around two-thirds of the countries classified as 'fragile' by these three agencies are low-income economies, and one-third are lower-middle-income economies.

The remainder of this paper is structured as follows. The next section discusses the situation of the MDGs in fragile states and non-fragile developing states. The subsequent section argues that social institutions play a key role in gender inequality, particularly in the fragile states. The last section offers some concluding remarks.

Fragile states and the MDGs

In the last decade many countries have experienced major economic and social progress towards the MDGs, allowing households and individuals to move out of poverty (Harttgen and Klasen, 2010). However, this achievement has been uneven among countries, and fragile states have been lagging behind. Wracked by conflict and weak governance, fragile states present hard governance challenges for effective development (World Bank, 2009). Thus, fragility is associated with poor MDG levels and trends, characterised by performance of policies, institutions and governments (Harttgen and Klasen, 2010). It is estimated that by 2015 half of the population living on less than USD 1.25 per day will reside in fragile states (OECD, 2013). The United Nations (UN) highlights that MDG progress at the global level is driven by large and middle-income countries (UN, 2012). Sapkota and Shiratori (2013) suggest that while achievement of the MDGs at the global level has been a success, poor progress in the most disadvantaged regions and countries indicates the urgency of a general change of policy, oriented towards more inclusive development. They also emphasise the risks associated with armed conflicts, natural disasters, and financial or other types of crises for poor and vulnerable people and propose developing social resilience through the establishment of a local, regional and global framework for social protection.

This section compares selected MDG indicators in developing countries between the years 1990 and 2010. The main comparison uses available data corresponding to the group of 47 'fragile states'[4] as defined by the OECD (2013), and a group of 85 other developing, non-fragile states.

It has been argued that the indicators that best describe the achievement of MDGs are poverty, childhood malnutrition, primary completion rates and under-5 mortality rate (Bourguignon et al., 2008; Harttgen and Klasen, 2013). Table 12.1

Table 12.1 Comparison of levels of selected MDG indicators in 2010 by fragile states and non-fragile states, according to the classification by the OECD (2013)

Indicator	*Observations*		*Mean (SD)*		*T statistic (p-value)*
	Non-fragile states	*Fragile states*	*Non-fragile states*	*Fragile states*	
Primary completion rate (% of relevant age group) year 2010	54	27	90.3104 (15.1553)	68.4219 (21.7288)	5.2788 (0.0000)
Primary completion rate (% of female relevant age group) year 2010	52	26	89.7645 (16.0357)	64.1904 (24.0914)	5.5847 (0.0000)
Primary completion rate (% of male relevant age group) year 2010	52	26	89.7843 (14.8565)	71.3066 (20.4934)	4.5468 (0.0000)
Secondary completion rate (% of relevant age group) year 2010	48	31	74.0078 (35.3169)	66.4819 (36.1416)	0.9164 (0.3623)
Secondary completion rate (% of female relevant age group) year 2010	47	30	74.1480 (37.2004)	67.1300 (38.3443)	0.7977 (0.4276)
Secondary completion rate (% of male relevant age group) year 2010	47	30	72.2560 (33.7921)	65.5087 (35.4594)	0.8382 (0.4046)
Under-5 mortality rate (per 1,000 live births) year 2010	81	46	36.5395 (31.5423)	84.7326 (47.6493)	-6.8455 (0.0000)
Under-5 mortality rate (per 1,000 live female births) year 2010	81	46	33.5346 (29.8985)	79.3391 (45.7479)	-6.8145 (0.0000)
Under-5 mortality rate (per 1,000 live male births) year 2010	81	46	39.3877 (33.1639)	89.8109 (49.4496)	-6.8619 (0.0000)
Proportion of seats held by women in national parliaments (%) year 2010	78	42	17.3436 (9.7345)	15.3691 (12.1944)	0.9684 (0.3348)
Ratio of female to male primary enrolment (%) year 2010	62	29	97.6070 (3.9282)	91.7890 (10.6105)	3.8132 (0.0003)
Ratio of female to male secondary enrolment (%) year 2010	58	21	100.5163 (11.0798)	83.4552 (20.1937)	4.7754 (0.0000)
Ratio of female to male tertiary enrolment (%) year 2010	50	22	114.8809 (37.9804)	75.9352 (42.7546)	3.8564 (0.0003)
Share of women employed in the non-agricultural sector (% of total non-agricultural employment) year 2010	44	13	40.1900 (10.2623)	28.5231 (12.2034)	3.4490 (0.0011)

Source: Authors' elaboration based on data from World Development Indicators (WDI) http://databank.worldbank.org/data/reports.aspx?source=world-development-indicators [Accessed: 18 June 2014].

Note: The T-statistic corresponds to a two-group mean comparison test (t-test) using as the two groups the non-fragile states and fragile states.

compares fragile and non-fragile states according to levels of primary and secondary education completion rates, under-5 mortality rate and some indicators related to the third MDG (Promote Gender Equality and Empower Women) for the year 2010. Results from a two-group mean comparison test (*t*-test), using as the two groups fragile and non-fragile states, suggest that fragility is associated with poorer levels of several outcomes: lower levels of primary completion rates; higher levels of under-5 mortality rates; lower ratios of female to male enrolment (primary, secondary and tertiary); and a lower share of women employed in the non-agricultural sector.

In terms of MDG achievement, it is often observed that fragile states are off track and will probably not achieve the goals by 2015 (Vandemoortele, 2012). According to the Global Monitoring Report (World Bank, 2009), 30 per cent of fragile states are off track in achieving the poverty reduction targets. With regard to promoting gender equality and empowerment of women, some progress has been made in achieving the goal related to education, but the fragile states still have a lot to do in this area as well.

Figure 12.1 presents MDG achievements in terms of percentage point changes for selected indicators: primary education completion rate, under-5 mortality rate and the ratio of female-to-male primary and secondary education enrolment between 1990 and 2010 for fragile and non-fragile states. It is important to note, however, that this information can only be computed for a low number of countries in both groups, especially for the education indicators, and so caution is needed when interpreting these results. The information is presented using box plots. As discussed by Cox (2009), box plots summarise helpful information corresponding to a variable related to location or levels (median), spread (interquartile range and range), asymmetry about the median and possible outliers. We observe that with regard to male primary completion rates, both fragile and non-fragile states have made similar progress. However, with regard to female primary completion rates, some fragile states have performed better in relative terms, probably as they started from lower levels in 1990. A similar pattern is observed for the ratios of female-to-male primary and secondary enrolment. Regarding the reduction of male and female under-5 mortality rates, it seems that fragile states have lagged behind.

In order to achieve the MDGs and eliminate poverty, it is necessary to ensure that poverty-reducing interventions are effective and beneficial to all poor people. Currently, women are discriminated against in every aspect of development opportunities, and thus remaining as the disadvantaged poorer segment of the society; this also affects their dependents and the next generation (Beall and Piron, 2005). Women and girls constitute at least 50 per cent of the world's population, but their presence among the poorest and most-excluded groups is observed to be disproportionately high.

Although there has been some progress among fragile states in terms of income levels, they are still home to one-third of the world's poor population, being more vulnerable to internal or external shocks than stable countries (OECD, 2013). Therefore, donors should rethink their approach and interventions for these

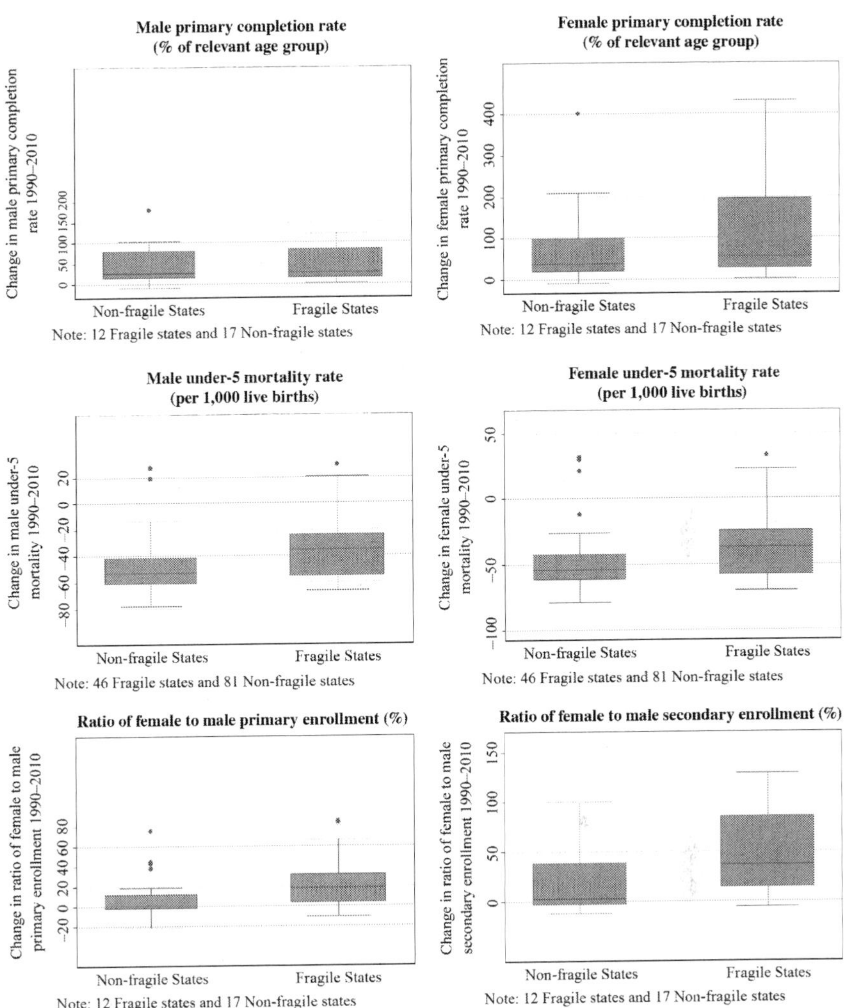

Figure 12.1 Change of selected MDG indicators (growth rate as a percentage) between 1990 and 2010 in fragile states and non-fragile states, according to the classification by the OECD (2013)

Source: Authors' elaboration based on data from World Development Indicators (WDI) http://databank.worldbank.org/data/reports.aspx?source=world-development-indicators [Accessed: 20 June 2014].

countries in order to enhance the aid effectiveness and development impacts. In this context, Sapkota and Shiratori (2013) stress upon inclusive development and resilient society for the post-2015 agenda in order to not leave behind the LICs and fragile states.

The relevance of social institutions related to gender inequality in fragile states

When thinking about the post-MDG agenda, it has been pointed that a new framework for fragile states will be required which will involve building security, legitimacy, governance and economy to bring security and development together (Zoellick, 2008). A country's extent of fragility may have varying causes. Collier (2014), for example, identifies as possible causes problems with (i) the economy, (ii) the society or (iii) the government.

We argue in this paper that gender considerations seem to be even more important in fragile states than in non-fragile states. Baranyi and Powell (2005, 1) claim that gender inequality is "a central feature of state fragility." There seems to be an emerging consensus that the post-MDG framework should apply an approach sensitive to gender and conflict and include measures to build and develop capacity for data collection and analysis on gender-related issues, particularly in fragile and conflict-affected contexts (Cordaid, 2013). The relevance of gender considerations in fragile states can be more easily understood if one recalls that (i) men and women are affected differently by state fragility and (ii) gender roles and relations are crucial to understanding opportunities and obstacles to state building (Baranyi and Powell, 2005).

Nevertheless, even if gender issues are clearly relevant for fragile countries, the topic of 'gender and fragility' remains relatively under-researched. Harcourt (2009, 1) identifies gender and fragility as an emerging new theme in the development literature and an important component of the current policy debate around peace and security and aid effectiveness of fragile states. Among the existing studies, few deal with the empowerment of women in fragile states (e.g. Armendáriz and Roome, 2008), and only a couple relate to gender inequality and conflict. For instance, Caprioli (2005) finds that gender inequality increases the chances of intra-state conflict even when controlling for economic factors. Similarly, Melander's (2005) study suggests a significant relationship between women's level of educational attainment and their representation in parliament and lower levels of conflict within a country. Concerning women's attitudes towards peace, Yablon (2009) reports that women are more positively consistent in their attitudes towards peace than are men.

The measurement at the country level of social institutions related to gender inequality

In this paper, we follow a relatively new strand of literature on gender inequality that appears particularly pertinent for fragile states. We focus on the measurement of social institutions related to gender inequality at the country level, defined as societal practices and legal norms that frame gender roles and the distribution of power between men and women in the family, the market, and social and political life (e.g. De Soysa and Jütting, 2007; Branisa et al., 2014). Branisa et al. (2014) use 12 variables from the OECD Development Centre's Gender, Institutions and

Development (GID) Database (Morrisson and Jütting, 2005; Jütting et al., 2008) to construct several composite measures of social institutions related to gender inequality. All the variables in the database, as well as the proposed composite measures, are coded between 0 and 1, where 0 means 'no or very low inequality', and 1 indicates 'high inequality'. Some of the variables are continuous, but most measure social institutions on an ordinal scale.

It is useful to briefly describe the five subindices proposed by Branisa et al. (2014). Each subindex is designed to provide a summary measure of one dimension of social institutions related to gender inequality. The aggregation of variables corresponding to each subindex is performed using polychoric principal component analysis.[5] Only countries with non-missing values for all the variables corresponding to a subindex are assigned with a value for the subindex. The subindex *Family Code* measures the decision-making power of women in the household, and includes the variables parental authority, inheritance, early marriage and polygamy. The subindex *Civil Liberties* captures the freedom of social participation for women, and includes the variables freedom of movement and freedom of dress. The subindex *Physical Integrity* comprises the indicators violence against women and female genital mutilation. The subindex *Son Preference* reflects an extreme manifestation of son preference under scarce resources using the variable missing women that measures gender bias in mortality (Sen, 1992; Klasen and Wink, 2003). Finally, the subindex *Ownership Rights* proxies access of women to several types of property and include women's access to land, women's access to bank loans and women's access to property other than land. For a full description of these variables and the coding scheme used, please refer to Branisa et al. (2014) and the supplemental content on the publisher's website.

Using the five subindices described before as inputs, Branisa et al. (2014) propose a multidimensional composite index named Social Institutions and Gender Index (SIGI) which reflects the deprivation of women caused by social institutions related to gender inequality. Only countries with non-missing values for all the subindices get a value for SIGI. The objective of SIGI is to capture the institutional basis of gender inequality. As it was the case for all variables and subindices, the index value is between 0 and 1, where 0 reflects 'no or very low inequality' and 1 denotes 'high inequality'.

Issues around social institutions related to gender inequality in fragile states have received little attention to date. As far as we are aware, no systematic study has been conducted on the topic, i.e. the measurement of social institutions related to gender inequality in fragile states, and the relevance of these institutions to the MDGs, and for the post-MDG development agenda.

Social institutions related to gender inequality in fragile states

The question remains whether gender inequality is a cause or an outcome of fragility in states. This certainly goes beyond the scope of this paper, and a complete answer probably needs to be based on multiple case studies. Nevertheless, following Branisa, Klasen and Ziegler (2013) we conceive gender inequality related to social institutions are long-lasting norms, values and codes of conduct that are frequently expressed in traditions, customs and cultural practices, and informal and formal laws. They shape up the gender roles and the distribution of power between men and women in the family, market, and social and political life. Gender inequalities seem to be rooted in gender roles that evolve from these institutions. It is possible that these same institutions are also related to some of the problems with economy, society or government, as stressed by Collier (2014) (details discussed earlier in this section). The idea presented by Jones et al. (2008) when reflecting on state building appears relevant here. They suggest that a focus on formal and informal governance structures which address inequality and promote accountability is likely to promote stability over time. All this, of course, remains highly speculative for the time being.

Another aspect that deserves attention for policy implications is that fragile states will experience difficulties in implementing policies to change social institutions related to gender inequality. As clearly stated by the (OECD, 2013, 15), a fragile state is one that "has weak capacity to carryout basic governance functions, and lacks the ability to develop mutually constructive relations with society [. . .] vulnerable to internal or external shocks such as economic crises or natural disasters [. . .] and low capacity and legitimacy of governing a population and its territory." These countries require support to improve their situation.

This being said, the main question we seek to address in this section is whether measures of social institutions related to gender inequality are, on average, different between fragile states and other non-fragile developing countries. As already noted, we follow the OECD (2013) by classifying countries as fragile or non-fragile.

We perform two formal tests to check whether there are differences between fragile and non-fragile countries concerning social institutions related to gender inequality. Results are presented in Table 12.2. The first test is a two-group mean comparison test (*t*-test) using as the two groups the fragile and non-fragile states. As the data might be interpreted as being ordinal rather than cardinal, we also perform a Wilcoxon rank-sum test,[6] which is based exclusively on the order in which the observations from the two groups fall (Wilcoxon, 1945; Mann and Whitney, 1947) and is a non-parametric alternative to the two-sample *t*-test. Results from both tests point in the same direction, and reject at the 1 per cent level that fragile and non-fragile states have both been drawn from the same population when considering the SIGI and the subindices *Family Code*, *Physical Integrity* and *Ownership Rights*.

Until now, we have dealt mainly with composite measures. We would also like to know which of the underlying variables are the ones driving the results. As a next step, we repeat both statistical tests (the *t*-test and the Wilcoxon rank-sum test) for the 12 variables used in the construction of the subindices of the SIGI (Table 12.3). This is interesting because we have more observations for the variables than for the subindices and the SIGI, and having more observations increases the statistical power of the tests. As stressed before, only countries with no missing values for each of the variables are assigned a value for the corresponding

Table 12.2 Mean-comparison test and Wilcoxon rank-sum test between fragile and non-fragile states [according to the classification by the OECD (2013)] for the Social Institutions and Gender Index (SIGI) and its five subindices – Family Code, Civil Liberties, Physical Integrity, Son Preference and Ownership Rights, year 2009

Index	*Observations*		*Mean (SD)*		*T statistic (p-value)*	*Rank sum*		*Expected*		*Wilcoxon test Z-statistic (p-value)*
	Non-fragile states	*Fragile states*	*Non-fragile states*	*Fragile states*		*Non-fragile states*	*Fragile states*	*Non-fragile states*	*Fragile states*	
SIGI	71	31	0.0852 (.0890)	0.2189 (.1380)	−5.8547 (0.0000)	2952	2301	3657	1597	−5.1260 (0.0000)
Family Code	78	34	0.2630 (.2136)	0.4719 (.1710)	−5.0372 (0.0000)	3682	2647	4407	1921	−4.5910 (0.0000)
Civil Liberties	85	38	0.1279 (.2323)	0.2306 (.3019)	−2.0584 (0.0417)	4966	2660	5270	2356	−2.0050 (0.0450)
Physical Integrity	77	37	0.3002 (.1663)	0.4772 (.1860)	−5.1179 (0.0000)	3600	2956	4428	2128	−5.0290 (0.0000)
Son Preference	84	39	0.1280 (.2376)	0.1474 (.2481)	−0.4168 (0.6776)	5115	2511	5208	2418	−0.6370 (0.5243)
Ownership Rights	84	38	0.2022 (.2132)	0.5107 (.2496)	−7.0100 (0.0000)	4146	3357	5166	2337	−5.8030 (0.0000)

Source: Authors' elaboration based on data from Branisa et al. (2014) and OECD (2013).

Table 12.3 Mean-comparison test and Wilcoxon rank-sum test between fragile and non-fragile states [according to the classification by the OECD (2013)] for the variables used in the subindices – Family Code, Civil Liberties, Physical Integrity, Son Preference and Ownership Rights, year 2009

Variable	*Observations*		*Mean (SD)*		*T statistic (p-value)*	*Rank sum*		*Expected*		*Wilcoxon test Z-statistic (p-value)*
	Non-fragile states	*Fragile states*	*Non-fragile states*	*Fragile states*		*Non-fragile states*	*Fragile states*	*Non-fragile states*	*Fragile states*	
Parental authority/legal guardian of a child during marriage	83	39	0.3313 (.4152)	0.5641 (.3835)	−2.9572 (0.0037)	4595	2909	5105	2399	−3.0130 (0.0026)
Inheritance rights of spouses	82	39	0.2927 (.3234)	0.5256 (.2797)	−3.8610 (0.0002)	4383	2998	5002	2379	−3.8020 (0.0001)
Percentage of women married between 15–19 years old	82	34	0.1599 (.1068)	0.3132 (.1685)	−5.8803 (0.0000)	4028	2759	4797	1989	−4.6690 (0.0000)
Polygamy acceptance or legality if acceptance is missing	85	39	0.3588 (.3827)	0.6026 (.4003)	−3.2455 (0.0015)	4773	2978	5313	2438	−3.0970 (0.0020)
Female genital mutilation	78	37	0.0682 (.2036)	0.2354 (.3215)	−3.3857 (0.0010)	3911	2759	4524	2146	−4.5070 (0.0000)
Violence against women	84	39	0.5163 (.2356)	0.7008 (.2252)	−4.0956 (0.0001)	4483	3144	5208	2418	−4.0090 (0.0001)
Freedom of movement	85	38	0.1235 (.2302)	0.2237 (.3008)	−2.0213 (0.0455)	5000	2626	5270	2356	−1.8830 (0.0597)
Dress code in public	85	39	0.0941 (.2112)	0.1795 (.3138)	−1.7814 (0.0773)	5121	2630	5313	2438	−1.4600 (0.1443)
Son preference	84	39	0.1280 (.2376)	0.1474 (.2481)	−0.4168 (0.6776)	5115	2511	5208	2418	−0.6370 (0.5243)
Women's access to land	84	38	0.2619 (.2741)	0.5263 (.3277)	−4.6363 (0.0000)	4504	2999	5166	2337	−4.0830 (0.0000)
Women's access to bank loans	84	39	0.1548 (.2325)	0.4744 (.2797)	−6.6416 (0.0000)	4306	3320	5208	2418	−5.5780 (0.0000)
Women's access to property other than land	84	39	0.1667 (.2494)	0.4744 (.2797)	−6.1219 (0.0000)	4339	3287	5208	2418	−5.3510 (0.0000)

Source: Authors' elaboration based on data from Branisa et al. (2014) and OECD (2013).

subindex, and only countries with no missing values for all the subindices are assigned a value for the SIGI. The results confirm that there are differences in all nine variables corresponding to the subindices *Family Code, Physical Integrity* and *Ownership Rights*, but not for the variables corresponding to the subindices *Civil Liberties* and *Son Preference*.

We conclude that fragile states perform worse than other non-fragile developing countries when considering social institutions related to gender inequality, and in particular in the dimensions (1) *Family Code*, which measures the decision-making power of women in the household and includes the variables, such as parental authority, inheritance, early marriage and polygamy; (2) *Physical Integrity*, which comprises the indicators on violence against women and female genital mutilation; and (3) *Ownership Rights*, which proxies access of women to several types of property and include women's access to land, women's access to bank loans and women's access to property other than land.

The importance of social institutions related to gender inequality for fragile and non-fragile states

Why are these all pertinent for the post-2015 development agenda? We think that this is related to the view championed by Amartya Sen (e.g. Sen, 1999), who reasons that freedom is both intrinsic and instrumental to development.

First, from the *intrinsic* perspective, it should be clear that in all developing countries, and particularly in fragile sates, policies focusing on changing gendered development outcomes should take into account inequalities in social institutions as relevant constraints. As already shown, fragile states perform worse than other developing countries in the dimensions *Family Code, Physical Integrity* and *Ownership Rights*. This, of course, does not mean that the issue is not relevant for *all* developing countries, and it should be addressed explicitly as it reflects the deprivation of women. Attempting to remove this deprivation is essential.

Second, Sen (1999) argues that different kinds of freedom interrelate with one another, and freedom of one type may to a great extent help in advancing freedom of other types. From this *instrumental* perspective we should consider the studies at the cross-country level that show that social institutions related to gender inequality are associated with, and appear to be relevant for, several development outcomes such as female education, child mortality, fertility and governance in developing countries. The empirical results from Branisa, Klasen and Ziegler (2013), for example, suggest that apart from geography, the political system, level of economic development and religion, one should also consider social institutions related to gender inequality to better account for differences in development outcomes among developing countries. This line of research indicates that trying to address these gendered institutional constraints in fragile states should be high on the agenda when trying to promote development outcomes in general.

One could think of including a special set of indicators reflecting social institutions related to gender inequality in both fragile states and non-fragile states as part of the post-MDG agenda.[7] As a start point, one could use the 12 variables described in Branisa et al. (2014), which are used to build the five subindices or composite measures of different dimensions of social institutions related to gender inequality described already. *Family Code* measures the decision-making power of women in the household and includes the variables parental authority, inheritance, early marriage and polygamy. *Civil Liberties* captures the freedom of social participation of women and includes the variables freedom of movement and freedom of dress. *Physical Integrity* comprises the indicators on violence against women and female genital mutilation. The subindex *Son Preference* reflects an extreme manifestation of son preference under scarce resources using the variable 'missing women' that measures gender bias in mortality (Sen, 1992; Klasen and Wink, 2003). Finally, the subindex *Ownership Rights* proxies access of women to several types of property and includes women's access to land, women's access to bank loans and women's access to property other than land. For a complete description of all variables and the coding scheme, please refer to Branisa et al. (2014) and the supplemental content on the publisher's website.

Also, one could consider special measures to help fragile states improve the situation and reduce gender inequality as part of the new global partnership towards a new spirit of solidarity, cooperation and mutual accountability. We believe that Vandemoortele (2012) is right when he claims that the post-2015 agenda must be global and universal, and it should not include targets for particular regions or specific types of countries.

Conclusions

The paper shows that social institutions related to gender inequality, defined as societal practices and legal norms that frame gender roles and the distribution of power between men and women in the family, market, and social and political life (e.g. De Soysa and Jütting, 2007; Branisa et al., 2014), appear even more important for fragile states that for non-fragile states. We argued that indicators related to this issue are relevant for both fragile and non-fragile states when reflecting upon the post-2015 agenda.

These indicators should be considered explicitly as part of the post-MDG discussion, because these social institutional constraints play both an intrinsic and an instrumental role in development (Sen, 1999). From an intrinsic point of view, social institutions related to gender inequality reveal the deprivation of women, which cannot be tolerated if we are to take seriously the first transformative shift of 'leaving no one behind', proposed by the UN High-Level Panel (2013). In addition, and from an instrumental perspective, it has been argued that reducing gender inequality could benefit not only women but the whole society, as social institutions related to gender inequality are associated with, and appear to be relevant for, several development outcomes including female education, child mortality, fertility and governance in developing countries.

Notes

1 A longer version of this paper, with more details, tables, graphs, etc. is available at: http://southernvoice-postmdg.org/wp-content/uploads/2015/02/SV-OP-21.pdf
2 For more detail on the harmonised list, see http://go.worldbank.org/BNFOS8V3S0; on the FSI, see http://global.fundforpeace.org/index.php
3 The present study has checked the robustness of all empirical results using the three aforesaid alternative definitions of fragile countries. The results are similar.
4 For details on the selection of the 47 fragile states, see OECD (2013).
5 For details, please see http://southernvoice-postmdg.org/wp-content/uploads/2015/02/SV-OP-21.pdf
6 The Wilcoxon rank-sum test is also known in the literature as Mann-Whitney U test, Mann-Whitney-Wilcoxon test and Wilcoxon-Mann-Whitney test.
7 Apart from the composite indices presented before from Branisa et al. (2014), which have been modified and updated by the OECD (www.genderindex.org), systematic information proxying social institutions related to gender inequality at the cross-country level is scarce. Much effort is needed to collect and evaluate information concerning social institutions related to gender inequality in both fragile and non-fragile states. This should be seen as part of a wider process to better understand the distribution of power in these countries.

References

Armendáriz, B. and Roome, N. (2008) *Empowering Women via Microfinance in Fragile States*. CEB Working Paper no. 08/001. Brussels: Centre Emile Bernheim.

Baranyi, S. and Powell, K. (2005) *Fragile States, Gender Equality and Aid Effectiveness: A Review of Donor Perspectives*. Canada: Canadian International Development Agency (CIDA). Available from: http://www.nsi-ins.ca/wp-content/uploads/2012/10/2005-Fragile-States-Gender-Equality-and-Aid-Effectiveness-A-Review-of-Donor-Perspectives.pdf [Accessed: 3 October 2014].

Beall, J. and Piron, L. H. (2005) *DFID Social Exclusion Review*. London: Overseas Development Institute (ODI). Available from: http://www.odi.org/sites/odi.org.uk/files/odi-assets/publications-opinion-files/2301.pdf [Accessed: 29 September 2014].

Bourguignon, F., Benassy-Quere, A., Dercon, S., Estache, A., Gunning, J. W., Kanbur, R., Klasen, S., Maxwell, S., Platteau, J. P. and Spadaro, A. (2008) *Millennium Development Goals at Midpoint: Where Do We Stand and Where Do We Need to Go?* Brussels: European Commission. Available from: https://ec.europa.eu/europeaid/sites/devco/files/study-millenium-development-goals-200810_en.pdf [Accessed: 6 October 2014].

Branisa, B., Klasen, S. and Ziegler, M. (2013) Gender inequality in social institutions and gendered development outcomes. *World Development*. 45 (1). pp.252–268.

Branisa, B., Klasen, S., Ziegler, M., Drechsler, D. and Jütting, J. (2014) The institutional basis of gender inequality: The Social Institutions and Gender Index (SIGI). *Feminist Economics*. 20 (2). pp.29–64.

Caprioli, M. (2005) The role of gender inequality in predicting internal conflict. *International Studies Quarterly*. 49 (2). pp.161–178.

Collier, P. (2008) *The Bottom Billion: Why the Poorest Countries Are Failing and What Can Be Done about It*. New York: Oxford University Press.

Collier, P. (2014) *Fragile African States: What Should Donors Do?* France: Fondation Pour Les Études Et Recherches Sur Le Développement International (FERDI). Available from:

http://www.ferdi.fr/sites/www.ferdi.fr/files/publication/fichiers/wp95_collier_web.pdf [Accessed: 25 September 2014].

Cordaid. (2013) *Gender Inequality and Fragility in the Post-MDG Framework*. The Hague: Catholic Organization for Relief and Development Aid. Available from: http://www.post2015hlp.org/wp-content/uploads/2013/05/Cordaid-7264–02-PP-The_New_Deal_and_UNSCR_1325-DEFHR-web.pdf [Accessed: 10 October 2014].

Cox, N. J. (2009) Speaking Stata: Creating and varying box plots. *Stata Journal*. 9 (3). pp.478–496.

de Soysa, I. and Jütting, J. (2007) Informal Institutions and Development: How They Matter and What Makes Them Change. In Jütting, J., Drechsler, D., Bartsch, S. and de Soysa, I. (eds.) *Informal Institutions: How Social Norms Help or Hinder Development* (pp.29–43). Paris: OECD Development Centre.

FFP. (2014) *The Failed State Index 2013*. Washington, DC: The Fund for Peace. Available from: http://library.fundforpeace.org/library/cfsir1306-failedstatesindex2013–06l.pdf [Accessed: 18 October 2014].

Harcourt, W. (2009) *Literature Review on Gender and Fragility*. Available from: http://erd.eui.eu/media/review-by-w-harcourt.pdf [Accessed: 6 October 2014].

Harttgen, K. and Klasen, S. (2010) *Fragility and MDG Progress: How Useful Is the Fragility Concept?* CRC Discussion Paper No. 41. Goettingen: Courant Research Centre. Available from: http://www2.vwl.wiso.uni-goettingen.de/courant-papers/CRC-PEG_DP_41.pdf [Accessed: 10 October 2014].

Harttgen, K. and Klasen, S. (2013) Do fragile countries experience worse MDG progress? *The Journal of Development Studies*. 49 (1). pp.134–159.

Jones, B., Chandran, R., Cousens, E., Slotin, J. and Sherman, J. (2008) *From Fragility to Resilience: Concepts and Dilemmas of Statebuilding in Fragile States*. OECD/DAC Discussion Paper. Paris: Organisation for Economic Co-operation and Development (OECD).

Jütting, J., Morrisson, C., Dayton-Johnson, J. and Drechsler, D. (2008) Measuring gender (in)equality: Introducing gender, institutions and development database (GID). *Journal of Human Development*. 9 (1). pp.65–86.

Klasen, S. (2013) Do fragile countries experience worse MDG progress? *The Journal of Development Studies*. 49 (1). pp.134–159.

Klasen, S. and Wink, C. (2003) Missing women: Revisiting the debate. *Feminist Economics*. 9 (2, 3). pp.263–300.

Mann, H. B. and Whitney, D. R. (1947) On a test of whether one of two random variables is stochastically larger than the other. *Annals of Mathematical Statistics*. 18 (1). pp.50–60.

Melander, E. (2005) Gender equality and intrastate armed conflict. *International Studies Quarterly*. 49 (4). pp.695–714.

Morrisson, C. and Jütting, J. (2005) Women's discrimination in developing countries: A new data set for better policies. *World Development*. 33 (7). pp.1065–1081.

OECD. (2012) *The Missing Piece: Improving International Support to the Peace Process*. Paris: Organisation for Economic Co-operation and Development (OECD).

OECD. (2013) *Fragile States 2013: Resource Flows and Trends in a Shifting World*. Paris: Organisation for Economic Co-operation and Development (OECD).

Sapkota, J. B. and Shiratori, S. (2013) *Achieving the Millennium Development Goals: Lessons for Post-2015 New Development Strategies*. JICA-RI Working Paper No. 62. Japan: Japan International Cooperation Agency Research Institute (JICA-RI). Available from: http://jica-ri.jica.go.jp/publication/assets/JICA-RI_WP_No.62_2013.pdf [Accessed: 30 September 2014].

Sen, A. (1992) Missing women. *British Medical Journal*. 304, March. pp.586–587.

Sen, A. (1999) *Development as Freedom*. New York: Alfred A. Knopf.

UN High-Level Panel. (2013) *A New Global Partnership: Eradicate Poverty and Transform Economies through Sustainable Development*. New York: United Nations. Available at: http://www.un.org/sg/management/pdf/HLP_P2015_Report.pdf [Accessed: 1 October 2014].

United Nations. (2012) *The Millennium Development Goals Report 2012*. New York: United Nations. Available from: http://www.un.org/millenniumgoals/pdf/MDG%20 Report%202012.pdf [Accessed: 1 October 2014].

Vandemoortele, J. (2012) *Advancing the Global Development Agenda Post-2015: Some Thoughts, Ideas and Practical Suggestions*. New York: UN System Task Team on the Post-2015 UN Development Agenda. Available from: http://www.un.org/millennium goals/pdf/jan_vandemoortele_Aug.pdf [Accessed: 3 October 2014].

Wilcoxon, F. (1945) Individual comparisons by ranking methods. *Biometrics*. 1 (6). pp.80–83.

World Bank. (2007) *Global Monitoring Report 2007*. Washington, DC: The World Bank. Available from: https://www.imf.org/External/Pubs/FT/GMR/2007/eng/gmr.pdf [Accessed: 11 September 2014].

World Bank. (2009) *Global Monitoring Report 2009*. Washington, DC: The World Bank. Available from: http://siteresources.worldbank.org/INTGLOMONREP2009/Resources/ 5924349–1239742507025/GMR09_book.pdf [Accessed: 12 September 2014].

Yablon, Y. B. (2009) Gender differences in the consistency of attitudes towards peace. *Women's Studies International Forum*. 32 (4). pp.305–310.

Zoellick, R. B. (2008) Fragile states: Securing development. *Survival*. 50 (6). pp.67–84.

Governance and capacities

13 Ensuring good governance and effective institutions

Can we afford to ignore capacity issues?

Subrat Das

The context

The framework of the Sustainable Development Goals (SDGs) formulated by the United Nations (UN) acknowledges the criticality of improving governance. The SDGs recognise some aspects of governance as core elements of well-being as well as enablers of development, which include among others: free, safe and peaceful societies; access to fair justice systems; and participatory democracy. Some of the other important parameters of governance have been recognised primarily as enablers of development, for instance: effective, accountable and inclusive institutions at all levels; reducing corruption and bribery in all their forms; and reducing illicit financial flows and the recovery and return of stolen assets. Though a range of issues relating to the quality of governance and effectiveness of institutions has been highlighted in the discourse on SDGs, it is necessary to probe deeper into this area from a fiscal policy perspective.

Goal 16 of the SDGs is accompanied by a number of targets, some of which emphasise specific features of good governance and effective institutions. These include the targets pertaining to developing effective, accountable and transparent institutions at all levels; ensuring responsive, inclusive, participatory and representative decision-making at all levels; ensuring public access to information and protecting fundamental freedoms; substantially reducing corruption and bribery in all their forms; and promoting the rule of law and ensuring equal access to justice for all.

The emphasis on some of the key parameters of good governance and effective institutions – such as space for people's participation, transparency and accountability – is indeed commendable. However, the problem of erosion in governance capacity, which can be a serious challenge in any country struggling to deal with long-term public expenditure commitments because of weaknesses in its fiscal policy, does not seem to have received due attention.

With regard to the investments required to be made in 'capacities' for sustainable development, the emphasis seems mainly to be on skills and technical know-how. One of the targets accompanying Goal 17 of the SDGs focuses on capacity building; it calls for enhancing "international support for implementing effective and targeted capacity building in developing countries to support national plans to implement all the sustainable development goals, including through North–South, South–South and triangular cooperation" (United Nations, 2015). However, the issue of shortsighted fiscal consolidation measures leading to weakening capacity of the executive and government apparatus in a country, which in turn results in different kinds of governance failures over time, is a glaring omission.

The fiscal policy-induced failures in governance could potentially create major hurdles in the journey towards SDGs in a number of countries, especially in those developing countries that allow a gradual deterioration of public service delivery because of the limitations in their fiscal policy regimes. The present paper attempts to throw light on this potential challenge with the help of a brief account of how India has been witnessing serious problems in public service delivery, one of the primary factors underlying the erosion in state capacity resulting from a conservative fiscal policy regime being followed in the country for most part of the last two decades.

Weakening capacity of government apparatus

The experience of public policies and their implementation in India over the past decade indicates that acute shortage of staff, especially skilled employees, across a range of administrative units at the subnational level, who are vested with the responsibilities of planning and implementing government interventions for crucial social sectors, has resulted in poor quality of public expenditure in these sectors. This is one of the main reasons for the persistence of development deficits in the country despite increases in the magnitudes of budget outlays for development programmes.

In the Indian context, it can be argued that the shortage of staff, particularly in the regular cadres of state government departments and local bodies responsible for social sectors such as education, health, water and sanitation, rural development and agriculture, among others, is one of the main factors affecting the coverage as well as quality of government interventions in these crucial sectors across many states. Several micro studies commissioned by government and independent organisations have pointed out that the shortage in quality human resources is one of the major challenges faced by the system of public service delivery in India. It is important to note that the gap is more acute for skilled/technical staff positions – programme managerial staff, finance and accounts staff, and skilled service providers – than the unskilled/support staff positions.

As shown in Table 13.1, the total employment in the public sector in India (including the central government, state governments, local bodies and quasi-government institutions such as the public sector enterprises) has shrunk in absolute numbers from 19.3 million in 2000 to 17.6 million in 2012. In terms of implementing most of the public-funded development programmes in the country, the state governments and local bodies play the most important role. The total employment in the state governments has declined from 7.46 million in 2000 to 7.18 million in 2012, and the decline in total employment in local bodies over the same period is from 2.25 million to 2.11 million. While this decline in absolute

Table 13.1 Total employment in India's public sector (as on 31 March) (million persons)

Authority	*1991*	*1995*	*2000*	*2004*	*2005*	*2006*	*2007*	*2008*	*2009*	*2010*	*2011*	*2012*
Central government	3.41	3.39	3.27	3.03	2.94	2.86	2.80	2.74	2.66	2.55	2.46	2.52
State governments	7.11	7.35	7.46	7.22	7.20	7.30	7.21	7.17	7.23	7.35	7.22	7.18
Local bodies	2.31	2.19	2.25	2.12	2.12	2.12	2.13	1.97	2.07	2.09	2.05	2.11
Quasi-governments	6.22	6.52	6.32	5.82	5.75	5.91	5.86	5.79	5.84	5.87	5.81	5.80
Total	19.05	19.46	19.31	18.19	18.01	18.19	18.00	17.67	17.80	17.86	17.54	17.61

Source: Compiled by the author based on data from Government of India (2015) and Government of India (2012).

Note: Data for the year 2012 are provisional.

numbers does not appear very drastic, we have to take into account not just the growing population of the country, but also the fact that the number of development programmes (especially in the social sectors) and the magnitude of overall funds allocated for those witnessed a visible increase during the past decade. Thus, the workload on the existing staff in the state governments and local bodies would have grown significantly over that period.

It would be worthwhile to look at the availability of total staff in the public sector as a proportion of the country's population for India and a few other countries, as is depicted in Table 13.2. As of 2010, India had 1.5 government sector personnel for every 100 residents – this includes personnel in the central government of India, Indian Railways, state governments, urban and rural local governments and public sector undertakings. This is a relatively low figure when compared to the much higher figure of 5.9 government sector personnel for every 100 residents in Brazil, or even the figure of 3.9 government sector personnel for every 100 residents in Mexico.

It is well known that in the past decade, both the central government and the state governments in India have been hiring large numbers of temporary workers in many sectors. To date, the government has not attempted any estimation of the total strength of either the temporary workers hired with fixed short-term contracts or those hired simply as casual workers (the latter includes labourers who work on public works programmes as well as the 'honorary' or 'voluntary' workers in some development programmes who are paid only some 'performance-based incentives' or small amounts of 'honorarium' less than even the minimum wages). However, an independent study (Indian Staffing Federation, 2014) has attempted such an estimation based on the latest Employment–Unemployment Survey of India's National Sample Survey Organisation and various statistics published by different government sources. The said study indicates that as of 2011–12, India

Table 13.2 Total staff in the public sector as a percentage of the country's population: comparison across selected countries (per cent)

Country	*2001*	*2002*	*2003*	*2004*	*2005*	*2006*	*2007*	*2008*	*2009*	*2010*
Brazil	–	–	–	5.3	5.3	5.6	5.7	5.8	5.9	–
Canada	9.8	9.8	10.0	10.0	10.0	10.2	10.3	10.5	10.6	10.6
France	10.8	10.9	11.0	10.8	10.6	10.6	–	–	–	–
Germany	7.5	7.4	7.4	7.2	7.0	7.1	7.1	7.1	7.2	7.3
India	1.8	1.7	1.7	1.6	1.6	1.6	1.5	1.5	1.5	1.5
Mexico	4.6	4.5	3.9	3.9	3.9	3.9	3.9	3.9	3.9	–
South Africa	3.2	3.1	3.1	3.1	2.4	3.3	–	–	–	–
United Kingdom	9.5	9.6	9.9	10.0	10.1	10.0	9.8	9.7	10.1	10.0

Source: Compiled by the author from the following sources:

(i) ILO Laborsta database (http://laborsta.ilo.org/STP/guest) for figures on public sector employees in the selected countries [Accessed: 14 September 2015] and (ii) World Bank's database (http://databank.worldbank.org/) for data on population of the selected countries [Accessed: 14 September 2015].

Note: (a) The figures for Public Sector Employment in India for the years 2006 to 2010 used in the calculations presented above are from a different source, viz. *Economic Survey* of the Ministry of Finance, Government of India (as presented earlier in Table 13.1). The figures from this source are fully comparable with the ILO Laborsta figures for India for the years 2001 to 2005.

(b) The Public Sector is composed of a general government sector and a public corporation sector. This includes employment of general government sector as defined by the System of National Accounts (1993) plus employment of public-owned enterprises and companies, resident and operating at central, state (or regional) and local levels of government.

had around 1.8 million persons working for the government at various levels who had fixed short-term contracts of three years or less; many of these were employed as teachers or teaching associates in government schools, or as data-entry operators or clerks in various government offices, among other things. Even when we add this number to the total number of staff in the public sector on regular employment, the country had around 1.6 government sector personnel for every 100 residents as of 2011–12. Thus, the government sector in India is understaffed as a proportion of the country's population as compared to not only some of the developed Organisation for Economic Co-operation and Development (OECD) countries, but also some of the other developing countries.

Table 13.3 presents comparable figures for a few states in India. Only a limited set of states could be covered here due to the unavailability of such data for most of the other states. At the level of the state government, the number of government personnel for every 100 residents varies from 1.53 in Haryana to 1.01 in Madhya Pradesh. But it is worth noting here that, among the six states covered, the three poorer states (viz. Madhya Pradesh, Odisha and Rajasthan) had a lesser number of state government personnel per 100 residents as compared to the three economically better-off states (viz. Haryana, Kerala and Andhra Pradesh). Thus, it may well be the case that the problem of staff shortage in the government sector could be more serious in the poorer states in India, which actually need a stronger intervention from the government for promoting human development.

Table 13.3 Public sector employees as a percentage of the state's population: selected states in India

State	*Reference year*	*Public sector employees per 100 persons in the state**
Haryana	2013–14	1.53
Kerala	2013–14	1.50
Andhra Pradesh	2011–12	1.39
Rajasthan	2012–13	1.29
Odisha	2011–12	1.11
Madhya Pradesh	2011–12	1.01

Source: Compiled by the author based on data from Das and Shrivastava (2014).

Note: * includes employees in state government departments, government-aided institutions, state public sector undertakings, and rural local bodies and urban local bodies in the state.

Regarding the shortage of government personnel at the subnational level in India, the sectors that are believed to be worst affected are mostly the social sectors, such as education, health, water and sanitation, and rural development and agriculture, among others. It is important to note that the total number of government employees available in these sectors at present includes a sizable proportion of personnel hired on fixed short-term contracts, i.e. those hired on a contract basis for a few months or at most for a couple of years, who are usually less qualified and paid much less than those recruited as regular or permanent cadre employees. For instance, it has been reported that a staggering 40 per cent of 933,000 teachers in the higher education system (comprising universities and colleges) of the government sector in India are 'contractual' teachers, and a large number of such teachers do not have the desirable levels of qualification, such as post-graduate or doctoral degrees, are paid meagre salaries and are hired on contracts for a duration of six to eight months (Varma, 2013).

The acute shortage of government personnel, particularly personnel with requisite qualifications and skills, is not confined to higher education – it is prevalent in most of the social sectors in India. For instance, a recent study had indicated that the overall shortage of allied health professionals in India amounted to more than 6.4 million (Public Health Foundation of India, 2012); given that healthcare delivery in the country is dominated significantly by the private sector, it can be safely assumed that the availability of such skilled health workers in the public health sector in India would be far less than the numbers required.

However, capacity has numerous dimensions. It is necessary to add here that the shortage of staff in terms of the numbers of skilled staff available is only one of the several dimensions of the problem of weak capacity of the government apparatuses across social sectors in India. Skewed geographical distribution of the existing staff (i.e. a higher concentration of government sector staff in urban areas at the cost of the neglect of rural areas) and low productivity of some of the staff (in terms of the low 'value for money' derived from the under-performing staff) are other important dimensions of this problem.

In fact, serious concerns have been raised over the past decade about the low productivity of some government personnel, which have a range of consequences for the social sectors. For instance, *Annual Status of Education Report* surveys over the past few years have indicated that learning outcomes in terms of reading and arithmetic levels for children in government schools in India have been poorer compared to those for children in private schools, and the gap appears to be widening over time (see, for instance, ASER Centre, 2014).

Studies conducted by the World Bank about a decade ago had pointed out absenteeism of teachers and medical personnel in the government sector as a major problem in the public delivery of essential services in India (as was the case in a number of other developing or less developed countries surveyed). The survey had inferred that on average 25 per cent of teachers in India's government primary schools used to be absent from work on any given day, and a similar problem of absenteeism was reported for government medical personnel as well.

In this context, it is obvious that a strengthening of the capacity of governance in terms of improvements in the availability of staff for relevant functions does not imply any spontaneous improvement in the productivity of government personnel. But a number of policy alternatives have been put forward to address the problem of low productivity of government staff in the Indian context, and some measures have also been pursued vigorously over the past few years. Narayan and Mooij (2010) highlight three policy strategies that are being pursued or have been proposed to deal with teacher absenteeism in government primary schools in rural India – forming local-level institutions that can hold teachers accountable, relying on contractual teachers instead of regular cadre teachers, and introducing a voucher system to promote competition between government and private schools. Forming local-level institutions like school management committees and village health and sanitation committees to hold government staff involved in frontline service provision accountable and relying heavily on contractual staff in almost all development schemes are two such policy measures that have been pursued intensely in development planning in the country over the last decade.

However, the critical issue that policymakers in India have missed is the shortage of staff vis-à-vis the numbers of skilled staff required for carrying out various functions in social sectors and its consequences in the domain of public service delivery. How does such weak capacity of government apparatuses in the social sectors affect the delivery of public services in those sectors?

Consequences in the domain of public service delivery

The consequences of acute staff shortage in government apparatuses at the subnational level in terms of inadequate coverage and poor quality of government interventions in the social sectors in India are not difficult to visualise. The most widespread manifestation, however, is the poor resource absorption (or fund utilisation) capacity of states. A number of studies by the Centre for Budget and Governance Accountability (CBGA) on programmes in the social sectors in Indian states have revealed that shortages of staff have weakened the state government apparatuses, which consequently have not been able to effectively utilise budget outlays provided for these programmes (CBGA and UNICEF, 2011a, 2011b, 2011c and 2011d).

This phenomenon of underutilisation of the available budgetary resources for programmes in the social sectors in most states has been cited by many policy-makers and policy analysts as the current key problem in India. More importantly, it has also been used by the central Ministry of Finance as the main rationale for discouraging any significant increases in budgetary provisions for these sectors.

The findings of the studies by CBGA throw light on a set of institutional and procedural constraints that need to be addressed in order to enable states to effectively utilise greater magnitudes of budget outlays in the social sectors. These studies analysed the implementation of some of the major programmes/schemes in the social sectors, such as *Sarva Shiksha Abhiyan* (a scheme for universalising elementary education in the country), National Rural Health Mission, Integrated Child Development Services and Total Sanitation Campaign, at the district level in selected states (see CBGA and UNICEF, 2011a, 2011b, 2011c, 2011d).

These studies find that over the past decade, two key problems have been observed across various states with regard to the utilisation of available budgetary resources in social sector programmes/schemes, particularly in the relatively backward states. First, many states' capacity to effectively spend on the schemes is low, which is evident from noticeable levels of unspent budget outlays due to the low levels of actual spending as compared to the approved budgets for the schemes. Second, the quality of spending/fund utilisation by many states in the development schemes is poor. Fund utilisation levels are skewed across the four quarters of a fiscal year; typically, a large share of spending occurs in the last two quarters. Fund utilisation levels are also skewed across different components in a scheme; spending on certain components increases quickly when it is easier to disburse funds as compared to other components that require greater efforts from implementing agencies. Finally, fund utilisation levels are skewed across different regions within a state.

The studies also identified a number of factors responsible for the aforementioned problems in fund utilisation in development schemes, which can be broadly divided into three causal factors. The first causal factor is the deficient decentralised plans (or need assessment documents) being prepared in most of the schemes. Deficiencies in planning in the schemes are caused by staff shortages that hinder need assessment activities at the grassroots level and the lack of emphasis on training and capacity building of staff and community leaders for decentralised planning. The second causal factor is the delay in the flow of funds to the grassroots level where services are being delivered. The delay in fund flow is related, among other factors, to the slowness in preparation, submission and subsequent approval of decentralised plans, a result of shortages of skilled staff responsible for carrying out the decentralised planning work in the schemes. The third causal factor is the systemic weaknesses in state government and local government apparatuses, particularly in the relatively backward states. Shortages of trained regular staff who assume various important roles, such as management, finance and accounts, and frontline service provision, have weakened the capacity of government apparatuses to implement development schemes.

In addition to the aforesaid problem of poor fund utilisation in development schemes, staff shortages, particularly shortages of frontline service providers, could also be aggravating the problem of corruption in India.

It can be argued that there are primarily three forms of corruption in the country. First, institutional corruption by government officials involved in major decisions pertaining to public procurement (contracts given to private parties for construction of roads, flyovers and so on), extractive industries (contracts given to private parties for mining and fossil fuel extraction), and other natural resources (for instance, the sale of land owned by the government to private parties). Second, oppressive corruption in the enforcement of laws and regulations (for example, the enforcement of traffic laws, building regulations and regulations for carrying out commercial activities). Third, corruption in the delivery of public services (for instance, in the issuance of passports and driver's licenses and the provision of drinking water and sanitation facilities).

Different factors enable the aforementioned types of corruption. Institutional corruption is linked to the lack of transparency in government decision-making processes and weak accountability mechanisms. Oppressive corruption is possible due to vulnerabilities of different sections of the population, such as the lack of education, caste, religion, gender, age and migration. Corruption in public service delivery is inherently related to the demand in terms of scale and frequency for certain public services far exceeding the supply of these services. Since corruption in the delivery of public services is facilitated by the inadequate supply of services, it is plausible that the shortage of government personnel can aggravate this problem.

As stated at the outset, the weakening capacity of the government apparatus in India is primarily a result of shortsighted fiscal consolidation measures pursued in the country over the last one and a half decades. The following section attempts to explain this phenomenon.

Fiscal policy discouraging long-term public expenditure commitments

The main cause of the problem of staff shortages in the regular cadres of state government departments in India seems to be rooted in the kind of fiscal consolidation strategies that state governments have followed over the last one and a half decades. In their attempts to eliminate the revenue deficits[1] in their budgets (and show a revenue surplus, in some cases), many states appear to have limited their long-term expenditure commitments, particularly in social sectors, by freezing recruitment of regular cadres in their departments. An analysis of the fiscal policies of states, especially those striving to eliminate revenue deficits in their budgets such as Odisha, Chhattisgarh and Bihar, among others, reveals similar trends of freezing recruitment in regular cadre posts for a long time.

In India, the total expenditure from the budget is categorised separately as plan expenditure and non-plan expenditure. Plan expenditure refers to all kinds of government expenditure incurred on the development programmes/schemes adopted through the Five Year Plans. Non-plan expenditure refers to all kinds of government expenditure that remains outside the purview of the Five Year Plan (such as, expenditure on defence, law and order, interest payments, pension and other retirement benefits for regular cadre government employees, and the expenditure towards the sustenance of government institutions in the development sectors, among others). A very large part of non-plan expenditure in the states is meant for the salaries of staff working for the government.

It can be argued that non-plan expenditure determines the strength of a state government apparatus in terms of the availability of regular qualified staff who carry out various kinds of functions including the planning, implementation and monitoring of development programmes/schemes. Over the last one and a half decades, non-plan expenditure in social sectors has been checked by many states due to the emphasis of prevailing fiscal policy on the reduction of deficits through the curtailment of public expenditure.

Sharing of resources between the central government and state governments has been one of the most important aspects of India's federal fiscal architecture. Since the early 1990s, the fiscal policy in India has strengthened the central government's position vis-à-vis the states in terms of control over fiscal resources. The trends in gross devolution and transfers (GDT) from the central government to states as percentages of the country's gross domestic product (GDP), as well as the trends in GDT as percentages of aggregate disbursements by state governments, show a decline over the last two and a half decades, as demonstrated in Table 13.4. Thus, the overall volume of fiscal resources transferred from the central government to the states has not kept pace with the growth in expenditure commitments for the states. Moreover, the composition of the overall volume of fiscal resources transferred from the central government to the states had also changed in terms of the share of untied resources in total annual transfers falling in the last decade and a half.

India's policies in the domain of centre-state sharing of resources over the past decade and a half had neglected the need for greater magnitudes of untied resources to be transferred to state governments. Transfers of resources tied to the conditionalities and guidelines of central government ministries had increased during this period. The transfer of such resources did not quite enable state governments to increase or even sustain their existing levels of long-term expenditure commitments, especially those regarding staff in the regular cadres of their departments.

For instance, the central Ministry of Human Resource Development has been running a programme at the level of elementary education called Sarva Shiksha Abhiyan since 2001, for which resources are transferred to the states every year for implementation. These resources are tied to the expenditure norms and guidelines of the scheme. In this scheme, the states are required to hire only contractual teachers, who are paid meagre salaries of around Rs. 5,000 per month as compared to the salaries of regular teachers, which would be at least four times higher. They cannot hire regular or permanent cadre teachers with these resources. Had

Table 13.4 Sharing of resources between centre and states in India: gross devolution and transfers from centre to states

Year	*GDT from centre to states* (Crore Rs.)*	*GDT as % of GDP*	*GDT as % of aggregate disbursements of states*
1988–89	30,333	7.1	45.2
1989–90	32,862	6.7	42.8
1990–91	40,859	7.2	44.9
1998–99	102,268	5.8	39.1
1999–00	95,652	4.9	31.1
2000–01	106,730	5.1	31.4
2001–02	119,213	5.2	32.3
2002–03	128,656	5.2	31.4
2003–04	143,783	5.2	28.0
2004–05	160,750	5.0	29.0
2005–06	178,871	4.8	31.8
2006–07	220,462	5.1	33.5
2007–08	267,276	5.4	35.5
2008–09	297,980	5.3	33.8
2009–10	324,090	5.0	31.9
2010–11	392,460	5.0	33.9
2011–12	438,430	4.9	30.6
2012–13	497,900	5.0	30.5
2013–14	595,630	5.2	–

Source: CBGA (2013).

Note: * GDT include states' shares of central taxes, grants from the centre and gross loans from the centre.

the states been given these resources every year as untied resources, they could have filled the vacancies in the positions of regular cadre teachers in schools.

The declining share of untied resources in total annual transfers from the central government to the states and the absence of any significant increase in own tax revenue collection by the states[2] had constrained the abilities of state governments to make long-term expenditure commitments, such as those on regular cadre staff. As a result, most state governments could not fill the vacancies in regular cadre staff positions in various sectors, even though the number of sanctioned positions of the regular cadre staff would most likely be smaller than the required number of personnel given that the population to be served is growing. When state governments are compelled to increase the human resources in a sector, they are relying primarily upon temporary workers, some of whom are hired on fixed short-term contracts, and many are hired effectively as casual workers. The expenditure towards the salaries for these contractual staff is much less as compared to regular cadre staff, but their lack of competence for skilled jobs as well as lack of motivation due to the poor work conditions has been a major concern.

Recently, the Fourteenth Finance Commission of India has introduced visible changes in the domain of centre-state sharing of resources, which would be applicable for the five years from 2015–16 to 2019–20. It would change the composition of the resources transferred to states significantly in favour of untied funds; though state governments may not get much higher volumes of resources transferred from the centre, they would certainly have a much greater autonomy now in designing their public expenditure priorities. However, this has happened at the cost of the central government reducing its own budgetary spending on a large number of development programmes; the state governments would need to use much of their untied funds to sustain such development programmes. This issue has been a subject of heated public debates in the country since the changes in centre-state sharing of resources and the restructuring of the central budget were announced in February 2015. This issue of the state governments being given more untied funds primarily at the cost of reduced central government support in the ongoing development programmes is rooted in the country's low tax-GDP ratio and the absence of any strong policy measure to increase the same significantly.

It needs to be emphasised that one of the root causes of the inadequate supply of public services lies in the low magnitude of the tax-GDP ratio in India. Over the past decade, the country's tax-GDP ratio – the combined figure for taxes raised by the central government and states – has been around 17 per cent or less, which is much lower than the tax-GDP ratios of many of the other Group of Twenty (G-20) countries and some of the other BRICS (Brazil, Russia, India, China and South Africa) countries. For instance, the tax-GDP ratio for the year 2010 was just 16.3 per cent for India, while it was a much higher 33.2 per cent for Brazil and 33.8 per cent for the OECD countries on an average (Figure 13.1). Thus, the overall magnitude of public resources available to the government in India has been inadequate in comparison to several other countries; India cannot address the inability

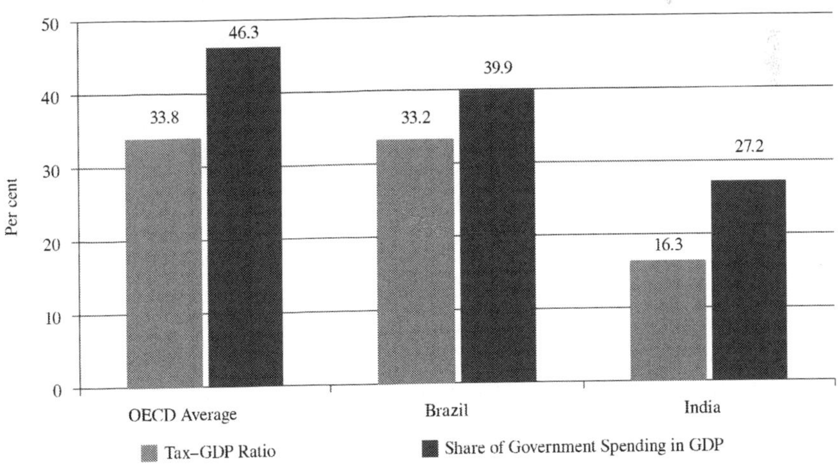

Figure 13.1 Tax-GDP ratio and total government spending as per cent of GDP for India, Brazil and OECD average (as of 2010)

Source: CBGA (2014).

of its state governments to make long-term expenditure commitments so long as its tax-GDP ratio continues to be low.

Another development in India over the past two decades has further constrained the abilities of state governments (as well as the central government) to hire regular cadre staff – the pressure to increase salaries through salary scale revisions at regular intervals. The central government appoints a pay commission once every decade and then implements its recommended salary scale revisions. The Fourth Pay Commission's recommendations were implemented beginning in January 1986, the Fifth Pay Commission's recommendations were implemented beginning in January 1996 and the Sixth Pay Commission's recommendations were implemented in the latter half of the subsequent decade. It has been argued that the Fifth Pay Commission, deviating from the trend of previous pay commissions, recommended sharp increases in pay scales at higher levels of government staff in the central government.

It is worthwhile to note that the sharp increases in pay scales for higher levels of government staff recommended by the Fifth Pay Commission were implemented in the post-liberalisation era of the Indian economy, during which salaries for senior corporate executives in the private sector had started to increase rapidly. This development, the result of a number of factors after the opening up of the Indian economy in the early 1990s, is believed to have had an impact on the recommendations of the Fifth Pay Commission.

Usually, most state governments follow the central government's pay scale revisions with similar increases in their own pay scales for employees, though it is not mandatory. Hence, following the Fifth Pay Commission's recommendations, the salary scales of regular cadre employees were increased sharply in the central government and in most states as well. The consolidation of this development at the end of the 1990s pushed many states towards the policy of freezing recruitment in regular cadre positions in various sectors. The intertwined trend of increasing salaries for regular cadre staff in the central and state governments, on the one hand, and growing shortage of the total number of regular cadre staff, on the other hand, has continued since the Sixth Pay Commission's recommendations were implemented. For instance, the figures for average salaries of regular cadre staff in the government sector provided by the Fourteenth Finance Commission (Government of India, 2014) indicate that the per employee annual salary of regular cadre civilian staff of the central government has gone up from 3.7 times the per capita income of the country in 2007–08 to 4.6 times the per capita income in 2012–13; and, the per employee annual salary of regular cadre staff in the state governments in 2012–13 varied from 3 to 7.7 times the per capita income of the country across states.

The report of the Seventh Pay Commission set up by the central government is expected to be available by the end of 2015; unless this Pay Commission takes a holistic view of the situation, the problem of reluctance and weakening abilities of state governments to address the shortages of skilled staff could aggravate further in the coming years. Also, the state governments need to be persuaded by the fiscal policymakers in India to use the Fourteenth Finance Commission–induced autonomy in expenditure priority-setting adequately to improve the availability of skilled human resources in their government apparatuses, especially in the development sectors. However, as indicated earlier, no long-term or substantive policy measure to address this issue can be pursued in India until its tax-GDP ratio remains very low.

Policy recommendations for the framework of SDGs

The problem of staff shortages in the social sectors has constrained the abilities of state governments in India to fully and effectively utilise budgetary resources being provided for programmes and schemes. Moreover, the problem of staff shortages, especially those pertaining to skilled service providers, can aggravate corruption in the delivery of some public services. India thus needs to address the issue of weakening capacity of the executive and government apparatuses if it wants to ensure good governance and effective institutions, which would no doubt be a strong enabler of sustainable development. Addressing other issues such as space for people's participation, transparency and accountability are absolutely necessary but not really adequate for the country.

It is certainly not the case that the erosion of the capacity of governance in terms of staff shortages in key sectors is the only serious problem with the delivery of public services in India. Problems relating to limited scope for community participation, lack of transparency and weak mechanisms of accountability are equally serious problems in this regard. In the present framework of the SDGs, parameters like space for people's participation, transparency and accountability have been well incorporated, but the issue of the erosion of the capacity of governance due to problems with a country's fiscal policy has been omitted.

The situation regarding capacity of governance in India could be similar to those in numerous other countries. In fact, in the context of the fiscal consolidation measures being adopted in many of the OECD countries in the wake of the economic recession a few years ago, an OECD study (OECD, 2012) cautioned that drastic measures of 'rightsizing' the government sector with the objective of fiscal consolidation through budget cuts might result in a reduction of capacity to deliver the public services needed or a demoralised workforce.

Thus, it is necessary to incorporate a strong fiscal policy perspective on governance and institutions in the discourse on SDGs and the associated national targets in order to highlight the significance of governance capacity in the journey towards SDGs, especially in the developing and less-developed countries. Given that the weakening of governance capacity can be rooted in the fiscal policy, including the taxation policy, being adopted in a country, the targets and indicators associated with the SDGs could also incorporate substantive policy directions to encourage developing and less-developed countries to pursue fiscal policies that would create enabling environments for good governance and effective institutions.

Notes

1 In India, the central government and state governments are required to have two accounts stated in their budgets, the capital account and revenue account. A government's financial transactions that have an impact on its assets or liabilities – such as expenditure

on construction of a factory or a hospital building, repayment of the principal amount of a loan, selling off a public sector undertaking company – are reported in the capital account of the budget. Its transactions that have no impact on the assets or liabilities – such as payment of salaries and wages, expenditure on scholarships, receipts from taxes, user charges – are reported in the revenue account. When expenditure exceeds receipts in the revenue account in a fiscal year, there is a revenue deficit. Some economists argue that a government should not run a revenue deficit, as that would imply that it is financing revenue expenditure, which does not generate any flow of income in the future, by borrowing. However, such fiscal orthodoxy has been strongly challenged by other economists.

2 In the Indian tax system, the central government collects two-thirds of the total tax revenue, while states collect one-third. Most of the buoyant taxes are in the central government's tax system.

References

ASER Centre. (2014) *Annual Status of Education Report (Rural) 2013*. New Delhi: ASER Centre.

CBGA. (2013) *How Has the Dice Rolled? Response to Union Budget 2013–14*. New Delhi: Centre for Budget and Governance Accountability (CBGA).

CBGA. (2014) *Has the Tide Turned? Response to Union Budget 2014–15*. New Delhi: Centre for Budget and Governance Accountability (CBGA).

CBGA and UNICEF. (2011a) *Integrated Child Development Services*. Budgeting for Change Series. New Delhi: Centre for Budget and Governance Accountability (CBGA) and United Nations Children's Fund (UNICEF), India.

CBGA and UNICEF. (2011b) *National Rural Health Mission*. Budgeting for Change Series. New Delhi: Centre for Budget and Governance Accountability (CBGA) and United Nations Children's Fund (UNICEF), India.

CBGA and UNICEF. (2011c) *Sarva Shiksha Abhiyan*. Budgeting for Change Series. New Delhi: Centre for Budget and Governance Accountability (CBGA) and United Nations Children's Fund (UNICEF), India.

CBGA and UNICEF. (2011d) *Total Sanitation Campaign*. Budgeting for Change Series. New Delhi: Centre for Budget and Governance Accountability (CBGA) and United Nations Children's Fund (UNICEF), India.

Das, S. and Shrivastava, S. (2014) Erosion in governance capacity at the sub-national level. *Budget Track*. 10 (1–2). pp.24–26.

Government of India. (2012) *Economic Survey 2011–12*. New Delhi: Ministry of Finance, Government of India.

Government of India. (2014) *Report of the Fourteenth Finance Commission*. New Delhi: Government of India.

Government of India. (2015) *Economic Survey 2014–15*. New Delhi: Ministry of Finance, Government of India.

Indian Staffing Federation. (2014) *Indian Staffing Industry Research 2014 – Flexi Staffing in Government and Public Sector*. New Delhi: Indian Staffing Federation.

Narayan, K. and Mooij, J. (2010) Solutions to teacher absenteeism in rural government primary schools in India: A comparison of management approaches. *The Open Education Journal*. 3. pp.63–71.

OECD. (2012) Current Trends in the Compensation of Public Employees in OECD Countries. In *Public Sector Compensation in Times of Austerity* (pp.17–40). Paris: OECD Publishing.

Public Health Foundation of India. (2012) *From 'Paramedics' to Allied Health Professionals: Landscaping the Journey and Way Forward.* New Delhi: Public Health Foundation of India.

United Nations. (2015) *Transforming Our World: The 2030 Agenda for Sustainable Development.* New York: United Nations.

Varma, S. (2013) Indian higher education: 40% of college teachers temporary, quality of learning badly hit. *The Times of India*, November 10.

14 Mind the data gap

Evaluating MDGs' contribution to the improvement of statistical capacities in Bolivia, 2000–2013

Katerine F. Saravia Olivarez and Wilson Jiménez Pozo

Introduction

Since the early years of the 21st century, Bolivia has undertaken activities for monitoring the Millennium Development Goals (MDGs) through national reports based on data from the statistical systems of the central government.

Seven reports of the MDG progress have been published by official entities between 2000 and 2013. The first two reports were promoted by the United Nations Development Programme (UNDP), while from 2004 the Bolivian government agreed to the creation of an Interagency Committee of the Millennium Development Goals (CIMDM). This was led by the Analytical Unit for Social and Economic Policies (UDAPE) and involved the National Statistics Institute (INE), Ministries of Education and Health, as well as the executive on water and basic sanitation and Vice-Ministry of Public Investment and External Financing (VIPFE).

CIMDM generated a methodological basis to define and build indicators, established guidelines for strengthening the MDG monitoring system, and proposed to improve data collection records in the Bolivian health sector. Despite CIMDM's initial momentum that promoted its establishment, in subsequent years, MDG monitoring activities have been declining. Consequently, the information continually lagged behind (see Annex 14.2) and had an impact on institutional weakness of entities that form the national statistical system.

The present paper describes the MDG monitoring process in Bolivia, based on documents and analysis of national Statistical Information System (SIS) activities, focusing on the sources, processes and results related to the MDGs' monitoring. Furthermore, interviews and surveys were conducted with identified relevant participants, who were particularly responsible for tracking and following the MDGs from the initial stages of the setting up. The purpose of the aforesaid exercise was to evaluate the institutional capacities and come up with a proposal for an evaluation framework in view of the post-2015 agenda. The data collection methodology for this study is detailed in Annex 14.1.

Background

Between 2000 and 2013, Bolivia experienced political, institutional and social changes which slowed progress towards achieving the MDGs. The economic growth rate accelerated from 2.51 per cent in 2000 to 6.78 per cent in 2013 (INE, 2014). Between 2000 and 2005, economic average growth was 3 per cent, and between 2006 and 2013 it was 5 per cent. Macroeconomic policies privileged stability, so inflation remained at low levels despite the effects of the international financial crisis in the early years of the last decade. Between 2006 and 2013, fiscal surplus was achieved by Bolivia under an international context characterised by high prices of commodities, especially oil, mining and other agricultural products.

Between 2000 and 2005, Bolivia experienced a period of high social tension, political instability and social conflict. In this backdrop, Morales won the 2005 election with 54 per cent of the votes. Between 2006 and 2013, tax revenue increased and determined an expansion of public investment and expenditures. Central government pursued higher investment levels in infrastructure, besides distributing surpluses in natural resources to vulnerable groups through social protection policies.

Social changes in Bolivia that led to a decrease in inequality were not accompanied by institutional changes of the same magnitude. The entities that perform monitoring and assessment of development and population welfare have fallen behind.

Research questions

Nowadays, many entities and institutions have been asking themselves about the situation and advances made towards monitoring of the MDGs. It is important because each country needs to know precisely its successes or failures, which depends on the quality of the statistical systems. Furthermore, the international community is preparing the post-2015 Sustainable Development Goals (SDGs) and the tools for their implementation. Consequently, an evaluation is needed of the achievements, changes and improvements done for the MDGs, to correct mistakes and make the necessary changes. Bolivia is not an exception and needs to take into account the situation of its follow-up and monitoring mechanisms, so that we acknowledge how reliable and accurate the provided data are. The research proposes the following *questions* focused on institutional capacity and a statistical evaluation, because they constitute the basis for monitoring the MDGs:

- Has attention to the need for strengthening institutional capacities in statistics increased, in order to track indicators of development including the MDGs?
- Do MDGs coincide with the priorities of the Bolivian national agenda?
- Were there partnerships between national and international statistical systems to strengthen the production of statistics and indicators of development?
- Has coordination within Bolivia between government agencies improved, to enhance the national and subnational reports?
- Have the MDGs contributed to improving data quality indicators for development at the national and international statistical systems?
- Have the MDGs developed new statistical methodologies to guide changes in the data availability, quality and comparability, besides the promotion and adoption of international agreements with international standards?
- What was the role of institutions in the task of monitoring targets and indicators in the context of the MDGs?

The main objective of this paper is to assess statistical capacity of Bolivia to build indicators on social development, and then respond to the challenges of post-2015 SDGs. The Bolivian case study is focused on national statistical capacity, in order to propose challenges for an appropriate monitoring of the SDG agenda.

National monitoring of the MDGs

First, this paper reviews the socio-political context in Bolivia over the 13 years since the Millennium Declaration. After that, there follows a brief description of the principal tools implemented by the entity responsible for the MDG tracking and monitoring process.

Bolivian institutional frame of the MDGs' tracking and monitoring

In the early 2000s, Bolivia published its Poverty Reduction Strategy Paper (PRSP). It was an initiative originating from international cooperation that benefited several countries with the aim to reducing external debt, in exchange for directing resources to the fight against poverty.

After a process of national dialogue in 2001, the Bolivian PRSP was approved; it contained commitments related to 42 priorities regarding employment opportunities and income, productive capacities, security and protection, participation and social integration. In order to track its development, an inter-institutional board for strategy monitoring (namely, the Interagency Council for Monitoring and Evaluation – CISE) was created, aiming to evaluate the strategy and adjust to result management.

Implementation of the Bolivian PRSP was not a success story, mostly due to various external factors. These included deteriorating macroeconomic conditions, a fiscal crisis, institutional weaknesses and design of poverty reduction in a centralised framework. It was led by a Directory of Funds, which transferred resources to debt relief municipal accounts with several rules that reduced leeway.

At the same time, UNDP was promoting the MDGs and preparing a national report. In 2004, CIMDM was formed as a government council that developed the basis for monitoring the MDGs. In 2006, it set the basis for matching the MDGs with the National Development Plan. Even though CIMDM promoted coordination meetings of SIS, this achievement did not generate actions to improve the monitoring tools.

Information systems for national monitoring

The national statistical information system is regulated by a decree law (14100) promulgated in 1976. Since then, no authority could adopt a modernisation of that system. The absence of a regulatory framework prevents strengthening the statistical capacities of state entities and generates uncertainty over the participation of society in activities of public statistics.

National entities developed statistical activities with overlapping functions and a lack of clarity in the definition of the official public statistics. INE is part of regional initiatives to improve the measurement of welfare statistics through household surveys from 1999 to date. It also developed health surveys and collected a survey of employment information. INE has conducted demographic and health surveys under the supervision of the World Health Organization (WHO) that supported the design and processing of these surveys. However, the data processing was delegated to a company, causing the loss of some legitimacy due to the estimates yielded. Finally, no mention was made by CIMDM regarding the changes in how indicators were calculated from the records.

Tracking information and indicators related to the MDGs are the responsibility of the UDAPE, which is in charge of collecting the data organised according to each MDG. UDAPE, as CIMDM chair, presented three tools for monitoring the MDGs:

- *Indicators Group:* composed of 47 indicators and 15 goals selected for monitoring the MDGs; they vary in disaggregation among themselves. UDAPE's website presents a summary sheet for each indicator, including a methodological explanation; however, only the data up to 2009 are available.
- *Programs and Projects Group:* generated by entities related to UN or the Bolivian government. It presents information related to human development interventions (only the data up to 2008 are available). It details coverage and financial resources. In case of the most important programmes, there is a standardised summary.
- *Report Group:* composed of seven national reports presented until 2013 (at departmental level there are short reports for 2010 and 2011 on some topics).

Information systems applied for monitoring

HOUSEHOLD SURVEY

INE has been conducting household surveys for several years, with different levels of coverage and emphasis. Since 2003, the household survey has been increasing its coverage, and adding multi-thematic questionnaires including questions on health, education and employment, among others (between 1999 and 2002 there were only surveys on measurement of living conditions).

NATIONAL DEMOGRAPHIC AND HEALTH SURVEY (ENDSA)

These surveys are carried out every five years to provide databases to enable informed decision-making, strengthen technical capacity, expand the base, etc.[1] The last ENDSA-registered data referred to fertility, family planning, exposure to risk of pregnancy, mortality, reproductive health of adults, etc. However, the 2003 ENDSA does not present some data in its index clearly, such as maternal mortality.

Information systems for sectoral monitoring

EDUCATIONAL INFORMATION SYSTEM (SIE)

This system is designed to respond to the present needs of the plurinational educational system and disseminate reliable information. However, access to information platforms is not available to the public, because it requires the entry of a username and the correct password, or the page is disabled. Only administrative information is available.

The method of data collection from the records of primary and secondary education was recently changed. Until 2007, the data was collected manually in the SIE. The new Register of Students (RUDE) has helped improve the quality of educational data through control and automatic processing. Changes in the registration system caused unexpected trend variations of education coverage indicators.

NATIONAL SYSTEM OF EPIDEMIOLOGICAL SURVEILLANCE AND HEALTH

This unit provides health data and information needed for decision-making and proper implementation of public health policies. It has information subsystems and plans to establish committees of analysis. Its website has epidemiological information, production services, laboratory information, evaluation of solid waste, network services, human resources (2007, 2009 and 2011, and only in some cases prior to 2001) and demographic information (less detailed for 2001–2006 than for 2007–2012), among others. Disaggregated data can be obtained according to different categories.

INFORMATION SYSTEMS OF THE MINISTRY OF ENVIRONMENT AND WATER

This ministry has various information systems, such as the Information System on Water and Sanitation Sector (SISAS) and the National Environmental Information System (SNIA). However, it requires a username and password for access. The platform SIAS (Water and Sanitation Information System) is not available.

EXTERNAL FINANCING INFORMATION SYSTEM (SISFIN)

This system was created to collect, process and disseminate information related to resource management, allocation, and implementation and monitoring of external financing. The database was not available when this study was being carried out, because its public access platform was still being developed.

PUBLIC INVESTMENT MAP

The map, available at the website of the VIPFE, is an educational resource that shows the number of projects being developed in each region. It also shows the percentage of allocation for these projects by sectors and donors. Nonetheless, it does not allow a review by series, since it only presents the current project. Moreover, it is statedly a draft version (reviewed on 13 September 2014).

Results

We present the main results from the following sources: (i) CIMDM reports, (ii) national and sectoral systems, and (iii) opinion of eight qualified interviewees. We combine and compare the results from these different sources to provide inputs for the analysis of the MDG monitoring activities in Bolivia.

The follow-up and monitoring systems implemented by UDAPE were validated to prove its availability and use as instruments of measurement and analysis. The validation process enabled us to show how systematic and periodic the information in the MDGs' reports is, and how it measures the advances towards reaching the goals. During the process, it is possible to point to the technical, institutional and political difficulties that influence the quality of the data presented. The application of the systems of monitoring provides key elements for the evaluation of policies applied by general and subnational governments. Thus, it is possible to improve the policies and get better results that foster human development.

Changes in the institutional capacity

The government developed more capacities for monitoring and evaluating the MDGs since the second report of the MDGs' advances (UDAPE and UNDP, 2002). This happened because the MDGs were perceived as an incentive for the consolidation of the national system of statistical information. The report emphasises data sources, such as census, surveys and administrative records, which enabled the implementation and monitoring of public policies. Therefore, more emphasis was put on the investment on data generation and analysis. However, the results did not match expectations. UDAPE was strengthened as head of the CIMDM, but the other members did not increase their capacities to accompany the process (Interviewee 7, personal communication, 20 June 2014).

According to the interviews, INE has an institutional weakness attributed to different causes. First, the government has centralised many of the decisions, and therefore the public entities (such as INE) have a narrow scope of action. INE has been in charge of data generation for monitoring the MDGs, but it does not have an active role in the CIMDM, especially in the methodological aspects in the elaboration of statistics. The workers' incentives in INE and other public entities are not competitive. For example, the mobile nature of work at the INE is not attractive for skilled workers (Interviewee 6, personal communication, 13 August 2014). Another example comes from the recent national census, where INE announced three different population estimates and modified the distribution of variables between the different official census publications (Interviewees 1, 2 and 6, personal communication, June and August 2014).

A positive aspect is the strengthening of the statistical capacity fostered by the need to monitor the MDGs. To complete such tasks, the methods of data recollection to estimate key indicators were clarified and updated. For example, data on water and basic sanitation were released; the United Nations Children's Fund (UNICEF) provided a methodology based on international standards and UDAPE implemented them (Interviewee 5, personal interview, 15 July 2014). However, an important source of information to estimate health indicators, such as the DHS,[2] was not conducted in 2013, and the previous is a survey from 2008.

Finally, UDAPE made the necessary efforts to estimate indicators for the last MDG, which were not previously available. These indicators were presented in the last report, but the statistical capacity to estimate them continuously has not been strengthened.

Coordination within the government

Since the different monitoring and evaluation systems were established during the first years of the Bolivian Poverty Reduction Strategy (BPRS), different institutions adopted specific roles. UDAPE led the information process and INE became the information provider (Interviewee 2, personal interview, 12 June 2014).

Different institutions were responsible for the first few MDGs reports. For example, the UN promoted the first report, while UDAPE, INE and the national office of the UNDP worked together on the second report. The role of UDAPE in monitoring the BPRS increased its legitimacy over other public entities. International cooperation led to the creation of the CIMDM, but it only considered national institutions (leaving behind the international cooperation) (Interviewee 1, personal interview, 12 June 2014).

The CIMDM aimed to generate information, analyse and promote the MDGs oriented to public policies, but made insufficient progress (Interviewees 1 and 2, personal communication, 12 June 2014). UDAPE generated all necessary information to create the reports that corresponded to each member of CIMDM and did not always use the statistics information system. Furthermore, the institutions of the CIMDM did not complement each other. Even INE did not play a key role, although it could have helped in the estimation of several indicators. None of the preliminary reports was a joint effort of the members of the committee. Instead, UDAPE was left in charge of all the tasks and the other members did not play an active role in the monitoring and evaluation tasks (Interviewee 1, 2, 3 and 7, personal communication, June 2014).

INE, the most important institution in charge of the data provision for monitoring the MDGs, did not have the capacity to carry out regular surveys. It also could not work with other members of the CIMDM to improve the design of administrative records and did not have the incidence capacity in the elaboration process of the first MDG reports (Interviewee 2, personal communication, 12 June 2014). This element, strengthened by political changes, caused INE's institutional weakness and its low credibility in recent years[3] (Interviewee 1, personal interview, 12 June 2014).

MDGs and the national agenda

BPRS had a broad approach to fighting poverty; it comprised different sectors such as education and health. As a result of the BPRS, different indicators linked to the MDGs were already incorporated into the statistical system, though integration of indicators was not complete.

In spite of the positive circumstances for improving the SIS, the government did not adequately disseminate the information. By the time the MDGs were being diffused in Bolivia, the government did not emphasise some of the goal areas enough. However, the BPRS was an instrument that helped guide the process (Interviewee 3, personal interview, 20 June 2014).

In 2003, the national government evaluated the implementation of the BPRS and detected severe problems concerning the information system for monitoring and evaluating the strategy. Moreover, the necessary resources were not available (Gray, 2003). Under the circumstances, the first stage was to establish the CISE with the aim of helping in the monitoring and evaluation of the BPRS. Later, different institutions worked on the adaptation of the BPRS towards the complete implementation of the MDGs in Bolivia.

New statistical methodologies

To improve the monitoring of progress toward the MDGs, official authorities expanded the set of indicators. The third report (2003) added indicators, targets and objectives of each of the MDGs. The CIMDM presented the methodology of each through a specialised publication (UDAPE, 2005).[4] At the same time, the Ministry of Finance's information system on budget execution was presented, which supplemented the analysis of public resources oriented to the MDGs.

Between the fourth and the last report (UDAPE, 2013), more indicators and detailed information were included, which was disaggregated at the municipal level, by ethnicity, linguistic groups and wealth level. The 2008 report also incorporated indicators and targets that assess the progress, which means a step forward toward integration of sources that were underutilised. The sixth report (UDAPE, 2010) identified gaps related to levels of employment by sector, geographical disparities and socio-economic inequalities, demonstrating the need for more information to guide policy action.

For the malnutrition indicator that informs the first goal, there is no data available since the national information system on health (http: snis.minsalud.gob.bo/snis/) is still under construction. Also, short-term employment indicators are not available since the government halted data collection from the employment survey (data collected only between 2009 and 2010).

With regard to Goal 2, achieving universal access to primary education, the monitoring tool introduced a significant change after the implementation of the RUDE that began in 2007. In previous years, the net enrolment rate of primary education was calculated based on the SIE. However, the data show a different pattern. These differences are attributed to the management of information, based on self-reports of the educational units on the number of students in each grade, which are derived from the registers made at the beginning of the year, drop-outs during the year, and approvals and disapprovals at the end of the year. There was no strict control of the name of pupils or transfers of school during the schooling year. Many schools also had an incentive to report more students, which would ensure that they do not lose a number of contracts for teachers. The data from RUDE and SIE have different methodologies and the comparability is weak. The RUDE register has a better design and stronger controls, but accessibility to this system is still limited.

The interviewees highlighted the availability of information to the public as an issue (Interviewees 1, 2, 4 and 6, personal interviews, June to August 2014). Some institutions developed and improved the ability to generate information, but it is not available to users. UDAPE and INE are not spreading the data and placed restrictions through the use of electronic keys in the websites. For example, the Population and Housing Census reveals a decline in the availability of data. A few months after the collection of data from the 2001 Census, estimates of poverty and infant mortality were openly available, whereas the same indicators are not available from Census 2012 (Interviewee 4, personal interview, 26 June 2014).

Technological progress facilitates access to information and reduces delays in the delivery of data. However, some statistical information systems do not have data online yet (Interviewee 5, personal interview, 15 July 2014). For example, health indicators require a password to access the National Health Information System (SNIS). Moreover, the platform of the Ministry of Health had severe problems in its applications installer.[5]

Furthermore, indicators related to access to water and basic sanitation were developed and improved in the past years, but still have access restrictions. UNDP used linear projections, whereas the government institutions refer to data from censuses of 1992 and 2001, together with estimates of the household surveys, without showing the complete series. UNICEF supported the initiative to develop linear projections on water and sanitation (Interviewee 5, personal communication, 15 July 2014).

Data quality

In early 2000, there were some difficulties with the information systems and data availability for monitoring and evaluation of the MDGs. The government chose UDAPE as the institution to define the baseline and indicators and the implementation of the MDG monitoring system. UDAPE came across much difficulty in accomplishing its set task due to weak data quality.[6] The omitted information system data for recent years, for example, the base year, presented a critical situation, especially for indicators related to maternal mortality that was absent from the report, causing uncertainty about the initial level in this important goal.

The report of sectoral progress had to resolve errors on administrative records, especially in health indicators, in the absence of instances that verify the quality of data collected. Sometimes there were different values for the same indicator in the same period, and differences between publications of national institutions that are part of the CIMDM. Sectoral information systems had a technological lag and caused delays in the information. The data was questionable and the training of the people who conduct the registers was inadequate because they were unfamiliar with the importance of the information (Interviewee 2, personal interview, 12 June 2014).

While official data from INE are perceived to be of low quality by most of those interviewed, it is attributed to the interference of the central government (Interviewee 1, personal interview, 12 June 2014). Once again cited is poverty reduction that contains measurement errors (Interviewee 7, personal interview, 13 August 2014). Child mortality indicators also contained errors, though not so critical (Interviewee 5, personal interview, 15 July 2014). These errors cause less reliance on published information.

The institutional weakness of INE is an additional constraint. Household surveys have weaknesses that result from the application of different sampling frames. Sample designs are not the same every year and they have lack of transparency in results dissemination. Statistical series on poverty and inequality have little coherence with other Bolivian economic data. Statistical processes are sometimes incomplete and reflected in different trends estimated by agencies such as the World Bank and UN Economic Commission for Latin America and the Caribbean (UN-ECLAC).

On the fifth MDG objective, the rate of teen pregnancy is reported from the SNIS; however, there is a gap in periods corresponding to the calculated indicator. It might be due to a failure of communication for the government during a specific period of application of the data. In the case of child and maternal mortality, there are problems of estimation: There is a high error margin, and there could be a problem of overestimation.[7]

As a result, information related to MDG targets needs to be corrected and verified in order to find out accurately about the achievements in Bolivia.

Challenges for monitoring the post-2015 agenda

In designing a monitoring system for the post-2015 agenda, the lessons of the MDG process monitoring should be taken into cognisance so that problems associated with institutional weaknesses are not repeated. Recommendations of experts which could help improve the information in Bolivia include the following:

- It should be made mandatory to update the legal framework of the SIS. The new information law should ensure statistical activity as a strategy for measuring economic and social progress. It should strengthen the role of national and sectoral statistical systems and help as territorial subsystems for the generation, processing and use of statistical information.
- International cooperation should provide guidelines or best practices that can be appropriated by the government from the lessons learned from other countries.
- It should strengthen the technical capacity of state agencies for data collection, processing and management of SIS.
- INE should decentralise statistical processes, but establish technical guidelines, adopt a regulatory role and validate the produced data.
- The data collection process should consider the data needed for public policy.

- It should improve the ability of INE through a bigger budget and internal organisational changes.
- Processes should be implemented to ensure data quality.
- It should require open access from different information systems that provide indicators related to MDG for all users.
- The processes performed for MDG monitoring should be transparent and more visible.
- The social accountability system should be strengthened for users, stakeholders, academics and researchers.

For strengthening statistical operations that measure welfare indicators, it may be helpful to define a plan of survey for a whole decade. It should have a dynamic sampling frame to update the population, defining a set of core variables and establishing coordinated work with local authorities.

It should empower statistical users. Participation of users in the statistical information system overall should be promoted; they should be engaged in data generation through research, especially on issues related to the agenda of post-2015 development. At the same time, improving the quality of the data will allow generation of research and knowledge about the causes of changes in welfare indicators. Information systems must also address priority information needs of Bolivian Agenda 2025, beginning with the assessment of changes in multidimensional indicators.

Bolivia's government should strengthen or redirect CIMDM through the participation of local stakeholders, academia and the private sector related to data collection and social research.

Conclusions and final thoughts

This paper discussed issues related to the ability of the SIS for monitoring the MDGs and the prospects for improvement in monitoring the post-2015 agenda. After the evaluation, we arrive at the following conclusions:

- The international community promoted statistical projects to improve capacities at the local level. Setting the data collection standards should be a priority. Consequently, national authorities ought to give more importance to results of policies rather than processes. However, the lack of a framework of the national SIS limited the capabilities of system entities to develop data sources.
- The MDG framework created a basis for guiding the actions of public policy towards the well-being of the population. Bolivia already has a history of a poverty reduction strategy in the framework of the international initiative for Heavily Indebted Poor Countries (HIPC). In 2004, Bolivia drafted a revised PRSP based on the MDGs. However, it adopted the MDGs as part of the national strategy, excessively centralising the monitoring goals, excluding other actors in society or the subnational levels of government.
- Weakness of the institutions of the national statistical system caused the agenda linked to the MDGs to have poor reception at subnational levels. Few

initiatives could generate department-level MDG reports as the UN does. Inter-institutional coordination only served to generate periodic reports at the national level, so had no force to communicate the achievements in human development at other sectors of the state and society. After the research process, it has been detected that the statistical capacity for tracking and monitoring is strongly affected by a poor performance in coordination among the different institutions, which have not worked jointly to draft each of the official reports.

- MDGs should improve the quality of data on indicators about human development at national and subnational levels. Results in Bolivia are mixed. First, it improved the attention of authorities in indicators of result and impact, an aspect that allowed for financing on some tools, such as the household survey data on water and sanitation improvement. However, far from improving the quality of data from household surveys, these had severe problems for monetary poverty measurement. Likewise, this was not on the agenda of a statistical plan for the health sector.
- Initially, CIMDM was allowed to create methodological guidelines to build indicators that allow the temporal comparability and higher quality data. However, as the MDG reports were published, they were not accompanied by actions to improve transparency in the data generation. Poverty indicators were not revised, poverty lines were not updated and the comparability of household surveys is weak.
- Civil society generated contesting initiatives, such as the route of the census, which was critical to the census process. There has been no support from the national authorities.

Notes

1 There are reports for 1989, 1994, 1998, 2003 and 2008.
2 National Demographic and Health Survey.
3 In July 2014, INE announced a variation in the census data of 2012 that increased the size of the population. The new population was 10,059,856, an increase of 32,602 with respect to the initial reports announced by INE itself. The variation was caused by changes in the geo-referenced registers of each community in the census base between 2001 and 2012, and the verification with the Agricultural Census of 2013 (Oxígeno, 2013).
4 The report contained selected indicators for tracking the achievements of the MDGs.
5 The Ministry of Health and Sports software section was updated on 1 September 2014.
6 For example, the Demographic and Health Survey was not updated.
7 UNICEF and the Bolivian Government led the survey of post-census mortality after 2001, but it was not possible to apply it to the 2012 population census due to the delay in the publication of results.

References

Gray, G. (2003) Logros y dificultades en la implementación de la EBRP. In Centro de Estudios para el Desarrollo Laboral y Agrario (CEDLA) (ed.) *Memoria del Seminario:*

A un año de Implementación de la Estrategia Boliviana de Reducción de la Pobreza (pp.9–14). Centro de Estudios para el Desarrollo Laboral y Agrario.

INE. (2014) *Producto de Bolivia Registro Tasa de Crecimiento Histórica de 6.78%.* Available from: www.ine.gob.bo/pdf/boletin/NP_2014_54.pdf [Accessed: 25 April 2014].

Oxígeno, R. (2013) *El INE cambia datos del Censo 2012 y ahora dice que Bolivia tiene 10.059.856 habitantes.* Available from: http://oxigeno.bo/node/1934 [Accessed: 10 September 2014].

UDAPE. (2004) *Tercer Informe sobre los Objetivos de Desarrollo del Milenio.* Available from: http://www.undp.org/content/dam/undp/library/MDG/english/MDG%20 Country%20Reports/Bolivia/3er%20Informe%20de%20Progreso%202004.pdf [Accessed: 8 April 2014].

UDAPE. (2005) *Indicadores seleccionados para el seguimiento del logro de los Objetivos de Desarrollo del Milenio (ODMs).* Available from: http://www.fam.bo/contenidos/ compendio_de_informes_de_los_objetivos_de_desarrollo_del_milenio_en_boliviado cumentosindicators per cent20Seleccionados.pdf [Accessed: 24 April 2014].

UDAPE. (2006) *Cuarto Informe sobre los Objetivos de Desarrollo del Milenio.* Available from: www.udape.gob.bo/portales_html/portalSIG/ . . . /4toinformeODM.pdf [Accessed: 8 April 2014].

UDAPE. (2008) *Quinto Informe sobre los Objetivos de Desarrollo del Milenio.* Available from: http://www.udape.gob.bo/portales_html/ODM/Documentos/InfProgreso/5to%20 Informe%20de%20Progreso.pdf [Accessed: 10 April 2014].

UDAPE. (2010) *Sexto Informe sobre los Objetivos de Desarrollo del Milenio.* Available from: http://www.udape.gob.bo/portales_html/ODM/Documentos/InfProgreso/7moper cent20Informepercent20depercent20progreso.pdf [Accessed: 10 April 2014].

UDAPE. (2013) *Séptimo Informe sobre los Objetivos de Desarrollo del Milenio.* Available from: http://www.udape.gob.bo/portales_html/ODM/Documentos/InfProgreso/7moper cent20Informepercent20de per cent20progreso.pdf [Accessed: 15 June 2014].

UDAPE and UNDP. (2002) *Segundo Informe sobre los Objetivos de Desarrollo del Milenio.* Available from: http://www.udape.gob.bo/portales . . . /2dopercent20Informe percent20de percent20Progreso.pdf [Accessed: 9 April 2014].

UNDP. (2001) *Primer Informe sobre los Objetivos de Desarrollo del Milenio.* Available from: www.udape.gob.bo/ . . . /1er%20Informe%20de%20Progreso%202001.pdf [Accessed: 8 April 2014].

Annexes

Annex 14.1 Data collection methodology

Data collection tools

Interviews under the present study were conducted using semi-structured questionnaires. These included questions about perception, details of the implementation and tools for monitoring the MDGs. The actors associated with the monitoring tasks in governmental institutions were identified through an exercise of stakeholder mapping. The actors include participants at the central state level and the representation of the UN system in Bolivia. They participated in processes such as the preparation of reports, analysis and composition of indicators and related activities.

Most were direct participants from the CIMDM and the UN system. The research followed the procedure outlined here:

- MDG monitoring activities conducted by the CIMDM were prioritised.
- The interviews were conducted with those who held executive positions in institutions part of the CIMDM, emphasising members from UDAPE and INE.
- The representatives of the UNDP were considered for the support offered to the process through a programme of public policy for the MDGs in the decentralised level.
- Once key participants were identified, the survey was carried out with the help of questionnaires applied.

Online questionnaires were administered to respondents who did not have time available for a personal interview, but who could provide valuable information to describe the process, as well as those who no longer held executive positions, but had been part of the process.

As a complementary tool, an extensive review of SIS was conducted. When available, the presented data was compared with published information on each of the reports. Through this exercise, some problems were detected in monitoring the MDGs.

Interview procedure

The interviews were semi-structured, asking:

- Name
- Institution to which the person belongs/belonged when monitoring/evaluating the MDGs
- Which tools or methods were used to monitor? Why that tool?

- What were the characteristics of the methods and tools used for monitoring the MDGs?
- What were the tasks performed to monitor and evaluate the MDGs?
- What were entities or institutions with which you coordinated for the provision of data and development of indicators?
- Which institutions financed/finance the SIS?
- What were the characteristics of the information used for monitoring and evaluation of the MDGs?
- What difficulties or errors were detected in the SIS?
- Were tasks performed to reformulate the SIS? What were they and who did them?
- What was the strategy of data dissemination?
- Did the monitoring and evaluation of the MDGs contribute to public policy?
- How do you think the process of tracking and monitoring the MDGs in our country could be improved?

The questionnaires were customised according to the role of the interviewee or the person's relevant organisation. The online survey had similar questions, but with a more general orientation.

Annex 14.2 Lag estimation (in years)

Goal		Indicators	Report						Goal 2015	Base line	Lag mean	
			2	3	4	5	6	7				
1. Eradicate extreme poverty and hunger	1A. Halve the proportion of people whose income is less than $1 a day	1. Percentage of population in extreme poverty (impact)	37.3	41.3 (2005)	38.2 (2005)	37.7 (2006)	26.1 (2009)	21.6 (2012)	24.1	41.2 (1996)	1.2	MEAN OBJ: 1.309
		2. Extreme poverty gap ratio				18.2 (2006)	12.8 (2009)	10.3 (2012)		22.5 (1996)	1.33	
		3. Share of the poorest quintile in national consumption	3.01 (2001)			1.9 (2006)	2.6 (2009)	3.1 (2012)		1.5 (1996)	1.33	
		4. Percentage of population in moderate poverty	64.4 (2001)			42.7 (2006)	50.6 (2009)	43.4 (2012)		64.8 (1996)	1.33	
	1B. Achieve full and productive employment and decent work for all, including women and young people	1. Growth rate of GDP per person employed					0.8 (2009)	2.7 (2012)		1.9 (1990)	1	
		2. Employment-to-population ratio (%)					63 (2009)	59.6 (2012)		66.5 (1996)	1	
		3. Proportion of employed people living below $1.25 per day					24.2 (2009)	19.7 (2012)		42.0 (1996)	1	
		4. Proportion of won-account and contributing family workers in total employment	54 (2001)				55.4 (2009)	53.7 (2012)		66.1 (1996)	1	
	1C. Halve the proportion of people who suffer from hunger	1. Percentage of children under-three years of age with chronic underweight		24.2 (2003)	24.2 (2003)	25.5 (2003)	20.3 (2008)	18.5 (2012)	21	41.7 (1996)	2.4	
		2. Percentage of children under 5-years old with global under nutrition					6.1 (2008)	3.6 (2012)	4.1	8.3 (1996)	1.5	

(*Continued*)

Annex 14.2 (Continued)

Goal		*Indicators*	*Report*						*Goal 2015*	*Base line*	*Lag mean*	
			2	*3*	*4*	*5*	*6*	*7*				
2. Achieve universal primary education	2A. Ensure that children everywhere will be able to complete a full course of primary schooling	1. Net enrolment ratio in primary education	97 (2001)	97.1 (2003)	94 (2005)	92.7 (2006)	90 (2008)	82.2 (2011)	100	94.1 (2000)	1.5	MEAN OBJ: 1.6
		2. Proportion of pupils starting grade 1 who reach last grade (6th, 8th)	72.7 (2001)	75 (2003)	77.8 (2005)	75.6 (2006)	77.3 (2008)	90 (2011)	100	69.1 (1992)	1.5	
		3. Literacy rate of 15–24 year olds, women and men	86.72	86.7	94.9 (2004)	98.5 (2006)	99.4 (2009)	99.5 (2011)	100	97.4 (1997)	1.8	
3. Promote gender equality and empower women	3A. Eliminate gender disparity in primary and secondary education and in all levels of education	1. Ratios of girls to boys in primary (8th)	104 (asymmetry in primary)	3.4 (2003)	0.3 (2005)	−0.6 (2006)	−1.8 (2008p)	−1.2 (2011)	0	9.7 (1992)	1.6	MEAN OBJ: 1.85
		2. Ratios of girls to boys in secondary (4th)	111 (asymmetry in secondary)	−0.1 n/a	−0.4 (2005)	−1.5 (2006)	−1.4 (2008p)	−5.3 (2011)	0	3.2 (1992)	1.75	
		3. Literacy rate of 15–24 year-olds, women and men	97.72 for both		5 (2004)	89.1 (2006)	99.6 (2009)	1.002 (2012)	1	0.980 (1997)	1.5	
		4. Share of women in wage employment in the non-agricultural sector			32 (2005)	34.6 (2006)	34.7 (2009)	36.4 (2012)		31.3 (1999)	1.25	
		5. Proportion of women in the Parliament				16.9 (2005)	23 (2009)	23 (2009)			2.67	
		6. Proportion of seats held by women in national parliament				28.5 (2004)	43 (2010)	43 (2010)		19 (2004)	2.33	
4. Reduce child mortality	4A. Reduce by 2/3 the under-5 mortality ratio	1. Rate of child mortality					63 (2008)	58 (2011)	43.1	129.4 (1989)	2	MEAN OBJ: 1.83233
		2. Infant mortality rate	55.6 (2001)	54 (2003)	54 (2003)	53.6 (2003)	50 (2008)	48.6 (2011)	27.3	81.9 (1989)	2.33	
		3. Coverage of Pentavalent Vaccination until third dose for under-one-year olds (%)	90 (2001)	80 (2003)	84.5 (2005)	82.6 (2006)	84.5 (2009)	79.7 (2012)	95	68 (1994)	1.167	

5. Improve maternal health	5A. Reduce by 3/4 the maternal mortality ratio	1. Maternal mortality ratio	234 (2000) (Different and non-comparable methodology)	229 (2003)	229 (2003)	229 (2003)	229 (2003)	229 (2003)	104	416 (1989)	4.5	MEAN OBJ: 4.1666667
		2. Proportion of births attended by skilled health personnel (%)	54 (2001)		61.9 (2005)	65 (2006)	67 (2009)	70.8 (2012)	70	33 (1996)	6.5	
	5B. Achieve, by 2015, universal access to reproductive health	1. Contraceptive prevalence rate (%)					60.6 (2008)	60.6 (2008)		30.3 (1989)	3.5	
		2. Adolescent birth rate (15–19 years)					88.8 (2008)	88.8 (2008)		94.3 (1989)	3.5	
		3. Antenatal care coverage					72.3 (2008)	72.3 (2008)		31.9 (1989)	3.5	
		4. Unmet need for family planning (%)					20.2 (2008)	20.2 (2008)		23.2 (1989)	3.5	
6. Combat HIV/ AIDS, malaria and other diseases	6A. Have halted and begun to reverse the spread of HIV/ AIDS	1. HIV prevalence	25.1 (2001)	13.4 (2004)	19.3 (2005)	19.2 (2006)	82.6 (2009)	83.4 (2012)	80–85	2.3 (1996)	1	MEAN OBJ: 1.65714
		2. HIV prevalence among population aged 15–24 years					599 (2009)	973 (2012)			1	
		3. Proportion of 15–24 aged population who have extensive and correct knowledge						Women 22.4 Men 27.7 (2008)			5	
	6B. Achieve universal access to treatment for HIV/AIDS	1. Proportion of population with advanced HIV infection with access to antiretroviral drugs						2.278 (2012)		382 (2006)	1	

(*Continued*)

Annex 14.2 (Continued)

Goal		*Indicators*	*Report*						*Goal 2015*	*Base line*	*Lag mean*	
			2	*3*	*4*	*5*	*6*	*7*				
	6C. Have halted and begun to reverse the incidence of malaria and other major diseases	1. Incidence and death rates associated with malaria	5 (2001)	4.1 (2004)	5.5 (2005)	5.2 (2006)	2.8 (2009)	2.1 (2012)	2	7.5 (1990)	1.2	
		2. Percentage of municipalities with higher infestation rate than 3% with chagas disease		31 (2004)	19 (2005)	30.4 (2006)	19.6 (2009)	35.3 (2012)	0	56 (2003)	1	
		3. Percentage of patients with healed tuberculosis of the patients reported		81.2 (2004)	78.7 (2005)	76.3 (2006)	81.5 (2008)	84.2 (2011)	95	71.2 (2000)	1.4	
7. Ensure environmental sustainability	7A. Integrate the principles of sustainable development into country policies and programmes	1. Proportion of land area covered by forest	47.5 (2001)		47.5 (2005)	47.5 (2005)	53.4 (2009)	53.9 (2010)			2	MEAN OBJ: 1.7668
		2. National Surface of protected areas	16 (2002)		17.2 (2005)	17.1 (2006)	17.1 (2008)	17.1 (2011)	17.2	16.8 (2001)	1.75	
		3. Consumption of ozone-depleting substances (tons of PAO)			30.8 (2005)	36.4 (2005)	9 (2008)	0 (2011)	0	80.3 (2001)	2.75	
	7B. Halve the proportion of people without sustainable access to safe drinking water and basic sanitation	1. Proportion of population using an improved drinking water source	70.3 (2001)	72.3 (2004)	71.7 (2005)	73.1 (2006)	74.6 (2008)	78.9 (2012)	78.5	57.5 (1992)	1.167	
		2. Proportion of population using an improved sanitation facility	61.7 (2001)	41.6 (2004)	43.5 (2005)	55.7 (2006)	48.4 (2008)	49.8 (2012)	64	28 (1992)	1.167	

8. Develop a global partnership for development	8A. Addressed due problems of developing countries through national and international measures	1. Official development assistance as a percentage of income of donor countries	0.15 (2005)	0.48 (2008)	0.3 (2012)	0.7	2	MEAN OBJ: 1.4528
		2. Debt service as a percentage of exports of goods and services	22 (2006)	4.2 (2009)	4.2 (2012)		1.33	
	8B. Make available the benefits of new technologies	1. Percentage of homes with mobile-cellular subscription	50.3 (2006)	89% (2008) (includes mobile and fixed telephones)	87.1 (2012)		1.67	
		2. Percentage of over 5-year aged population with mobile-cellular subscription			61.3 (2012)		1	
		3. Percentage of homes with fixed-telephone subscriptions	18.1 (2006)		21.7 (2012)		1.5	
		4. Percentage of homes with Internet subscription	38.4 (2006)	31.2 (2008)	10.7 (2012)		1.67	
		5. Percentage of over 5-year aged population that uses Internet			35.5 (2012)		1	

Source: Prepared by the authors based on data from UNDP and UDAPE's National Reports (UNDP, 2001; UDAPE and UNDP, 2002; UDAPE (2004, 2006, 2008, 2010 and 2013)).

15 Intergovernmental fiscal transfers and gender-sensitive education financing

Khalida Ghaus and Muhammad Sabir

Introduction

Sustainable development begins with the development of the human resource. Access to education services that generates several positive externalities is among the basic human rights of each individual. Unfortunately, there exist inequalities in the access to education services between males and females in many countries such as Pakistan. In the presence of inequalities, Goals 2 and 3 of the Millennium Development Goals (MDGs) cannot be achieved by Pakistan. An exploration of education statistics indicates that progress made towards Goal 2 (universal primary education) and Goal 3 (promoting gender equality and empowering women) is currently slow. For example, against the MDG target of 100 per cent net enrolment in primary education (5–9 years of age) by 2015, only 56 per cent could be achieved by 2010–11.[1] Similarly, the Gender Parity Index (GPI) (0.88 in 2010–11[2]) shows that fewer girls than boys of primary age attend school. A closer examination shows that a combination of cultural, social and economic factors impede progress, which is further compounded by gender-insensitive policy formulation despite initiatives such as the Gender Reforms Action Plan (GRAP).

The overall literacy rate in Pakistan has improved by 31 percentage points since 1996. Among people aged 10 years and older, it marginally increased to 58.5 per cent in 2010–11 from 57.7 per cent in 2008–09. This is in comparison to the target of a 100 per cent literacy rate in 2015, which is now unlikely to be met. The completion/survival rate up to Grade 5 decreased between the years 2005–2009. This implies that more than a quarter of students enrolled in primary schools do not complete their education. Given this progress, it seems highly unlikely that Pakistan will be able to achieve MDG 2 by 2015. Among females, literacy rate improved more than it did for males. Despite this, the gender disparity reduction has been nominal and negates any claim of gender parity being ensured. In addition, urban literacy rate showed stronger improvement it did for rural areas. The variations also exist among the various districts of the four provinces of Sindh, Balochistan, Punjab and Khyber Pakhtunkhwa. All of the above three differentials (though in varying degrees) indicate the similarities in the challenges confronted by the MDGs. However, the factors impeding the progress clearly were multi-faceted. It includes structural factors to availability of resources, and from traditional (socio-customary) to governance (non-functionality of schools) factors and backwardness. Faced with adverse conditions and multiple challenges, Pakistan's journey towards the MDG targets has been shaky and slow. Following are some of the steps taken by the government to meet the MDG 2:[3]

- National Education Policy (NEP) 2009
- Education Sector Reforms Programme (ESRP)
- One UN Programme
- 10th Five Year Plan (FYP) 2010–2015

Despite the fact that the policies/programmes were introduced, not much success was achieved in attaining gender parity either in primary and secondary education. There are several reasons attributed for this slow progress in meeting MDG 2 targets. The funding allocated by the National Finance Commission (NFC) to each of the provinces is not monitored to oversee the progress made in achieving the goal at the provincial level. Provinces, especially the smaller ones, do not have a strong commitment or understanding of what it means to achieve the MDG in the education sector. In addition, the budget allocated to education is low. Currently, the budget for education remains at less than 2 per cent of gross domestic product (GDP), out of which more than 90 per cent is spent on administrative items such as salaries and 10 per cent is for new initiatives.

At the federal level, the government failed in identifying the relevant mechanisms much needed to assess the status of the programmes implemented and their impact on education sector outcomes. Clearly, due to the absence of coordinated and concerted plans and policies between the different tiers of governments, it is difficult to evaluate the success or failure of interventions made in the education sector. The poor quality of education, discriminatory cultural practices, long distances to schools, and illiteracy among parents are some of the other causative factors. Education utilises the private sector to deliver services; however, the cost of private institutions cannot be borne by people in the lower income strata, thus making it difficult to provide equitable education at all levels. Pakistan has been off track in achieving satisfactory progress in improving the net primary enrolment ratios, ensuring an improvement in the completion rate of those studying in Grade 1 to 5, and also in improving the overall literacy rate. The indicators in all three categories respectively were 57 per cent, 50 per cent and 58 per cent, showing a negligible improvement from the figures for the same in 1990–91. All the six indicators in Table 15.1 indicate that Pakistan continues to remain far behind and faces serious gender inequality issues. Although there is a slight increase in the GPI (primary education) from 0.73 in 1990–91 to 0.9 in 2011–12, the 0.01 increase in GPI (secondary education) between the years 2008–09 to 2011–12 is almost negligible. Additionally, the marginal increase in youth literacy GPI from 0.51 (1990–91) to 0.81 (2011–12) indicates that Pakistan will not be able to achieve its set goal for Gender Equality and Women's Empowerment by the year 2015.

One of the instrumental impediments sighted for gender-insensitive policy formulation is the intergovernmental fiscal transfers constituted through NFC Award. While these transfers are said to be the financial lifeline of the provincial

Table 15.1 Goals 2 and 3: achieving universal primary education and promoting gender equality (in per cent)

Indicator	*1990–91*	*2008–09*	*2010–11*	*2011–12*	*MDG targets 2015*	*Status*
Net primary enrolment ratio	46	57	56	57	100	Off track
Completion/survival rate (Grade 1 to 5)	50	49	49	50	100	Off track
Male	*n/a*	*59*	*59*	*60*	100	Off track
Female	*n/a*	*38*	*39*	*40*	100	Off track
Literacy rate	35	57	58	58	88	Off track
Male	*48*	*69*	*69*	*70*	*n/a*	–
Female	*21*	*45*	*46*	*47*	*n/a*	–
GPI (primary education)	0.73	0.88	0.88	0.90	1.00	Off track
GPI (secondary education)	n/a	0.80	0.85	0.81	0.94	Off track
GPI (youth literacy)	0.51	0.78	0.79	0.81	1.00	Off track
Share of women in wage employment in the non-agricultural sector	8.07	10.64	10.45	n/a	14.00	Off track
Proportion of seats held by women in the national assembly (% of seats)	0.9	22.2	22.2	22.2	n/a	On track
Proportion of seats held by women in senate (% of seats)	1.1	17.0	17.0	17.0	n/a	On track

Source: Pakistan Millennium Development Goals 2013, Ministry of Planning, Government of Pakistan.

governments (representing more than 70 per cent of provincial revenues), they do not appear to be gender sensitive. Transfers made through the NFC Award played a vital role in the financing of all social services, including in the sector of education. The provincial governments have overlooked the gendered context of education financing.

With a comparatively lower spending on girls' education, it is important to undertake a systematic evaluation of the effects of NFC transfers on public spending in primary and secondary levels of education, besides identifying such plausible options that would help the provincial governments make these transfers gender sensitive.

Role of public sector in education

In 1972, the Government of Pakistan nationalised private schools and became the sole provider of education as a part of its campaign to provide free and universal basic education. However, very soon it realised that without the help of the private sector, the objective of universal basic education could not be achieved. Since this realisation, the government has encouraged the private sector to help improve the literacy percentage and the quality of education at all levels of education, i.e. from primary to tertiary. The institutionalisation of the National Education Assessment System (NEAS) also did not help in ensuring the quality of education. During the previous decade, Pakistan has witnessed the mushrooming of private institutions across all provinces. However, despite this proliferation, the public sector continues to play a major role in the provision of education. Even today, the government is the major provider of primary, secondary and tertiary education. Though the share of public schooling declined during the last decade, it continues to cover at least two-thirds of primary, secondary and tertiary education in all the provinces.

Education financing

An equitable and efficient level of funding for education requires a well-functioning financing system. However, a closer look at the management of public finances does not reveal encouraging improvement. The geopolitical conditions along with the economic shock (such as the increase in the oil prices) and internal security conditions narrowed the fiscal space for the federal and at least the three provincial governments that resulted in the reduction of financial resources for education and other social sector expenditures. For instance, the oil price shock in 2008 and floods in 2010 negatively affected the financing of education in Pakistan.

Public expenditure on education as percentage of GDP is widely used in the literature to compare the public spending among different countries. A comparison of public expenditure on education of the countries of the South Asian Association for Regional Cooperation (SAARC) shows that the Maldives, Nepal, Bhutan and India spent a greater share of their GDP on education than did Pakistan. Across South Asia, spending in the education sector averaged 2.8 per cent of GDP. In the case of Pakistan, the spending was only 2.4 per cent. Another comparison of 105 countries as per World Development Indicators (WDI) shows that Pakistan was among only 5 per cent of countries which spent its lowest share of public expenditures on education as a percentage of GDP in 2010. Education as a percentage of total government budgets has also been widely used in the literature to compare the public expenditure of the regional states. Among SAARC countries, Pakistan stands at the lowest, spending only 9.9 per cent of its budget on education.

Role and financial contributions of provincial governments in the education sector

The role of provincial governments in the financing of education services strengthened after the introduction of the 18th Constitutional Amendment in April 2010. The amendment devolved powers to provincial governments including that of education. Prior to it, both the federal and provincial governments had a role in the delivery and financing of educational services. Thus, the provincial governments are now largely responsible for the delivery and financing of educational services. Moreover, the amendment inserted article 25-A in the Constitution of

Pakistan which guarantees the right to free and compulsory education to all children between the ages of 5 and 16 years. Although both the federal and provincial governments are included in the constitutional definition of the state, the greater responsibility lies with the provincial governments.

Figure 15.1 shows the share of federal and provincial governments in total expenditure on education before (2000–01) and after the 18th Amendment (2011–12). It indicates that more than 80 per cent of public spending on education was already being borne by the provincial governments, which further increased in 2011–12 after the 18th Amendment.

Education in Pakistan is overseen by the Federal Ministry of Education, as well as the provincial governments. The federal government is mainly responsible for the development of curriculum, accreditation and the financing of higher education, research and development. In other words, delivery of education services in Pakistan is the responsibility of provincial governments, not the federal/central government. The role of federal government in the delivery of education services is confined to areas, which falls under the federal domain including the Federally Administrated Tribal Area (FATA), Gilgit Baltistan and Islamabad Capital Territory. The role of the provincial governments has been strengthened by the constitutional amendment. Provincial governments are responsible for the provision of education services in their respective provinces, from elementary to university level. Since the federal government is not directly involved in the delivery of education services in the provinces, the focus of this paper is the provincial government. Moreover, since the consumer no longer has to choose between federal and provincial government services and the public and private sector, the

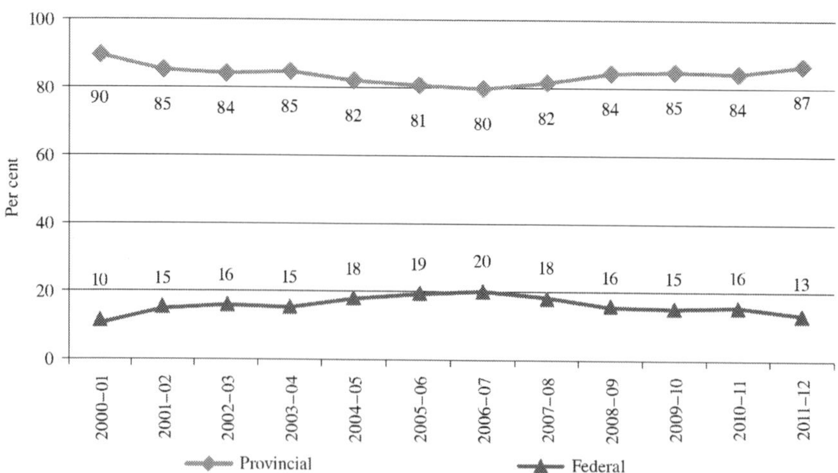

Figure 15.1 Share of federal and provincial governments in education expenditures

Source: Based on PRSP Budgetary Expenditures (various years), Government of Pakistan.

analysis mainly focuses on public and private rather than federal vs. provincial governments.

Public spending on education by gender

Gender disparity persists at all educational levels and in all provinces in Pakistan. In other words, public spending on education was biased against females. For instance, in Punjab in 2010–11, 47.6 per cent of spending was allocated to females at the primary level, 43.8 per cent at the secondary level and 48.6 per cent at the tertiary level. The remainder was spent on males. In the other three provinces, a greater share of public spending also benefitted males. The gender gap in public spending on education is lowest at the primary level, where females received 40.9 per cent, 44 per cent and 34.8 per cent of the total spending for primary education in Sindh, Khyber Pakhtunkhwa and Balochistan respectively in 2010–11. The gender gap gradually increases with education level and is greatest at the tertiary level in all three provinces.

Table 15.2 presents per capita estimates of public spending on education at the various levels for 1998–99, 2004–05 and 2010–11. It shows that gender disparity persists at primary, secondary and tertiary levels of education in all the four provinces of Pakistan. The table clearly indicates that the pattern of public spending on education is biased against females. However, there are differences in relative gender gaps in public spending on education among provinces by level of education. The relative gap is the lowest in Punjab and the highest in Balochistan.

National Finance Commission (NFC) Awards and public spending on education

One of the reasons for a low share of public spending allocated to education in Pakistan is a lack of available resources at provincial levels. Taxes such as those on income, sales tax on goods and customs and excise duties are vested in the federal domain, whereas residual taxes, like agriculture income tax, sales tax on services, motor vehicle tax and others, are in the provincial domain. This leaves little scope for provincial resource mobilisation besides relying on federal transfers to finance their expenditures. These intergovernmental fiscal transfers are constituted through NFC awards and are said to be the financial lifeline of the provincial governments. This is because they constitute more than 70 per cent of provincial revenues and because of their vital role in financing social services such as education.

According to the constitution of Pakistan, the president of the country constitutes NFC after every five years. This commission allocates or awards the total resources or revenues collected during a fiscal year between the federal government and provincial governments by devising a formula for resource transfers and revenue sharing for five years. Hence, the decision made by the commission is called the NFC Award.

Table 15.2 Per capita public spending on education (in rupees)

Year	*Punjab*			*Sindh*			*Khyber Pakhtunkhwa*			*Balochistan*		
	Male	*Female*	*Relative gender gap*	*Male*	*Female*	*Relative gender gap*	*Male*	*Female*	*Relative gender gap*	*Male*	*Female*	*Relative gender gap*
Primary level												
1998–99	1,475	1,233	0.84	1,422	1,011	0.71	1,492	945	0.63	1,019	636	0.62
2004–05	2,318	2,180	0.94	1,989	1,356	0.68	2,410	1,520	0.63	2,112	1,208	0.57
2010–11	6,019	5,833	0.97	6,383	5,008	0.78	2,397	2,192	0.91	5,655	3,421	0.60
Secondary level												
1998–99	670	455	0.68	1,034	626	0.61	1,694	679	0.40	1,563	539	0.34
2004–05	1,278	943	0.74	1,913	1,168	0.61	2,967	1,374	0.46	2,322	967	0.42
2010–11	4,442	3,817	0.86	5,962	4,085	0.69	4,234	2,739	0.65	8,248	3,447	0.42
Tertiary level												
1998–99	310	256	0.83	531	181	0.34	720	297	0.41	770	118	0.15
2004–05	490	506	1.03	872	563	0.65	997	348	0.35	1,198	479	0.40
2010–11	915	836	0.91	1,869	1,251	0.67	3,164	1,516	0.48	3,835	1,333	0.35

Source: Estimates based on PRSP Budgetary Expenditures, Pakistan Integrated Household Survey (PIHS) 1998–99; Pakistan Social and Living Standards Measurement (PSLM) Surveys 2004–05 and 2010–11.

Vertical distribution of the divisible pool

The provincial share in the divisible pool of NFC awards indicates that until the 4th NFC Award, provincial governments had been receiving 80 per cent of two major federal taxes: 'sales tax' and 'income and corporation tax', which were the most buoyant sources of revenues. In contrast, the 5th NFC Award included all federal taxes in the divisible pool and decreased the provincial share from 80 per cent to 37.5 per cent. The *Distribution of Revenues and Grants-in-Aid (Amendment) Order (DRGO) 2006* promulgated by the president of Pakistan increased the provincial governments share to 41.5 per cent in 2006–07, which gradually increased to 46.25 per cent in 2010–11. Later, the 7th NFC Award further enhanced the provincial share to 56 per cent in the divisible pool in 2010–11 and then to 57.5 per cent for the rest of the award period. This means that the share of the federal government in the net divisible pool would be 44 per cent in 2010–11 and 42.5 per cent during the remaining period.

Horizontal distribution of the divisible pool

The formula for horizontal distribution of the divisible pool in NFC awards demonstrates that the entire distribution of divisible pool among provinces in the first three conclusive NFC awards and in DRGO was based only on population. However, the 7th NFC Award framed the distribution of the divisible pool based on four weighted factors. These include population (82 per cent), poverty and backwardness (10.3 per cent), revenue collection/generation (5 per cent) and inverse population density (2.7 per cent).

Trend in federal transfers and provincial education expenditure

Figure 15.2 shows the trend in real per capita federal transfers to provinces channelled through NFC Awards and real per capita provincial expenditure on education. It helps in bringing forward the divergences between the federal transfers and provincial spending on education since 1986–87. While the federal transfers increased substantially between 1990–91 and 1996–97, education spending did not show much improvement during the same period. Moreover, high growth in federal transfers to provinces since 2006–07 also was not translated into the provincial spending on education.

Gender sensitisation of the NFC Awards

The concept of gender-sensitive budgeting is not new in Pakistan. The introduction of Gender Responsive Budgeting was proposed for the first time in Pakistan by the Ministry of Women's Development in a paper on gender and poverty submitted to the Poverty Reduction Growth Facility (PRGF) in 2001. Later, the Social Policy and Development Centre (SPDC) conducted pioneering capacity-development workshops for government officials and civil society on the gender-responsive

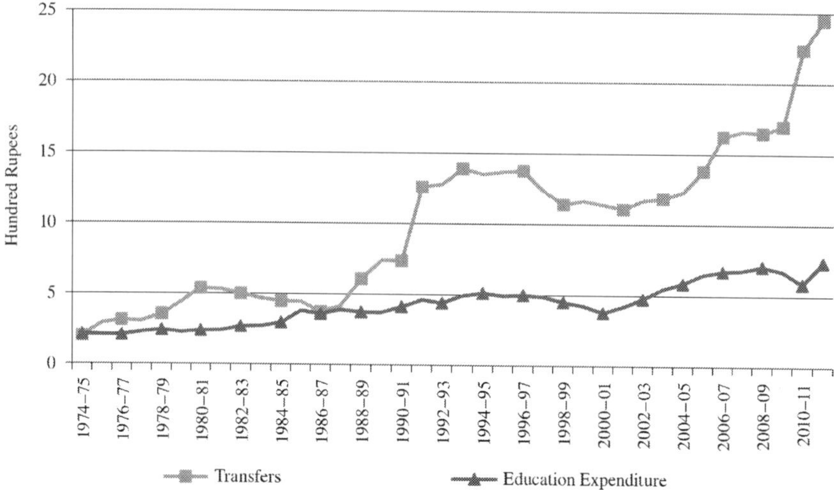

Figure 15.2 Trend in real per capita federal transfers and provincial education expenditure

Source: Based on data from Pakistan Economic Survey, Province-wise Annual Budget Statement and PRSP Budgetary Expenditures.

budgeting in Pakistan. Since then, several attempts have been made in Pakistan to gender sensitise the spending on social services, including education. However, these attempts were limited to 'either analysing existing education spending through a gender lens or getting feedback from the beneficiaries'. The approach did not help to improve the amount of education spending in relation to GDP.

Despite slow progress towards the MDG targets related to education, higher federal transfers to provinces were not translated into higher growth in spending on education. This apparent disconnection between the federal transfers to provinces and provincial spending can largely be attributed to the absence of a gendered approach, particularly in the distribution of resources among provinces. The design of NFC awards did not link financial resources to fiscal needs to educate girls and boys. In other words, financial resources transferred to provinces were not linked with the MDG costing exercise conducted earlier to bring in children that were out of school. Neither was it linked with the output indicators such as enrolment and completion rates. Therefore, any increase in federal transfer to provinces did not necessarily generate an increase in provincial spending on education.

Conceptual framework and empirical strategy

The gradual increase in provincial resources after the 5th NFC Award led to the question of the likely impact of increase in federal transfers on public spending on education. In order to understand the linkages that exist between the intergovernmental transfers and education spending, a review of the existing literature was conducted, which is presented below.

Review of the literature

A review of the existing research does not indicate sufficient empirical work that has tested the response of change in intergovernmental transfers on education expenditures. The available literature addresses aspects of intergovernmental transfers with respect to fiscal competition among subnational governments (Musgrave, 1997); market incentives of federalism (Qian and Weingast, 1997); intergovernmental transfers and deadweight losses in the tax system (Smart, 1996); coordination failure (De Mello Jr., 2000); survey of approaches in designing intergovernmental fiscal transfers (Bird and Smart, 2002); principles and practices of intergovernmental transfer (Boadway and Shah, 2007); and social policy and state revenues (Hinojosa et al., 2010). Unfortunately, the normative question of consequences of any change in the designed mechanism of intergovernmental transfers on provincial expenditures remains unexplored.

Xiaobo (2011) and Litschig and Morrison (2013) have produced work that stands apart from the general stream of literature. The first study investigates the relationship between intergovernmental transfers and country education spending during the period of 1994–2000 in China, and found little evidence that supports a positive effect of transfers on education spending. The second study found that extra transfers in Brazil increased local government spending per capita by about 20 per cent over a four-year period with no evidence of crowding out own revenue or other revenue sources. It also showed that schooling per capita increased by about 7 per cent and literacy rates by about 4 percentage points.

Ghaus and Pasha (1994) developed and tested an econometric model for Pakistan to evaluate the consequences of the 1991 NFC Award. They analysed the budgetary consequences of increases in transfers and found corresponding increases in provincial government services delivery expenditures along with the crowding out of provincial revenues. Sabir (2001) and Sabir (2010), while analysing the impact of change in the design of transfers on social sector expenditures, found that other expenditures tend to increase more than the expenditure on social services due to increase in transfers. Moreover, any shortfall in transfers largely affects expenditures on social services. However, the two studies treated social sector expenditure at the aggregate level, and did not consider education separately. Due to this, no direct link has so far been established on the role of transfers on public spending on education in Pakistan.

Conceptual framework

The conceptual framework is based on the assumption that politicians/officials want to maximise the utility of a typical (median) consumer in their jurisdiction subject to budget constraint. For the sake of simplicity, the consumption basket of a typical consumer can be divided into two broad groups: goods and services provided by the provincial government[4] *(A)*, and goods and services provided by private sector *(B)*. Utility *(U)* was assumed to depend positively on the quantity of both goods and services provided by the provincial government *(A)*, and goods and services provided by the private sector *(B)*.

$$U = U(Q_A, Q_B) \tag{1}$$

The goods and services provided by the provincial government can be divided into education services (Q_{AE}), and goods and services other than education (Q_{AO}).

$$U = U(Q_{AE}, Q_{AO}, Q_B) \tag{2}$$

The quantity of demand of each good and service depends upon the expenditure (public/private) on it. In the case of private goods and services, expenditure would be equal to real per capita disposable income of the consumer or $(Y–R)$, where Y is the real per capita income and R is the real per capita revenue collected by both the federal and provincial governments. Similarly, in the case of publicly provided goods and services, per capita expenditure would be equal to provincial government per capita expenditure on education services *(EE)* and other services *(OE)*. Therefore, the utility function of a typical consumer can be rewritten as:

$$U = U(EE, OE, Y–R) \tag{3}$$

R includes both tax and non-tax revenues, while *EE* and *OE* consist of both recurring and development expenditures on education services and other services provided by provincial governments. Payments for the servicing of debt are excluded, as these do not benefit citizens directly through the provision of services.

The sources of revenues for provincial government, except its own revenues, are federal transfers from the divisible pool, development and non-development grants and borrowings. Therefore, the budget constraint of the provincial government (at current prices) can be expressed as:

$$p_2(EE + OE) = p_1R + T + B + G \tag{4}$$

where, Y = real per capita income
R = Real per capita provincial revenue (include both tax and non-tax revenues)
EE = Real per capita public expenditures on education
OE = Real per capita other expenditures
p_1 = General price level (Consumer Price Index – CPI)
p_2 = Price index of public expenditure
T = Per capita total intergovernmental transfers
B = Per capita borrowing by the provincial government

G consisted of two types of grants from the federal government to provincial governments. These are lump sum grants (G_O) (which consist heavily of development grants) and deficit grants (G_D) (heavily consists of non-development and non-obligatory grants). Therefore, the total flow of grants is given as:

$$G = G_O + m[p_2(EE + OE) - p_1R - T - G_O],\ 0 < m < 1 \tag{5}$$

where, m = proportion of the revenue deficit financed by deficit grants.

Deficit grant played a very significant role in the provincial finances before 1991, but this option was curtailed in the 1991 NFC Award. However, lump sum grants are still provided to the provinces for their development projects.

Substituting (5) into (4) we obtain:

$$p_2(EE + OE) - p_1R + T + G_O + G_D + B \tag{6}$$

After applying first order condition and solving for public expenditure on education, we get Equation 7, which is the expenditure equation for empirical estimation.

$$EE = \alpha_1(1 - a_1)\frac{p_1Y}{p_2} - a_0\alpha_1\frac{p_1}{p_2} + \alpha_1\frac{(T + G_0)}{p_2} + \frac{\alpha_1}{(1-m)}\frac{B}{p_2} + \{(1-\alpha_1)EE_0 - \alpha_1 OE_0\} \tag{7}$$

Empirical strategy

Keeping in line with the scope of study, empirical estimation is restricted to the Equation 7 derived for education expenditures. The slight changes are made in the Equation 7 for econometric specification, which can be rewritten in the following form:

$$EE = c_0 + c_1\frac{p_1Y}{p_2} - c_2\frac{p_1}{p_2} + c_3\frac{(T + G_0)}{p_2} + c_4\frac{B}{p_2} \tag{8}$$

So far, the equation has not contained any terms to capture the impact of gender-sensitive programmes on education expenditures. Pakistan's history indicates that a small number of government interventions can be classified as gender sensitive in the education sector. One such intervention is Prime Minister Junejo's Five-Point Programme initiated in December 1985.

> The program was multidimensional in nature. The main objectives were to induct a new and progressive civilian order, establish institutions of social justice, introduce an egalitarian economy, increase employment opportunities, strike hard at corruption and other social evils, liberate at least 50 per cent of the people from illiteracy, and to start socio-economic development of the country.[5]

Other interventions were also initiated and implemented between 2005 and 2008. During this period, various gender-sensitive education interventions were made, including gender-responsive budgeting along with the second phase of ESRP. In addition, the Education for All (EFA) Plan of Action (2001–2015) has been developed through broad-based consultations with principal actors and other stakeholders. The priorities under EFA include (i) universal primary education and quality education for all, (ii) adult literacy rate of 86 per cent for both males and females, (iii) reducing illiteracy by 50 per cent with a focus on reducing the gender gap and (iv) quality education and technical and skill development programmes. The government is also in consultation with development partners of the Education for All Fast Track Initiative to enhance quality and coverage in education. While the ESRP and EFA plans of action have been developed for 2001 to 2015, their implementations gained momentum between 2005 and 2008.

In order to capture the impact of these interventions, Equation 9 is further augmented by adding an incremental dummy *(DUM)* and being rewritten as follows:

$$EE = c_0 + c_1 \frac{p_1 Y}{p_2} - c_2 \frac{p_1}{p_2} + c_3 \frac{\left(T + G_0\right)}{p_2} + c_4 \frac{B}{p_2} + DUM \tag{9}$$

Estimation

Due to limits on the availability of key macroeconomic variables such as data on provincial GDP and province-level inflation, analysis using panel data for provinces is not possible. Given this constraint, the model was estimated by combining the four provincial governments and using macroeconomic data of Pakistan.

Sources of data

Annual budget statements of each province were used to generate the aggregate database for key provincial budgetary magnitudes, including education expenditures, intergovernmental transfers, borrowing and grants. The data of general price level (CPI), price index of public expenditure, population and GDP at market price is taken from various issues of Pakistan Economic Survey. Values of the dummy variable that range between 1 and 2 during 1985 to 1988 and between 0.25 to 0.5 during 2005 and 2008 capture the impact of the Five-Point Programme and gender-sensitive interventions respectively.

Results

Equation 9 is estimated using annual data for the period 1972–73 to 2011–12. The dependent variable in the equation is real per capita provincial expenditure on education, whereas the independent variables are the ratio of general price and public expenditure price index (p_1/p_2); per capita GDP multiplied by the ratio of prices (p_1Y/p_2); real per capita intergovernmental transfers and grants $((T+G_0)/p_2)$; real per capita provincial borrowing (B/p_2); and a dummy variable *(DUM)* for

Table 15.3 Results of estimation: 1972–73 to 2011–12 (dependent variable: real per capita provincial expenditure on education)

Independent variable	*Constant*	(p_1Y/p_2)	(p_1/p_2)	$(T+G_O)/p_2$	(B/p_2)	*DUM*
Coefficient	+ 0.595	+ 0.009	−1.255	+ 0.176	+ 0.186	+ 0.583
t-statistic	(0.735)	(1.829)	(−1.740)	(3.185)	(2.981)	(4.030)
Adjusted R^2	0.958			Durbin-Watson stat	1.435	

Source: Authors' estimation.

gender-sensitive interventions in the education sector. Results of estimation are given in Table 15.3.

The signs of all the estimated coefficients are theoretically consistent. Each coefficient is significantly different from zero at a 5 per cent significance level except GDP and price ratio, which are significantly different from zero at 10 as apparent from the *t*-statistics. The value of adjusted R^2 indicates that the model explains almost 96 per cent of variation in provincial education sector expenditures.

According to the estimated equation, an increase or decrease of Rs. 100 in either the real federal transfers or lump sum grants can affect the real per capita expenditure on education by Rs. 17.60. It is important to note that the impact of borrowing is greater than that of intergovernmental transfers and grants. One of the possible explanations of this result could be the nature of provincial borrowing. Historically, provincial borrowing consisted of cash development loans, which afterwards changed into project loans. Both of them were largely used to finance development expenditures in social sectors where the education sector is a greater component. Larger coefficient and negative sign of the price ratio indicates that an increase in general price levels causes an increase in interest rates, which ultimately increases the cost of provincial borrowing and shifts resources from education to debt servicing. Finally, the positive sign and lower magnitude of GDP indicates that any growth in GDP marginally affects provincial education expenditures through indirect channels, such as increases in revenues from motor vehicle tax or urban immovable property tax. It is also important to note that the dummy for gender-sensitive intervention is significant and on average had a greater impact on provincial education spending.

Conclusion and policy recommendations

The results presented in this paper show that increasing the amount of resources to provincial governments through intergovernmental fiscal transfers and grants constituted through NFC awards leads to a marginal increase in provincial expenditure on education. This marginal increase is less than the desired level of education spending needed to achieve MDGs 2 and 3. Moreover, the Five-Point Programme and borrowing had a greater impact on provincial expenditure on education, which is generally linked to the development project. One possible explanation for this trend is the nature of NFC transfers and their design. For instance, these transfers are not linked to gender-sensitive output indicators such as higher enrolments for boys and girls, or higher literacy for men and women. Moreover, prior to the 7th NFC Award, backwardness was used to make a case for higher constitutional subventions and grants, without any condition to tackle backwardness and illiteracy through higher resources. In the 7th NFC Award, backwardness is used as one of the criteria to determine the share of provinces in a divisible pool. On a positive note, this criterion allocates more resources to relatively backward provinces. It also simultaneously provides them with a negative incentive to stay backward in order to claim higher resources in future NFC awards. The danger of this negative incentive to stay backward is contributing towards the failure in achieving the MDGs.

One striking finding is the greater positive impact of provincial borrowing and gender-sensitive interventions on education expenditures. This leads to two policy choices:

- Provincial governments could be asked to design and implement gender-sensitive projects in the education sector on federal directives without making it conditional in NFC awards, as in the case of Junejo's Five-Point Programme and during the period 2005–2008.
- Gender-sensitive interventions could be integrated into the design of NFC awards and then be properly monitored through the NFC.

While the first choice helped in raising resources for education in the past, it was ad hoc in nature and did not ensure sustainable resource flows to the sector. Therefore, this study recommends the second approach for sustainable resource flow to education. The following suggestions should be incorporated in future NFC awards:

- The distribution of resources among provinces is not linked to the MDG costing exercise undertaken in this paper to address non-attendance in schools, which in Pakistan is higher among girls. It is also not linked to output indicators like enrolment and completion rates. Establishing an explicit link between federal transfers to provinces and MDG costing for education will help reduce the gender gap in education.
- Gender-sensitive indicators of the net enrolment rate and completion rates of primary education for girls and boys should be used to help determine the share of provinces in the divisible pool.
- Additional incentives should be provided to the provinces by granting a higher share in the divisible pool. These incentives would help reduce gender inequality in education. For instance, provinces with high enrolment rates in public schools could get a higher share in the divisible pool to finance the cost of retaining a higher number of students in public schools, particularly for female students.
- The share in NFC awards should be made conditional so that the provincial share is linked to spending of the (agreed) distribution of resources on

education. A failure to do so must result in withholding their respective share of resources from the divisible pool.

- A post-MDG framework when developed by the government must incorporate the role and responsibility of subnational governments in the delivery of social services to achieve the desired targets.

These suggestions would help link the intergovernmental transfers with the education outcomes along with encouraging gender-sensitive changes in the future design of NFC awards. Moreover, it would facilitate an increase in the level of resources allocated to education as a percentage of GDP, which would help in achieving gender equality in the sector.

Notes

1 Pakistan Economic Survey 2012–13.
2 Pakistan Economic Survey 2012–13.
3 The NEP 2009 aimed at addressing the challenges of the education sector and also to formulate an action plan to ensure universal primary education for all. ESRP primarily aimed at providing the missing facilities to the middle/primary schools and also to establish polytechnic institutes at the district level. Under the One UN Programme and the 10th Five Year Plan also the government expressed its commitments towards universal primary education, girls' literacy, standardisation of curriculae and the examination system. The latter also committed up 4 per cent of gross domestic product (GDP) on education.
4 In line with the scope of this paper, the analysis is limited to provincial expenditure, ignoring the impact of federal expenditures on the utility of consumers. Details explained in the second section.
5 http://storyofpakistan.com/muhammad-khan-junejo-becomes-prime-minister/ [Accessed: 9 August 2015]

References

Bird, R. and Smart, M. (2002) Intergovernmental fiscal transfers: International lessons for developing countries. *World Development*. 30 (6). pp.899–912.

Boadway, R. and Shah, A. (2007) *Intergovernmental Fiscal Transfers: Principles and Practice*. Public Sector Governance and Accountability Series. Washington, DC: The World Bank.

De Mello Jr., L. R. (2000) Fiscal decentralization and intergovernmental fiscal relations: A cross-country analysis. *World Development*. 28 (2). pp.365–380.

Ghaus, A. F. and Pasha, H. A. (1994) Dynamic budgetary consequences of the 1991 NFC Award. *Pakistan Development Review*. 33 (4-II). pp.627–645.

Hinojosa, L., Bebbington, A., Barrientos, A. and Addison, T. (2010) *Social Policy and State Revenues in Mineral-Rich Contexts*. Social Policy and Development Programme Paper No. 44. New York: United Nations Research Institute for Social Development (UNRISD).

Litschig, S. and Morrison, K. (2013) The impact of intergovernmental transfers on education outcomes and poverty reduction. *American Economic Journal*. 5 (4). pp.1–35.

Musgrave, R. A. (1997) Devolution, grants and fiscal competition. *Journal of Economic Perspectives*. 11 (4). pp.65–72.

Qian, Y. and Weingast, B. R. (1997) Federalism as a commitment to preserving market incentives. *Journal of Economic Perspectives*. 11 (4). pp.83–92.

Sabir, M. (2001) Dynamic consequences of the 1997 NFC Award: Provincial social sector expenditures. *The Pakistan Development Review*. 40 (4-II). pp.967–984.

Sabir, M. (2010) Financial implications of the 7th NFC Award and the impact on social services. *The Pakistan Development Review*. 49 (4-II). p.387.

Smart, M. (1996) *Taxation Incentives and Deadweight Loss in a System of Intergovernmental Transfers*. Working Paper No. msmart-96–03 Department of Economics, University of Toronto.

Xiaobo, L. (2011) *Do Inter-governmental Transfers Enhance Local Education Spending in China*? Paper presented at the *American Political Science Association (APSA) 2011 Annual Meeting*. 1–4 September, Seattle, USA.

Financing the new development agenda

16 Exploring domestic financing options for post-2015 development agenda in selected Sub-Saharan African countries

Eberechukwu Uneze and Adedeji Adeniran

Introduction

Many developing countries will not meet the Millennium Development Goals (MDGs) due to a number of factors, among which finance is paramount. The importance of finance, therefore, has been recognised in the various discussions leading up to the post-2015 development agenda. While the MDGs focused on foreign aid as its major source of financing, the post-2015 agenda is essentially emphasising domestic resource mobilisation and private sector funding. In this instance, a sustainable financing strategy will be crucial to achieving the ambitious targets and goals being proposed in the post-2015 development agenda.

In the past, the prospect of financing development through domestic resource mobilisation in Sub-Saharan Africa (SSA) countries was viewed with scepticism, due to weak economic growth and lack of technical capacity for effective tax administration (Aryeetey, 2004). However, over the last two decades, the weaknesses of external sources of finance have become more evident. For example, the external debt financing model that was adopted in the 1970s and 1980s in many developing countries resulted in a debt crisis that had a debilitating effect on their economies (Ajayi, 1997). Also, foreign aid has, in recent times, become increasingly unpredictable and unsustainable as economic uncertainty pervades the world (Greenhill and Prizzon, 2012). This has resulted in a rethink in the development financing strategy, with greater emphasis on domestic resource mobilisation, especially since the strong growth experienced by many countries in the African continent.

A number of domestic financing sources for post-2015 have been identified in the development finance literature.[1] In this paper, we examine the revenue potentials of five of these financing sources for five SSA countries across the four regional blocs. These sources include three existing financing sources: tax revenue, domestic savings and capital flight, and two of the emerging financing sources: financial transaction tax and domestic philanthropy.

Our objective is to shift the focus of the debate on financing for post-2015 from 'what options are available' to 'what options are viable'. While recent literature has identified a wide range of domestic financing options from which developing countries could draw for the post-2015 development agenda, the revenue potentials of these channels have not been critically examined. It is therefore crucial to understand which among the financing options would be effective and what factors would enable their effectiveness.

Understanding these issues has important policy implications for both designing the financing strategy and setting the goals and targets for the post-2015 development. By providing an insight into the revenue potential of key domestic financing sources, policymakers are better informed on the expected financial flows. Hence, the post-2015 goals and targets will be aligned with available and potential resources.

The rest of this paper is organised as follows. The second section gives a brief review of the preliminary cost estimate for post-2015 agenda. The third section examines the revenue potential of the identified financing options in the selected countries. Finally, conclusions and recommendations are given in the last section.

A review of the financial estimates for the post-2015 agenda

The cost estimate of the post-2015 development agenda will only be known with some precision when the goals and targets are clearly set out. Nonetheless, there seems to be a consensus that the post-2015 goals will be broad, as it will encompass the unfinished MDGs plus goals on sustainability – objectives promoting climate change and energy access for all. It is on this assumption that several attempts have been made to estimate the cost of the post-2015 development agenda. In this case, we move on to review some of the preliminary estimates in the literature.

As Greenhill and Ali (2013) argue, there are two ways to quantify the cost of implementing the post-2015 agenda: by taking a sectoral approach and a sustainable growth approach. The sectoral approach involves assessing the financial requirement of achieving a given set of targets across some specific sectors that are likely to be included. Based on this approach, Greenhill and Ali estimated that between USD 586 billion and 1,086 billion per annum will be required, across five main sectors: sustainable energy, food security and agriculture, education, health, and water and sanitation. The sustainable energy sector takes the bulk of the expenses at between USD 434 billion and USD 934 billion, followed by food security and agriculture (USD 50.2 billion), education (USD 38 billion), health (USD 37 billion), and water and sanitation (USD 26.8 billion).

In a more detailed review of the sectoral cost, the UN Task Team Working Group on Sustainable Development Finance (2013) reported that the "unfinished" MDG sectors will require an additional USD 20 to USD 200 billion per year. New goals, such as infrastructure financing, will require between USD 1 and USD 3.2 trillion a year, with a significant proportion allocated for maintenance cost. The sustainability goal, which comprises objectives promoting climate change mitigation and energy access for all, has an estimate of about USD 820–1,635.4 billion. This is spread across five main areas: climate change mitigation (USD 400–1,200 billion), climate change adaptation (USD 50–170 billion), energy access and full energy security (USD 55–130 billion), renewable energy (USD 136–718 billion) and global commons (USD 235–547 billion).

The sectoral approach to estimating the cost requirement for the post-2015 agenda is not without its limitations. The main shortcoming of the approach is that it neglects the interdependencies among sectors. For example, the achievement under the poverty goal has a positive spillover on health, education and other goals, implying that aggregating the estimate for each of the sectors could result in double counting. This key weakness has led to the use of the sustainable growth approach. This approach assesses the level of financial resources that will be required to achieve sustainable growth that will raise enough income to meet other goals.

Although there is no clear way of identifying the specific sectors that will promote sustainable growth, one important aspect, the green economy initiative, seems to be well recognised. At the Rio+20 Conference in 2012, it was agreed that green economy initiatives be integrated into the post-2015 development framework. Green economy focuses on achieving sustainable development through poverty eradication and protection of the environment through sustainable production and consumption. In essence, the sustainable growth approach estimates the cost of post-2015 indirectly by estimating the cost of achieving poverty reduction and the sustainability goals.

Several estimates for achieving green economy in developing countries have been provided in the literature. For example, UNDESA (2011) estimates that USD 1.1 trillion per annum will be required. A more conservative estimate is provided by the World Bank (2010), which calculates that between USD 407–740 billion per annum will be required for efforts at climate change mitigation, while between USD 75–100 billion per annum is needed for aspects relating to climate change adaptation. Compared with the sectoral estimates, the amount of financial needs, though slightly lower, is still substantial. Also, a comparison of the World Bank (2010) estimate for post-2015 with the most recent estimate of financing requirement for the MDGs by Atisophon et al. (2011) shows that developing countries will require as much as between four to seven times the resources put into the MDGs each year.

Scope for scaling up domestic resources

Our review in the previous section has shown that the resource requirement for the post-2015 agenda is huge and far outweighs the current flow of resources to SSA countries. This financing gap means that not only would existing sources of financing be scaled up, innovative sources should also be explored. This section therefore focuses on the role of domestic resources mobilisation, its potentials and magnitude.

Tax revenue

Tax revenue is the largest source of domestic resource mobilisation available to governments in SSA (Bhushan, Samy and Medu, 2013). More importantly, resources mobilised through taxation have higher prospects of being channelled to development activities. In fact, improving the efficiency of the tax system in developing countries was an integral part of the MDGs financing strategy, and over the last 10 years tax revenue has increased sharply, rising about three-fold in SSA.

According to data from African Economic Outlook (2013), most African countries have recorded a positive trend in their tax revenue in recent years, with the magnitude of revenue generated reflecting the size of the economy. For example, among the selected countries, the data shows that South Africa has the highest tax revenue, followed by Nigeria, Ghana, Gabon and Ethiopia. However, a breakdown of the tax level according to revenue sources shows that the improvement is largely due to an increase in resource taxes, which accounted for 43 per cent of tax revenue of SSA over the period (see African Economic Outlook, 2013). It is estimated that non-resource-related taxes in SSA increased by less than 1 per cent of the gross domestic product (GDP) over the past three decades (Gupta and Tareq, 2008). This highlights the nature and problem of resource dependency for many countries in SSA.

Tax effort

There are two approaches to measure the revenue potential from taxation. First is the tax ratio, which is defined as tax revenue as a percentage of GDP. A ratio of 15 per cent (excluding resource taxes) is considered ideal for any country. The other measure is the tax effort, which is the actual tax ratio as a proportion of potential tax ratio. Tax effort is preferred to tax ratio for three important reasons. First is that tax ratio is based on an arbitrary threshold of 15 per cent. In this case, it may not be a sound basis to gauge the performance of the tax system or to determine the potential for additional tax revenue. For example, a government's drive to increase the tax revenue could, at the same time, reduce GDP and make the economy worse off. Second is that tax ratio does not provide any indication to the potential revenue that could be raised by improving tax effort. Finally, tax effort factors into its computation the political and institutional variables that determine the revenue potential.

TAX EFFORT IS CALCULATED AS:

$$\frac{ATR}{PTR} \tag{1}$$

where, *ATR* is actual tax ratio and *PTR* is potential tax ratio.

Tax effort has a benchmark of 1. Countries that have a tax effort lower than 1 have the capacity to generate additional tax revenue, while countries with tax effort that is greater than 1 are generating the maximum possible tax revenue, and effort to scale up will only come at the cost of reduced economic growth or investment.

The potential tax ratio gives a counterfactual estimate of revenue feasible for a given country based on its structural characteristics. To estimate the potential tax ratio, we use the predicted tax capacity model proposed by Bird, Martinez-Vazquez and Torgler (2008) and Le, Moreno-Dodson and Rojchaichaninthorn (2008). The model expresses potential tax ratio as a function of the level of economy's development, trade openness, level of industrialisation and institutional quality. A detailed analysis and regression results are presented in the Annex 16.1.[2]

The estimated tax effort index shows that South Africa (1.63), Ghana (1.03) and Ethiopia (1.08) have tax effort of more than 1, implying that the potential for additional tax revenue is low. For Nigeria (0.46) and Gabon (0.66), the estimates are lower than 1 and this means that both countries are currently generating less taxes than expected. Using the average GDP between 1996 and 2012, a projected estimate of around USD 9 billion and USD 529 million additional tax revenue could be generated in Nigeria and Gabon, respectively. This analysis does not imply, however, that additional tax revenue cannot be generated in countries with high tax effort. Implementation of policies that promote economic growth and increase administrative capacity for tax collection could improve potential tax.

Also, there are opportunities to improve tax revenue by expanding the tax bracket in order to capture the shadow economy. Recent estimates of the size of the shadow economy in SSA by Elgin and Oztunali (2012) show that it could be more than one-third of the current GDP. In the selected countries, Elgin and Oztunali (2012) estimates show that, in 2008, the percentage of shadow economy to GDP is highest in Nigeria at 49.94 per cent, followed by Gabon at 47.37 per cent; Ghana at 37.42 per cent; Ethiopia at 32.86 per cent and South Africa at 24.87 per cent. Reducing the size of the shadow economy, as well as the level of informality, will therefore help improve the potential tax revenue. Potential policy options could include strengthening the capacity of revenue collection institutions, reducing the tax burden in order to lower incentives for tax evasion and instituting a legal framework that penalises non-registration of specific activities within the shadow economy.

Domestic savings

Domestic savings are another important domestic financing option, but these are often neglected in the financing strategy of many SSA countries. Savings provide short- and long-term resources which can be put into development projects and programmes. Domestic savings include public sector savings (i.e. sovereign wealth funds, budget surplus), and private sector savings (i.e. household saving, pension fund, insurance funds and companies' retained earnings). Worldwide, the SSA region has the lowest savings rate, which according to UNCTAD (2007) stood at about 17.6 per cent of the continent's GDP. In addition, a large proportion of savings is concentrated in the informal financial sector, where it is hardly used to generate productive investment (UNCTAD, 2007). As argued by Ratha, Mohapatra and Plaza (2008), this low savings rate contributed to the large financing gap which has held back development in SSA.

Measuring saving deficiency

In most studies, saving rate (saving as percentage of GDP) is used as an indicator of a country's potential to mobilise additional savings. However, saving rate is a poor indicator of potential saving, as it neglects the opportunity cost involved in saving by economic agents. In this case, a measure of saving deficiency (or the golden saving rate) for a country is required. Following McKinnon (2013), we measure saving deficiency as the current account deficit of a country relative to its GDP. Current account deficit is the difference in claims between a country and the rest of the world, and it indicates the extent to which a country depends on external borrowing as against domestic saving. The result of the saving deficiency for the selected countries between 2005 and 2010 is presented in Figure 16.1. This is as far as data could allow. Nigeria and Gabon show no sign of saving deficiency, and this could imply that there is little scope to mobilise additional savings from the existing channels. Interestingly, South Africa, Ghana and Ethiopia have enormous potential to expand their current levels of domestic savings. This result needs to be interrogated further, since it may be difficult to conclude that any country in SSA has exhausted its potential to mobilise savings.

While gross domestic savings levels in Nigeria and Gabon are impressive, both countries fell short of the optimum level of 'genuine' savings – the saving rate necessary to offset the declining stock of non-renewable resources. According to World Bank (2005), genuine savings for Nigeria and Gabon are −35.7 per cent and −6.7 per cent, respectively.

Other components of savings that are generally low in SSA are savings by the formal financial sector and corporate savings (UNCTAD, 2007). With the exception of South Africa, the level of financial development in SSA is low, and this

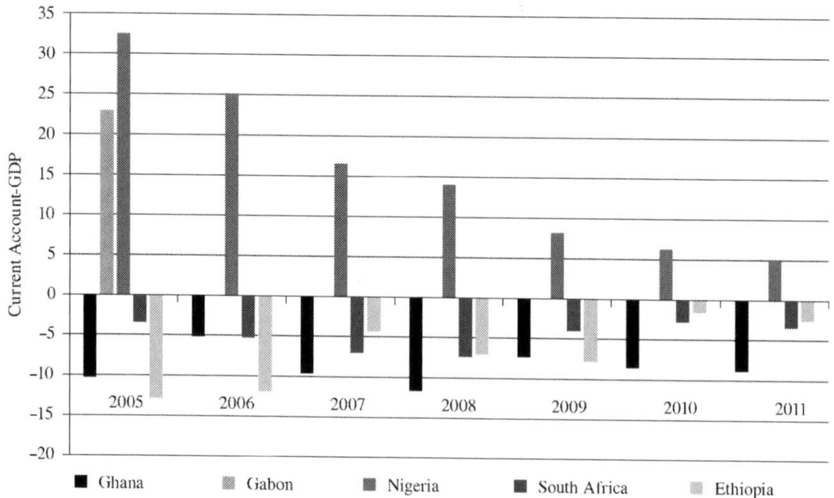

Figure 16.1 Savings deficiency in selected countries

Source: World Development Indicators (2014).

hinders the mobilisation of these forms of savings. An important advantage of formal financial and corporate savings is that they can be more easily targeted or mobilised for investment.

However, the nature of productive investment mobilised through formal financial and corporate savings could deviate from prioritised developmental activities. The profit motive argument dictates that savings mobilised within the formal financial sector will be allocated to high return yielding investments. This means that private investors might underinvest in social sectors or public goods with low return. In SSA, private savings are estimated at about USD 1.1 trillion, and if deployed for development purposes, the financing gap will reduce down significantly. Therefore, creating an incentive system that will encourage private investors to allocate resources to social sectors is critical to the post-2015 financing.

The first important step towards mobilising private investment in the social sectors is for government to provide an enabling investment climate and public infrastructure. In addition, regulatory and policy frameworks need to be stable in order to mitigate the problem of information asymmetry. Government interventions will also be essential in reducing investment risk in the social sectors. A potential strategy in this regard is the provision of insurance facilities for investment in social sectors to help spread the risks. Another viable strategy is to grant tax credits and premium prices to firms operating within the sectors. Overall, a well-structured public-private partnership (PPP) is essential to ensuring the mobilisation of private sector resources for development activities.

Capital flight

Capital flight arises because of either economic and political uncertainty that increases investment risk or illicit transactions and activities such as money laundering among public officials, tax evasion and trade misinvoicing by multinational firms.[3] For many SSA countries, the incidence of capital flight has been observed due to illicit transactions and activities rather than strategic portfolio diversification by investors. Between 1970 and 2010, about USD 23.5 billion per annum was lost to capital flight in 33 SSA countries, with 72 per cent of the loss taking place in the oil-rich countries (Boyce and Ndikumana, 2012).

Using Boyce and Ndikumana's (2012) cross-country estimates, we identify a similar pattern for the selected countries. As shown in Figure 16.2, capital flight as a percentage of GDP was higher in Gabon (41 per cent) and Nigeria (4.7 per cent) than in Ghana (1.3 per cent), South Africa (1.4 per cent) and Ethiopia (0.8 per cent). In terms of magnitude, Nigeria and South Africa, the two largest economies in the region, recorded the biggest loss between 1970 and 2010. Nigeria alone lost about USD 25 billion to capital flight between 2001 and 2010 (Boyce and Ndikumana, 2012). This is more than the combined capital expenditure of all sectors over the same period. In essence, capital flight has become an endemic problem across the region and a substantial threat to domestic resource mobilisation effort. It holds back resources that could be channelled into development.

Therefore, understanding the channels and means through which this leakage occurs will be an important step towards reducing the incidence of capital

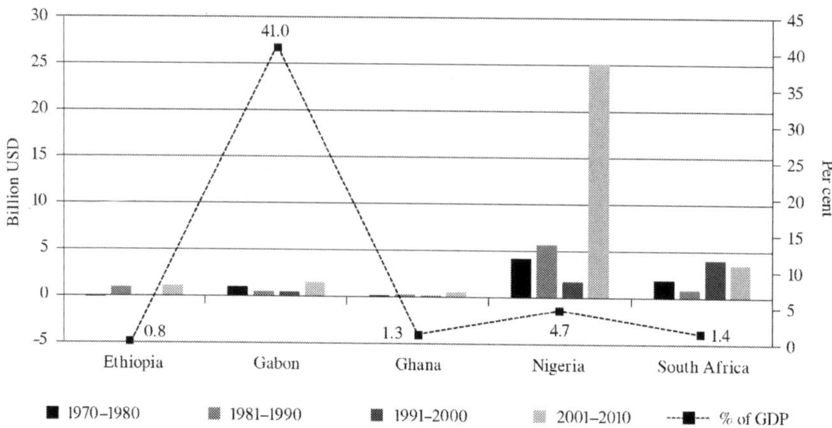

Figure 16.2 Trends in capital flight

Source: Boyce and Ndikumana (2012).

flight. This will require not only improved governance at domestic level, but also international cooperation to curb both outflows from developing countries and inflows to developed countries. The recent initiative by the United Nations Office on Drugs and Crime and the World Bank – Stolen Assets Recovery (STAR) is a right step in this direction, but it can be taken a step further by integrating the concerns about capital flight into post-2015 development agenda. Specifically, development partnership under the post-2015 framework should involve collaboration towards eliminating capital flight in developing countries.

Essentially, domestic policy that prevents revenue leakages through money laundering, strategic tax evasion by multinational firms and other avenues for capital flight remains the most effective strategy for addressing capital flight. Presently, there are enabling laws against money laundering in many SSA countries, but institutional framework for implementation remains weak and susceptible to abuses from the political class. For example, Nigeria and Ethiopia in 2011 and South Africa in 2004 reformed their existing regulations on money laundering – stipulating a stiffer penalty for money laundering as well as empowering anti-money-laundering agencies. Nigeria, Ghana, Gabon and South Africa have also introduced transfer pricing regulation to curb trade mispricing by multinational firms and are also members of Egmont Group – an informal network of financial intelligence units (FIUs) collaborating to reduce money laundering through information exchange, training and sharing of expertise. The main challenge therefore lies in strengthening the effectiveness of the existing institutions. Some policies in this regard include improving the technical capacity of these institutions, intensifying the level of collaboration among relevant stakeholders and institutions, and ensuring independence of anti-money-laundering institutions.

Domestic philanthropy or giving sector

Philanthropic organisations have played a major role in the financing of the MDGs, and more resources can be harnessed from this sector for the post-2015 development agenda, especially in developing countries. In 2010, an estimated USD 56 billion was mobilised for developing countries from philanthropy, with the United States alone contributing about USD 39 billion. In SSA, the level of financial giving remains very low, as indicated in a recent survey (CAF, 2010) that found only 21 per cent of the population in the region are willing to give money to organisations. This lack of willingness could be due to high incidence of poverty in the region. However, home-grown philanthropists are rapidly emerging among the growing affluent population of the region. For example, many African industrialists, namely Aliko Dangote, Tokyo Sexwale, Moi Ibrahim and Tony Elumenu, have recently established foundations dedicated to promoting global development, with large amount of grants already disbursed. Also, African leaders have contributed resources to charities within and outside the region, for example the Mandela Foundation, the Desmond Tutu Foundation, and the Kofi Annan Foundation, among others.

Corporate philanthropy within the domestic front is also expanding rapidly. For example, a study by GIZ (2013) on corporate social responsibility (CSR) of local and multinational firms in Africa observed a remarkable improvement in the number of firms reporting their CSR as well as increasing awareness about environmental sustainability and development of their operating communities. Public goods and social sectors were also found to be priority areas of their interventions. Other important beneficiaries of charitable donations are non-government organisations (NGOs) and civil society organisations (CSOs), which play a crucial role in the coordination and implementation of development initiatives. NGOs and CSOs in developing countries are largely financed through donations from local and foreign philanthropists and foundations. The philanthropic sector is therefore critical to the financing of the post-2015 development agenda.

Although data on the level of domestic giving in SSA is not available, effective public policies and tax incentives could promote giving as well as improve the contribution of domestic philanthropy to economic and social development. The potential will be higher in countries with high per capita income, large industrial presence and high propensity to give. Gittell and Tebaldi (2006) found that countries with higher per capita income have a higher giving rate. Lastly, propensity to give differs remarkably across countries; the CAF (2010) survey found that the percentage of the population willing to give money to organisations to be as low as 4 per cent in Lithuania and as high as 83 per cent in Malta. Although this is a subjective measurement of giving culture, it indicates the dynamics in giving across countries.

Table 16.1 presents the indicators of size of the philanthropy sector. South Africa shows the greatest potential based on income per capita and number of listed domestic companies, although the willingness to give is also the lowest. Nigeria and Gabon also show strong potentials in expanding the level of

Table 16.1 Indicators of potential revenue from the philanthropy sector

Country	*Giving culture as on 2010 (% of the population willing to give)*	*Per capita income as on 2013 (constant, USD)*	*Total listed domestic companies as on 2012*
Ethiopia	10	268.23	–
Gabon	12	6937.71	–
Ghana	27	766.05	34
Nigeria	30	1097.96	192
South Africa	14	5916.46	348

Source: Giving culture is based on CAF (2010). Other indicators are from World Development Indicators (2014).

philanthropy, given the size of the various indicators. In Ghana and Ethiopia, the potential to raise funds through philanthropy appears low. However, this result should be treated with caution. It is difficult to identify any of the indicators without a shortcoming. For example, none of the indicators captures the level of social and economic inequality and social justice among economic classes, which can significantly affect the propensity to give.

A more robust indicator of potential to generate funds from philanthropy, although equally difficult to measure, is the presence of vibrant media and a well-informed public that put corporate practices and wealthy individuals under constant scrutiny. Callan (2012) noted that, in the past two decades, risk of bad public relations has made firms more accountable to communities within their domain. But the most important means of translating this potential into actual resource flow is through better public policy that offers favourable tax treatment to charitable donations. Presently, Nigeria and South Africa have regulations that provide tax incentive for charitable donations. The Nigerian Company Income Tax Act provides for tax deduction on charitable donation for firms, if the donation does not exceed 10 per cent of the annual profit. There is also a private bill currently in the parliament that will mandate businesses to spend 3.5 per cent of their gross profit on CSR. South Africa also has similar laws on tax deductions and regulations that provide incentive for firms to contribute to charity. For Ghana, Ethiopia and Gabon, we observe no clear rules for tax deductions on charitable donations. Surprisingly, existing laws in Nigeria and South Africa focus largely on companies, excluding individual donations to charity. Also, the scope of the laws is limited, as they are restricted to specific sectors. For example, donations to the agriculture sector which are not related to research are presently not eligible for tax deduction. In this case, additional reforms are needed in these countries to fully realise the revenue potentials of domestic philanthropy.

Financial transaction tax (FTT)

FTT is a tax imposed on various classes of financial instruments ranging from financial securities (equities, stocks and debts) to financial contract (derivatives), bank debits and credits. FTT serves two important purposes: It helps to stabilise the financial market and generates revenue for the government. A global FTT is one of the innovative and new options being proposed for financing post-2015 initiatives. Given the volume of financial transactions globally, a small tax rate will generate a sizeable level of funds for development. Nevertheless, the possibility of a unilateral FTT by developing countries needs to be considered. Between 2001 and 2008, South Africa realised USD 7 billion through FTT and was the highest globally relative to GDP (Beitler, 2010). Different forms of FTT are already being implemented in many countries and these could be expanded.

Based on the experiences of developing countries currently implementing FTT, the potential revenue depends on the level of financial development, the size of financial markets and financial instruments and economic size. Following the literature, we measure the level of financial development by the ratio of broad money to GDP. The size of the financial market and instruments are measured by the value of market capitalisation of companies in the stock market as a percentage of GDP and the value of portfolio inflows (investment plus bond), respectively. Economic size is proxied by the level of real GDP. These indicators are presented in Table 16.2.

In terms of prospect to mobilise funds through FTT, South Africa is followed by Nigeria. This is evidenced by the strength of the economy and the financial market. For similar reasons, FTT may be a less effective source of revenue for Ethiopia, Ghana and Gabon. Introducing FTT in these economies may be counterproductive, as the effect might disrupt the evolving financial sector and economic development. However, as financial markets develop in these countries, there may be a need to introduce FTT.

Grabel (2005) provides a rough projection of the potential revenue to be generated from FTT for 60 developing countries, including South Africa, Nigeria and Ghana, based on the value of their stock markets and different scenarios (rates) of FTT. For Ghana, the projected revenue is as low as USD 45 to 255 thousand per annum, while Nigeria has the potential to generate about USD 0.885 to

Table 16.2 Indicators of prospect for FTT

Country	*Financial development (M2 % of GDP as on 2012)*	*Portfolio investment, bonds (current USD million as on 2012)*	*Market capitalisation of listed companies (% of GDP as on 2012)*	*GDP as on 2013 (Constant USD 2005 million)*
Ethiopia	41.50*	0.00	–	27.21
Gabon	21.45	−4.00	–	11.60
Ghana	30.51	0.00	8.30	19.84
Nigeria	20.86	350.00	12.26	190.62
South Africa	75.57	2455.88	160.14	313.47

Source: World Development Indicators (2014).

Note: * is the trend value, given that the actual value for 2012 is not available.

4.29 million per annum and South Africa as high as USD 102 to 514 million per annum. This therefore places more financially developed SSA countries at greater advantage to explore FTT for development financing. But most importantly, it underscores the benefits to financial development.

Conclusion and recommendations

This paper has examined the revenue potential of key domestic financing options which could be used to finance the post-2015 development agenda in SSA. The study finds that the revenue potential of each financing option differed remarkably across countries. Overall, while the revenue potential is enormous in some countries, it is weak in others. However, each country has strong revenue potentials in, at least, one of the five financing options considered. While this does not suggest that the potential revenue will be enough to meet the financing requirements, it demonstrates the viability of domestic sources of revenue and the need to explore them, if only to complement the existing financing options, especially foreign aid.

Furthermore, the paper finds that the magnitude of potential revenue corresponds to the country's economic size. As it were, Nigeria and South Africa have more potential to mobilise domestic resources than the other countries examined. The other key issues that emerge from this study are that

- Government has to play a leading role in every area and stage of domestic resource mobilisation process. In most SSA countries, the present realities demonstrate clearly that the institutional capacity to mobilise domestic resources is weak and susceptible to corruption. Therefore, measures to promote accountable and transparent governance while strengthening the capacity of institutions responsible for revenue collection will be important.
- The set of goals for post-2015 development agenda must be flexible enough to allow 'domestic government ownership'. Unlike in the past when countries depended on external resources, the post-2015 agenda should draw on domestic and other innovative financing options.
- The proposed governance goals for post-2015 should include fiscal accountability and transparency as part of its target. Present discussions on governance have mostly focused on improving human rights, ignoring issues on fiscal accountability. While countries should be allowed to manage their resources to their best interest, there is a need to provide mechanisms to guide against the mismanagement and misallocation of scarce resources. With external resources, donors could condition their support on the continuous improvements in specific areas of governance.

Finally, there is a need for a broader country-level assessment of the financing requirement for the post-2015 agenda and the revenue potential of various domestic financing sources. This will better provide a sense of the magnitude of the financing gap and alternative financing options that could be explored.

Notes

1 A detailed review of the financing channels and sources for post-2015 can be found in UNCSD (2012); World Bank (2013) and Greenhill and Ali (2013).
2 Countries included in the regression are Angola; Benin; Botswana; Burkina Faso; Cameroon; Congo, Dem. Rep.; Ethiopia; Gabon; Gambia; Ghana; Kenya; Lesotho; Liberia; Madagascar; Mali; Mauritania; Mauritius; Namibia; Nigeria; Senegal; Sierra Leone; South Africa; Togo; Uganda and Zambia.
3 Capital flight refers to the transfer of assets abroad in order to reduce loss of principal, return or control over one's financial wealth (Epstein, 2005).

References

African Economic Outlook. (2013) *Database on African Fiscal Performance*. Available from: http://www.africaneconomicoutlook.org/en/database-on-african-fiscal-performance [Accessed: 19 March 2014].

Ajayi, S. I. (1997) *An Analysis of External Debt and Capital Flight in the Severely Indebted Low-Income Countries in Sub-Saharan Africa*. IMF Working Paper No. 97/68. Washington, DC: International Monetary Fund (IMF).

Aryeetey, E. (2004) *Financing Africa's Future Growth and Development: Some Innovations*. G-24 Discussion Paper. Washington, DC: Intergovernmental Group of Twenty-Four (G-24).

Atisophon, V., Bueren, J., De Paepe, G., Garroway, C. and Stijns, J. (2011) *Revisiting MDG Cost Estimates from a Domestic Resource Mobilization Perspective*. OECD Development Centre Working Paper No. 306. Paris: OECD Development Centre.

Beitler, D. (2010) *Raising Revenue: A Review of Financial Transaction Taxes throughout the World*. Report prepared for Health Poverty Action and Stamp Out Poverty. London: Stamp Out Poverty.

Bhushan, A., Samy, Y. and Medu, K. (2013) *Financing the Post-2015 Development Agenda: Domestic Revenue Mobilization in Africa*. North-South Institute Research Report. Ottawa: The North-South Institute (NSI).

Bird, R., Martinez-Vazquez, J. and Torgler, B. (2008) *Societal Institutions and Tax Efforts in Developing Countries*. Working Paper No. 4/6. USA: Andrew Young School of Policy Studies, University of Georgia.

Boyce, J. K. and Ndikumana, L. (2012) *Capital Flight from Sub-Saharan African Countries: Updated Estimates, 1970–2010*. PERI Research Report 144. Amherst: Political and Economic Research Institute, University of Massachusetts.

CAF. (2010) *The World Giving Index 2010*. London: Charities Aid Foundation (CAF). Available from: http://www.3sektorius.lt/docs/WorldGivingReport_Interactive_070910_2013–02–27_17_08_21.pdf [Accessed 8 April 2014].

Callan, M. (2012) *What Do We Know about the Private Sector's Contribution to Development?* Development Policy Centre Discussion Paper No. 11. Canberra: Crawford School of Public Policy, Australian National University.

Elgin, C. and Oztunali, O. (2012) *Shadow Economies around the World: Model Based Estimates*. Working Paper 2012/05. Istanbul: Department of Economics, Bogazici University.

Epstein, G. A. (2005) *Capital Flight and Capital Controls in Developing Countries*. Northampton: Edward Elgar Publishing.

Gittell, R. and Tebaldi, E. (2006) Charitable giving: Factors influencing giving in US states. *Nonprofit and Voluntary Sector Quarterly*. 35 (4). pp.721–736.

GIZ. (2013) *Shaping Corporate Social Responsibility in Sub-Saharan Africa: Guidance Notes from a Mapping Survey*. Bonn and Eschborn: Deutsche Gesellschaft für Internationale Zusammenarbeit (GIZ).

Grabel, I. (2005) Taxation of international private capital flows and securities transactions in developing countries: Do public finance considerations augment the macroeconomic dividends? *International Review of Applied Economics*. 19 (4). pp.477–497.

Greenhill, R. and Ali, A. (2013) *Paying for Progress: How Will Emerging Post-2015 Goals Be Financed in the New Aid Landscape?* ODI Working Paper No. 366. London: Overseas Development Institute (ODI).

Greenhill, R. and Prizzon, A. (2012) *Who Foots the Bill after 2015? What New Trends in Development Finance Mean for the Post-MDGs*. ODI Working Paper No. 360. London: Overseas Development Institute (ODI).

Gupta, S. and Tareq, S. (2008) Mobilizing revenue. *Finance and Development*. 45 (3). pp.44–47.

Le, T. M., Moreno-Dodson, B. and Rojchaichaninthorn, J. (2008) *Expanding Taxable Capacity and Reaching Revenue Potential: Cross-country Analysis*. Policy Research Paper No. 4559. Washington, DC: The World Bank.

McKinnon, R. (2013) The US saving deficiency, current-account deficits, and deindustrialization: Implications for China. *Journal of Policy Modeling*. 35 (3). pp.449–458.

Ratha, D., Mohapatra, S. and Plaza, S. (2008) *Beyond Aid: New Sources and Innovative Mechanisms for Financing Development in Sub-Saharan Africa*. Policy Research Paper 4609. Washington, DC: The World Bank.

UNCSD. (2012) *Finance for the Transition to a Green Economy in the Context of Sustainable Development and Poverty Eradication*. Rio+20 Issue Brief No. 16. New York: United Nation Conference on Sustainable Development (UNCSD).

UNCTAD. (2007) *Economic Development in Africa: Reclaiming Policy Space Domestic Resource Mobilization and Developmental States*. UNCTAD/ALDC/Africa/2007/1/. Geneva: United Nations Conference on Trade and Development (UNCTAD).

UNDESA. (2011) *The Great Green Technological Transformation*. United Nations Publication E/2011/50/Rev.1/ST/ESA/333. New York: United Nations Department of Economic and Social Affairs (UNDESA).

UN Task Team Working Group on Sustainable Development Finance. (2013) *Financing for Sustainable Development*. New York: United Nations.

World Bank. (2005) *Where is the Wealth of Nations? Measuring Capital for the 21st Century*. Washington, DC: The World Bank.

World Bank. (2010) *The Costs to Developing Countries of Adapting to Climate Change*. Washington, DC: The World Bank.

World Bank. (2013) *Finance for Development: Post-2015*. Washington, DC: The World Bank.

World Development Indicators. (2014) Washington, DC: The World Bank. Available from: http://data.worldbank.org/data-catalog/world-development-indicators [Accessed: 15 March 2014].

World Governance Indicators. (2014) Washington, DC: The World Bank. Available from: http://data.worldbank.org/data-catalog/worldwide-governance-indicators [Accessed: 16 March 2014].

Annex

Annex 16.1 Tax effort: regression

We adopt a linear model, which is specified in equation 1 as:

$$TGDP = \alpha_0 + \alpha_1 INDUST + \alpha_2 TO + \alpha_3 LogGNI + \alpha_4 INQ + \mu \qquad (1)$$

Where[1],
$TGDP$: Actual tax-GDP ratio
$INDUST$: Level of industrialisation (measured by the share of agriculture in GDP)
TO : Trade openness (measured as ratio of export plus import to GDP)
GNI : Gross national income per capita (at constant 2005 USD)
INQ : Institutional quality (measured by the level of corruption)

Theoretically, the tax ratio is expected to vary directly with trade openness and GNI, and inversely with agricultural share of GDP and institutional quality. Using a Pooled Ordinary Least Square (POLS) regression, we estimate the equation 1 for the SSA countries for which data are available between 1996 and 2012. The estimated coefficients are then used to derive the average tax effort for the five selected countries.

Annex Table 16.1 shows the results, which indicate the variables are rightly signed and statistically significant. We also test the model using a random effect model to check the robustness of our results. The results show that the model is robust to alternative specification: the sign and magnitude of the point estimates are similar.

Annex Table 16.1 Results: tax effort regression

Variables	*Tax Ratio*	
	Pooled OLS	*Random Effect Model*
Agriculture value added	−0.003** (0.001)	−0.003* (0.001)
Trade openness	0.089** (0.029)	0.040 (0.040)
Log GNI per capita	0.059*** (0.017)	0.056* (0.232)
Corruption	−0.052*** (0.015)	−0.053** (0.018)
Constant	−0.208 (0.139)	−0.145 (0.192)
R-squared	0.314	0.3096

Note: Standard errors are in parentheses and * $p < 0.05$, ** $p < 0.01$, *** $p < 0.001$.

Note

1 Data sources of variables included in the regression are: tax revenue (African Economic Outlook, 2013); corruption (World Governance Indicators, 2014); data GDP, trade openness, GNI per capita, agricultural value added (World Development Indicators, 2014). The sample period covers 1996 to 2012.

17 Illicit financial flows in view of financing the post-2015 development agenda

Towfiqul Islam Khan and Mashfique Ibne Akbar

Introduction

As the 2015 deadline for the Millennium Development Goals (MDGs) approaches, the international community is gearing up in finalising the next global development agenda. Many stakeholders view the MDGs as a historical breakthrough in terms of accelerating progress on an array of key indicators. Hence, the post-2015 development agenda has inspired significant policy formulation efforts and advocacy activities.

Global leaders, specifically heads of state and governments, should carry forward the spirit of the Millennium Declaration and the best of the MDGs, but they must also take into cognisance the lessons learned during the MDGs period to make the most out of the post-2015 agenda. Hulme (2013) points out that the MDGs only interested the 'big global players' on a limited scale. As a result, the weakest performance on the MDGs was observed in the area of MDG 8 that deals with the global partnership for development, particularly concerning pledged volumes of official development assistance (ODA) (MDG Gap Task Force, 2013). The conceptualisation of global partnership over the last six decades has been defined by developed countries issuing a package of commitments on promoting development via making conditional financial transfers, providing technical assistance, granting trade preferences and affording special and differential treatment to developing countries. At the 2002 United Nations International Conference on Financing for Development in Monterrey, Mexico, developed countries jointly made the commitment to provide a sufficient amount of development finance to attain the MDGs. The conference concluded with the so-called Monterrey Consensus, in which countries of the Development Assistance Committee (DAC) of the Organisation for Economic Co-operation and Development (OECD) were encouraged to ensure that at least 0.7 per cent of their respective gross national income (GNI) would be disbursed as ODA. Nevertheless, these countries have not been able to keep to their commitment (MDG Gap Task Force, 2013). Vandemoortele (2008) argues that the MDGs were essentially based on an extrapolation of past trends at the global level. Accordingly, discussions on the need for innovative finance for development have ramped up (Sobhan, 2013).

The World Bank (2013) stresses that financing the post-2015 agenda will require using available resources more effectively and strategically catalysing additional financing by both the public and private sectors. A largely marginalised issue, curbing illicit financial flows (IFFs) can help finance development by mobilising more domestic resources through tax collection and by saving foreign exchange reserves. Tackling IFFs can help finance the implementation of the post-2015 agenda, while simultaneously prompting a fairer global taxation regime and a more just global system in general. The post-2015 agenda can focus attention on addressing the challenges of making more efficient and effective use of the various available sources of finance. Success on this front will require governments to work together in order to establish the right policy environments at the national and international levels (Dafe, Hartwig and Janus, 2013).

IFFs have become a common phenomenon in developed and developing countries alike. IFFs from developing countries, however, are leaving deeper scars compared to their developed counterparts. Clark (2011) has defined IFFs as financial flows that include, but are not limited to, "cross-border transfers of the proceeds of tax evasion, corruption, trade in contraband goods, and criminal activities such as drug trafficking and counterfeiting." The United Nations Economic Commission for Africa (2013, 3) classifies IFFs into "(i) the proceeds of theft, bribery and other forms of corruption by government officials; (ii) the proceeds of criminal activities including drug trading, racketeering, counterfeiting, contraband, and terrorist financing; and (iii) the proceeds of tax evasion and laundered commercial transactions." Curiously, proceeds of laundered commercial transactions by multinational corporations (MNCs) constitute the largest share of IFFs, followed by the proceeds of criminal activities and corruption in turn (Baker, 2005).

This study explores the relevance of IFFs in the post-2015 context. It identifies options with regard to targets that could be considered during ongoing intergovernmental negotiations on the post-2015 agenda. The study also outlines the determinants of IFFs by using econometric estimation techniques. The rest of the study is organised as follows. The second section discusses the relevance of IFFs in the context of post-2015 development framework and the related targets. The third section discusses methodology of the econometric exercise, the findings of which are presented in the fourth section. Concluding remarks and ways forward are covered in the final section.

IFFs in the context of post-2015 development framework

One of the appealing aspects of having a common global development agenda is that it can unite countries on development issues that require close international cooperation. Indeed, an agenda that addresses IFFs would necessitate cooperation between and among member countries, as it encompasses policies which require reforms at the global level. In this context, a target on IFFs is certainly one of the deserving candidates for inclusion in the post-2015 agenda given the potential of IFFs for financing the agenda.

The scale of IFFs is so severe in some developing countries that illegal financial outflows tend to outpace ODA inflows (Kar and LeBlanc, 2013). IFFs deprive local economies of a considerable portion of the resources that would otherwise be employed for development financing. Hence, they undermine domestic investment and ultimately hinder long-term economic growth. Recent evidence indicating that Sub-Saharan Africa (SSA) is a 'net creditor' to the rest of the world is compelling – assets held by Africans abroad exceed the liabilities of Africans to the rest of the world (AfDB and GFI, 2013).

Considerable interest has recently arisen over the extent to which IFFs have developmental consequences for both developing and developed countries (see, for instance, Baker, 2005; Ndikumana and Boyce, 2008). Notably, the Istanbul Programme of Action for the Least Developed Countries for the Decade 2011–2020 (IPoA), adopted by the United Nations Fourth Conference on the Least Developed Countries (UN LDC IV) in 2011, highlighted the issue and outlined various actions (United Nations, 2011). World Bank (2013) urges the developing countries to step up efforts to finance their own development by improving domestic resource mobilisation through, for example, strengthening tax administration, better harnessing natural resource revenue and curbing of the IFFs. It comes as no surprise that IFFs have been included in a number of civil society debates on the future of development cooperation under the post-2015 agenda.[1]

Academic contributions highlight the need for targets that address IFFs in the post-2015 agenda. Recently, Bhattacharya, Higgins and Kindornay (2014) under the goal area 'Establish a global partnership for sustainable development' have proposed the target 'Create an enabling environment for sustainable development'. One of the suggested candidate indicators for this target is suggested as 'Existence of laws for ensuring country-by-country reporting by multinational corporations, disclosure of beneficial ownership and preventing money laundering', which is also included as one of the candidate indicators in 'global minimum standards' or 'zero targets'. Cobham (2014) proposes three candidate targets: (i) reduce to zero the legal persons and arrangements for which beneficial ownership information is not publicly available, (ii) reduce to zero the cross-border trade and investment relationships between jurisdictions for which there is no bilateral automatic exchange of tax information and (iii) reduce to zero the number of multinational businesses that do not report publicly on a country-by-country basis. Rowe et al. (2014) have conducted a survey involving 27 experts to help identify consensus on desirable policy options regarding IFFs. The survey identified 10 policy options that could be considered 'consensually desirable', including disclosure of beneficial ownerships, reforms of the international tax rule, transparency in international taxation, enhancement of developing country tax authority capacity, implementation of automatic exchange of tax-relevant information and public country-by-country reporting for MNCs, and harmonisation of anti-money laundering regulations.

Regrettably, certain major global and regional contributions towards shaping the post-2015 agenda did not directly mention the need for curbing IFFs (UN System Task Team on the Post-2015 UN Development Agenda, 2012; Economic Commission for Europe et al., 2013; SDSN, 2013, 2014; United Nations Global Compact, 2013). The UN System Task Team on the Post-2015 UN Development Agenda (2013), however, urges for a renewed global partnership that could enhance government capacity to efficiently and effectively mobilise public and private domestic resources in order to promote good corporate governance and combat IFFs. The United Nations General Assembly (2012) stressed that member states should fight corruption and IFFs at both the national and international levels.

Two key United Nations (UN) processes flagged IFFs and related issues for the post-2015 agenda. The report of the United Nations High-Level Panel of Eminent Persons on the Post-2015 Development Agenda (HLP) explicitly highlighted the need to tackle IFFs. The High-Level Panel of Eminent Persons on the Post-2015 Development Agenda (2013) urged developed countries to 'co-operate more effectively to stem aggressive tax avoidance and evasion, and illicit capital flows'. In its illustrative goals and targets, the High-Level Panel of Eminent Persons on the Post-2015 Development Agenda (2013) recommended the target 'Reduce illicit flows and tax evasion and increase stolen-asset recovery by $x' under the goal 'Create a global enabling environment and catalyse long-term finance' (Goal 12). It mentioned that further technical work to identify appropriate indicators is necessary. Indeed, there is a lack of consensus about the appropriate methodology to estimate IFFs. Available estimates suggest that IFFs from developing countries appear to have grown during the last decade (Kar, 2011; Kar and Freitas, 2012; Kar and LeBlanc, 2013), hence a comprehensive assessment will be required to finalise the related indicator(s).

To date, the final proposal of the intergovernmental Open Working Group on the Sustainable Development Goals remains the most influential document in the context of shaping the post-2015 agenda (Bhattacharya, Khan and Salma, 2014). Unfortunately, the scope for addressing IFFs narrowed subsequently during the negotiation process, which is evident from the content analysis presented in Annex 17.1. The two earlier versions of the proposal, the 'Zero Draft' (Open Working Group, 2014a) and 'Zero Draft Rev 1' (Open Working Group, 2014b) included targets that strongly addressed the issue of IFFs. The final proposal (Open Working Group, 2014c), surprising to an extent, was revised in a way that significantly reduced the scope for curbing IFFs.

In its final proposal, the Open Working Group (2014c) suggested target (16.4) 'By 2030, significantly reduce illicit financial and arms flows, strengthen recovery and return of stolen assets and combat all forms of organized crime'. At least three other proposed targets are closely related to – and can address the objective of – curbing IFFs: (16.5) 'Substantially reduce corruption and bribery in all its forms'; (16.6) 'Develop effective, accountable and transparent institutions at all levels'; and (17.1) 'Strengthen domestic resource mobilization, including through international support to developing countries, to improve domestic capacity for tax and other revenue collection'. Notably, a number of potential means of implementation targets remain absent (Bhattacharya, Khan and Salma, 2014). One may recall that an earlier version of the Zero Draft included two important means of implementation targets, 'Cooperate globally to reduce substantially international tax evasion and avoidance', and 'Cooperate globally to combat illicit financial flows and transfers, recover stolen assets and return them to their countries of origin'. On a welcome note, at the Third International Conference on Financing for Development, the member states pledged to "redouble efforts to substantially reduce illicit financial flows by 2030, with a view to eventually eliminating them, including by combating tax evasion and corruption through strengthened national regulation and increased international cooperation" (United Nations General Assembly, 2015, 8).

The World Bank (2013) argues that country efforts to address IFFs need to occur at two levels. A more complex and difficult path involves tackling the underlying dynamics that help drive IFFs. Other approaches aim to directly reduce IFFs, rather than targeting their underlying causes, such as improving transparency in the declaration of revenues and payments by MNCs, tightening the regulation of tax havens and secrecy jurisdictions, and strengthening efforts to curb money laundering. A particularly effective approach for governments working with private companies is ensuring beneficial ownership information on legal entities and legal arrangements.

IFFs are an issue on which progress is relatively difficult to measure, as IFFs apparently fall under the so-called soft areas of development. However, this challenge cannot stand in the way of adequately addressing the issue in the post-2015 agenda, particularly in view of strong evidence for their negative impact on overall development outcomes. The best way to address IFFs is to include policy targets that can help curb them. If the aforementioned academic contributions (Bhattacharya, Higgins and Kindornay, 2014; Cobham, 2014; Rowe et al., 2014) on the post-2015 agenda are analysed in view of IFFs, it can be observed that there is more emphasis on policy targets (e.g. disclosure of beneficial ownership, country-by-country reporting by MNCs) than outcome targets (e.g. reduce illicit financial flows by x per cent). The issue of IFFs could perhaps be addressed while setting the indicators against the finalised targets. Either way, as Bhattacharya, Khan and Salma (2014) have mentioned, it is critical to ensure that the language on monitoring of the goals, targets and indicators, including those addressing IFFs, and accountability is stringent enough to promote and accelerate implementation of the post-2015 international development framework.

Methodology

Given the apparent growth of IFFs during the last decade, developing countries have been missing out on opportunities to invest domestic funds in the local market because of illegal transfer of resources to other destinations, mostly developed countries (Kar, 2011). It is evident from the above sections that IFFs from developing countries, especially low-income countries (LICs), are an ongoing concern alongside the inherent LIC characteristics of low domestic investment. While the issue of IFFs has been flagged by national governments and the international community, very few concerted efforts have been made. This situation calls for a discussion about why resources are being directed to other destinations despite investment opportunities in the home countries.

Studies on IFFs are often limited to estimates of their scale and so far have largely not attempted to understand the underlying causes driving these outflows.

Kar (2011) and Kar and Cartwright-Smith (2008) highlight a number of possible issues underlying IFFs, such as macroeconomic, structural, external and institutional attributes. This study performs an econometric analysis with the aim of identifying determinants of IFFs from developing countries. A panel data[2] exercise that analyses available data[3] for 84 developing countries from 2002 to 2011 was carried out. The analysis employs a pooled ordinary least square (POLS) regression model, fixed effects (FE) and random effects (RE) estimation models. Advantage of panel data analysis over other econometric techniques pertains to the ability of the methodology to control for variables that cannot be measured or observed. Furthermore, the methodology allows for the control of other variables such as those that change over time but not across entities, together with controlling for factors that could cause omitted variable bias if the respective variables are omitted.

The study employs recent estimates of IFFs by Kar and LeBlanc (2013).[4] Towards this end, the study compiles the latest available estimates of IFFs and juxtaposes them with other secondary data. Data are compiled from a number of sources including IFF estimates by Kar and Freitas (2012), the World Bank's World Development Indicators,[5] United Nations Conference on Trade and Development statistics,[6] Polity IV database,[7] and the PRS Group database.[8] Macroeconomic variables included in the analysis are per capita gross domestic product (GDP) (current United States Dollars (USD)),[9] degree of openness of the economy, exchange rate, capital formation, rate of inflation, average tax rates and capital account convertibility. Other indicators included are type of institutional democracy, level of corruption, state of law and order and degree of political stability. Additionally, regional dummies,[10] specifically East Asia and the Pacific, Europe and Central Asia, Latin America and the Caribbean, the Middle East and North Africa, South Asia, and Sub-Saharan Africa, are included in the analysis.

The POLS regression model runs a simple ordinary least square (OLS) regression by stacking the time series data of the cross-sections, one above another. The following equation encapsulates the POLS model:

$$
\begin{aligned}
IFF_{it} = {} & \alpha_0 + \alpha_1 \ln PCGDP_{it} + \alpha_2 OPEN_{it} + \alpha_3 ER_{it} + \alpha_4 \ln CAPFOR_{it} + \alpha_5 INF_{it} \\
& + \alpha_6 TAX_{it} + \alpha_7 DEM_{it} + \alpha_8 CORR_{it} + \alpha_9 LAW_{it} + \alpha_{10} POL_{it} \\
& + \alpha_{11} CAPCNV_{it} + \alpha_{12} EASTDUM_{it} + \alpha_{13} EURDUM_{it} + \alpha_{14} LATINDUM_{it} \\
& + \alpha_{15} MENADUM_{it} + \alpha_{16} SOUTHDUM_{it} + \alpha_{17} SUBAFRDUM + \epsilon_{it}
\end{aligned}
$$

where, IFF = illicit financial flows as a percentage of GDP
PCGDP = per capita GDP (current USD)
OPEN = degree of openness of the economy
ER = exchange rate (local currency against USD)
CAPFOR = gross capital formation
INF = rate of inflation
TAX = average tax rates
DEM = index of institutional democracy
CORR = index of corruption within the political system

LAW = index of the state of law and order
POL = index of political stability
CAPCNV = index measuring a country's degree of capital account convertibility
EASTDUM = dummy variable for the region East Asia and the Pacific
EURDUM = dummy variable for the region Europe and Central Asia
LATINDUM = dummy variable for the region Latin America and the Caribbean
MENADUM = dummy variable for the region the Middle East and North Africa
SOUTHDUM = dummy variable for the region South Asia
SUBAFRDUM = dummy variable for the region Sub-Saharan Africa
ln = natural logarithm of the variables

The FE estimation model is employed with a rationale to explore if country-specific issues (e.g. government policy) affect IFFs. This model recognises that cross-sectional elements have different attributes which are not captured in the model, but assumes that for a given cross-section, they will remain time-invariant. The effects of these attributes are captured in the intercepts. Thus, the model estimated through this approach is:

$$
\begin{aligned}
IFF_{it} = {} & \alpha_i + \alpha_1 \ln PCGDP_{it} + \alpha_2 OPEN_{it} + \alpha_3 ER_{it} + \alpha_4 \ln CAPFOR_{it} + \alpha_5 INF_{it} \\
& + \alpha_6 TAX_{it} + \alpha_7 DEM_{it} + \alpha_8 CORR_{it} + \alpha_9 LAW_{it} + \alpha_{10} POL_{it} \\
& + \alpha_{11} CAPCNV_{it} + \epsilon_{it}
\end{aligned}
$$

where, the symbols represent corresponding variables, as outlined above, and the $_i$ of the intercept, which in this model is assumed to remain fixed over time, indicates the unobserved individual country-specific factors.

Unlike in the FE estimation model, the variation across entities is assumed to be random and uncorrelated with the independent variables in the RE estimation model. RE model assumes that the error terms are not correlated with the explanatory variables, which allows for time-invariant variables to play the role of explanatory variables. Hence, the RE model captures both country and time-specific effects.

$$
\begin{aligned}
IFF_{it} = {} & \alpha_0 + \alpha_1 \ln PCGDP_{it} + \alpha_2 OPEN_{it} + \alpha_3 ER_{it} + \alpha_4 \ln CAPFOR_{it} + \alpha_5 INF_{it} \\
& + \alpha_6 TAX_{it} + \alpha_7 DEM_{it} + \alpha_8 CORR_{it} + \alpha_9 LAW_{it} + \alpha_{10} POL_{it} + \alpha_{11} CAPCNV_{it} \\
& + \alpha_{12} EASTDUM_{it} + \alpha_{13} EURDUM_{it} + \alpha_{14} LATINDUM_{it} \\
& + \alpha_{15} MENADUM_{it} + \alpha_{16} SOUTHDUM_{it} + \alpha_{17} SUBAFRDUM + \mu_{it} + \pi_{it}
\end{aligned}
$$

where, the symbols represent corresponding variables, as outlined above, the μ_{it} captures the between-entity component and the π_{it} captures the within-entity component.

The rationales for the inclusion of the macroeconomic indicators are as follows. Per capita GDP (current USD) is included in the model because it is assumed that the level of a country's development influences capital outflow, either in terms of trade mispricing or other money laundering measures. LICs are typically unable to contain capital outflows due to low regulatory capacity, but high incidence of corruption can be attributed as another main reason. The degree of openness is measured by considering exports and imports as a percentage of GDP (current USD). The greater the openness of a country's economy, the more that economy is integrated with the global economy and the greater the rationale to invest in countries other than the home country by means of illegal channels. It is assumed that the exchange rate (local currency against USD) stimulates IFFs in the sense that a depreciation of the local currency impedes confidence among both local and foreign investors. Gross capital formation (in current USD), or gross domestic investment, indicates the status and growth of investment in the domestic economy. It is expected that the level of capital formation in the domestic economy will have a significant impact on the determination of capital outflows from the home country. In connection to investment, it is assumed that the rate of inflation substantially determines IFFs by eroding purchasing power and increasing the costs of doing business in the home country. Investors, irrespective of the level of capital formation, are assumed to base their expectations on current levels of inflation. It is assumed that commercial tax rates are a determinant of IFFs. If the primary concern of companies is to generate profit, a higher tax rate would inevitably push finances from the home country to foreign destinations where business operations can be carried out at lower costs. The Chinn-Ito index (2006) is considered in the analysis to account for a country's degree of capital account convertibility. The rationale for the inclusion of the variable lies in the assumption that capital account convertibility will presumably influence IFFs.

The first of the governance-related indicators is the index of institutional democracy, which provides insight into the type of regime that a particular country is governed by.[11] Furthermore, it is assumed that corruption stimulates IFFs. Klitgaard (1998) states that corruption includes "bribery, extortion, influence peddling, nepotism, fraud and embezzlement." Certain factors appear to be equally important in motivating corruption, such as complicated tax laws, excess power vested in tax administrators, weak legal and judicial systems, low salaries in the public sector, and lack of accountability and transparency in tax administration (Tanzi, 1998). The index of the state of law and order indicates the level of strength and impartiality of a country's legal and judicial system (together with the assessment of the rule of law). Index of political stability (political risk rating index)[12] is a variable that provides an assessment of political stability. The regional dummy variables included in the regressions take a value of 1 if the point of interest is valid; otherwise 0.

Multicollinearity is often a problem in OLS estimations, hence tests were performed to assess it. The primary concern that arises from collinearity between one and more of the variables is that regression estimates of the coefficients can become flawed with the standard errors of the coefficients becoming inflated. To check for multicollinearity, variance inflation factor (VIF) values were calculated for each of the variables. It was found that there exists no multicollinearity with the VIF values of the variables being less than 10 in each instance. Other tests such as the condition number test and Farrar-Glauber test were also carried out to test for multicollinearity and there were no deviations from the results.

The Cameron-Trivedi decomposition of the information matrix test and Breusch-Pagan/Cook-Weisberg test were also performed to test for heteroskedasticity, which both assess the null hypothesis that the variance of the residuals is homogenous (not heteroskedastic). Both of the tests rejected the null hypothesis, indicating that the residuals are heteroskedastic. Accordingly, adjustments were made in the regressions to account for heteroskedasticity.[13] Robust standard errors were obtained by applying the Huber-White (Huber, 1967; White, 1980, 1982) estimator to each of the regressions. The estimator is robust to misspecification, keeping in mind that the observations to which the estimator is applied are independent.

Model selection and empirical results

A range of estimations was carried out to address the difficulties of estimating the dependent variable, IFF. It needs to be mentioned at the outset of the analysis that time-fixed effects were considered for both the FE and RE models. The rationale for this deviation from established custom is derived from the fact that the econometric exercise does not aim to distinguish the variation between countries. Rather, the analysis aims to probe into the collective properties of the countries and hence does not separate the outcomes.

The Breusch-Pagan Lagrange multiplier (LM) test was carried out first to choose between the POLS and RE models. With a null hypothesis that there is no variation across entities, the LM test rejected the null hypothesis, indicating that co-variance is zero across units. The RE model is therefore the preferred model in the current exercise because there is significant difference across time periods. The Hausman Test (HT) was then carried out to choose between FE and RE models. The HT, which tests the null hypothesis that the unique errors (μi) are uncorrelated with the regressors (FE model) against the alternative hypothesis that the μi are correlated (RE model), cannot reject the null hypothesis, indicating that the RE model is the more appropriate model for the dataset at hand (probability > $chi^2 = 0.9492$).

Although both the POLS and FE models were rejected by tests of model specification, the POLS estimation is presented in Table 17.1 to act as a benchmark for the RE estimations which follow: generalized least square (GLS) and maximum likelihood (ML) regressions. Since estimates of IFFs are prone to errors, having three estimations lends a dimension of robustness to the analysis. It can be observed from Table 17.1 that some variables are significant in all estimations, while others are only significant in selected estimations.

Per capita GDP (current USD), with a negative sign, was found to be significant across all the estimations at the 1 per cent significance level. This indicates that with increasing levels of income, IFFs decrease. Such a situation can arise as a result of improved law and order incorporating judicial amendments or changes in the mind set of citizens to be more like that of a developed country. The degree of openness of the economy, with a positive sign, is also significant across the estimations at the 1 per cent significance level. It is common for capital outflows

Table 17.1 Regression results

Variable	*POLS*		*GLS*		*ML*	
	Coefficient	p-*value*	*Coefficient*	p-*value*	*Coefficient*	p-*value*
lnPCGDP	−4.454443	0.046**	−4.454443	0.014**	−4.454443	0.001***
OPEN	0.2787158	0.002***	0.2787158	0.006***	0.2787158	0.000***
ER	−0.0004221	0.041**	−0.0004221	0.000***	−0.0004221	0.173
lnCAPFOR	0.8282569	0.387	0.8282569	0.334	0.8282569	0.212
INF	−0.000776	0.000***	−0.000776	0.000***	−0.000776	0.305
TAX	−0.465764	0.005***	−0.465764	0.028**	−0.465764	0.013**
DEM	0.135991	0.030**	0.135991	0.001***	0.135991	0.134
CORR	−0.9207053	0.458	−0.9207053	0.186	−0.9207053	0.582
LAW	1.198796	0.180	1.198796	0.108	1.198796	0.295
POL	−0.2547866	0.014***	−0.2547866	0.000***	−0.2547866	0.128
CAPCNV	6.108627	0.077*	6.108627	0.020**	6.108627	0.030**
EASTDUM	4.622584	0.783	−13.13849	0.001***	−13.13849	0.001***
EURDUM	9.637813	0.493	−8.123264	0.000***	−8.123264	0.008***
LATINDUM	17.76108	0.209	n/a		n/a	
MENA-DUM	10.14618	0.451	−7.614898	0.002***	−7.614898	0.047**
SOUTH-DUM	11.34839	0.432	−6.412683	0.000***	−6.412683	0.206
SUBAFR-DUM	19.53103	0.146	1.769955	0.528	1.769955	0.570
Constant			17.76108	0.174	17.76108	0.225
R^2	0.4421		0.3343		n/a	

Source: Authors' calculations.

Note: The dependent variable is IFF.

n/a is not applicable.

Regional dummy for Latin America and the Caribbean was omitted from the regressions to avoid perfect multicollinearity.

* represents significance at 10 per cent level; ** represents significance at 5 per cent level; *** represents significance at 1 per cent level.

to increase as integration with the global economy increases. Capital account convertibility was also found to be significant with a positive sign, although at varying levels of significance across estimations, which implies that IFFs increase with the extent of capital account convertibility, but this is not generalisable (with the current data). Keeping in mind that only developing countries form the sample, such a conclusion can be established, as capital from developing countries will flow more easily to other stable destinations given the relaxed restrictions on capital transfers.

Exchange rate (local currency against USD), rate of inflation, institutional democracy and political stability were found to be significant in the POLS and GLS estimations, but not the ML estimation. Exchange rate has a negative sign in both of the estimations where the variable is significant. This indicates that IFFs increase as the local currency depreciates, in line with our assumptions. Inflation too takes a negative sign, which follows the assumption that with higher levels of inflation, the gradual erosion of purchasing power and increase in the costs of doing business cause IFFs to rise. Political stability has a negative sign across the estimations, indicating towards political instability having a significant influence on IFFs.

Average tax rates were also found to be significant across the estimations, but with a negative sign. This contradicts the assumption about the variable. Nevertheless, an investigation into how increasing tax rates can lead to lower levels of IFFs is certainly an area for future study. Institutional democracy has a positive sign in the POLS and GLS estimations, but it is unclear whether this indicates that more loopholes in more democratic and decentralised countries lead to increases in IFFs. This can also serve as an area for future study.

Regional dummies that were found to be significant include those for East Asia and the Pacific, Europe and Central Asia, and the Middle East and North Africa. These dummies are significant in the GLS and ML estimations, but not the POLS estimation. This reflects that the above-mentioned regions have higher incidences of capital outflows than the other regions, namely South Asia and SSA.

Variables that were considered in the analysis but did not provide significant results in determining IFFs from developing countries include capital formation, corruption within the political system as well as the state of law and order. However, these findings could also stem from data discrepancies.

Conclusions and way forward

Although IFFs are prominent in the ongoing post-2015 discussions, they are largely marginalised and left unattended in major global and regional contributions towards shaping the post-2015 development agenda. This study has argued that not only it is important to have dedicated targets and indicators on curbing IFFs in the post-2015 agenda, it is also necessary to understand the underlying factors that influence growth of IFFs. The results of the econometric analysis are intuitive in certain respects and confirmative in others. Per capita GDP, the degree of openness of the economy and capital account convertibility were found to be significant determinants of IFFs from developing countries. The exchange rate, rate of inflation, institutional democracy and political stability also appear to influence illicit financial outflows, but these variables should be interpreted with caution since they were not found to influence IFFs in all of the estimation techniques considered in the analysis. Overall, the present study highlights that both economic and institutional variables influence IFFs.

Since resources lost as IFFs have the potential to finance a large proportion of the post-2015 agenda, it is critical that continuous efforts are put in place to battle IFFs while implementing the post-2015 development agenda. It is likely that a concrete monitorable IFF-relevant indicator (e.g. total volume of IFFs) will be adopted to measure global progress as regards the proposed Target 16.4 under the post-2015 development agenda. However, it is important to recognise that without the required policy actions, the global post-2015 development target as regards IFFs will remain unattainable. In this context, institutional and legal reforms at both country and global levels, a number of which have been mentioned above, is critically important to curb the IFFs.

Notes

1 For a Southern perspective, see Southern Voice on Post-MDG International Development Goals (2013).
2 Panel data analysis is conducted since observations are examined over a period of time.
3 Data unavailability for some developing countries was a major concern. Additionally, data available for some countries were not available for others. Hence, some developing countries were dropped from the analysis during cross-country comparison and dataset matching.
4 Estimates by Kar and LeBlanc (2013) are prone to errors because of irregularities in the compilation of balance of payments data, a component of an overall IFF estimate for a country. It should be mentioned that earlier estimates are available in Kar and Freitas (2012).
5 http://databank.worldbank.org/data/reports.aspx?source=world-development-indicators [Accessed: 8 October 2014].
6 http://unctadstat.unctad.org/wds/ReportFolders/reportFolders.aspx?sRF_ActivePath=p,4&sRF_Expanded= (p.4) [Accessed: 12 November 2014].
7 http://www.systemicpeace.org/polity/polity4.htm [Accessed: 15 October 2014].
8 http://epub.prsgroup.com/country-database/country-data [Accessed: 15 October 2014].
9 Since IFF estimates are available in terms of current values, other explanatory variables are also considered in current values.
10 According to the World Bank classification of developing countries.
11 The index of institutional democracy includes three components: (a) presence of institutions and procedures, (b) existence of institutional constraints on the exercise of power by the executive and (c) assurance of civil liberties to all the citizens of the country and in participation of political participation (Marshall, Gurr and Jaggers, 2014).
12 Components employed to calculate the political risk rating index include government stability, socio-economic conditions, investment profile, internal conflict, external conflict, corruption, military in politics, religious tensions, law and order, ethnic tensions, democratic accountability and bureaucratic quality (Howell, 2011).
13 It is recognised that Blackburne III and Frank (2007) recommended using the mean-group estimator and pooled mean-group estimator instead of making such adjustments. However, they also pointed out that the technique is applicable when the number of groups and number of time series observations are both large. Given the nature of the dataset available for this study, the present technique was followed.

References

AfDB and GFI. (2013) *Illicit Financial Flows and the Problem of Net Resource Transfers from Africa: 1980–2009*. Tunis and Washington, DC: African Development Bank (AfDB) and Global Financial Integrity (GFI).

Baker, R. (2005) *Capitalism's Achilles Heel: Dirty Money and How to Renew the Free-Market System*. Hoboken: John Wiley & Sons.

Bhattacharya, D., Higgins K. and Kindornay, S. (2014) *Methodology and Implementation Guide*. Dhaka and Ottawa: Centre for Policy Dialogue (CPD), the North-South Institute and Southern Voice on Post-MDG International Development Goals.

Bhattacharya, D., Khan, T. I. and Salma, U. (2014) A commentary on the final outcome document of the Open Working Group on SDGs. *SAIS Review of International Affairs*. 34 (2). pp.165–177.

Blackburne III, E. F. and Frank, M. W. (2007) Estimation of nonstationary heterogeneous panels. *Stata Journal*. 7 (2). pp.197–208.

Chinn, M. D. and Ito, H. (2006) What matters for financial development? Capital controls, institutions, and interactions. *Journal of Development Economics*. 81 (1). pp.163–192.

Clark, H. (2011) *Illicit Finances Divert Resources away from Development*. Opening Remarks at the Special Event on *Illicit Financial Flows: Perspectives on Issues and Options for LDCs*, at the Fourth United Nations Conference on the Least Developed Countries. 11 May, Istanbul, Turkey. Available from: http://www.undp.org/content/undp/en/home/presscenter/speeches/2011/05/11/clark-illicit-finances-divert-resources-away-from-development.htm [Accessed: 10 November 2014].

Cobham, A. (2014) *Benefits and Costs of the IFF: Targets for the Post-2015 Development Agenda*. Copenhagen: Copenhagen Consensus Center.

Dafe, F., Hartwig, R. and Janus, H. (2013) *Post-2015: Why the Development Finance Debate Needs to Make the Move from Quantity to Quality*. Bonn: German Development Institute/Deutsches Institut für Entwicklungspolitik (DIE).

Economic Commission for Europe, Economic and Social Commission for Asia and the Pacific, Economic Commission for Latin America and the Caribbean, Economic Commission for Africa & Economic and Social Commission for Western Asia. (2013) *A Regional Perspective on the Post-2015 United Nations Development Agenda*. New York: United Nations.

High-Level Panel of Eminent Persons on the Post-2015 Development Agenda. (2013) *A New Global Partnership: Eradicate Poverty and Transform Economies through Sustainable Development*. New York: United Nations.

Howell, L. D. (2011) *International Country Risk Guide Methodology*. East Syracuse: The PRS Group.

Huber, P. J. (1967) *The Behavior of Maximum Likelihood Estimates under Nonstandard Conditions*. Proceedings of the Fifth Berkeley Symposium on Mathematical Statistics and Probability. 1. pp.221–233. Berkeley: University of California Press.

Hulme, D. (2013) The Post-2015 Development Agenda: Learning from the MDGs. *Southern Voice Occasional Paper No. 2*. Dhaka: Southern Voice on Post-MDG International Development Goals.

Kar, D. (2011) *Illicit Financial Flows from the Least Developed Countries: 1990–2008*. New York: United Nations Development Programme (UNDP).

Kar, D. and Cartwright-Smith, D. (2008) *Illicit Financial Flows from Developing Countries: 2002–2006*. Washington, DC: Global Financial Integrity (GFI).

Kar, D. and Freitas, S. (2012) *Illicit Financial Flows from Developing Countries: 2001–2010*. Washington, DC: Global Financial Integrity (GFI).

Kar, D. and LeBlanc, B. (2013) *Illicit Financial Flows from Developing Countries: 2002–2011*. Washington, DC: Global Financial Integrity (GFI).

Klitgaard, R. (1998) International cooperation against corruption. *Finance and Development*. 35 (1). pp.3–6.

Marshall, M. G., Gurr, T. R. and Jaggers, K. (2014) *Polity IV Project: Data Users' Manual; Political Regime Characteristics and Transitions, 1800–2012*. Vienna, VA: Center for Systemic Peace.

MDG Gap Task Force. (2013) *The Global Partnership for Development: The Challenge We Face*. New York: United Nations.

Ndikumana, L. and Boyce, J. K. (2008) *New Estimates of Capital Flight from Sub-Saharan African Countries: Linkages with External Borrowing and Policy Options*. Amherst: Political Economy Research Institute, University of Massachusetts.

Open Working Group on the Sustainable Development Goals. (2014a) *Introduction and Proposed Goals and Targets on Sustainable Development for the Post-2015 Development Agenda*. Available from: http://sustainabledevelopment.un.org/content/documents/4528zerodraft12OWG.pdf [Accessed: 12 October 2014].

Open Working Group on the Sustainable Development Goals. (2014b) *Introduction and Proposed Goals and Targets on Sustainable Development for the Post-2015 Development Agenda*. Available from: https://sustainabledevelopment.un.org/content/documents/4523zerodraft.pdf [Accessed: 12 October 2014].

Open Working Group on the Sustainable Development Goals. (2014c) *Open Working Group Proposals for the Sustainable Development Goals*. New York: United Nations.

Rowe, G., Bolger, F., Payne, R. and Shubert, E. (2014) *Policy Options for Addressing Illicit Financial Flows: Results from a Delphi Study*. New Haven: Academics Stand Against Poverty (ASAP).

SDSN. (2013) *An Action Agenda for Sustainable Development: Report for the UN Secretary-General*. New York: Sustainable Development Solutions Network (SDSN).

SDSN. (2014) *Indicators and a Monitoring Framework for Sustainable Development Goals: Launching a Data Revolution for the SDGs*. Revised Working Draft, 25 November. New York: Sustainable Development Solutions Network (SDSN).

Sobhan, R. (2013) *Innovation and Additionally for Development Finance: Looking at Asia*. CPD Working Paper No. 102. Dhaka: Centre for Policy Dialogue (CPD).

Southern Voice on Post-MDG International Development Goals. (2013) *First Approximations on Post-MDG International Development Goals*. Southern Voice Occasional Paper Special Issue 1. Dhaka: Southern Voice on Post-MDG International Development Goals.

Tanzi, V. (1998) *Corruption around the World: Causes, Consequences, Scope and Cures*. IMF Working Paper No. 98/63. Washington, DC: International Monetary Fund (IMF). Available from: https://www.imf.org/external/pubs/ft/wp/wp9863.pdf [Accessed: 12 October 2014].

United Nations. (2011) *Programme of Action for the Least Developed Countries for the Decade 2011–2020*. A/CONF.219/3/Rev.1. Istanbul: United Nations.

United Nations Economic Commission for Africa. (2013) *The State of Governance in Africa: The Dimension of Illicit Financial Flows as a Governance Challenge*. E/ECA/CGPP/3/2. Addis Ababa: United Nations Economic and Social Council.

United Nations General Assembly. (2012) *The Future We Want*. A/RES/66/288. New York: United Nations.

United Nations General Assembly. (2015) *Addis Ababa Action Agenda of the Third International Conference on Financing for Development (Addis Ababa Action Agenda)*. A/RES/69/313. New York: United Nations.

United Nations Global Compact. (2013) *Corporate Sustainability and the United Nations Post-2015 Development Agenda: Perspectives from UN Global Compact Participants on Global Priorities and How to Engage Business towards Sustainable Development Goals*. New York: United Nations Global Compact (UNGC).

UN System Task Team on the Post-2015 UN Development Agenda. (2012) *Realizing the Future We Want for All: Report to the Secretary-General*. New York: United Nations. Available from: http://www.un.org/millenniumgoals/pdf/Post_2015_UNTTreport.pdf [Accessed: 12 October 2014].

UN System Task Team on the Post-2015 UN Development Agenda. (2013) *A Renewed Global Partnership for Development*. New York: United Nations. Available from: http://www.un.org/en/development/desa/policy/untaskteam_undf/glob_dev_rep_2013.pdf [Accessed: 12 October 2014].

Vandemoortele, J. (2008) Making sense of the MDGs. *Development*. 51 (2). pp.220–227.

White, H. (1980) A heteroskedasticity-consistent covariance matrix estimator and a direct test for heteroskedasticity. *Econometrica*. 48 (4). pp.817–838.

White, H. (1982) Maximum likelihood estimation of misspecified models. *Econometrica*. 50 (1). pp.1–25.

World Bank. (2013) *Financing for Development Post-2015*. Washington, DC: The World Bank.

Annex

Annex 17.1 Chronological evolution of international financial flows in the Open Working Group documents

Zero Draft (Open Working Group on the Sustainable Development Goals, 2014a)	*Zero Draft Rev 1 (Open Working Group on the Sustainable Development Goals, 2014b)*	*Final Proposal (Open Working Group on the Sustainable Development Goals, 2014c)*
Proposed Goal 16. Achieve peaceful and inclusive societies, rule of law, effective and capable institutions 16.3 by 2030 reduce illicit financial flows by x% and reduce money laundering and all forms of organized crime including human trafficking and illicit trade in arms, drugs and wildlife **Proposed Goal 17. Strengthen and enhance the means of implementation and global partnership for sustainable development** 17.45 cooperate globally to reduce substantially international tax evasion and avoidance 17.46 cooperate globally to combat illicit financial flows and transfers, recover stolen assets and return them to their countries of origin	**Proposed Goal 16. Achieve peaceful and inclusive societies, access to justice for all, and effective and capable institutions** 16.3 by 2030 reduce illicit financial flows by x% globally, increase stolen asset recovery and return by y% globally, fight all forms of organized crime, and reduce corruption and bribery in all its forms and at all levels and ensure accountability and transparency	**Goal 16. Promote peaceful and inclusive societies for sustainable development, provide access to justice for all and build effective, accountable and inclusive institutions at all levels** 16.4 By 2030 significantly reduce illicit financial and arms flows, strengthen recovery and return of stolen assets, and combat all forms of organized crime

Source: Authors' compilation.

Note: Goals are in bold, while the targets are not.

Appendix

Sustainable Development Goals (SDGs)

(adopted at the 70th General Assembly of the United Nations in September 2015)

Goal 1. End poverty in all its forms everywhere

Goal 2. End hunger, achieve food security and improved nutrition and promote sustainable agriculture

Goal 3. Ensure healthy lives and promote well-being for all at all ages

Goal 4. Ensure inclusive and equitable quality education and promote lifelong learning opportunities for all

Goal 5. Achieve gender equality and empower all women and girls

Goal 6. Ensure availability and sustainable management of water and sanitation for all

Goal 7. Ensure access to affordable, reliable, sustainable and modern energy for all

Goal 8. Promote sustained, inclusive and sustainable economic growth, full and productive employment and decent work for all

Goal 9. Build resilient infrastructure, promote inclusive and sustainable industrialization and foster innovation

Goal 10. Reduce inequality within and among countries

Goal 11. Make cities and human settlements inclusive, safe, resilient and sustainable

Goal 12. Ensure sustainable consumption and production patterns

Goal 13. Take urgent action to combat climate change and its impacts[1]

Goal 14. Conserve and sustainably use the oceans, seas and marine resources for sustainable development

Goal 15. Protect, restore and promote sustainable use of terrestrial ecosystems, sustainably manage forests, combat desertification, and halt and reverse land degradation and halt biodiversity loss

Goal 16. Promote peaceful and inclusive societies for sustainable development, provide access to justice for all and build effective, accountable and inclusive institutions at all levels

Goal 17. Strengthen the means of implementation and revitalize the global partnership for sustainable development

Note

1 Acknowledging that the United Nations Framework Convention on Climate Change is the primary international, intergovernmental forum for negotiating the global response to climate change.

Index